PSYCHOLOGY OF DECISION MAKING IN LEGAL, HEALTH CARE AND SCIENCE SETTINGS

Psychology of Decision Making in Legal, Health Care and Science Settings

Gloria R. Burthold

Editor

Nova Science Publishers, Inc.

New York

For permission to use material from this book please contact us:
Telephone 631-231-7269; Fax 631-231-8175
Web Site: http://www.novapublishers.com

NOTICE TO THE READER

The Publisher has taken reasonable care in the preparation of this book, but makes no expressed or implied warranty of any kind and assumes no responsibility for any errors or omissions. No liability is assumed for incidental or consequential damages in connection with or arising out of information contained in this book. The Publisher shall not be liable for any special, consequential, or exemplary damages resulting, in whole or in part, from the readers' use of, or reliance upon, this material.

Independent verification should be sought for any data, advice or recommendations contained in this book. In addition, no responsibility is assumed by the publisher for any injury and/or damage to persons or property arising from any methods, products, instructions, ideas or otherwise contained in this publication.

This publication is designed to provide accurate and authoritative information with regard to the subject matter covered herein. It is sold with the clear understanding that the Publisher is not engaged in rendering legal or any other professional services. If legal or any other expert assistance is required, the services of a competent person should be sought. FROM A DECLARATION OF PARTICIPANTS JOINTLY ADOPTED BY A COMMITTEE OF THE AMERICAN BAR ASSOCIATION AND A COMMITTEE OF PUBLISHERS.

LIBRARY OF CONGRESS CATALOGING-IN-PUBLICATION DATA
Psychology of decision making in legal, health care and science settings / Gloria R. Burthold, editor.
    p. cm.
  Includes index.
  ISBN-13: 978-1-60021-932-0 (hardcover)
  ISBN-10: 1-60021-932-2 (hardcover)
  1. Decision making. I. Burthold, Gloria R.
BF448.P98 2007
153.8'3--dc22
                    2007028964

Published by Nova Science Publishers, Inc. ✦ New York

CONTENTS

PREFACE

In a fast-moving world, the necessity of making decisions, and preferably good ones, has become even more difficult. One reason is the variety and number of choices perhaps available which often arenot presented or understood. Alternatives are often unclear and complex paths to them confusing and misleading. Thus the process of decision making itself requires analysis on an ongoing basis. Decision making is often made based on cultural factors whereas the best alternative might be quite different. The subject touches ethics aspects as well as psychological considerations. This new book presents important research on the psychology of decision making related to law and law enforcement, health care and science.

Chapter 1 - This Chapter explores applications of decision-making primarily in health care but also examples dealing with environmental challenges and international affairs. It gives recent evidence of failures in each of these sectors and attempts to explain how such errors recur. It then describes some medical approaches to decision-making, evidence-based medicine, guidelines, epidemiology, risk assessment, prevention and screening and how they might apply beyond the world of medicine, even to international affairs. Guidelines and decision-making in medical practice are frequently premised on fundamental logical fallacies and questionable assumptions. These include faulty end points, surrogate indicators and a failure to understand the difference between causation and association. Such mistakes, also occur in international affairs, and seem to be related to narrowly reductionist, 'scientistic' or 'Realist' approaches, which ignore biases and distortions to objective decision-making. Reasons for acceptance of such failures include perceived self-interest and various cognitive distortions promoted in each sector by corporate use of media, think tanks, key opinion leaders, consumer or citizen groups, all which appeal to fears and uncertainties. Recommendations are made for changes to achieve more robust decision-making in each of medicine, environment and international affairs.

Chapter 2 - In recent years the Iowa Gambling Task has become an important tool in the development of theoretical models of decision-making and has greatly added to the authors understanding of the underlying neural mechanisms. The Iowa Gambling Task is a repeated choice situation in which participants must choose a card from any one of four decks. Two of the decks are advantageous in the sense that although they have a relatively low immediate reward with repeated selection they result in a high overall reward. The remaining two decks are disadvantageous in the sense that they have a higher immediate reward but result in an overall loss with repeated selection. As such, consistent choice of the advantageous decks is rational while consistent choice of the disadvantageous decks is impulsive. These behavior patterns clearly discriminate between clinical and healthy participants. Despite this, behavior in the Iowa Gambling Task, and in particular the motivations for individual choices, are poorly understood. The authors report two of experiments in which we compared choices between pairs of decks that varied in frequency and magnitude of both reward and punishment to better understand the bases of decision making in the Iowa Gambling Task.

Chapter 3 - Previous research has shown that jurors who are legally considered death qualified (DQ) significantly differ from those considered non-death qualified (NDQ). For example, it has been found that DQ and NDQ jurors differ in punitiveness (including use of evidence and deliberation, conviction-proneness, and sentencing), as well as gender and race. The purpose of this paper is to address the strengths and weaknesses of using social dominance theory to account for these differences. In addition, the author suggests other theories, as well as combinations of theories, which may be more appropriate to help researchers understand the differences between DQ and NDQ jurors and in turn how these differences affect jury decision making. Possible areas for future research are also discussed.

Chapter 4 - In the present analysis, research subjects were asked to rate four adult males, shown individually in black-and-white photographs, on twelve factors related to physical appearance and personality characteristics (i.e., attractiveness, honesty, etc.). After rating each photograph, research subjects were told that all four of the men photographed were convicted of capital murder and sentenced to either life or death by a capital jury. The research subjects were then asked to decide what punishment a jury imposed on each murderer.

Data gathered by the Capital Jury Project (CJP) provided evidence about the sentencing verdicts reached by juries in 48 death penalty cases. From this information, Department of Corrections' websites in four states were searched to locate photographs of these offenders. Cases were sought to fulfill the following research design: 24 Black murderers (12 from cases resulting in a death sentence and 12 from cases resulting in a life sentence) and 24 White murderers (12 from cases resulting in a death sentence and 12 from cases resulting in a life sentence).

During no part of the experiment did the participants have knowledge about the crime or details about the murder that was committed. Findings indicated that 1) certain factors related to physical appearance and personality characteristics were associated with trial outcomes; 2) offender race significantly impacted ratings on the twelve factors and also students' decision-making about trial outcomes; and 3) accuracy for choosing the correct trial outcome was at a rate greater than expected by chance alone.

Chapter 5 - The sunk-cost effect describes a common type of non-optimal decision in which humans contribute additional resources to a failing endeavor as a function of previous expenditures of resources (time, effort or money, the "sunk costs"). This phenomenon is intriguing because it appears to result from considering prior costs in decision making rather than basing decisions solely (and rationally) on marginal costs and benefits. The authors review different types of sunk-cost effects including those embodied in our laboratory's explorations of the factors controlling sunk-cost behavior in both humans and pigeons. These experiments suggested that sunk-cost behavior should be minimized if salient cues directed the participants' attention to the marginal costs and benefits. This finding led to one of the three experiments reported in this paper: By presenting the participant with precise economic forecasts we produced a "reverse" sunk-cost effect in which past expenditure of resources made future spending less (not more) likely. Two additional experiments explored the notion that poor decision-making behavior sometimes reflects inappropriate application of learned aversion to waste (as in "Waste not, want not"). This possibility was explored with both sunk-cost and Ultimatum Game scenarios. In each case support was found for the possibility that non-optimal decisions may be based in part on an aversion to waste. Just as there are different types of sunk-cost behavior, there are multiple causes of these behaviors. From an applied standpoint, however, it appears that presenting information in a complete and transparent manner may minimize such non-optimal decisions.

Chapter 6 - Decision-making capacity is a developmentally regulated process. Among the determinants of that capacity are the age and developmental status of the individual, their relative health, the nature of the choice to be made and the stress under which that person finds themselves. This article will focus on the influences of stress and culture on decision-making by parents whose children are critically ill. The two stressors highlighted in this discussion will be 1) the child's severity of illness and the critical care environment, and 2) potential culture/language discordance between the parents (or surrogates) of the patient and the healthcare team. Treatment decisions for the critically ill child demands the most astute decision-making capacity during a time that that capacity is severely strained. This article will define the environment impacting those decisions and offer some suggestions for improving the ability of parents to make these difficult decisions during a very stressful time.

Chapter 7 - The high performance development model (http://vaww.va.gov/hpdm/) enables leaders within the Veterans Health Administration (VHA) to function more effectively in the highly competitive environment in which they operate. The model is based on eight core competencies expected of VHA leadership, including personal mastery, interpersonal skills, creative thinking, technical skills, flexibility, systems thinking, organizational stewardship, and customer service. The impact of each of these on decision making is significant both for the individual leader and for healthcare leadership. A 360-degree assessment is used in the VHA to compare actual performance (as perceived by the rater) and preferred performance. This model encourages continuous growth of leaders and is an effective and efficient way of teaching and effecting good decision-making skills.

Chapter 8 - This study examined the effects of note-taking and justice-vengeance motives on juror decision making in a criminal trial. The study predicted that (1) jurors who took notes would render more appropriate decisions and recall more evidentiary content, (2) jurors high in vengeance would sentence the defendant more harshly and recall less probative information, and (3) note-taking would interact with justice and vengeance motives and impact upon sentencing and the recall of information. The sample of 149 jury eligible participants recruited from the Central Queensland community were assigned to one of two conditions (note-taking or non note-taking). All participants viewed the same murder trial and subsequently, rendered a verdict and sentencing decision, as well as recalled the trial facts. Lastly, they completed the Justice-Vengeance scale (Ho, ForsterLee, ForsterLee, & Crofts, 2002). Results of the study indicated that (1) jurors who took notes recalled more probative information than their non note-taking counterparts, (2) jurors high in vengeance sentenced the defendant more harshly and recalled fewer case-related facts, and (3) note-taking offset the vengeance motive for punishment, suggesting that note-taking would be a useful memory aid for vengeance-oriented jurors. The implications of these findings are discussed, as well as recommendations for future research in the field of juror decision-making.

Chapter 9 - The implementation of feedback systems into routine clinical practice has been recognized as a promising way to enhance treatment outcomes in outpatient psychotherapy. These feedback systems rely on the monitoring of individual treatment progress during the course of psychotherapy and the feedback of this information to therapists in a timely manner. If necessary, therapists can then use this information for adaptive treatment planning. However, since the problems of the clients seeking psychotherapy are manifold and, hence, not all clients have the same prospect for treatment success (at least not within the same amount of time), such feedback systems should also take into account an estimation of how much change or improvement can be expected for a given client until a given point of time in therapy based on his or her individual characteristics. By contrasting the actual treatment progress of an individual client and his or her expected treatment response, the actual client state is set into perspective. The approaches to predict individual treatment courses on the basis of client intake characteristics and previous treatment progress can be classified into two broad classes: *Rationally-derived decision rules* are based on judgments of experts, who determine the amount of progress that a client has to achieve until a given treatment session to be considered 'on track'. *Empirically-derived decision rules,* on the other hand, are based on statistically-derived expected recovery curves. In this chapter, examples of such decision support systems are presented and their potential to identify clients at risk for treatment failure during ongoing treatment courses is demonstrated. Furthermore, the potential of providing feedback to therapists based on these decision rules with respect to the enhancement of treatment outcomes is discussed.

Chapter 10 - Reactivation and the subsequent transformation of previously established memories are among the major topics of current psychobiological research [1, 7, 10, 26, 31]. Despite controversy about the nature of reconsolidation, there is growing acceptance that memory is a dynamic in nature and that reactivation returns a consolidated engram to a labile sensitive state, in which it can be modified, strengthened, or possibly even erased [9-11, 26]. Whereas significant efforts were applied to pharmacological dissection of reconsolidation, in an attempt to discover clear distinctions between cellular-molecular mechanisms of consolidation and reconsolidation [1, 6-7, 14-15, 17, 39, 41], the variety of roles that systemic consolidation and reconsolidation can play in actual-choice behavior is still largely unknown [1, 5, 10, 41]. Recently, the authors reported several new findings on hidden learning and ranking of memories and behavioral strategies in the matching-to-sample task on the radial maze [34]. Initially, the possible function of consolidation and reconsolidation, underlying these phenomena was not elucidated. In the current paper, the new extended research framework has been delineated. According to this, hidden learning and ranking can be explained by systemic consolidation and reconsolidation of matching skill, and by its effect on post-reactivation dynamic interactions of engrams in working memory. It is suggested that in a choice process, ranking of co-existing memories and behavioral strategies can be an important function of consolidation and reconsolidation. Further research for understanding the features and the functional significance of systemic consolidation and reconsolidation was shown to be critical for grasping dynamic aspects of decision-making in multiple-choice situations.

Chapter 11 - While research focusing on decision making by laypersons is quite ample, research focusing on the decision making processes conducted by experts is a bit less abundant. This is especially true for studies conducted in actual life settings instead of the popular excerpt or hypothetical bets settings used in most existing studies. The two studies depicted herein examined decision making processes conducted by laypersons and personnel psychologists regarding the congruence of candidates' various characteristics with the requirements and demands of a professional job.

One hundred and six candidates applying for prestigious legal positions in a large government agency participated in the first study. They have taken a selection test battery including aptitude tests as well as personality and interpersonal skill tests. The results were judged by I/O psychologists specializing in HR selection. To test the decision-making processes of these experts, the information sources (the test scores) were used as predictors of the final decision criterion in a series of stepwise regression models.

In the second study, 68 candidates for a service oriented position in a technological organization were screened using a standard aptitude battery, and then were screened using an assessment center, observed by both skilled psychologists and HR managers from the organization. The candidates accepted were followed up until the end of their training program in the organization. The training course grades served as a performance criterion.

The same method as described above was used to compare the structure and validity of the psychologists' decision making process vis-à-vis the HR managers decision making (based on a simple averaging formula).

The results show patterns consistent with existing research on human perception and decision making: Experts showed the same biases as laypersons in their decision making process. Moreover – the validity of the experts' decision was found to be lower than the validity of a simple averaging formula utilized by the HR managers.

The results are discussed in light of existing research on human perception and information processing. In addition suggestions for additional research and possible practices in the field of HR decision making are raised.

In: Psychology of Decision Making...
Editor: G. R. Burthold, pp. 1-67

ISBN: 978-1-60021-932-0
© 2007 Nova Science Publishers, Inc.

Chapter 1

APPLICATIONS OF SCIENCE-BASED DECISION-MAKING: MEDICINE, ENVIRONMENT AND INTERNATIONAL AFFAIRS

Neil Arya

University of Waterloo Environment and Resource Studies University of Western Ontario Family Medicine McMaster University Family Medicine

ABSTRACT

This Chapter explores applications of decision-making primarily in health care but also examples dealing with environmental challenges and international affairs. It gives recent evidence of failures in each of these sectors and attempts to explain how such errors recur. It then describes some medical approaches to decision-making, evidence-based medicine, guidelines, epidemiology, risk assessment, prevention and screening and how they might apply beyond the world of medicine, even to international affairs. Guidelines and decision-making in medical practice are frequently premised on fundamental logical fallacies and questionable assumptions. These include faulty end points, surrogate indicators and a failure to understand the difference between causation and association. Such mistakes, also occur in international affairs, and seem to be related to narrowly reductionist, 'scientistic' or 'Realist' approaches, which ignore biases and distortions to objective decision-making. Reasons for acceptance of such failures include perceived self-interest and various cognitive distortions promoted in each sector by corporate use of media, think tanks, key opinion leaders, consumer or citizen groups, all which appeal to fears and uncertainties. Recommendations are made for changes to achieve more robust decision-making in each of medicine, environment and international affairs.

Keywords: evidence based medicine, international affairs, epidemiology, screening, cognitive distortions, risk analysis, medical decision-making, scientism, risk assessment

THE FAILURE OF MEDICAL DECISION-MAKING

Over the last fifteen years as a family physician, I have observed developments in the field of medicine. As a graduate of chemical engineering, an adjunct professor of environmental studies and sitting on committees for the environment for my city and for my provincial college of family physicians and now on government advisory panels, I have followed current issues in the nuclear power, petroleum and pesticide industries. As a leader in a physicians' peace group, I have reflected on military affairs, small arms and the arms trade.

Since I began medical school, conventional medical practice has reversed itself on many issues, from beta blockers being contra-indicated in heart failure to being used to treat it, from forbidding breastfeeding because of 'breast milk jaundice', to encouraging more frequent breastfeeding to deal with neonatal jaundice, from enforcing the prone position in newborns to avoid aspiration, to advocating 'back only' sleep position to avoid SIDS, from treating low back pain with forced immobilization, then with active mobilization and finally allowing activity as tolerated.

Such reversals in medical practice are not uncommon and, I believe, represent faults and biases in the decision-making process. While this Chapter primarily addresses such issues in the domain of medicine, drawing on lessons from medical failures to the present day across the spectrum of medical practice, from management of infections to chronic disease cancers, heart disease and risk factors, I will also use analogies from aspects of environmental and international affairs with which I am most familiar.

I will try not to suggest particularly how others should weigh the evidence, but to clarify assumptions behind medical decision-making, to understand cognitive distortions of such decision-making, to consider values that underlie our decisions and to suggest certain considerations to evaluate risk benefit with explicit criteria, in order to make the most honest, transparent and resilient decisions with the best scientific information available. I will suggest how we may design a more effective robust system for making decisions not just in medicine, but in other sectors, including international affairs and environmental policy.

DECIDING WHAT'S SAFE AND WHAT'S NOT

Three Phases of Introduction of a New Drug

The medical "magic bullet", the subject of daily newspaper headlines, is often much less impressive than initially touted. Undesirable side effects may appear even years after its introduction. In medical school, I was taught that new drugs introduced to the market often go through three phases, the three 'P's, panacea, poison and pedestrian.

Panacaea

When it first comes out, a drug may be thought to be God's gift to humankind, curing everything from warts to heart attacks. In fact when we find one drug that seems highly effective for a particular situation, the natural tendency is to look at more general applications. Fluoxetine (Prozac), sildenafil (Viagra) and tamoxifen (Nolvadex), each have been considered, for a time, to be so beneficial that the pharmaceutical industry, certain allied physicians and media declared that indications should be expanded to the worried well, to all men and women with sexual dysfunction, and to all women without breast cancer, respectively, until studies proved them not to possess such advantages. Expensive anti viral drugs such as zanamivir (Relenza) and oseltamivir (Tamiflu), meant for immune-compromised individuals, were marketed for flu-like illness and used for common cold in some countries. Despite equivocal efficacy and dangers, even for treatment of the flu, (including behavioral aberrations) and though they have never been tested against 'bird flu', they are now being considered to be a major part of the armamentarium to prevent a pandemic.

Poison

Later, when major side effects are 'discovered', some former panaceas come to be seen as poisons; if not subject to withdrawal from the market, they may become objects of major lawsuits. Sometimes side effects are discovered early on by the drug company which developed the drug, but as occurred with Vioxx, this evidence may not be fully communicated to the medical profession and to the public for years. But more often it is just that problems aren't discovered until a drug is used widely. The prokinetic agent cisapride (Prepulsid), once considered an ideal drug because it worked on all parts of the gut and was used to treat gastro-esophageal reflux (heartburn) and motility disorders such as gastroparesis, was withdrawn from the market because of its arrhythmogenic properties; it can cause irregularities of the heart rate, increasing the risk of sudden death. [1, 2]

Pedestrian

When, with the passage of time, the risks and benefits are properly weighed, drugs often becomes mediocre or pedestrian, something that we recognize when we meet on the street, but don't consider extraordinary, with advantages and disadvantages that must be balanced. Day before yesterday's panacea became yesterday's poison and but today may be used judiciously, in selected cases. In medicine we have seen doxylamine succinate the main component of Bendectin, which was banned, return as a component of Diclectin in Canada, currently the *only* 'safe' agent for nausea and vomiting in pregnancy. [3] The bacteriostatic antibiotic agent chloramphenicol, known to cause aplastic anemia in an irreversible, idiosyncratic way in less than 1:25000 cases, can be useful to treat some serious systemic infections such as typhoid. Even thalidomide, which caused major malformations, now has made a comeback to treat leprosy and cancer. [4]

Three Phases in the Environmental Sector

Similar errors occur in the environmental sector. The organochlorine pesticide, DDT began as a panacea after World War II, before becoming the villain in Rachel Carson's widely acclaimed *Silent Spring* in the early 1960s. Though it is now known to be a carcinogen with terrible consequences for many species and ecosystems, it may be making a comeback in areas where malaria is endemic, where benefits seem to outweigh the risks. [5]

Nuclear power, a panacea in the 50s, became a poison by the 80's, following accidents at Chernobyl and Three Mile Island. By this time the issues of nuclear waste management and disposal were unresolved, evidence pointed above ground nuclear testing in the 50s and 60s may have led to millions of premature deaths, and the nuclear establishment was perceived to be secretive with each of these matters. Now in the era of climate change and Peak Oil, it has among its advocates, solid environmentalists such as James Lovelock, developer of the Gaia hypothesis. [6][1]

Public Health and Environmental Measures that Remain Life-savers and those that Remain Killers

But not all interventions have balanced effects. Even though sometimes procedures may be carried to an extreme, there are many public health measures whose benefits become more apparent as the years go on. Despite the skepticism of much of 19th century society [7] and Semmelweiss' colleagues at the Vienna Allgemeines Krankenhaus who rejected his advice for years, hand-washing and hygiene on the obstetrics ward led to major reductions in mortality. [8] Speed limits, seatbelts, crash helmets, air bags, and penalties for drinking and driving all have helped decrease morbidity and mortality, far more than medical practice.

Clearly there are some drugs and therapies that remain 'poisons', never becoming 'pedestrian' because of major adverse or unacceptable effects, Lasser [9] found that of 548 new chemical entities approved by the FDA between 1975 and 1999, 45 (8.2%) acquired a black box warning and 16 (2.9%) were pulled from the market. The estimated probability over a 25 year period, of acquiring a new black box warning or being withdrawn from the market was 20%.

In the environmental sector, types of poisons are also multifold. Persistent organic pollutants (POPs) which bioaccumulate are banned under the 2001 Stockholm protocol;[2] [10, 11] so are chlorofluorocarbons (CFCs) under the 1987 Montreal protocol. [12] Reduction of exposure to asbestos, has led to decrease in mesothelioma. Mercury in water and lead in paints and gas have few redeeming qualities. Cosmetic use of pesticides (to kill weeds in lawns and gardens to create 'healthy' lawns) has few benefits and carries uncertain risks and is becoming unacceptable in many western countries. [13]

The three phases of societal perception of drugs, chemical substances in household and industrial usage and new technologies may reflect evolution in scientific knowledge.

However is there a basis for rational decision-making, a way to determine what may be a true panacea, what is a real poison and what is somewhere in between much earlier on, or must we remain guinea pigs losing lives as science progresses?

---

[1]   The hypotheses central to the thinking of environmental ethics views the earth as a self-regulating living system that maintains the conditions for the perpetuation of life. The earth has finite resources, sustainability limits. Human beings have a responsibility as stewards, to preserve the function of this within the various delicate margins necessary for life.

[2]   This class of long-lasting and dangerous chemicals is based on the criteria of toxicity, persistence, bioaccumulation, and long-range transport and includes polychlorinated biphenyls (PCBs), dioxins, furans and nine pesticides

SCIENCE AND SCIENTISM

Science

The scientific ideal is a relatively simple iterative process of observation, hypothesis development and hypothesis testing producing new evidence and debate leading to conclusions that are increasingly refined and reliable and cover more situations though are never certain.

By contrast, the sociological process of the diffusion of new beliefs is more complex. This sociological process often involves power struggles in which all sides of the debate claim that their old opinion is supported by the best evidence, but overlooking flaws in evidence that supports their opinions whilst discounting evidence that does not. Demosthenes once said that *"Nothing is easier than self-deceit. For what each man wishes, that he also believes to be true"* [14]. It is normal to wish to be proven to have been right all along and that wish can blind us to the reality that we were wrong from the start.

Some people regard the panacea, poison, pedestrian sequence as evidence of something wrong with the scientific ideal. People may believe that their belief that a new drug is a panacea is justified by science, but science never justifies such beliefs. However when a drug is new there is very limited evidence available- the only valid scientific conclusion is that it is not yet known if the drug is a panacea, a poison, or pedestrian. While we cannot blame science for its misuse, for extrapolations beyond the evidence, for claims that it supported the false beliefs, we must realize that when key constituencies have something to gain, hyping of the value of therapies is common.

The beliefs given as examples above, (beta blockers in heart failure, breast feeding, prone position), were due to overconfident misinterpretation of inadequate evidence. Sometimes science had it right on the benefits, but was missing or underestimating toxicity based on inadequate information (cisapride) or we knew about the benefits and downsides, but didn't have an appropriate view of the balance (chloramphenicol).

Scientism

I too, am a believer in science and the scientific method, but not in 'Scientism', which I will define as the generalized, unexamined belief in narrowly, 'evidence—based', reductionist, scientific studies on which the above faulty decisions were made. [15] Scientism is more religion than science and distorts our ability to weigh evidence and act in our longer-term interests. It involves the unintentional, over-enthusiastic use of data without looking at its assumptions, sources, their vested interests, biases and even deliberate, fraudulent manipulation of the data.

Scientism's True Believers remain convinced that, despite major failures in decision-making based on such 'science' in the past, in the future, medical science, scientific experts or the military will solve each of the world's problems; from medical diseases as cancer and heart disease to environmental and social problems such as pollution, climate change, hunger or poverty to the political and security problems of ridding the world of dangers of weapons of mass destruction and terrorism.

I will argue that many errors we in medicine have made were not merely part of scientific development and either predictable or knowable much earlier. I have seen similar assurances that decision-making is better in the environmental and military sectors despite various environmental failures and now with major US military debacles in Iraq and arguably, in Afghanistan. In each sector, with each failure or reversal, the name and tools change slightly, but the basic methods do not change. When analogous failures continue to occur over and over in several sectors, it may suggest a collective failure of societal memory, and of decision-making.

Even in the couple of months it was found that the majority of angioplasties, (one million in the US annually at costs of billions of dollars, added little to optimal medical management of stable patients, that a recent class of diabetic medications, the thiazolidinediones, may be dangerous increasing heart attacks and eye problems, which good control of diabetes was meant to help.-These will be discussed in more detail later.

In the 19th century studies of 'time proven' treatments of bleeding, cupping, purging and enemas compared to bed rest, nutrition, and observation for conditions such as typhoid fever and delirium tremens found doing nothing to be superior leading to an era of "therapeutic nihilism". [16] But I am not advocating inaction.

Through a decade and a half of decision-making in general practice, a healthy skepticism has served me well. Before prescribing drugs, both new and old, I had explained risks and possible drawbacks, both known and unknown. Despite many drug recalls and re-labeling of even common drugs, I have never had to re-call patients to tell them that I had inadvertently given them a dangerous drug. I will try to draw on such experience to help assess for example, in what situations a drug is likely to do more good than harm.

Such an approach might equally be applied to other sectors of decision-making as opposed to a current 'scientistic' approach where each reversal seems novel and unpredictable. In designing a better system, it is helpful to look at how decisions are currently made.

OBJECTIVITY IN MEDICAL DECISION-MAKING

Decision-making

Decision-making is a cognitive process of making a selective judgment or choice. It typically follows a process where a problem or opportunity is identified, aims are determined, relevant information gathered, alternatives developed and evaluated. On this basis, a decision is made to implement the best alternative. Subsequently there is follow-up and evaluation. Depending on the situation, this may be a more cyclical process. Structured, rational decision making is a must for all science-based professions, where specialists apply their knowledge in a given area to making informed decisions. The reasoning process may be based on explicit or tacit assumptions, ideas or opinions and usually defines a course of action.

Medical decision-making often involves making a particular diagnosis and/or selecting an appropriate treatment. So how are objective decisions made in medicine?

Evidence-based Medicine

The term Evidence-based Medicine (EBM) was coined by the McMaster University research group led by David Sackett and Gordon Guyatt. and first entered the medical literature in Guyatt's 1991 paper entitled 'Evidence-Based Medicine'. [17] Guyatt's aim was to differentiate clinical decision-making based on evaluation of evidence from obedience to dogma. The British Medical Journal now considers Evidence-based Medicine to be among the top 15 medical innovations since 1840. [18]

EBM is a conscientious, explicit, judicious and systematic process of finding, appraising, and using current best evidence from scientific studies and integrating that with clinical experience and information about an individual patient's condition, values and preferences.

The fundamental precepts of EBM include beginning with an open mind and formulating a clear and appropriate clinical question regarding a patient's problem, finding and critically appraising relevant data for its validity and usefulness and applying judgements about the inductive quality of evidence.

"By best available external clinical evidence we mean clinically relevant research, often from the basic sciences of medicine, but especially from patient-centered clinical research into the accuracy and precision of diagnostic tests (including the clinical examination), the power of prognostic markers, and the efficacy and safety of therapeutic, rehabilitative, and preventive regimens." [19]

Developing Guidelines in Medicine

Out of the best available evidence, experts ideally may develop clinical practice guidelines (CPGs), which may be integrated with clinical expertise and patient values in order to make decisions. One set of guidelines, *The Medical Letter on Drugs and Therapeutics* has provided relatively independent, unbiased, critical evaluations of new drugs and sometimes, older drugs when important new information becomes available since 1959. Occasionally new non-drug treatments or diagnostic aids are reviewed. *The Medical Letter* receives no pharmaceutical revenue nor allows any drug advertising in the publication.

The Cochrane Centres of evidence-based medical research, and the international organization, the Cochrane Collaboration, named after Scottish epidemiologist Archie Cochrane, author of *Effectiveness and Efficiency: Random Reflections on Health Services* (1972), focuses on studies with the best methods for answering the question including best qualitative studies, and meta-analyses. The Cochrane Database of Systematic Reviews synthesizes such evidence, providing overall assessment based on the best relevant well conducted individual studies, so researchers can then critically analyze and assess the quality and relevance of the evidence. [20] Cochrane reviewers have explicit instructions not to make recommendations but to summarize information, searching the literature according to a pre-specified system to minimize bias. Unfortunately the Cochrane Reviews are still far from comprehensive and many important questions in Medicine have yet to be subjected to Cochrane scrutiny.

There are benefits to ensuring a consistent acceptable standard of care. Medical students and physicians often want guidelines and algorithms including immunization schedules, lipid and hypertension management guidelines, which they feel improves their decision-making efficiency and patient care. [21] They understand that these may change when new evidence becomes available.

Medical algorithms may include computations, formulae, nomograms, or tables, useful in healthcare, but usually employs flow charts (i.e. if symptoms A, B, and C are evident, then use treatment X) or binary decision trees (if X do Y, if not X, do Z). Decision trees analysis may begin with all the options then splits into all the possible outcomes giving each a probability and a utility.

Most Western countries have national bodies for developing medical management guidelines. These bodies, for example, exist in Canada [22], the US [23], Britain, [24] France, [25] and Germany [26] to name just a few. International bodies such as the Guidelines International Network compile national guidelines. Such compilations also demonstrate that even evaluating the same evidence may lead to different conclusions resulting in varied guidelines among countries. [27]

The Canadian Task Force on the Periodic Health Examination, [28] begun in 1976, and used a standardized methodology for evaluating the effectiveness of preventive health care interventions and for developing clinical practice guidelines based on the evidence from published medical research. The rules were refined in collaboration with the U.S. Preventive Services Task Force *(USPSTF)* [29] in the 1980s and the latter's efforts continue. The basic premise- to form recommendations of graded strength based on the quality of published medical evidence remains unaltered. Grades of Recommendations vary from 'Good evidence' to support the recommendation that the condition be specifically considered in a General Physical Examination (PHE), to 'fair evidence' to 'Good evidence' to support the recommendation that the condition be specifically excluded from consideration from a PHE. The latest development in rating quality of evidence and strength of recommendations (the GRADE approach) was introduced in 2004 [30] and so far has been endorsed by WHO, Cochrane, UpToDate, NICE, ACP, BMJ, and 10 other major guideline groups.

Epidemiology in Medicine

Epidemiology and biostatistics are fundamental to the science of medical decision-making. Last defines epidemiology as *"the study of the distribution and determinants of health-related states or events in a specified population and the application of this study to the control of health problems."*

Hippocrates said *"To know the cause of a disease and to understand the use of the various methods by which disease may be prevented amounts to the same thing in effect as being able to cure the malady."* [31]

An epidemiologist determines frequencies and patterns of disease, causes of disease, mode of transmission and factors related to susceptibility, exposure and risk. Clinical medicine focuses on treating sick patients while public health, the sector of medicine based on epidemiology, focuses on reducing disease in the future. Common goals of each may be to prevent disease, improve disease outcome, and to promote the health of populations, but perspectives differ in clinical and public health sciences. Data collection for the clinician is primarily the history, physical exam and technological investigations, but for the epidemiologist, surveillance and analyses. A clinician treats individuals one at a time, which may ultimately impact the community but an epidemiologist examines benefits of community interventions, which may ultimately impact individuals.

In medicine, epidemiology may help to describe the natural history of disease, identify individual risks, and search for causes. Epidemiology identified associations of sudden infant death syndrome with sleeping on the side or prone, mesothelioma with asbestos, use of the oral contraceptive pill (OCP) with increased risk of DVT, and fluoridated water supplies with lack of cavities. In public health it may be used to study historical patterns, assess the health of the community, or evaluate health services.

In 1965 Bradford Hill [32] examined criteria to determine whether there was a probable causation between for example, smoking and lung cancer. He asserted that the greater the *Strength of Association* the more likely it is causal; *Consistency* across a variety of populations, times and circumstances with multiple studies and study designs will enhance this conclusion; *Specificity* of a single type of exposure with a single disease will strengthen the chance of causation (but the absence doesn't refute it); *Temporality*-the exposure must take place before disease (cross sectional and case control studies can't establish causality); there may be a *Biological gradient* (increasing the dose resulting in an increasing response), but there may also be a minimum dose threshold before which no effect is noted; *Plausibility* is based on existing biological and social models, but having a plausible 'explanation' for the relationship is not essential, since putative explanations for observed phenomena often turn out to be wrong; there must be *Coherence*-it must not contradict what it known, though we must be prepared to reinterpret what is known; analogy with other diseases similarly strengthens associations.

The links between exposures and outcomes are complex in medicine, but even more so with environmental issues and international affairs. The simplest situation to analyze is single agent cause and single effect that has no other causes. A slightly more complex framework is the epidemiological triad involving host, agent and environment. However for many environmental or social problems, causal pies full of necessary and sufficient causes or webs of causation are more accurate.

Epidemiologic studies typically look for a common association between exposures and outcomes for a defined population. Study designs may differ in terms of data collection methods, timing, units of observation and subjects. Cases studies and case series and cross sectional studies seek association; ecologic and case control studies are somewhat stronger and generate hypotheses. Cohort studies may be prospective or retrospective and generate more information on the incidence and natural history of disease. Cohort studies are also critical in defining associations between environmental occupational or drug exposures and specific diseases.

Non-randomized trials, opinions of respected authorities based on clinical experience, descriptive studies, or reports of expert committees each have their place but for treatment–oriented questions, the 'gold standard' test, from an experimental or statistical point of view, with highest levels of evidence to test an intervention's ability to affect the natural history of a disease, is a properly designed randomized controlled trial. [33]³ RCTs are often quite

---

3   Sackett et al further state, *"Evidence based medicine is not restricted to randomized trials and meta-analyses. It involves tracking down the best external evidence with which to answer our clinical questions." "Because the randomized trial, and especially the systematic review of several randomized trials, is so much more likely to inform us and so much less likely to mislead us, it has become the "gold standard" for judging whether a*

expensive to conduct and either prove impractical or require smaller sample sizes. Meta-analyses are meant to draw experience of several similar studies to increase the power of studies and systematic reviews.

Risk Assessment

Often in medicine, environmental and international affairs, we are left with trying to determine risk and benefits of choices-for example whether to use a drug or chemical. Policy makers also have to make decisions on whether to allow or force withdrawal of a drug on market, whether or not to ban a pesticide or to promote alternative energy sources, whether to choose military action or diplomatic means to achieve goals.

Risk assessment is the process of quantifying the probability of a harmful effect from certain human activities to individuals or populations and the classification of hazards including estimate of risks and uncertainties. *Risk evaluation* is concerned with assessing probability and impact of individual risks, taking into account any interdependencies or other factors outside the immediate scope under investigation: *Risk management* concerns evaluation and implementation of options based on scientific, political and socio-cultural considerations.

On safety issues in Public Health or in industry, risk assessment begins with identification of the hazard (circumstances which result in adverse outcome), quatification of exposure and assessment of response. Probability is the evaluated likelihood or frequency of a particular outcome actually happening. Impact is the evaluated effect or result of a particular outcome actually happening. Risk is a product of the probability and the impact.

Responses to risk include prevention-terminating the risk, reduction-treating the risk to limit its impact to acceptable levels, transferring the risk- passing it to third party via, for instance, an insurance policy and accepting or tolerating the risk. The last choice may be made because nothing can be done at a reasonable cost to mitigate it or the likelihood and impact of the risk occurring are at an acceptable level. In that case contingency plans may be developed with actions planned and organized to come into force, if and when the risk occurs. We need to understand that in some circumstances, particularly in the social realm, risk is more difficult to evaluate, but nonetheless controllable and we might attempt to reduce harm. More complex models would include benefits and consider the nature and probability of each benefit and harm, attempting to maximize benefits and minimize harms.

"Prevention" and Screening in Medicine

Confusingly, the term prevention which implies reducing risk to zero is generally used to mean merely reducing risks. In medicine it is preferable and often cheaper, to reduce risks where possible, rather than reacting to full- blown disease. Important preventable health deficits such as lung cancer, cirrhosis and melanoma, which may be mitigated simply by reduced exposure to the causative smoking, alcohol and sun respectively. Increasing exercise,

---

treatment does more good than harm. However, some questions about therapy do not require randomized trials (successful interventions for otherwise fatal conditions) or cannot wait for the trials to be conducted."

decreasing meat consumption and increasing fiber in diet are generally useful preventive measures to improve health. However sometimes the "prevention" is worse than the disease. This can occur when the "preventative" activity is expensive and/or poorly effective and/or has its own risks.

"Primary prevention" refers to the prevention of diseases, reducing exposure to risk factors before their biological onset: Examples include pasteurization and immunization. Sometimes *"primordial prevention,"* is used to refer to modification or elimination of risk factors or behaviors prior to them causing a problem. *"Secondary prevention"* refers to the prevention of clinical illness through the early detection prior to symptoms that, if left undetected, would likely become clinically apparent and harmful. This is often referred to as *"screening."* *"Tertiary prevention"* refers to the prevention of disease progression and additional disease complications after overt clinical diseases are manifest. [34] Confusingly many doctors use the term secondary prevention for tertiary prevention.

'*Screening*' refers to a technique for the presumptive identification of people with early disease by application of tests to separate those within a broad population who are likely to suffer from a particular condition from those without a condition. These tests, which include procedures such as mammograms and PAP smears, are meant to diagnose disease at a pre-symptomatic or early symptomatic stage when intervention may alter the natural course of the disease.

A suitable disease is an important health problem which, if left untreated, goes on to serious consequences, one where early detection in asymptomatic persons leads to a significantly better outcome related to response to treatment or to individuals changing their lifestyle in a protective way.

A suitable test is one with few side effects and the ability to detect accurately with low false negative and false positive rates and is cost effective. A reliable screening test gives the same test result each time a test is done while a valid test gives the correct result each time. A sensitive test correctly detects cases, while a specific one correctly identifies non-cases. A test with inadequate sensitivity means a significant proportion of persons with the disorder will escape detection. Such false negative results may give a false sense of security, resulting in inadequate attention to risk reduction and delays in seeking medical care even after warning symptoms become present. An excessively sensitive test will mean that many normal people (false positives) are caught in the net and subjected to unnecessary and potentially dangerous additional testing and/or treatment.

SCIENCE-BASED DECISION-MAKING IN INTERNATIONAL AFFAIRS

The powerful methods of EBM applied judiciously to other sectors.

Evidence-based International Affairs

In specific instances such as Bosnia or Sierra Leone in the early 90s or East Timor over the last quarter of the 20th century, early military intervention by the international community may arguably have done more good than harm for the survival and well being of the majority of people in the area. Yet, generalizing successes of possible military ventures to other situations or using the military for tasks for which it was not designed, from delivering aid, to conflict resolution, to policing to post-conflict rebuilding and development of schools, water supply, electricity and sewage may not be the most efficient use of resources.

In an article appearing just prior to the 2003 Iraq war entitled 'Ask the Right Questions', I attempted to apply precepts of evidence-based medicine and risk assessment to evaluating the merits of the war to see if using EBM techniques might lead US and British leaders to draw different conclusions about Saddam Hussein and Iraq. [35] The questions 'they' appeared to be asking were 'Is Saddam Hussein a liar and does he hang out with a bad crowd? and Does Saddam Hussein defy international order and like weapons of mass destruction?'

I proposed instead, that before launching a war the Bush administration and the American public ought to ask clear and appropriate questions according to EBM - 'How imminent and credible is the threat? What will this do to the Iraqi people? What will this do for countries and peoples in the region? What will it do for our own safety? What will this do to the economy? What will it do to international institutions? What are alternatives?'

After analyzing answers to the above using the best available evidence, it appeared that the chance of usable WMD that could be any threat to those in the region or as claimed by some to US and IK territory in the near future were nil. The conclusions were most likely that the war could only be bad for the Iraqi people with damage predicted by others, that it was likely to be destabilizing for the region and to promote terror (rather than acting in a domino way to promote democracy) and to cost over $50-200 billion (a major underestimate), and undermine any sense of international governance. Other goals to ensuring adequate energy supplies could have been accomplished more cheaply by conservation.

I then proposed alternatives to war[4] concluding, "These are cheaper, more effective and sustainable alternatives to war. Let's choose them; let's choose peace."

Of course, the decision-making of the Bush administration involved not only explicit logic, but included values, ideology and politics and perhaps self-deception. In spite of the objective evidence for lack of benefits for Americans or the international community let alone Iraqis, whether it was oil, the mutual hatred of Saddam and the senior Bushes, the symbol of Saddam remaining in power for the region, the chance to democratize the Middle East through a domino effect, the Bush administration drew different conclusions. Similar analyses could have been done in Afghanistan [36]

---

4   These included 1.supporting international law, multilateral processes and institutions: the International Criminal Court, the Biological Weapons Convention, the Anti-Ballistic Missile treaty, Landmines Treaty, and even the Kyoto Protocol to reduce our dependence on fossil fuels 2. de-linking military sanctions from economic sanctions 3. supporting regional arms control 4.genuine moves on the part of the Nuclear Weapons States to abolish nuclear weapons as mandated by Article VI of the Nuclear Non-Proliferation Treaty to reduce the threat of proliferation and support for inspection and verification regimes to get rid of biological and chemical weapons would add moral strength to such efforts, 5. encouraging regional peace processes, particularly a just solution to the Israeli-Palestinian question 6. promoting human rights monitors, tribunals for violations and rewarding progress by allowing Iraq's reintegration into the international community and failing this nurturing democratic movements within Iraq supporting civil society opposition to Saddam through nonviolent regional and international non-governmental organizations.

Epidemiology in International Affairs

No randomized trials are conducted in international affairs, but epidemiology can be quite useful in improving decision-making in that sector. Randomization and blinding would be difficult if not impossible, for most environmental exposures on humans and in any case, would contravene the Conventions of Nuremberg, Helsinki, Tokyo and Geneva, developed in response to the Second World War medical experimental crimes of the Nazis and the Japanese military government. Further, the ethical boundaries on experimentation, for instance on informed consent, increase as the proposed effects of the intervention increase, and become more uncertain.

Tragically, one of the best-conducted and most well resourced studies occurred on radiation victims after Hiroshima. The Life Span Study of 93,000 survivors and 27,000 unexposed individuals used *longitudinal cohort* and *case-control* designs to study the life-long health risks of cancer and radiation effects. [37] In 1962 Physicians for Social Responsibility projected Hiroshima's devastation and health effects to Boston, Massachusetts, estimating the impact of firestorm, blast wave and gale causing projectile debris on mortality, physical trauma, and the short-term and long-term radiation effects: 98 % of medical personnel would die within the central city; the entire U.S. would not have enough burn beds to deal with this one city's victims; environmental radiation would cause cancers years after an attack. [38] Leading medical voices were thus able to prove there could be no meaningful medical response to a nuclear war. International Physicians for the Prevention of Nuclear War (IPPNW) later demonstrated the likely effects of accidental nuclear war or a terrorist attack and using such data convinced the leadership in various countries of the merits of disarmament, winning the Nobel Peace Prize in 1985 [39].

Epidemiology has also been used to describe the nature of the small arms damage to health and possible interventions. [40] In the United States almost 30,000 people are killed each year with firearms, second only to motor vehicles as the most frequent cause of injury or death for 15-24 year olds. One innovative study design has been to compare geographically and demographically similar cities with differing prevalence of gun ownership: Seattle, USA (41%) vs. Vancouver, Canada (12%). During the study period, while robbery, home burglary, and aggravated assault rates were nearly comparable, rates of assault with firearms were 7.7 times higher and homicides involving firearms 4.8 times higher in Seattle than Vancouver. [41] Other work showed that households in the US with firearms are three times more likely to have suicides [42] and five times more likely to have homicides than those without firearms. [43] The lethality of handguns is far higher than other methods of homicide and suicide such as knives and ropes. [44]

Even war itself may be studied with epidemiological methods. International Physicians for the Prevention of Nuclear War predicted prior to the Gulf war that the war would cause between 50,000 and 250,000 deaths in the first few months during and after the war. [45, 46] Iraq Body Count (IBC) has sought to count the dead directly since the war. [47] Immediately prior to the 2004 US election, at a time when IBC reported 10,000 direct deaths, a retrospective study by Johns Hopkins University, showed 100,000 excess deaths, with general mortality being 2.5 times greater than pre-war and violent death 58 times greater. [48] A follow-up study determined an excess mortality of 650,000 Iraqi casualties in the 40 months post-invasion. [49][5]

Using such data may help guide international affairs, to decide whether the risk of potential harms of a particular proposed intervention is worth its purported benefits.

FAULTY ASSUMPTIONS OF SCIENTISM

While such objective decision-making, if practiced consistently, might serve us well in medicine and international affairs, this often doesn't occur in the 'real world'.

Faulty Models

Hormone replacement for post menopausal women was initially promoted for symptom relief, but was found to reduce osteoporosis and to have properties that might reduce risk factors for heart disease. At medical meetings throughout the 1990s, physicians were told that it was unethical and possibly fraught with medico-legal consequences to fail to recommend hormone replacement for all perimenopausal and post menopausal women. Some even conjectured that it could be good for "preventing" Alzheimer's disease. All this was before adequate randomized controlled trials had been done.

The Women's Health Initiative (WHI) randomized controlled trial and others, gave lie to many of these claims finding that hormone replacement increased breast cancer, stroke, early heart disease and even Alzheimer's- exactly the opposite to previous conjecture! [50][6]

In the end it seems that such initial guidelines by expert bodies recommending hormone treatment to all, were not truly evidence-based, beginning as they did with a flawed pathophysiological model and overconfidence about observational evidence.

Let us look at our limited models with regard to our bones. Many have assumed that if bones are heavier or denser then they will be stronger. Taking one of the early agents intended to strengthen bones, sodium fluoride to increase bone density actually may make bones more fragile. Drugs for osteoporosis such as bisphosphonates will make the bones more brittle if used for too long, and may occasionally cause the jawbone to die (osteonecrosis) and rarely even result in oesophageal perforation, which has very high

---

5   This study of 1,849 homes in 47 randomly selected community clusters, documented 629 deaths among 12,801 household members over a 4.4 year period. Crude mortality rates (all ages) rose from 5.5 per 1000 to 13.2; violent deaths rose from pre 2003 war levels of 2% to 60 %; 78% of which occurred among adult males 15-59 years. Though Tony Blair claimed these claims were flawed without giving a rationale, scientists from the British government validated its methodology.

6   This was multicentre cohort study of 161,809 women between the ages of 50-79, of the use of estrogen and progestin in women who had a uterus. The study itself was difficult to fund because of the general perception of the benefits of hormone replacement therapy HRT. In July 2002 the 'estrogen with progesterone' component of the WHI study was stopped early because of a 26% relative increase in breast cancer. Later the estrogen only arm was stopped because of an increase in strokes. Hormone replacement also increased the number of cardiac events from 30 to 37 per 10,000 women years of use. Though HRT also increases blood clots (DVTs), strokes, ovarian cancer and gallstones and uterine cancer if estrogen is unopposed (used without progesterone), it does appear to reduce colon cancer, slow bone mass loss, and help with menopausal symptoms. Some patients with severe menopausal symptoms may weigh the benefit of improving their quality of life as worth the calculated risk of possibly losing their life.

mortality. How about prevention measures for other problems? Recommendations to avoid sun because of skin cancer may actually increase the risk of osteoporosis because of a decrease in vitamin D. Now we find that proton pump inhibitors (PPIs), commonly used to suppress gastric acid production in the treatment of reflux oesphagitis, may interfere with calcium absorption through this decreased acid production and now are associated with increased hip fractures. [51] PPIs have also been linked to low serum Vitamin B12 levels which could cause neurological or blood disease.

Vitamin A and E, antioxidants, for the prevention of heart disease and lung cancer, were actually found to be neutral or slightly harmful for these diseases in high risk populations including smokers and those with higher exposure to asbestos. [52, 53, 54, 55, 56]

What is responsible for such errors? Let's look at a few very basic methodological errors that are commonly overlooked in design and evaluation of trials.

Reliance on Surrogate Indicators

"A surrogate end-point of a clinical trial is a laboratory measurement or a physical sign used as a substitute for a clinically meaningful end-point that measures directly how a patient feels, functions or survives."

Changes induced by a therapy on a surrogate end-point in cardiology trials, such as suppression of ventricular arrhythmias or reduction in cholesterol level or blood pressure, are expected to reflect changes in a clinically meaningful endpoint. A surrogate is not just a correlate; the effect of the intervention on the surrogate end- point predicts the effect on the clinical outcome.

"Surrogate end points can be useful in phase 2 screening trials for identifying whether a new intervention is biologically active and for guiding decisions about whether the intervention is promising enough to justify a large definitive trial with clinically meaningful outcomes. In definitive phase 3 trials, except for rare circumstances in which the validity of the surrogate end point has already been rigorously established, the primary end point should be the true clinical outcome." [57]

Cardiac arrhythmias are a major source of mortality after a heart attack. Two decades ago, anti-arrhythmics such as encainide and flecanide were approved by the Food and Drug Administration (FDA) to suppress ventricular arrhythmias which could produce severe symptoms or be life threatening. More than 200 000 persons per year eventually took these drugs in the United States to reduce these ventricular arrhythmias. Unfortunately drugs do not just have one set of properties and other properties of these anti-arrhythmics meant they actually killed more people than they saved.[7] [58, 59, 60][8]

Recently one of the newest classes of diabetic medications the thiazolidinediones, which controls blood sugar quite well, has been found to have negative effects on heart failure and

---

[7] The encainide flecainide trial was stopped when preliminary data 33 sudden deaths 56 total deaths occurred in patients taking either drug compared with only 9 (22 total in the matching placebo control group* final figures showed later 43 sudden deaths (63 total) in the intervention group and 16sudden (26 total) in control.

[8] A meta-analysis showed that a one-third reduction in the risk for ventricular tachycardia with lidocaine' (another antiarrhythmic) was accompanied by a one-third increase in death rate. Quinidine, which had been used to maintain normal sinus rhythm after patients with atrial fibrillation (a different arrhythmia) had been converted to sinus rhythm, increased the mortality rate from 0.8% to 2.9%.

peripheral edema, and at least some member of this class on myocardial infarction [61], fractures and possibly macular edema. The increase rather than decrease in heart attacks was unexpected to many, as it did help control diabetes, one of the major risk factors for heart disease. [62, 63, 64]

Cholesterol and Effects not on the Causal Chain

Surrogate indicators such as cholesterol levels are useful only if most of the effect on on the true clinical endpoint (eg. morbidity or mortality) is mediated biologically through a change in the surrogate marker, or closely related to something else which actually achieves the desired outcome. Consequently there should be a strong biological link between the intervention, the surrogate and the true clinical endpoint. One of the earliest cholesterol lowering agents, clofibrate, lowered cholesterol beautifully but actually increased all cause mortality. [65] Niacin also known to decrease cholesterol levels, did not reduce total mortality in the highly powered 7-year CDP trial. [66]

Simvastatin use however has been associated with decreased cholesterol levels and with a 25 to 30% reduction in total mortality in patients with angina pectoris or post MI. [67] Whether this reduction in mortality has a casual relation with the cholesterol lowering properties of simvastatin is unproven, and evaluating a treatment solely on that basis makes little sense.

Without clinical end points, such as total mortality, such drugs as fibrates and hormones could be in widespread use for their cholesterol-lowering effects.[9] Given the complex effects of each drug not just on blood vessels and not just mediated by LDL levels, even the findings of Framingham or intervention studies, do not support focusing on a 'target' LDL of 2.4 or 1.8 after a heart attack, let alone with healthy populations. [68] We don't really know if using these drugs on people with minimal elevations in cholesterol without established coronary artery disease where any positive effect may be minimal or whether the marginal benefit of increasing the dose of the statin actually benefits a population let alone an individual patient.[10] Lower cholesterol has also been associated with such conditions as Parkinson's

---

[9]   Gordon's meta-analysis. considering 50 randomized controlled trials of cholesterol-lowering interventions, including diet, fibrates, hormones, resins, and lovastatin, found an average reduction in cholesterol level of 10% and a reduction of death from coronary heart disease of 9%. Unfortunately, these cholesterol-lowering treatments as a group unintentionally increased the mortality rates associated with causes other than coronary heart disease by 24%. In these 50 trials, use of cholesterol-lowering agents actually led to a net 1% increase in overall mortality. Gordon DJ. Cholesterol lowering and total mortality. In: Rifkind BM, ed. Contemporary Issues in Cholesterol Lowering: Clinical and Population Aspects. New York: Marcel Dekker; 1994

[10]   De Lorgeril and Salen point out that most cardiac deaths for adults over 35 years of age were sudden cardiac deaths . The only indicator that seems to identify this group as being at risk is C-reactive protein (CRP) --- not LDL cholesterol levels or total cholesterol or any other lipid parameters. For women the risk indicators were diabetes or smoking while "blood cholesterol did not increase risk." Yet data (including an estimate from Merck) indicates there may be between 500,000 to 800,000 US women of childbearing age younger than 35 that the guidelines say are "at risk" because they have "high" cholesterol. de Lorgeril M and Salen P *Secondary prevention of coronary heart disease by diet* http://www.healthyeatingclub.com/APJCN/Volume14/vol14supp/fullArticles/deLorgeriltrial.pdf

Clinical trial evidence arguably is lacking for the benefit of statin therapy in women of all ages and men greater than 70 without heart disease or diabetes. Even manufacturer-sponsored trials PROSPER and SPARCL found significant problems with statins. PROSPER found a 25% increase in the risk of cancer among people age 70-82 treated with a statin for 3.4 years (p=0.02) while the SPARCL study of more than 4,700 people who

disease. [69] Cerivastatin (Baycol), [70] a recent statin, was withdrawn from market because of a rare but serious illness involving muscle destruction called rhabdomyolysis, a property shared to a lesser degree by other statins.

Hypertension and Use of Wrong End Point

Epidemiologic evidence establishes hypertension as another risk factor for cardiovascular-related mortality. Those with lower blood pressures have lower rates of stroke and cardiovascular-related mortality. [71] One of the early large studies of treatment for hypertension, the Hypertension Detection and Follow-up Program showed a 17% relative reduction in total mortality in patients with mild hypertension who were managed with a stepped treatment program. [72]

In the last couple of decades many different drugs were developed to treat hypertension in a primary prevention setting. Diuretics, which were found to reduce the stroke rate and had been around for years, were supplanted by scores of other (more expensive) drugs which reduced blood pressure, had good effects on cholesterol, on kidney function and on glucose tolerance, were cardio-selective, bio-available, lasted longer and improved other lab parameters. Most studies were not one to one comparisons with placebo or diuretics (this was considered unethical) and one end point they did not study was the effect on life expectancy. When this was finally chosen as an outcome measure, lo and behold, the ALLHAT trial [73] demonstrated that these earliest and cheapest anti-hypertensives were at least as, and often more, effective than these newer agents.

The earliest Calcium Channel Blockers, used to treat hypertension and meant to decrease cardiovascular mortality, actually increased it. [74, 75, 76] Most were withdrawn from market, only to be replaced by longer acting ones and a second generation of related compounds. The favorable antihypertensive effects of such agents may be offset by other mechanisms of action that are unanticipated, and unrecognized and undiscovered for years.

Confounders: Causation vs. Association

Physicians must recognize the difference between causation and association: this difference is captured by the concept of 'confounders.' For example, people who ingest a lot of alcohol also have higher rates of squamous cell carcinoma of the head and neck. But, this is not because of the alcohol, at least not directly, but rather because of the increased rates of tobacco use in people who ingest a lot of alcohol. Therefore, in this case alcohol was not causal but was associated and smoking confounded this effect because it was associated both with the "risk factor" alcohol, and the outcome, head and neck cancer.

---

had recently had a stroke or TIA found Lipitor to be not much better than placebo at preventing strokes While thrombotic strokes were reduced significantly, hemorrhagic strokes, were far more common in the Lipitor group with 55 cases, compared to 33 cases in the placebo group. While the authors reported a trend towards decreased cardiovascular mortality in a non statistically significant way, there was also a non statistically significant increase in cancer and all cause mortality. Welch K.M.A. et al The Stroke Prevention by Aggressive Reduction in Cholesterol Levels (SPARCL) Investigators. High-dose atorvastatin after stroke or transient ischemic attack. N Engl J Med. 2006;355 (6) 549-559 Aug 10, 2006.

Chlamydia pneumoniae has been associated with atherosclerosis and heart disease, but thus far not found to be causative. Searches for agents of immunodeficiency and respiratory failure turned up dozens of associated organisms (and non-infectious entities) before HIV and SARS were identified. Similarly, people who drink a lot of coffee are more likely to be overweight, than those who don't and problems linked to obesity such as diabetes may appear linked to coffee. Indeed such reasoning is analogous to supposing that, because most people die in hospital beds, if hospital beds are reduced, then fewer people would die.

In the Nurses Health Study, those who took HRT were more likely to be more health conscious and lead a healthy lifestyle, which inadvertently created the erroneous impression that the HRT was the reason for better outcomes.

Scientism Gone Amok - The Polypill

In what was hailed by British Medical Journal editor Richard Smith as the most important journal issue of the last half century, Nicholas Wald and Malcolm Law used extrapolations to describe a Polypill to prevent heart disease, composed of a statin for cholesterol, three antihypertensives (beta blocker, diuretic and ACE inhibitor), aspirin, and folic acid (to reduce homocysteine levels) which they predicted could prevent 90% of strokes and 80% of heart attacks, [77] exclusive of lifestyle changes, vitamins or alternative medicines.

Current treatment guidelines recommend multiple drugs for the secondary prevention of cardiovascular disease. In the area of primary prevention, however, the value of such a pill would have to be clearly demonstrated, rather than simply assumed. As Srinath Reddy says, *"Without such evidence, advocacy for the polypill would be a mere leap of faith."* [78][11]

Australian GP Ralph Faggotter viewed these recommendations with justified skepticism. Looking at additive or multiplicative positive effects without looking at possible negative implications both additive and multiplicative and then extrapolating to those without heart disease, is ludicrous, Faggotter asks ironically,

> "Imagine what could be achieved if they added a few more drugs to the mix. Along with the beta-blocker, they could add a little salbutamol and cortisone in case it caused asthma, and a little Viagra in case it caused impotence. Along with the aspirin they could add a little omeprazole in case it caused gastric bleeding. Along with the statin they could add a little codeine in case it caused aching muscles and a little Aricept in case it caused memory loss. "Along with the thiazide diuretic, they could add a little colchicine in case it caused gout. Along with the ACE inhibitor they could add a little cough mixture, in case it caused a cough. Some of these drugs, in combination, can stress the kidneys so a little EPO would help control any resultant renal anaemia." [79][12]

---

[11] The benefits in absolute numbers may not be as great as the authors' paper indicates even if all goes according to their extrapolations. Paul Rosch showed that for statins, the absolute risk reduction of cardiac events was 1.4% from 4.1 to 2.7% and the number needed to treat (NNT) was 71 for five years with some six percent side effects some possibly life threatening including a one percent increase in cancer risk which might persist well beyond the five year period. Rosch Paul J More on the Preposterous Polypill Panacea 2003 www.mercola.com/2003/aug/6/polypill.htm

[12] Perhaps a safer more natural tastier alternative to the Polypill is the Polymeal, Using data taken from the medical literature, the Framingham heart study and the Framingham offspring study the authors propose an evidence-based recipe included wine, fish, dark chocolate, fruits, vegetables, garlic, and almonds. Data assuming multiplicative correlations was used to model the benefits of the Polymeal in the general population

LIMITATIONS OF CONVENTIONAL
MEDICAL DECISION-MAKING PROCESSES

Why have guidelines led us astray? Part of the answer is failure to understand the limitations of our methods.

Limitations of Guidelines and EBM

After critical appraisal of evidence from well –designed studies from trusted sources, physicians must either be open to changing established practice patterns or have well thought-out arguments that they are prepared to intelligently defend. In some sectors, failure to adhere to CPGs can result in legal liability and disciplinary action against physicians. Some fear that guidelines will be hijacked by purchasers, managers or governments to cut the costs of health care.

There are concerns of partiality and commercial interest influencing Clinical Practice Guidelines (CPGs), especially those based on specialty consensus opinions. [80] Cultural factors, or personal foibles, politicians or lobby groups all may influence CPGs. Clinical decisions must also be consistent with a patient's individual values and preferences.

But many physicians misinterpret the EBM as being restricted to, and synonymous with, RCTs. These clinicians defend the tools of EBM (RCTs, metaanalyses and systematic reviews, sometimes of questionable and biased design) with religious fervor, often failing to recognize its limitations and experience outside of RCTs. Such physicians also may take clinical practice guidelines or expert consensus as representing the best data available. To paraphrase Frank Zappa – " *Data is not information, information is not knowledge and knowledge is not wisdom."* [81] To some it appears that its language and tools have been taken over by people in power and misused to justify harmful practices that are the opposite of the principles of EBM. [82, 83, 84]

Following dogma, or cookbook medicine is questionable ethically, impacts on physician autonomy, diminishes professional integrity, may compromise the physician-patient relationship and be sub-optimal in terms of quality of care – especially when arguably the cookbooks themselves, have been cooked up. [85]

The founders of EBM assert that *"Evidence based medicine is not "cookbook" medicine..... External clinical evidence can inform, but can never replace, individual clinical expertise, and it is this expertise that decides whether the external evidence applies to the individual patient at all and, if so, how it should be integrated into a clinical decision."* [86]

from age 50 which was found to reduce cardiovascular disease events by 76%. For men it would increase life expectancy by 6.6 years, and years free from cardiovascular disease by 9.0 years. Franco Oscar H, Bonneux Luc, de Laet Chris, Peeters Anna, Steyerberg Ewout W, Mackenbach Johan P,The Polymeal: a more natural, safer, and probably tastier (than the Polypill) strategy to reduce cardiovascular disease by more than 75% BMJ 2004;329:1447-1450 (18 December), doi:10.1136/bmj.329.7480.1447

Limitations of Epidemiological Methods

Randomized Controlled Trials (RCTs) are a useful tool limited to answering very specific questions within a clearly-defined framework or context and taking into account those things that are measured.

'Deliberately, and of necessity, it (an RCT) focuses on one tiny little piece of nature to the exclusion of all else. It doesn't look at underlying structural causes for problems, e.g., it may link poverty with ill-health but doesn't look at why poverty exists in the first place. RCTs cannot answer historical questions such as why the incidence of autism or attention deficit disorder has increased. Most social or philosophical questions; what is important in life, what is right and wrong what we should value and why, are not answered by epidemiology. Studies can tell us what we are but not who we are. Such broader philosophical decisions should not be left in the hands of scientists, the medical profession, the drug companies or any other particular group of 'stake-holders' but should be decided by society as a whole through the process of informed debate in a participatory democracy.' [87]

Many of the problems of RCTs stem from the fact that it usually is the company which owns the drug which is conducts and funds trial. [88] This seems analogous to asking parents to mark their own child's exam paper and then expecting an unbiased outcome! Yet surprisingly, this does not seem to particualy bother many in the medical profession or regulators as they feel enough safeguards are in place.

Published RCT studies may not be representative of the array of studies that are completed on a given topic (published and unpublished) because journals or funders with conflicts of interest may preferentially select for publication, studies with desired conclusions. (i.e. publication bias). To reduce this problem, since 2004 the International Committee of Medical Journal Editors including most major medical journals, has a policy of refusing to publish clinical trial results if the trial was not recorded publicly at its outset. However even with registration, we still cannot expect the literature to be balanced. We know that those trials with positive outcomes or something new, are still more likely to be published..

Trials are often carefully designed to have just sufficient power to detect predefined significant clinical effect but often without sufficient power to pick up rare but serious adverse effects. This may be because of budget constraints. However safety problems, such side effects as the proarrythmic effect of cisapride, often only come to light much later as the RCT duration was too short. Consequently as a minimum it is important to have our regulatory bodies require extensive post marketing surveillance as part of the requirements for licensing any new drug. But there are many limitations to purely observational studies to evaluate adverse effects of treatment. [89]

Studies are often designed with power to show how a drug may influence an "intermediate/surrogate endpoint" such as a test result (blood pressure, tumor size, glucose, or cholesterol levels), or even a clinical endpoint such as number of heart attacks, without having the power to show that it decreases overall mortality in a population or, considering side effects, has a net positive effect for the patient population.

While empirically scientific understanding of the pathophysiology of disease may be valuable in initiating effective treatment, we can be led down the wrong path when we don't understand complex systems and our own limitations in performing science correctly.

Statistical methods such as multivariate regression models to evaluate associations still have major limitations as prognostic tools. [90]

When occasionally a positive, meaningful result is found, clinicians, drug companies and the Media often assume these findings might be generalized to wider populations. Trials often fail to account for differences in gender, ethnicity and individual susceptibility including genetic polymorphism.

Another major limitation of clinical trials is their generalizability to many patients seen in an average practice. Internal coherence of data is important but we must remember that for many trials, less than 10% of screened patients meet entrance selection criteria because of factors such as comorbidities, poor prognosis etc. [91] Though patients are often excluded from studies for good reasons and we can know little about effects on populations not studied. While better in terms of research interpretation, such studies with restricted populations have less generalizable findings. Unfortunately therapeutic decisions in practice still need to be made on real life patients with complex problems and the results of many clinical trials cannot be directly extrapolated to these patients.

The more complex patient populations (more severe conditions, co-morbidities, multiple drugs) in the study, the more difficult it is to assess the treatment effects (i.e., treatment mean - control group mean), relative to the random variation (within group variation of both the treatment and control groups). We are less able to detect real differences for a given sample size.

The number of patients who would need to be treated (the NNT) for one patient to benefit (given patients with the same initial level of risk, treated for the same length of time with the same follow-up) is often a useful number. Even if statistically significant differences are found with treatment, with a large "number needed to treat", use of a treatment may not be in the best interest of individuals or the population, especially if a treatment is associated with significant harms relative to benefits (iatrogenic side effects, labeling, high cost, etc.). Rarely are numbers needed to harm recorded. Evidence may need to be supplemented with data from longitudinal cohort studies, registries, case reports, and post-marketing surveillance to capture rare or delayed adverse events.

For environmental exposures, studies such as RCTs usually can't be conducted for ethical reasons and those guarding public safety are forced to rely on lesser methods. Studies of pesticides are often conducted by industry itself using a single chemical exposure on other animal models. Regulators then employ a standardized, but scientifically unproven product safety factor- a fudge factor, meant to provide for differences between animals and people, and between different types of people (gender, age etc.) but in reality these may not adequately model real world exposure with multiple exposures, interactions and the effects of genetic pleomorphism.

Ecological studies are indirect – relying on limiting factors such as type of crop or job description and may have no true control group. Case Control studies may be flawed due to recall bias, low participation and loss to follow-up. However, for rare diseases or those with complex etiology, ecological and case control studies often remain the best studies available. [92]

Limitations of Prevention in Medicine

But primary prevention activities should not automatically be endorsed. Even a theoretically effective public health measure such as immunization can have harm. Adding new vaccines to the immunization schedule especially with additional needles may not only increase childhood pain and reluctance to come into the office, but also the chance that parents may refuse all vaccines or forget to make appointments for some basic vaccines. And some vaccine efficacy relies heavily on herd immunity, eg. to provide a substantial reduction in all cause mortality greater than 80% of the population needs to be effectively immunized. Such measures therefore could be counterproductive for public health.

A new vaccine against human papilloma virus (even if affordable, effective and not allowing problems later or selecting out non-covered serotypes[13]), could inadvertently increase adolescents' sense of invulnerability, increase the number of sexual partners they choose to have, decrease the frequency of PAP smears and condom use and ultimately increase the cervical cancer risk. The universal flu campaign in Ontario, Canada has not been shown to decrease the incidence of flu after five years. [93]

As primordial and primary prevention are largely the field of public health so we will concentrate on secondary and tertiary prevention aspects.

Limitations of Screening

Can there be harm from a test that is adequately sensitive and specific?

Direct damage from tests includes colonic perforation during screening sigmoidoscopy or fetal demise during amniocentesis to screen for congenital birth defects.

Important complications of the results of screening tests are the psychological effects of labeling. This is the damage done when we tell someone who feels well that they are sick. Historically children diagnosed with "heart murmurs" may have been "protected" with less physical activity and have been in danger of developing cardiac neurosis, portrayed, for example, in the film, 'The Secret Garden'. People found in workplace screening programs to be hypertensive, have increased work absenteeism, increased anxiety and other behavioral changes and even earn less, have worse self reported health status, regardless of whether their hypertension warranted treatment. [94]

Routine electrocardiograms in an asymptomatic individual may work to the patient's disadvantage by consuming time and resources that could be devoted to possibly more effective interventions for preventing heart disease, such as counseling regarding smoking, dietary fat intake or exercise.

---

13 Thus may have been a problem with other vaccines. 3 years after introduction of pneumococcal conjugate vaccine routine vaccination with heptavalent, overall invasive pneumococcal disease decreased 67% in Alaska Native children younger than 2 years (from 403.2 per 100,000 in 1995-2000 to 134.3 per 100,000 per year in 2001-2003, $P<.001$). between 2001-2003 and 2004-2006, 82% increase to 244.6/100,000 .($P=.02$). Non vaccine covered disease increased 140% while there was a 96% decrease in heptavalent vaccine serotype disease. Such an effect was not found in non–Native Alaska children who were less at risk years. Singleton Rosalyn J., Hennessy, Thomas W Bulkow, Lisa R Hammitt Laura L Zulz, Tammy Hurlburt Debby A Butler, Jay C. Rudolph, Karen Parkinson Alan, Invasive Pneumococcal Disease Caused by Nonvaccine Serotypes Among Alaska Native Children With High Levels of 7-Valent Pneumococcal Conjugate Vaccine Coverage *JAMA*2007;297(16):1784-1792. April 25, 2007

False positive test results may lead to unnecessary diagnostic work-up, interventions or treatment. Screening using unnecessary procedures such as electronic fetal monitoring may contribute to increasing the frequency of Caesarian sections. [95] Tests may cause unnecessary anxiety in the physician as well as the patient or lead to difficulty in obtaining life or health insurance. False positive results will be more common when screening for diseases that are relatively rare in populations. For this reason, and also that of resources, it is also at times appropriate to limit screening to populations with a higher prevalence of disease (high-risk groups such as Tay Sachs in Jews or colonoscopy in those with a family history of colon cancer) rather than screening general populations.

Currently, official bodies in Canada recommend that routine teaching of breast self-examination (BSE) be excluded from the periodic health examination for women of all ages as the manoeuvre hasn't been shown to increase survival and may cause unnecessary anxiety. [96, 97] Screening mammograms, at least in the general population under 50, may detect cancers early, but do not appear to save lives. [98, 99, 100, 101] They may cause psychological distress and result in unnecessary surgery, radiotherapy, chemotherapy, hormonal therapy. [102, 103] Advocates of annual breast cancer screening highlighted a 30% *relative* reduction in the risk of dying from breast cancer over a 10-year period, downplaying any risk of radiation, any pain or the fact that women having regular mammograms would have a 49% chance of being recalled for a biopsy [104] and little absolute change in mortality, even in the most positive studies. Radical mastectomy, the conventional treatment of choice for breast cancer forty years ago, caused terrible morbidity for patients.

The prostate specific antigen (PSA) blood test is somewhat effective at detecting cancer (along with digital rectal exam and trans-rectal ultrasound), but also does not appear to save lives when practised on the general population. Further, treatments which cause morbidity such as impotence and incontinence, may negate any benefits of early detection. For this reason the Canadian Task Force on the Period Health Examination, the Canadian Cancer Society, the U.S. Preventive Services Task Force and the National Cancer Institute in the United States do not recommend routine PSA testing. [105, 106, 107]

Prostate intraepithelial neoplasia and ductal carcinoma in situ of the breast, virtually unknown before the advent of widespread screening, now account for a substantial portion of all diagnosed prostate and breast tumors and may only rarely progress to death. It is possible that over-diagnosis of dangers maybe the equivalent of false positives and partly explain why general population screening has not appeared to substantially change death rates from these two cancers.

After his own random, positive test for blood on urine dipstick done in the course of an effort to teach techniques to medical students, GP Chris Del Mar launched his own EBM oriented investigation of asymptomatic hematuria (blood in urine) finding little evidence that he would benefit from further investigation and treatment. [108][14] Consequently, del Mar chose not to pursue further investigation.

---

[14] A British study showed found 2.5% of more than 10 000 men screened randomly were positive for asymptomatic hematuria by dipstick testing. Of these 60% were investigated further by their general practitioners.
"*Three had a serious condition that was amenable to cure, two had bladder cancer and one had reflux nephropathy. This study seemed to be fairly close to my ideal. It gave a prognosis of the outcome someone like me (my situation being similar to screening) would expect.* " [I was] "*unlikely to have a serious condition that was amenable to cure. Of course, even this may be an overestimate of the benefits of screening. Perhaps those*

How about diabetes?

After diagnosis, tight control of diabetes likely reduces the risk for blindness and end-stage renal disease (ESRD, and aggressive control of hypertension, lipid therapy, and aspirin use seems to reduce cardiovascular events,. As such many felt that early detection in the asymptomatic preclinical phase and earlier tighter control to prevent diabetic complications such as retinopathy and nephropathy would be of even greater value. However, the US *Preventive Services Task Force* found that *"additional benefit of initiating tight glycemic control during the preclinical phase is uncertain but probably small."*[15]

Screening for Lung Cancer

Each year in the US lung cancer will be diagnosed in an estimated 164,100 people and claim 156,900. Screening for lung cancer using frequent, routine, conventional chest X rays has been known to be useless or possibly even harmful since the mid 1980s, even in high risk group such as smokers. The Mayo Lung Project [109] showed such findings to hold even after tracking patients for 20 years. [110]

Hopes for screening as better imaging became available soared after a *New England Journal of Medicine* study published last year. [111][16] The 10-year survival rate was 80 percent for those screened with spiral CT compared with conventional figures of 10 percent, presumably because they were diagnosed and treated earlier when the cancer was curable. Yet this was seemingly disputed by a *JAMA* article this year, which had a higher detection rate, meaning that the population may have been even more at risk, but no change in terms of survival. [112] The *JAMA* [113] study was primarily funded by institutions such as Sloan-Kettering, Mayo as well as the National Cancer Institute, the Department of Defense, and several European government agencies. The NEJM study received support from General Electric, which makes CT scanners, and Eastman Kodak, which sells the film.

---

three people would have developed symptoms such as frank haematuria or dysuria sufficiently early to negate the beneficial effect of screening on their prognosis."
"Another study was done in California. Over 20 000 middle aged people were screened by dipstick for haematuria. An unexpected positive result was found in nearly 3%, 99% of whom were followed up. Over the next three years, three patients developed urological cancers (two prostatic and one bladder). This study is more relevant because it looked at the outcome of people whose dipstick test was not positive; their probability of developing urological cancer was no less than that of people whose dipstick test was positive. According to this study, the likelihood of my developing urological cancer was 0.5%, whether I had haematuria or not."

[15] Even given the most optimistic assumptions, the number needed to screen (NNS) to prevent 1 case of blindness in one eye by tight glycemic control for 5 years is about 4,300. "Until we have better evidence about its benefits, harms, and costs, the role of screening as a strategy to reduce the burden of suffering of diabetes will remain uncertain. Current evidence suggests that the benefits of screening are more likely to come from modification of CVD risk factors rather than from tight glycemic control." Harris Russell; Donahue Katrina, Rathore; Saif S.; Frame Paul,; Woolf Steven H.; Lohr Kathleen N. Screening Adults for Type 2 Diabetes http://www.ahrq.gov/clinic/3rduspstf/diabscr/diabrev.htm
  Between 30 and 50 percent of people who receive a diagnosis of impaired glucose tolerance (IGT) will revert to normoglycemia. Studies have found that between 12.5 and 42 percent of men who were found to have diabetes on screening reverted to normoglycemia after 2.5 to 8 years. Diagnosing them with IGT, not only may be inconvenient and waste time but may subject them to harmful treatments. Stewart-Brown, Sarah Farmer Andrew Screening could seriously damage your health Decisions to screen must take account of the social and psychological costs BMJ 1997;314:533 (22 February) http://www.bmj.com/cgi/content/full/314/7080/533

[16] Of 31,567 asymptomatic persons at risk for lung cancer screened using low-dose CT from 1993 through 2005, the investigators found 484 with lung cancer.

How do we interpret this information?[17] Even the earlier Mayo Clinic study with regular chest X rays had shown a doubling of the 10-year survival rate with screening without improving death rates. So cancers may rapidly or slowly progress to death, not progress at all, or even regress. Over-diagnosis drastically inflates survival statistics, even if mortality is unchanged.

Length bias is a systematic error as screening detects more individuals with more slowly developing, as opposed to rapidly progressive, disease. These individuals also will appear to do better, as their course will allow more opportunity to be found by screening, particularly if there is a long, pre-symptomatic phase. Lead time bias gives the perception of longer survival without altering the natural course of the disease as finding disease at an early stage, increases the time from detection to death. This is one of the reasons why mammography appears to be a more successful screening tool than it actually is.

Another bias to consider in evaluating screening tests without randomization and control groups include volunteer or referral bias means that people who choose healthier lifestyles are more likely to be attracted to a treatment arm (that seems to be why the nurses health study seemed to show an advantage to hormone replacement,

Otitis Media and Angioplasty - Two Examples of Early Intervention

In the US and Britain, acute otitis media (AOM) is one of the most common reasons for children to visit a physician and to receive antibiotics. Nearly $5 billion is spent each year in the United States in managing AOM. By their first birthday, nearly two thirds of American children are diagnosed with at least one episode of AOM [114]. In the Netherlands however, physicians treat AOM in children symptomatically with analgesics and antipyretics and reserve antibiotics for those whose symptoms persist beyond 3 days. Trials in the late 1980s and early 1990s seemed to back up this approach with no increase in serious complications such as –mastoiditis and meningitis - and little effect on pain. [115, 116, 117][18]

---

[17] The JAMA study followed 3,246 smokers or ex smokers (average smoking history 39 years) and finding 144 with lung cancer, 3 times as many as without screening and resulting in 10 times the number of surgeries. (The detection rate was higher than in the NEJM study because this study had older patients and longer follow-up.) 38 died from lung cancer — the same mortality rate expected for people of similar age and smoking history in the absence of screening.

People with positive screens get more procedures including bronchoscopy and CT-guided needle biopsy. with complications from these procedures include bleeding, infection, and discomfort. Depending on the size and location of the lesion, a thoracotomy, opening the chest to obtain a larger biopsy, may be recommended. The death rate from lung cancer surgery is 5 percent while 20 percent to 40 percent of people who have such surgery have serious complications, including heart attacks, pulmonary emboli, and pneumonia.

[18] A Cochrane review (8 RCTs, n=2,287) assessed the effects of antibiotics versus placebo in children with AOM finding a 7% absolute reduction in the risk of pain, or NNT of 15 children to prevent one extra child from having pain after two to seven days. Also for every 17 children treated with antibiotics, one suffered an adverse effect (e.g. vomiting, diarrhoea, rash). O'Neill P, Roberts T, Stevenson CB. Acute otitis media. *Clinical Evidence.* September 2006. Accessed from www.clinicalevidence.com
Glasziou PP, Del Mar CB, Sanders SL, et al. Antibiotics for acute otitis media in children. *Cochrane Database of Systematic Reviews* 2004, Issue 1. Art. No.: CD000219. DOI: 10.1002/14651858.CD000219.pub2. Accessed from www.thecochranelibrary.com Another meta-analysis found few serious complications with the only case of mastoiditis in the antibiotic treatment group. Del Mar C, Glasziou P, Hayem M. Are antibiotics indicated as initial treatment for children with acute otitis media? A meta-analysis. *BMJ* 1997; 314: 1526-1529.

Angioplasty or percutaneous coronary intervention (PCI) has been practiced increasingly in the last decade. In 2004, more than 1 million coronary stent procedures were performed in the United States, where approximately 85% of all PCI procedures are undertaken electively in patients with stable coronary artery disease. The COURAGE trial, a new randomized study compared the effect of adding PCI to what is assumed to be optimal medical therapy and lifestyle intervention (advice on diet, exercise and smoking cessation) [118] found that PCI did not reduce the risk of death, myocardial infarction, or other major cardiovascular events and only provided slight and temporary relief from chest pain.[19] This study was funded by the US Department of Veterans Affairs, the Medical Research Council of Canada and a host of drug companies, with stent makers refusing to participate in funding.

Masterful Inaction –'Don't just Do Something, Stand there'

Sometimes when we talk of prevention, we are talking instead about early pre-emption. The urge to intervene in medicine is overwhelming. If it is 'broke' we must fix it. It is often true that, as Voltaire said, *"The art of medicine consists in amusing the patient while nature cures the disease."*

Time itself often heals. Studies show that de-briefing after major trauma to mitigate the effects of post traumatic stress disorder (PTSD) may make things worse. [119, 120]

In my local hospital cleaning of umbilical cords with alcohol, as opposed to leaving them alone, was found to actually be harmful and the practice was stopped a decade ago. There are actually a whole host of interventions in child birth which were once universally practiced, but which have now been abandoned due to lack of evidence for their value, including routine pudendal shaves, enemas, stirrups, draping, masks, lying in the supine position during labor, frequent vaginal examinations, and regimented timed breast feeds. [121] Everything about the culture of childbirth is different to what it was 30 years ago, most often going back to nature.

Boils must be ripe to be lanced. 'Incidental' appendectomies, with cholecystectomies or any other intra-abdominal surgery, which were meant to reduce chances of major problems in the future, were actually found to be harmful in the elderly. [122] Such procedures actually reduced in frequency once insurers stopped paying for it. [123]

Might there be similar analogies in International Affairs?

Dutch patients had similar outcomes at two months compared to seven other countries where antimicrobial therapy is virtually universal. Froom Jack, Culpepper Larry Jacobs Max DeMelker Ruut A Green Larry A, van Buchem Louk, Grob Paul Heeren Timothy Antimicrobials for acute otitis media? a review from the international primary care network *BMJ* 1997;315:98-102 (12 July) http://bmj. bmjjournals.com/cgi/content/full/315/7100/98

Others have suggested that antibiotics may be beneficial in subgroups of patients, e.g. children under two years and those with fever or vomiting but even this has been questioned. Damoiseaux Roger A M J van Balen Frank A M, Hoes Arno W, Verheij Theo J M, de Melker Ruut A Primary care based randomised, double blind trial of amoxicillin versus placebo for acute otitis media in children aged under 2 years http:// www.bmj.com/cgi/content/full/320/7231/350 *BMJ* 2000;320:350-354 (5 February)

[19] Between 1999 and 2004 researchers randomized 2287 patients at 50 U.S. and Canadian centers, with myocardial ischemia and objective evidence of significant coronary artery disease), typically blockages in two arteries, but medically stable, and about 40 percent of whom had had a prior heart attack. Following patients for an average of 4.6 years, Heart-related hospitalization rates were similar for subgroups of smokers, diabetics, or older or sicker people.

SCIENTISM IN INTERNATIONAL AFFAIRS - THE FAILURES OF REALISM

Bruce Jentleson observed that US Foreign Policy decision-making has historically been guided by various forces termed the Four Ps: Peace, Power, Prosperity and Principles. [124] Realist Walter Mead represented this in the policies of four US historical leaders: Hamiltonian Commerce or Prosperity, Wilsonian Moral Principle, Jeffersonian Democratic System and Peace and Jacksonian Military Might or Power.

Mead observes a difference in American and European approaches to the world which he sees as inevitable given Europe's recent military weakness. (For Europeans) *"The United States is too unilateralist, too religious, too warlike, too laissez-faire, too fond of guns and the death penalty, and too addicted to simple solutions for complex problems.... When Jacksonian America does think about Europe, it sees what Sheriff Andy of Mayberry saw in Barney Fife—a scrawny, neurotic deputy whose good heart was overshadowed by bad judgment and vanity. The slow-talking, solid Andy tolerated Barney just fine, but he knew that Barney's self-importance would get him into one humiliating scrape after another."* [125]

Robert Kagan puts this in terms of Americans being from Mars and Europeans from Venus, [126] much as John Gray's popular *Men are from Mars, Women are from Venus* [127]

Both observers, while sympathetic to concerns about values and principles seem to see the "Realist' approach, concentrating on use of 'hard power' and coercion as generally more successful. Is this true?

In international affairs preemption is also often cited to justify intervention. We are also told that we should not be Chamberlains. Yet not every bad actor, 'madman', or tyrant is a Hitler who has to be stopped before he launches World War III and the next Holocaust. The US national security strategy (NSS) of forward defence, not waiting until the terrorist attack, seemed, on the surface, to be logical. The pre-emptive battle against Saddam Hussein and the threat of his alleged weapons of mass destruction before he got too strong is not proving to be the greatest poster child for preemption. Was this a false positive diagnosis in a 'test' which is too sensitive?! Doing nothing in Iraq may actually have been far preferable to intervening.

Those who suggest alternatives to war are pooh-poohed as naïve appeasers. But it is often the 'Realists' who are being naïve. Even Plato's *Republic* described the cycle of governments from autocracy to tyranny then to democracy as a natural cycle of events likely driven by human motivation and the natural human desire for autonomy and self-determination. Consequently it is natural to think that tyrants such as Saddam Hussein would eventually fall to a democratic organization through natural forces alone. We must remember that most dictators, Latin American military ones, Southeast Asian, African and even western and European ones, including such unseemly characters as Marcos, Milosevic and Suharto, were overthrown not by outside military intervention or even internal coups, but by popular and largely peaceful, civilian movements. Resultant governments tend to be more stable than those which achieve power through violent means- violence begets violence. With military intervention, legitimacy is seen to come from military power rather than popular assent, possibly leading to further opposition, military despotism and then further military coups. Sometimes with preemption, the operation might be a success "Mission accomplished" proclaimed a banner behind George Bush shortly after the end of this Gulf War ...but the patient dies.

Peter Bergen and Paul Cruickshank attempted to measure the 'Iraq effect' on global terrorism. [128][20] The report also points out that the US administration's own National Intelligence Estimate on 'Trends in Global Terrorism: Implications for the United States' -- partially declassified last October -- stated that " the Iraq war has become the 'cause célèbre' for jihadists ... and is shaping a new generation of terrorist leaders and operatives."

SUBJECTIVITY IN DECISION-MAKING

Assuming we are willing and able to make purely rational decisions, *should* we assess risk and benefits of our actions and inactions objectively? Sometimes values and morals render certain choices unacceptable regardless of evidence of, for example, economic or security benefits. For many, these include such issues as slavery, torture, committing genocide, capital punishment, and for some, reproductive choices for women or rights of the unborn. Decision-making in medicine, public policy, environmental and military affairs must be based not only on evidence but also on personal, cultural and philosophical values.

A rational decision to one person may appear quite different to someone else presented with the same problem. It is often important to be subjective, to let our own internal and external realities influence health decisions. Ideology though, is usually considered an undesirable influence, especially if imposed by with different beliefs or if it colors our perceptions of objective effects, and should be considered to reduce the adverse influences.

A physician who is a Jehovah's Witness may perceive the risks of transfusion as being greater and the benefits being less than those without such faith.[21] Not only may some on the US political Right still be searching for Saddam's weapons of mass destruction and his connections with Al Qaeda, but they genuinely may believe that the Iraqi people are better off with military intervention. Similarly people who categorically reject a military response may not realize that they condemn target populations to death by not intervening in Sierra Leone, Rwanda, East Timor or Darfur and perhaps may ultimately in the longer term, be putting themselves and their own societies at risk. [129]

The political environment in decision-making determines what is possible and is most resilient with broad public consultation. In some cases the political system limits free choice and does not support public consultation. Sometimes the situation is not conducive for the ideal solution, and a harm reduction approach is preferred. This may include issues such as graft or child labor in certain developing countries or resource poor environments.

The problem is when we fail to recognize assumptions behind action and inaction such as devaluing the disempowered. When we delude ourselves and others into believing that we are

---

20   *"Our study shows that the Iraq war has generated a stunning increase in the yearly rate of fatal jihadist attacks, amounting to literally hundreds of additional terrorist attacks... The study compared the period between 11 September 2001 and the invasion of Iraq with the period since the invasion began in March 2003. The count -- excluding the Arab-Israel conflict -- shows the number of deaths due to terrorism rose from 729 to 5,420. As well as strikes in Europe, attacks have also increased in Chechnya and Kashmir since the invasion."*

21   Interestingly it was concerns of Witnesses and blood contamination with HIV, Hepatitis B and C, that made it evident that we did not have to treat everyone with Hb under 100 (10 in US Units) and to realize that 'anemia' of pregnancy might have some physiological advantages.

acting objectively in such cases, we may inadvertently harm our own interests and those of others.

Personality traits and cognitive styles each may affect how we weigh risks to arrive at decisions. Behavioralist Isabel Briggs Myers (1962), believed that a person's decision making process depends to a significant degree on their cognitive style. Myers developed a set of four bi-polar dimensions, called the Myers-Briggs Type Indicator (MBTI). The terminal points on these dimensions are: *thinking* and *feeling*; *extroversion* and *introversion*; *judgment* and *perception*; and *sensing* and *intuition*. Other personality type issues may also affect decision-making. Some are more Type A; some cannot accept non- quantitative data and ignore data with uncertainty. Some think more concretely or in absolutist, black and white terms.

In health communication, people are known to have particular cognitive styles of receiving new health information for such problems as heart disease and cancer. 'Blunters' avoid information to cope with stress while 'monitors' seek information. Some physicians and patients avoid detail while others seek and find comfort in numbers, even irrelevant ones when challenged with information that is technical, frightening, where there is disagreement among experts as to consequences and management. The same may be true for generals, politicians and civil servants.

When frightened, people may mistrust the evidence or the messenger, considering them to be devious, cunning or duplicitous and display hostility towards the source, seeing no need to systematically evaluate such information. 9/11 conspiracy theorists find the US government capable of mass murder and able to keep thousands of accomplices silent but at the same time, unable to fake evidence for weapons of mass destruction in Iraq.

Human Assessment of Risk

In the US, the probability of dying in a motor vehicle accident in a year is 1/6500 of being struck by lightning [130], 1/400,000 of dying from West Nile virus, 1 in 2,000,000, and of a snake-bite 1/145,000,000. [131] Yet in the public's perception the risk of a snakebite or West Nile may seem greater than either being struck by lightning or dying in a motor vehicle accident.

We often assess our own capabilities as being greater than others. 80 percent of us assert that we are better than average drivers and a similar proportion believe we are smarter, more attractive, and more talented than average. [132]

Jim Holt and Trisha Greenhalgh [133, 134] each suggest cognitive and social influences that may prevent us from making fully objective decisions.. I will separate them into the Who, What, Where, When, Why and How.

Who

People seem to value the lives of some greater than others.[22] [135] Those making judgments about others tend to be less risk averse than those making judgments about

---

[22]   Tom Englehart shows that average award to relatives of victims of 9/11 was $1.8 million-thanks to the September 11th Victim Compensation Fund. http://www.cbsnews.com/stories/2004/01/16/national/ main593715.shtml This was consistent with court appointed costs for lost income.
However in Jalalabad, Afghanistan in what was found to be deliberate acts of retaliation or admitted "excessive force" murdering "12 people -- including a 4-year-old girl, a 1-year-old boy and three elderly

themselves or those with whom they identify. We are willing to accept more risks for people we don't know than we are for more than identifiable ones or those more vulnerable, such as pregnant women, children or future generations.

People in positions of power are more likely to risk the lives of the poor or people of other cultures. Decisions are made at the head offices of a multinational corporation are more likely to favor shareholders with whom they identify as opposed to anonymous workers in far off countries. In recent conflicts, militaries of western powers have been willing to risk very few casualties on their own sides-, often wanting zero risk. For example the US was forced to leave Somalia in 1993-94 after the loss of 18 soldiers.

Those of the underclass themselves, often take the same approach, perhaps for different reasons. In North America, many blacks, non-unionized workers and those in lower socio-economic groups, presumably with less to lose, are willing to take dangerous tasks just to keep their jobs. In Third World countries, children may find working to be the least negative, short-term, personal option, because of the immediate economic necessities and with the limited choices society offers, though at a long term cost of perpetual poverty,

What and Where

We find poorly understood and therefore frightening phenomena such as SARS or Ebola virus outbreaks or those with hidden, irreversible damage or those that occur after many years such as cancers to be less acceptable, even if such risks are known to be small. We have a preference for the status quo or usual practice. Most people are reluctant to change current behaviors, (such as starting or stopping a particular drug) even when we know we will be better off if we do change.

The unfamiliar or novel or 'far off' phenomena such as a hurricane or tsunami, may be perceived as riskier than chemical spills, which may be more familiar.

When

We value things in the here and now much more than in the future and insurers place a value on, for example, money and life saved, twice as much today as ten years in the future.

---

villagers" -- and wounded 34. After much protest in Afghanistan, according to David S. Cloud of the New York Times http://www.nytimes.com/2007/05/09/world/asia/09afghan.html, US Col. John Nicholson, a brigade commander, met with the families of the (now) 19 Afghans who had been killed and the 50 who had been wounded by the Marines. He offered this official apology: "I stand before you today, deeply, deeply ashamed and terribly sorry that Americans have killed and wounded innocent Afghan people." The families were given approximately $2,000 per death in "condolence payments" to family.
And in Iraq in 2005, through a American Civil Liberties Association Freedom of Information Act request, it was found that the value of life was similar, averaging about $2,500 per acknowledged wrongful death.. "ACLU Releases Files on Civilian Casualties in Afghanistan and Iraq," http://www.aclu.org/ natsec/foia/29316prs20070412.html "ACLU Releases Files on Civilian Casualties in Afghanistan and Iraq," Greg Mitchell offered this description: "What price (when we do pay) do we place on the life of a 9-year-old boy, shot by one of our soldiers who mistook his book bag for a bomb satchel? Would you believe $500? And when we shoot an Iraqi journalist on a bridge we shell out $2,500 to his widow -- but why not the measly $5,000 she had requested?" Mitchell Greg "Sorry We Shot Your Kid, But Here's $500." Editor & Publisher http://www.editorandpublisher.com/eandp/columns/pressingissues_display.jsp?vnu_content_id=1003571125 The families or spouses of two dozen innocent Iraqis slaughtered in another Marines-run-amok moment at Haditha also after an attack on a convoy of Humvees that wounded a Marine were also given the same amount. The $32million paid out for US acknowledged deaths leading to a figure of over 6,000 "incidents"

Why

We are more afraid of involuntary exposures, inescapable despite personal precautions. The 'Anthrax in the mail' scare in the USA post-9/11 caused more panic and probably prevented resources from being devoted to other security concerns. Some might say that random screening of shoes and toothpaste at airports may mean that other security needs are neglected.

How

We place different values on life lost depending on the mode of death or disability. When the Washington snipers were loose, the seven deaths from drive-by shootings did not even represent a blip on Washington's gun murder rate, though it received much press coverage and was the subject of much angst.

Framing

'The glass being half full' or 'half empty', or relative or absolute increase or decrease may change a response. Most people have not been introduced to the concepts of and really don't understand "relative risk", "absolute risk" and "odds ratio". [136] People more likely to avoid a loss than get a gain Preference for cancer therapy is known to be affected by whether it is framed in terms of dying or survival. [137]

Zero Risk

We really can't tell the difference in a meaningful way between miniscule risks such as 1/10,000 and 1/200,000; we may have different arbitrary acceptable risks for instance for behaviours such as smoking and lung cancer and vaccine complications. We value 'zero' risk although there is nothing like true zero risk; every activity entails some risk and even doing nothing has risks.) Attempting to reduce risk to zero, suppressing the risk-causing activity, ironically, often increases risk in another area. Preventing skin cancer by reducing sun exposure may lead to osteoporosis. Trying to reduce the risk of children being abducted to zero, results in them being kept inside and sedentary which leads to obesity and early death from heart disease.

Primed Decision-making

Interestingly though, some decisions which appear subjective may truly be based on objective criteria. In situations with time pressure, higher stakes, or increased ambiguities, experts use intuitive decision-making rather than structured approaches, following a recognition 'primed decision approach' to fit a set of indicators into the expert's experience and immediately arrive at a satisfactory course of action without weighing alternatives. This often leads to good decisions ... as Malcolm Gladwell explains in *Blink* using examples of experts in gambling, speed dating, tennis, military war games, the movies, malpractice suits, popular music, and predicting divorce, ...but also may lead to disaster. [138] Let us examine where we act against our own interests

COGNITIVE DISTORTIONS IN MEDICINE
AND INTERNATIONAL AFFAIRS

Operating on Faith in Medicine and International Affairs

Many physicians assume that newer technology will be safer and better; that each new blood pressure medication, cholesterol lowering agent or painkiller will be better than the last. New painkillers, the COXII inhibitors, rofecoxib (Vioxx) [139], and valdecoxib (Bextra) [140] which were meant to reduce the rate of gastric ulcers compared with other older NSAIDs, appeared to do so, but actually caused more heart attacks and strokes and needed to be withdrawn from the market.

Interestingly, more often than not, good effects are assumed to be class effects, but bad effects, individual. When rofecoxib and valdecoxib were considered to pose unnecessary risk, the other COX II inhibitors were not considered bad (or at least the manufacturers of Celebrex and Mobicox attempted to quarantine their drugs from the negative publicity surrounding Vioxx), and though first generation calcium channel blockers were considered to have negative cardiac effects, the second generation and longer acting ones were assumed not to have these but to have retained all of the good effects.

Changing the Rules of the Game

Sometimes we go further, changing the evidence directly to fit our assumptions.

Doctors note non-statistically significant trends to decreased cardiovascular mortality with cholesterol treatment but systematically ignore statistically significant increases in cancers, accidents, suicide or hemorrhagic strokes if they don't fit with our model.

Re-jigging the experiment occurs in the Military as it does in Medicine. When initial testing for missile defense failed, the US military 'doctored' the results by changing decoys and putting homing devices, wrapping their missiles in tin foil so they could get positive results. The same, all-too-human motivating factors apply whether we are talking about Vioxx or Star Wars. This also occurred before the Gulf War in US trials of a war on a 'hypothetical' country with features similar to Iraq.[23] [141]

---

[23] In the summer of 2002 just prior to the war on Iraq US military carried on a $250m rehearsal using over 13,000 troops and computer simulation. Millennium Challenge 02 was a mock war against a fictitiously named Persian Gulf country that resembled Iraq run by a crazed but cunning megalomaniac. Retired Lieutenant General Paul Van Riper was in charge of the "Red Force" (simulating the enemy) against the "Blue Force" (the United States). The "control group", the officers refereeing the exercise, informed him that US electronic warfare planes had zapped his expensive microwave communications systems.
"You're going to have to use cell phones and satellite phones now, they told me. I said no, no, no - we're going to use motorcycle messengers and make announcements from the mosques," Van Riper says. "But they refused to accept that we'd do anything they wouldn't do in the west." Van Riper was initially given a free hand using motorcycle messengers to transmit orders to Red troops, thereby eluding Blue's super-sophisticated eavesdropping technology, reckoned Blue would try to launch a surprise strike, in line with the administration's new pre-emptive doctrine, "so I decided I would attack first" and sank many of the Blue Forces' ships when they entered the Persian Gulf with suicide-bombers in speed boats.
"At that point, the managers stopped the game to "refloat" the Blue fleet, and resumed play. On several occasions the Red Force was directed not to use certain weapons systems against Blue, was forced to reveal the location of its units."

Each of these mistakes: assumptions that screening and pre-emption only could have benefits, failing to understand causal chains, uses of surrogate indicators, wrong end points, and mistaking association for causation each represented very basic failures of logic and decision-making. Some were expensive errors and all harmed patients in the medical examples; in international affairs our own foreign policy interests and populations were negatively affected. Why would this occur when we seem to have so many checks and balances in the system? The rest of the paper will look at why this might be so and how it might be remedied.

Heuristics

Why do many consider many of the harmful thoughts and actions to be scientific, legitimate, even "Realistic'? Heuristics refers to short cuts and rules of thumb we use to allow us to make quick, often efficient, judgments. They allow us to conserve cognitive energy and make sense of a complex world. We selectively filter any new information with prior knowledge, values, beliefs and emotions. We'll use heuristics when overloaded with information, when don't want to think about a problem, when stakes not important or when we have little or no information.

We rely on facts and material that are easily brought to mind, which may be overestimated in frequency or importance. Our recall is influenced by immediacy, strong emotions, and anything that increases memorability (such as press coverage and personal experience). An example might be concern about deaths due to shark attacks at the beach, when statistically far more people are killed by falling aircraft parts! Media and popular novels make shark attacks seem much more common than they are. Such *Availability bias* occurs in medicine when a doctor makes a decision, based on an experience that is at the forefront of her/his mind but which bears little relation to the patient being treated. We'll remember people apparently saved by early detection of cancers. Stories about the harmful effects of medicines have a particularly powerful impact on decision- making. When presented with a large amount of data we'll remember that which we first heard (Primacy) and last heard (Recency) better than the rest. Pharmaceutical representatives and TV advertising seek to keep evidence that they feel most relevant readily available to physicians and the public

With regard to our individual outcome or capabilities we may have an *Optimism bias*. This may also be because of a desire to be better than others or to shield ourselves from fear. With situations with which we have little personal experience, that which we think is controllable, that where we feel that early action can pre-empt a problem or that we see as very low probability this tendency is exaggerated. People engaging in the most unhealthy behaviours, such as smoking, drinking and street drug use, tend to be the most unreasonably optimistic about positive outcomes. In medicine, surgeons for example, generally feel that their success rate is far greater than statistics bear out. Groopman cites research that shows the worse the performance of radiologists, the more certain they seem to be that they are right! [142]

Eventually with such manoeuvres, the Blue team 'won'. The US now had 'proof' that it would win the war on Iraq.

Representativeness bias occurs when we seek similar data to our experience but have an under reliance on direct observation. We look for a typical case similar to something we know, rather than relying on base rate information. An example might be a feeling that something must be better, because it is more expensive. Having relatives with cancer or heart disease or, in the case of physicians, patients with particular conditions, will colour our interpretation of symptoms such as chest pain.

We'll find a particular number, concept or value for a condition that we feel we understand and then relate to particular cases, adjusting up and down depending on our judgment perception or belief of risk relative to this number (*Anchoring and adjustment*). Media stories of breast cancer tend to focus on young cases, with the result that women in their 40s typically overestimate by more than 20-fold their chance of dying of breast cancer within a decade. They overestimate the risk reduction from screening by a factor of more than 100. [143]

Confirmation Bias

We seek evidence that proves beliefs; new evidence is made to fit while contrary evidence is devalued or filtered out. We ignore rationally constructed guidelines, considering the studies to be good but extend these conclusions to unproven, off label use. We even make the evidence fit our assumptions. "Diagnostic momentum" takes over when we are unable to change course, even though the basis for the initial diagnosis may have been unclear.

In the BMJ Jenny Doust and Chris Del Mar examined reasons why physicians use ineffective or harmful treatments. [144] Many of these represented a confirmation bias. These included: Clinical experience (eg. arrhythmia suppression), Failure to Understand the Natural history of the illness (which might include the example of antibiotic treatment of otitis media), Love of the pathophysiological model (that is wrong which would include many of the examples described such as positioning of children to avoid aspiration and breast milk jaundice, Ritual and mystique (a belief in technological progress- stents, spiral CT for lung cancer, mammograms) No one asks the question or right question (hypertension HRT treatments), and Patients' expectations (real or assumed). All of these may explain errors in our attitudes towards screening for hypertension, cholesterol, and diabetes.

Sometimes we may have excessive confidence or trust in numbers, in experts, or in technology and therefore fail to ask critical questions. We recognize anti-depressants as helping with mood but dismiss agitation and possible increase in suicide risk. Even when we find things such as a reduction in breast cancer incidence or mortality researchers in Canada looked to mammograms as the cause for this reduction, rather than seeing the temporal association between reduction of hormone replacement therapy.[24]

---

[24] Prescriptions for HRT decreased by 38 per cent in the year after publication of the WHI and they continue to fall. The incidence of breast cancer fell most precipitously, 11.8 per cent, in women aged 50-69, those most likely to take HRT. In the 70 and over age group, the rate went down 11.1 per cent. But in women under the age of 50, where HRT use was probably not a factor, the breast cancer rate rose slightly, by 1.3 per cent. The new research shows too that almost all the decline was accounted for by a drop in estrogen-receptor-positive tumours – those that would be most directly affected by use of HRT. However while use of HRT continued to decrease in 2004 there seemed to be no continued decrease in breast cancer. Ravdin Peter M Cronin, Kathleen A Howlader Nadia, Berg Christine D., Chlebowski Rowan T Feuer, Eric J. Edwards Brenda K. Berry Donald

Confirmation bias is found frequently in international and domestic political affairs. With the murder of 32 at Virginia Tech or earlier with 12 at Columbine High School, some derived a lesson that more guns needed to be available so people could 'take out' the shooter early, rather than seeing the solution as taking guns out of the hands of people, at least with mental health histories. Now, despite enormous spending the weakness of US military efforts and the attempt to impose 'simple' solutions is becoming evident. The willingness to 'doctor' the Millennium Challenge War game or Missile Defence results may reflect this trend.

'Why is it that people don't see failures of the hawks or of *Realism*?

Daniel Kahneman Nobel laureate in economics and Jonathan Renshon author of Why Leaders Choose War: The Psychology of Prevention (Westport: Praeger Security International, 2006), [145] looked at why hawks are so influential in political or military affairs despite lack of evidence. Hawks favor coercive action, are more willing to use military force and are overly reluctant to make necessary concessions. They believe that hostile regimes only understand the language of force and don't notice subtle openings for dialogue. They misjudge how adversaries perceive them, assuming that outside observers grasp the constraints on their own behavior, but they are unable to see constraints on others. Some might say that these are reflective of availability and representativeness biases. In war they suffer from an optimism bias, exaggerating their strengths; and they commonly overestimate their future success assuming relatively quick and easy victory. Leaders on both sides of a conflict often share such perceptions as with the last Gulf War. Sometimes these assumptions make wars more likely to begin and more difficult to end. This may have produced the disaster of World War I.

From the point of view of much of the rest of the world, the US, far from being the practical, straight-talking, logical Sheriff Andy of Mayberry, actually exhibits many fallacies of logic.

BOUNDED RATIONALITY

Bounded rationality, in Herbert Simon's words, means a variant of "rational choice that takes into account the cognitive limitations of the decision maker--limitations of both knowledge and computational capacity" (Simon, 291). "Rather than consider all conceivable alternative courses of action, the boundedly rational actor conducts a limited search for a few alternative courses, often following standard operating procedures or incremental adaptation. She (sic) makes use of subjective beliefs, social norms, and cognitive shortcuts." Instead of optimizing, which is well beyond her computational capacity, she chooses "an alternative that meets or exceeds specified criteria, but that is not guaranteed to be either unique or in any sense the best" (Simon, 295). [146]

We are all 'bounded' in some measure, but may be able to expand our repertoire of making optimal decisions. Why do such findings of failures in medicine and international affairs not guide current practice? Why do they not enter the media or medical education? Is there effective control of information flow? Why do many Americans still trust their

---

A The Decrease in Breast-Cancer Incidence in 2003 in the United States NEJM 356: (16) 1670-1674 April 19 2007 http://content.nejm.org/cgi/content/full/356/16/1670

leadership and reject the opinion of experts about climate change as a phenomena and human influence on this process or if they accept it refuse to act on this information?

As with families of alcoholics denying issues related to alcohol, the elephant in the room that no one talks about, we have thus far not addressed two elephants distorting decision-making in medicine, environmental science and world affairs – the corporation and self-interest.

DISTORTING DECISION-MAKING-THE TACTICS AND GOALS OF THE CORPORATION

The Goals of the Corporation

I do not wish to demonize everything about corporate or military structures and the people working for them. I have friends and family in each sector from the lowest to highest levels of leadership, almost invariably good thoughtful people; with a few other turns in my own life, I might also have been part of one of those sectors. Corporations and the military often are the least discriminatory parts of societies focused as they wish to be, on the bottom line. Racial prejudices, gender and class issues are often, though not always, less than in other sectors of society. [147] The medical technology sector and military have been responsible for advances that have been applied to other sectors of society saving countless lives. Militaries sometime deliver emergency aid, with efficiency not found in the government, developmental and NGO sectors.

Though most people working in the pharmaceutical, energy or arms industries may start out with reasonable intentions, the corrupting effects of the marketing imperative and the need to comply with corporate culture in order to survive and to succeed within the corporate world, result in any sense of need to present the facts honestly being subsumed beneath corporate interests.

The major goal of a corporation's marketing arm is to favorably highlight some of the real or imagined differences between its product and other competing products on the market. Some might say that effective marketing means clever manipulation of emotions-based behavior, convincing people, be they doctors, politicians or the general public, to make less rational decisions based on distorted evidence.

Social cognition is used by marketers. People are primed; events are made more recent. Decoys are used to shift reference points as in the real estate agent who shows a more expensive, but overvalued, house first. Sometimes they will use dilutional effects, flooding the environment with neutral or irrelevant information to reduce the impact of negative aspects of their product or to extinguish negative responses. Military PR people use the same tactics.

Marketing is often directed to generate negative emotions (fear, envy, shame self-doubt, anxiety) in people to make them feel inadequate or unhappy, (or that there is something missing in their lives- be it their health, their home, their clothes, in order to get them to consume. Satisfied, centred people, fulfilled by the simple things in life, are poor consumers. Advertisers must undermine feelings of contentedness to sell products. They sell the idea that health and happiness come through, and only through, the purchasing of products. Media-induced hypochondiasis is one facet of the more general issue of the discontents induced by the Consumer Culture.

A British Medical Journal study of advertising to physicians in the BMJ shows how industry uses the power of promotion and the power of visual and linguistic imagery to tap into deeper meanings from metaphors and ancient myths to depict exaggerated therapeutic efficacy. [148]

As the magical Mirror of Erised in Harry Potter said "*I show not your face but your heart's desire.*"

Medicine-selling Fear

Corporate-sponsored "disease awareness campaigns" typically urge potential consumers to consult their doctor for advice on specific medications. "Once the need has been established and created, then the product can be introduced to satisfy that need/desire," states Harry Cook in the "Practical Guide to Medical Education," published by the UK-based *Pharmaceutical Marketing* magazine. [149]

In *Disease Mongering* [150] Lynn Payer described a confluence of interests of doctors, drug companies and media in exaggerating the severity of illness and the ability of drugs to "cure" them. "Since disease is such a fluid and political concept, the providers can essentially create their own demand by broadening the definitions of diseases in such a way as to include the greatest number of people, and by spinning out new diseases,"

But can industry actually create a new disease? Andrew Malleson shows the evolution of a relatively rare and short term diagnosis of neck strain after a motor vehicle accident to the medico-legal diagnosis of whiplash where it now costs $13 billion to $18 billion annually in the United States. [151]

Malleson does not deny that people suffer injury and a burden of disability, but attributes much of the growth in magnitude of the problem and the handicap produced to be due to the legal climate, to 'secondary gains' -- workers' compensation claims or lawsuits and noted the much poorer outcome of those with each. Of course some would say that people continue to suffer but not complain about things because no one is listening. He also shows how other illnesses such as "railway spine" and "repetitive strain injury" became rampant in other countries until laws allowing compensation were rescinded.

Ray Moynihan et al illustrate tactics used by industry to make and to market a disease. These include medicalizing natural functions or personal or social problems as medical problems or ailments requiring medication such as finasteride (Propecia) for baldness or antidepressants for social phobia. Mild symptoms (irritable bowel, restless legs) are given the title syndrome with the implication they may be portents of serious disease. A major conference in Australia showed other aspects of disease mongering. [152]

Risks factors such as osteoporosis or high blood pressure or cholesterol levels may be conceptualised as diseases in themselves. [153] Though the real diseases are fractures and cardiovascular problems, the drive by drug companies and individual investigators is to use surrogate endpoints in order to show efficacy rather than focusing on the real end points. There seems to be little alternative to medication to treating such risk factors.

Once the need for a new drug is established, Moynihan and Cassels show how industry may expand limited markets [154] to "persuade millions that they are sick. [155] Using the example of female sexual dysfunction, they demonstrate how science is co-opted.[25] Shortly after the introduction of Viagra industry began to promote it for this condition. [156]

We are in a society trained to fear risk factors. Well, young people 'need' to know their cholesterol level, their bone density, PSA. They 'must' regularly perform home blood pressure monitoring without any evidence that this improves their health. Medical journalist Alan Cassels reports that, even with an established disease such as diabetes, frequent monitoring of glucose may not be that helpful for non-insulin dependent diabetics.[26]

Citing statistics selectively and out of context, to maximize the size of a medical problems, advertising to patients to consult their doctors if they have certain risk factors for such conditions as osteopenia or andropause use of handy checklists for both doctor and patient, which seem to accentuate a perception of scientific certainty are all tactics used by the corporation. As the New York Times put it, if you have a pulse, you're sick. [157]

Environment - The Manufacture of Uncertainty

The strategy of "manufacturing uncertainty" entails questioning the validity of scientific evidence on which the regulation is based. It has been used with great success by polluters and manufacturers of dangerous products to oppose public health and environmental regulation most notably by the tobacco industry, but also by producers of asbestos, benzene, beryllium, chromium, diesel exhaust, lead, plastics, and other hazardous products to avoid environmental and occupational health regulation. [158]

Manufacturing uncertainty has become a business in itself; numerous technical consulting firms provide a service often called "product defense" or "litigation support" employing scientists for hire. The methods used by each industry - inventing an enemy, creating uncertainty - may at times appear reminiscent of the techniques of Nazi propagandist Joseph Goebbels.

David Michaels, [159] Assistant Secretary of Energy in the US between 1998 and 2001 examined the operations of the tobacco (and energy) industries. Despite incontrovertible evidence from Doll and Hill of the association of smoking to lung cancer 50 years ago, [160, 161] tobacco companies continued to throw doubt on lung cancer as being caused by smoking.[27]

---

25 Though male erectile function is easy to measure, female sexual dysfunction has not been. This condition has been medicalized to a level that *"some clinicians now recommend, along with a physical and psychosocial examination, a comprehensive evaluation that can include the measurement of hormonal profiles, vaginal pH, and genital vibratory perception thresholds, as well as the use of ultrasonography to measure clitoral, labial, urethral, vaginal, and uterine blood flow. Industry has sponsored studies of "vaginal engorgement insufficiency and clitoral erectile insufficiency."*

26 The Cochrane database of systematic reviews 2006, states there is *"... no valid randomized trial evidence that SMBG (self-monitoring of Blood Glucose) reduces either the number or severity of symptomatic episodes of hypoglycemia (or hyperglycemia)." "Getting people to test and retest their blood sugars did not improve peoples' quality of life, was expensive and even potentially harmful in that it increases patients' rates of depression, stress and worry."* http://commonground.ca/iss/0702187/cg187_chronic.shtml

27 They employed scientists who *"dissected every study, highlighted every question, magnified every flaw, cast every possible doubt every possible time. They also conjured their own studies with questionable data and foregone conclusions. It was all a charade, of course, because the real science was incontrovertible. But the uncertainty campaign was effective; it delayed public health protections, and compensation for tobacco's*

The same tactic was used with climate change, with vested interests often demanding impossible levels of proof or creating spurious diversions to prevent governments from taking common-sense precautions. Legitimate debate about the extent of global warming or of the degree of human contribution, is meant to sow doubts about whether it is happening at all.[28] The approach is now so common that it is unusual for the science *not* to be challenged by an industry facing regulation. Short term financial interests triumph over the long term future of the human species and the planet.

And in the environmental sector, more so than the pharmaceutical industry, there is sometimes overt manipulation of evidence. Last year the International Journal of Occupational and Environmental Health had a special issue on "Corporate Corruption of Science" including issues such as asbestos, leaded gas and industry. In it the editors address issues involved with policy setting.

"Although occupational and environmental diseases are often viewed as isolated and unique failures of science, the government, or industry to protect the best interest of the public, they are in fact an outcome of a pervasive system of corporate priority setting, decision making, and influence. This system produces disease because political, economic, regulatory and ideological norms prioritize values of wealth and profit over human health and environmental well-being. Science is a key part of this system; there is a substantial tradition of manipulation of evidence, data, and analysis, ultimately designed to maintain favorable conditions for industry at both material and ideological levels." [162]

International Affairs- The Sewing of Doubt and the Manufacturer of War

Herman Goering said, "… the people can always be brought to the bidding of the leaders. That is easy. All you have to do is tell them they are being attacked and denounce the pacifists for lack of patriotism and exposing the country to danger. It works the same way in any country." [163] In George Orwell's '1984', governments maintain constant war with the enemy changing from one day to the next and people willingly following along, forgetting yesterday's friend as today's enemy and vice versa.[29]

---

victims, for decades." Michaels, David. The Art of 'Manufacturing Uncertainty' LA Times June 24, 2005 http://www.latimes.com/news/opinion/commentary/la-oe-michaels24jun24,0,7062250

[28] Frederick Seitz, a physicist who served as president of the US National Academy of Sciences became chair of a group called the Science and Environmental Policy Project more than twenty years later and circulated the Oregon Petition, which has been cited by many who claim that climate change is a myth. Arthur B Robinson, with no qualifications on climate science, and his associate leader of the Oregon Institute of Science and Medicine, became the lead author of the "review" that followed Seitz's letter. The petition was printed in the font and format of the Proceedings of the National Academy of Sciences, encouraging anyone with a university degree to sign as an expert. Soon after the petition was published, the National Academy of Sciences released this statement: *"The NAS Council would like to make it clear that this petition has nothing to do with the National Academy of Sciences and that the manuscript was not published in the Proceedings of the National Academy of Sciences or in any other peer-reviewed journal. The petition does not reflect the conclusions of expert reports of the Academy."*

[29] The movie 'Wag the Dog' featured the manufacture of a virtual war, by a PR consultant working for a fictitious US president, which only existed on the nation's TV screens, in order to distract attention from a sex scandal which was threatening to derail the president. This insightful and prescient film seemed to anticipate the war on Yugoslavia and the manufacture or 'sexing up' of the evidence of Saddam's WMDs in the US and Britain. Despite the oppression, major human rights violations and a refugee situation in Kosovo, these turned out to be comparatively 'mild symptoms' compared to the genocide or major ethnic cleansing that Clinton and

It is natural for populations to wish to simplify the world around them; to demonize, to separate the self and other, the in-group to whom we feel some moral obligation and the outgroup to whom we have no obligation- and to view ourselves as just and the enemies, internal and external as unjust.[30] War propaganda tends to claim that only the enemy kills civilians, tortures POWs, and practices aggression and imperialism with the media, even in democracies suppressing all reports that "our boys" are committing similar atrocities to win a war. Lying, creating 'Saving Private Lynch' and 'Pat Tillman: Football hero turned war hero' fairy tales, only diminishes the reputations of the military. Jessica Lynch and the family of Army Ranger Tillman have shown true heroism in setting the record straight. [164]

Not diminishing the importance or the reality of terrorist threats, today in the US we see pathologically heightened fears of packages of white powder in the mail, of running shoes, toothpaste and of young Muslims praying on planes, all accentuated by colour-coded alerts. Governments stockpile stores of Ciprofloxacin, to deal with bioterrorism as during the US anthrax scare, leading to shortage of supply which is picked up by the media and consumers who try even harder to get some for themselves exacerbating the shortage and panic. It is a well known human behavior to overreact to something currently in favour. This is well known in the arena of economic psychology where people race to pay any price for a commodity during a "boom" only to have a collapse in the price such as the Holland tulip frenzy of 1636-7. [165]

Doubt is sown and the onus of burden of proof reversed. Donald Rumsfeld asserted that *"Absence of evidence* (of Saddam Hussein's weapons of mass destruction or ties with Al Quaeda) *is not evidence of absence."* [166]

The lack of evidence of efficacy of medicine or procedure, (which have defined cost and morbidity) is met with an argument that there is no evidence that it isn't effective.

Co-opting Decision-makers - 'Self Interest'

In domains of health and military security self interest or unconscious bias may colour judgment. Even doctors whom much of the public trusts as altruistic, may operate on self-interest or may view a patient through the limited lens of their specialties. Ear nose and throat surgeons once prescribed tonsillectomies routinely to all. When the evidence pointed to the lack of utility of such measures the number of tonsillectomies in the US plummeted from about one million per year to 250,000 over two decades. At the same time the ENTs

---

Blair claimed was ongoing. A far greater case for war could have been made a few years earlier in Bosnia over Srebernica and other incidents of mass murder.

[30]   Sam Keen's *"Faces of the Enemy"* Keen Sam Faces of the Enemy: Reflections of the Hostile Imagination San Francisco: Harper & Row, 1986.

political cartoons, posters and artwork showing depiction of the enemy in twentieth century war propaganda.

"In the beginning we create the enemy. Before the weapon comes the image. We think others to death and then invent the battle-axe or the ballistic missiles with which to actually kill them. Propaganda precedes technology."

Keen divides his illustrations into "archetypes of the hostile imagination." Including the Enemy as "Stranger", Aggressor," "Barbarian," "Criminal,", "Rapist," "Death," and Insect" One memorable cartoon panel illustrates tactics.

"Our enemies make nerve gas. So will we. They squander their wealth on armaments. So will we. They spy on their own citizens. So will we. They prevent their people from knowing what they do. So will we. We will not let our enemies impose their evil ways on us. We'll do it for them."

discovered increasing merits in myringotomies or insertion of tympanostomy tubes (grommets) which increased by 250%. Consumer Reports found these and other surgeries including cataracts, cholecystectomies, hysterectomies, C-sections, and those for sleep apnoea and low back pain often unnecessary. [167]

Radiologists and surgeons continue to recommend routine mammogram screening in some countries despite lack of evidence of benefit, especially below age 50, feeling that there are no harms and that we are developing better machines that will allow earlier detection and treatment that will be successful in the future.

Financial relationships among the pharmaceutical industry, scientific investigators, and academic institutions are widespread. Approximately one fourth of investigators have industry affiliations, and roughly two thirds of academic institutions hold equity in start-ups that sponsor research performed at the same institutions. [168]

In Talking Back to Ritalin, Breggin describes how the mental health industry was going broke in the US in the 1970's with psychiatrists facing competition from psychologists, social workers, and family therapists. The DSM was revised to make diagnoses more objective and more medications became available to treat these conditions. An economic and political partnership with the drug companies in the 1980s allowed the profession to promote the medical model with drug company money through advertising in their journals, grants, special projects, massive support for professorships, lecture series and labs at medical schools.[31]

This also applies to other sectors. In the US the Department of Defence supports 37 percent of all federal research in the computer sciences and 44 percent of all engineering research, as well as significant shares of research in mathematics and oceanography. [169] The military industrial complex exerts major control in many societies with global defence spending now approaching $1 trillion US per year, about half of that taking place in the US [170]. Wars may be used to promote stagnant economies or to provide new sources of natural resources.

Both the pharmaceutical and the arms industries have paid lobbyists in Washington, including former officials from Congress, or the government, think tanks, as well as the media. Both support candidates who vow to actively support their industries and provide jobs through favourable legislation, regulation and juicy contracts. [171] When it came to Reagan's Star Wars, contracts were given to companies in all 435 Congressional districts to give Congressional representatives a sense of at least short term benefits for their constituencies.

---

[31] In Psychiatric News, psychiatrist Lester Shapiro (1991) identified the shared interests of the American Psychiatric Association and the drug companies:
"I am aware that the interrelationship of APA and the pharmaceutical industry is a complex one. We share research needs, appropriate product evaluation, planning for long-range goals, and the overarching considerations inherent in biopsychosocial patient care. It is far better that we engage in a serious examination and dialogue of the issues I have raised than to act in collusion with an industry whose goal is to increase drug usage by broadening indications for their drugs, advocating long-term administration, minimizing side effects, overstating effectiveness, de-emphasizing adjunctive treatments, or denigrating generic drugs"

DISTORTING DECISION-MAKING - THE TOOLS OF THE CORPORATION

Think tanks, lobbyists, committees, consumer interest groups and news media are all employed to market the message of fear and uncertainty. Overloading with information, they attempt to distort our decision-making capacity.

Communicating the Message: Experts and Thinktanks

To convince doctors, drug companies help set up boards of experts with key opinion leaders and launch a series of advertorials in leading medical magazines featuring interviews with members of the company's advisory board. These paid consultants also speak at rounds and various meetings, write or have articles ghost-written for them extolling the virtues of their product.

The Union of Concerned Scientists [172] produced a document showing how ExxonMobil used the tobacco industry's disinformation tactics, as well as some of the same organizations and personnel, to fund an array of front organizations or those which receive a substantial part of their revenue much as Big Tobacco had a few years earlier.[32]

A national coalition intended to educate the media, public officials and the public about the dangers of 'junk science' [173] portrayed the danger of tobacco smoke as just one "unfounded fear" among others, such as concerns about pesticides and cell phones.[33]

In the 1950s, with the link between cigarette smoking and lung cancer becoming well established, the tobacco industry was in crisis. Its PR strategy, devised by the firm Hill & Knowlton, *was "entangling itself in the manipulation of fundamental scientific processes,"* [174]

"It was Hill & Knowlton's John Hill who "hit on the idea of creating an industry-sponsored research entity. Ultimately, he concluded, the best public relations approach was for the industry to become a major sponsor of medical research." This approach "implied that existing studies were inadequate or flawed," and made the tobacco industry "seem a committed participant in the scientific enterprise rather than a detractor." [175] The industry also created the "Tobacco Industry Research Committee."

Hill & Knowlton later became known for use of the 16 year old daughter of the Kuwaiti ambassador to the US in order to generate support for the first Gulf War. 'Nayirah' testified before Congress that she was a volunteer in a Kuwaiti hospital who had witnessed Iraqi

---

[32]   Think tanks such as the Cato Institute and the Heritage Foundation received money from bith Big Tobacco and Big Oil. Monbiot George The denial industry Tuesday September 19, 2006 http:// environment.guardian.co.uk/print/0,,329579929-121568,00.html Exxon has been a major funder of climate change deniers including the George C Marshall Institute and the Center for the Study of Carbon Dioxide and Global Change. Greenpeace Exxonsecrets.org

[33]   "Junk science" meant peer-reviewed studies showing that smoking was linked to cancer and other diseases. "Sound science" meant studies sponsored by the tobacco industry suggesting that the link was inconclusive. A memo from the tobacco company Brown and Williamson noted, "Doubt is our product since it is the best means of competing with the 'body of fact' that exists in the mind of the general public. It is also the means of establishing a controversy." Monbiot George The denial industry Tuesday September 19, 2006 http://environment.guardian.co.uk/print/0,,329579929-121568,00.html JunkScience.com was founded by Big Tobacco but received money from companies such as Exxon.

soldiers throwing babies out of incubators,. Hill & Knowlton now does work for the nuclear power industry.

PR firms work on multiple issues. Burson Marsteller, like Hill & Knowlton, is owned by WPP, now the biggest communication firm in the world. [176] Burson Marsteller consults for clients including repressive regimes, Big Tobacco and biotech companies and against various environmental concerns. [177]

PR consultants such as Patrick Moore, who left Greenpeace two decades ago has worked on a range of issues, where he has dismissed concerns about the impact of logging in the Amazon, supported Newmont Mining over controversies at its mines in the U.S., Ghana and Peru, defended the use of PVC in plastics and extolled the merits of genetically engineered crops. Since 2006 he has been a consultant to the Nuclear Energy Institute's front group, the Clean and Safe Energy Coalition.

Communicating the Message: Advocacy Groups

Teri Cox from Cox Communication Partners expressed enthusiasm about the benefits of funding patient advocacy groups in *Pharmaceutical Executive* Magazine asserts that *"Successful partnerships with third-party organizations such as patient and caregiver advocacy groups, professional associations, and thought leaders are powerful medicine for pharma companies."* [178]

"Industry-patient" partnerships, could "influence changes in health care policy and regulations to expand patient access to, and coverage for, earlier diagnoses and treatments ... recruit participants for clinical trials" and "speed the development and approval process for new therapies." *"Partnering with advocacy groups and thought leaders at major research institutions helps to defuse industry critics by delivering positive messages about the healthcare contributions of pharma companies."* Better still, an alliance with a non-profit group can deter inquisitive journalists. *"Without such allies, a skeptical journalist may see a company's messages as self-serving and describe them as such to their audiences,"* [179]

What happens if no organization exists for your problem? To get out a "grassroots message" corporations' PR departments sometimes have created and funded front groups supposedly composed of ordinary citizens. Such practices are described by some critics and PR people as "astroturfing"- the practice of disguising an orchestrated campaign as a spontaneous upwelling of public opinion on a corporate message. In response to reports about the effects of passive smoking Big Tobacco began to create their own fake citizens' group, the Advancement of Sound Science Coalition to fight "over-regulation". Such groups manage to stay 'on message' but risk being publicly unmasked and leading to blowback for the company or coalition of companies:

More common and less risky in the pharmaceutical area is agreeing to fund existing organizations rather than to create their own.[34] Some older "patient groups" or disease groups

---

[34] According to the Union of Concerned Scientists, ExxonMobil funneled nearly $16 million between 1998 and 2005 to a network of 43 advocacy organizations that seek to confuse the public and delay action on global warming science. Oil Company Spent Nearly $16 Million to Fund Skeptic Groups, Create Confusion ExxonMobil Report Jan 3, 2007 Monbiot George The denial industry Tuesday September 19, 2006 http://environment.guardian.co.uk/print/0,,329579929-121568,00.html
Both the tobacco and petroleum industries also sought to distance themselves from their own campaigns.

(The Arthritis Society, founded in 1947, and the Canadian Diabetes Association, founded in 1953) began receiving funding from industry specifically to lobby and pressure governments on drug and health policy at a time when industry was less powerful and these groups remained more independent.

Sponsoring cash poor patient advocacy groups, supplying them with information (thereby filtering their marketing messages through organizations that tend to engender trust) helps medicalize issues. Some consumer health organizations are more than willing accomplices. The Canadian Cancer Society advertised that "Partnership with the Canadian Cancer Society can assist your company in reaching your commercial objectives." [180] And the CCS is one of the best, having taken a courageous stand on hormone replacement. "Osteoporosis Australia, a medical foundation, which has received funding from pharmaceutical companies, issued a press release recently urging people to take a one minute test for their risk of osteoporosis. According to the foundation, *we call this disease a silent thief: if you're not vigilant, it can sneak up on you and snatch your quality of life and your long-term health.'* [181][35] Many other patient/consumer groups understanding such influences only decide to accept pharma funding after major internal debate and conflict.

Such tactics have been employed in the tobacco and energy sector. Communications firm APCO advised Philip Morris tobacco in forming the fake citizens' group: the Advancement of Sound Science Coalition. (TASSC) The chairman of Chesapeake Energy Corp, an Oklahoma City natural-gas-production company, set "Clean Sky Coalition, [182, 183] running ads in *The Wall Street Journal*, the *Washington Post* headlined *'Face It, Coal is Filthy.'* as well as on local buses and in the subway system, Some ads falsely claimed that Environmental Defense and the Sierra Club had "joined" the coalition. The ads were produced by Strategic Perception,

Regulatory Bodies

Close ties remain between regulatory bodies and the pharmaceutical industry the world over and industry is often seen as being the hand that feeds the regulator. In some countries, the regulator of an industry will be funded directly by payments from the industry it regulates - eg the Food and Drug Administration (FDA), in the USA, is funded directly by drug company fees. To some degree such relationships are necessary as people in the industry have some expertise but with cross-over in personnel, friendships and financial interdependence, regulators often see themselves as needing to correct public 'misconceptions' and 'fallacies' about their industrial friends.

In Britain, the Medicines and Healthcare products Regulatory Agency (MHRA) and the trade association of the industry it regulates, have engaged in drawing up blueprints for action

---

35   *New Scientist,* in the largest survey to date of industry donations to patient groups, found only two of 29 US patient organizations, ruled out drug company funding. Most were reliant on them for over one-third of their budget. The Colorectal Cancer Coalition receives approximately 81% of its budget from drug companies. Marshall Jessica Aldhous Peter Swallowing the best advice? New Scientist 27 October 2006 issue 2575 pp18-22
Every group in our survey that received a high proportion of funding from industry denied that it biased their mission. Sharon Batt of Dalhousie University in Halifax, Canada, found that organizations that accept pharmaceutical funding "tend to advocate for faster review and availability of drugs, greater insurance coverage." Groups that maintain financial independence, on the other hand, "emphasize safety over speed".

and have done lobbying together. With the nuclear power and pesticide industries, with which I am most familiar, such considerations are often unconscious. The IAEA, meant to regulate nuclear power, is entrusted also with a mandatory obligation to promote nuclear power as a desirable source of energy.[36] [184]

Government

If you have friends in government you can move the agenda further. A survey of 1,600 government scientists by the Union of Concerned Scientists found systemic tampering with the work of government climate scientists to eliminate politically inconvenient material about global warming. Nearly half (46%) of climate scientists at government agencies from NASA to the Environmental Protection Agency had been advised against using the terms "global warming" or "climate change" in speeches or in their reports. Forty-three percent of respondents said their published work had been revised in ways that altered the meaning of scientific findings. [185]

In each sector, from medicine to military security, to the environment, the interested corporate sector has managed to sell fear and manufacture uncertainty to sell its product. Each employs think tanks or key opinion leaders, advocacy groups and influences regulatory bodies and governments to build markets for its product and to disturb rational decision-making.

UNBOUNDING RATIONALITY - THE END OF SCIENTISTIC THINKING AND CORPORATE - MILITARY CONTROL OF DECISION-MAKING

'Stuff happens," "But in terms of what's going on in that country, it is a fundamental misunderstanding to see those images over and over and over again of some boy walking out with a vase and say, 'Oh, my goodness, you didn't have a plan' ... It's untidy, and freedom's untidy, and free people are free to make mistakes and commit crimes and do bad things. They're also free to live their lives and do wonderful things, and that's what's going to happen here." [186] -Quote from Donald Rumsfeld, former US Secretary of Defence and architect of the war on Iraq.

Stuff doesn't just happen. The effects of the Gulf War were predictable. In the worlds of medicine, environmental and international affairs, we are adrift, or worse, entirely on the wrong course. When current approaches don't seem to work, we must reverse gear and look at alternative approaches. In the Western World or Global North, supporting despotic oil

---

[36] ARTICLE II: Objectives
The Agency shall seek to accelerate and enlarge the contribution of atomic energy to peace, health and prosperity throughout the world. It shall ensure, so far as it is able, that assistance provided by it or at its request or under its supervision or control is not used in such a way as to further any military purpose.
ARTICLE III: Functions
A. The Agency is authorized:
1. To encourage and assist research on, and development and practical application of, atomic energy for peaceful uses throughout the world; ...

regimes, continuing reckless oil consumption and pumping out greenhouse gases is not in our long-term interests.

The Health Belief Model [187] was developed by social psychologists in the 1950s after the failure of a free TB screening program by the US Public Health Service. It was found that individuals take health- related action if they believe that the severity of consequences is major, that the consequence can be avoided, there is positive expectation taking action will avoid consequences and that they can successfully undertake action (that they have the skills and confidence) to do so.

Albert Bandura, a father of Social Learning theory explained in 1977, that there has to be an expectation that change will have positive consequences, made an expectancy it that it has value and should be made, that an individual feels capable, that they can monitor progress and that there are positive reinforcers. [188]

Public health physician John Last similarly describes social change occurring on public health problems when we are aware that the problem exists, know what causes the problem, believe that it is important, believe in our ability to control the cause and have the political will to make the changes. [189]

Until recently physicians may not have believed that the system could change or that they have agency and most people, even in democracies, either do not believe that they can change the international system. I believe that the time is ripe for change in each of these sectors.

A Need to Change: Failure of Current Approaches

To quote Dr. Rumsfeld again, *"There are known knowns. These are things we know that we know. There are known unknowns. That is to say, there are things that we know we don't know. But there are also unknown unknowns. There are things we don't know we don't know."* [190]

This paper has been largely designed to show problems in terms of scientism and corporate/military distortion in each of, the energy, environmental and international security. The problems are knowable and solutions too.

When we look at effectiveness what do we find? Policies that leave us somewhat less secure and unsustainable, increased terrorism, decreased resources, increased output of greenhouse gases and continuing to sell policies that all is OK if we'll just turn the other way. *"Of the seventy-eight drugs approved by the FDA in 2002, only seventeen contained new active ingredients, and only seven of these were classified by the FDA as improvements over older drugs."* [191] Just four new molecular entities (NMEs) were introduced in Europe and seven in the US in 2005," [192] The benefits of medical action may not be as great as we hope nor the risks of medical inaction as great as we fear.

As Marcia Angell, former editor of the New England Journal of Medicine declared the pharmaceutical industry is "…extraordinarily privileged. It benefits from publicly funded research, government-granted patents and large tax breaks whilst it reaps lavish profits." [193] The same might be said for the oil and gas, auto, and nuclear power sectors and of course the military industries. Such failures should be invite closer scrutiny and a search for alternatives.

Failures in the pharmaceutical area are multiple. Decisions made in world affairs bear little relation to long term goals. Looking at smart bombs, guns, cluster munitions and nuclear weapons to achieve security in the short term may ultimately increase dangers. On nuclear weapons we have moved from policies parading the benefits of unilateral possession of nuclear weapons in the 1940s and 50s, to bilateral possession/detente (Mutually Assured Destruction) in the 70s and 80s to today's claims that they are beneficial for our friends and allies but need to be proscribed for others.[37] [194]

We are looking at crises in terms of air quality, fossil fuel scarcity and climate change. Solutions such as the use of corn for ethanol which requires more energy to make than one gains are only profitable in the US because of farm subsidies, but do nothing to save energy.

It is the 'scientistic', as opposed to the scientific, approach that must be thrown out. A belief in scientific medicine for resolving empirical questions is not wrong. But what we often have now is attempting to answer non-empirical questions or answering the wrong question, a flawed belief in science for science's sake.

Pragmatism seeks to reconcile the competing philosophies of empiricism (concepts as inductive generalizations from sensory experience) and rationalism (concepts as mental phenomenon understood as prior to experience, thus conceiving of knowledge in deductive terms). Understanding the limitations of the 'scientistic' approach and judiciously applying it, knowing heuristics, cognitive distortions, how we mis-evaluate risk, making assumptions explicit, improving information flows and keeping information transparent, can only improve our decision-making. [195]

Barriers to Change: The Medico-pharma and Military-industrial Complexes

I am convinced that in medicine, such errors represent a systemic and systematic failure in the system due, for example, to 1. inadequate initial and then post-marketing surveillance 2. lack of transparency of studies 3. drug company control of medical education 4. lack of interest from the medical profession, 5, undue influence that business partnerships at times exert on the universities 6. poor regulation and 7. lack of political interest/will. Each of these has a parallel in environmental decision-making and international affairs where similar industrial, corporate and military control of agenda through research education, media and government is enabled by lack of interest or self-interest of decision-makers,

In Medicine and international affairs, these distorted assumptions and values allow decision-makers with fiduciary responsibilities such as doctors and political representatives, consciously or unconsciously, to act against the interests of their constituents or patients. Ultimately this will undermine confidence in the whole process and will not serve the long-term interests even of these sectors, which see themselves as beneficiaries.

As Dwight Eisenhower warned in 1961 [196]

---

[37] I said in a response to Charles Krauthammer's argument in an essay in Time magazine, entitled "The Terrible Logic of Nukes" that nuclear weapons protected the peace by maintaining a delicate balance of terror was that it *was just that: terrible logic. Iraq wants nuclear weapons to balance Israel's, which built them to balance Arab conventional superiority. Pakistan wanted to balance India, which had to balance China, which had to balance Russia, which had to balance the U.S. and its allies, which had to balance Russia's presumed European-theater superiority. Throughout this balancing act, the world has been no more than 30 minutes away from Armageddon. The only logical way to keep nuclear weapons out of the hands of madmen is to renounce them ourselves.*

This conjunction of an immense military establishment and a large arms industry is new in the American experience. The total influence -- economic, political, even spiritual -- is felt in every city, every State house, every office of the Federal government. We recognize the imperative need for this development. Yet we must not fail to comprehend its grave implications. Our toil, resources and livelihood are all involved; so is the very structure of our society.

In the councils of government, we must guard against the acquisition of unwarranted influence, whether sought or unsought, by the military-industrial complex. The potential for the disastrous rise of misplaced power exists and will persist.

James Madison warned in 1795, "Of all the enemies of public liberty, war is perhaps the most to be dreaded, because it comprises and develops the germ of every other." [197]

Both the pharmaceutical and military industries are considered sacrosanct in terms of legislation- accountable to the public neither in terms of budget, nor effectiveness. To ask real, meaningful or profound questions to do performance appraisals, may be perceived as unpatriotic, even dangerous. A culture of fear makes holistic, non-pharmacologic approaches to health and non-military approaches to security, seem less viable. The militaristic press and lobbyists tell us that a military response to conflict is the only one possible. Just as spokespeople from the pharmaceutical industry dominate the airwaves, a parade of military and ex-military analysts on US television before this last Gulf War monopolized the stage preparing the groundwork for 'war as the only alternative'.

Yes says the skeptic. *Defining the problem and solution is a theoretical exercise, in an ideal world in which a Plato-style philosopher-prince has to make public policy decisions. Looking at who is making the decision, what is their motivation, what is their desired outcome and why. What caused a particular decision to be made to achieve that outcome- what was the reasoning behind it? Was the reasoning sound? Were the putative reasons the real reasons or was there a hidden agenda? Will a decision help in the short-term but hinder in the long term? Who really made the decision for the US to go to war in Iraq not just who was the frontman? What were their motives? Who really gains from the implementation of the decision? Perhaps the ultimate decision-makers happy with results of Iraq or failure of drugs. Often the answer to this is complex - A cluster/cabal of self-interested parties will often have worked together to soften up the politicians, the public and professions to accept some new idea, which is supposedly in the interest of the public.* [198]

But even if true, such thinking neglects the Decision-making power that is still within the control of individuals, especially in democracies.

Even people working in the pharmaceutical, energy and military sectors who are usually well-intentioned and thoughtful but don't see a way out and don't see themselves as decision-makers. They suffer from a sense of powerlessness or inertia and resign themselves to a default position of rationalism that they are doing the least harm or naked self interest professionally and splitting personally. What can increase the will to change?

Will to Change

Human beings are among the most adaptable of species. Once our mind is made up to change this system, we are capable of major shifts. Rational changes inputs open processes

better system in medicine and world affairs As such we can create the political will to change decision-making processes. Malcolm Gladwell shows that once societies reach the tipping point, they may be capable of rapid and productive change. [199] Former US Vice President Al Gore believes that democracies are capable of a rapid and effective response once they make up their minds to act. People have been able to effect great social change despite resistance of leaders from the abolition of slavery, to universal suffrage to the end of overt colonialism or in the health sector to attitudes towards smoking and drinking and driving.

James O Prochaska and Carlo Di Clemente studied the way in which people are able to make decisions to improve their health such as quitting smoking. [200] The stages of change model ranges from Pre-contemplation (with little awareness of a problem and no anticipation of change), to Contemplation (awareness of a problem but no effective plan) to Preparation (intent and a valid plan) to Action (where an attempt has been made to change) followed by Maintenance (> 6 months free of the harmful behavior). Collectively, with regard to changes in our way of decision-making in Medicine and International Affairs, we are in the 'pre-contemplation' stage.

How do we push to the action stage described by Prochaska and Di Clemente?

Looking at things psychotherapeutically we must look at the small changes we can make in our own behaviour and the first step solution-focused, when confronted with a problem. The above attitudes/ rationalizations against change of 'scientism' represent distortions pointed out by Aaron Beck, [201] *All or nothing, Overgeneralization, Negative filter discounting the positive*. The main thing is to alter the decision-making balance for individuals and institutions to show on balance the pros of change outweigh cons.

People are often ahead of leaders on action related to issues such as Climate Change or, Third World Debt. They recognize the interdependence in this world and the need to change and are capable of changes. The medical system is also capable of change. Patients of all education levels and cultures are open to a dialogue on the relative merits and harms of interventions as well as uncertainties.

Militaries also saw no way to give up landmines, the cotton industry in the US to manage without slaves, Airlines and restaurants were unable to see their world without smoking, before such decisions were thrust upon them..

Recent events make the situation ripe to accept change. Intelligence 'sexed-up' or hyped in both the US and Britain prior to the last war may have undermined public confidence the next time either country tries to use information gained from secret sources to argue for war. The same might be said for the pharmaceutical industry, which has suffered repeated black eyes related to suppressed studies and the necessity for drug withdrawal. Such events lead to conflict with dearly held assumptions. 'Conflict' in Peace Studies, is seen as a situation with perceived incompatible goals but where there may be a chance to grow. This may be the time to make a change with balanced arguments and credible sources, allowing people to confirm or modify their opinions.

Negative behaviors by the US military including massacres of civilians at Jalalabad in March 2007. [202] and Haditha in November 2005 [203], torture at Abu Ghraib and the cover-ups afterwards have increased the strength of the insurgency and undermined support for the war effort at home.[38]

---

[38] In international and diplomatic negotiations, game theory which stemmed from research performed during world war II, has been used to quantitate the effect of certain decisions. In effect the best overall decision to

The Boomerang effect when companies like Exxon Mobil, Merck or Pepsi use front groups make such tactics less attractive. [204, 205, 206] Spin of the Day and SourceWatch expose disinformation by various sources, their backing and affiliations.

We are now more skeptical as a public, being "inoculated," or forewarned about the presence of front groups presence. One study indicated " *that exposure, which reveals the corporate sponsors and true motives of corporate front-group stealth campaigns, backfires, not only against efforts to shape the attitude object but also against the image, reputation, credibility and citizenship assessments of front groups and their corporate sponsors. In short, there is significant risk associated with front-group stealth campaigns, which sponsors ignore at their peril,*" [207]

One avenue of action used frequently in the US to fight back is the legal one- "Product Liability". Many class action drug cases have been successful. In the social realm class action suits are less frequent and more difficult.[39] *Some are suing in US courts related to damage from the War on Terror involving torture but as yet attempts to impeach the President or to force the Prime Minister of Britain from office for their conduct on the war on Iraq and for launching it with false information have failed.*

In the environmental sector though, regulators in both the pesticide and nuclear industries which I am involved with have become more cognisant of possible biases related to their relationship with industry in the last decade, perhaps in response to scandal or public pressure. Following the accidents at the Three Mile Island and Chernobyl reactors the regulatory requirements for nuclear power reactors all over the world has been upgraded. Also, many new reactor designs are much more robust than the previous reactors to deal with malevolent acts. The US Nuclear Regulatory Commission now tries to approach decision-making using probabilistic risk analysis. [208] It describes Principles of Good Regulation which include Independence, Openness, Efficiency, Clarity and Reliability while its Organizational Values include Integrity, Excellence, Service, Respect, Cooperation and Commitment.

Can we convince corporations and militaries not to use selling Fear or marketing Uncertainty as their primary modus operandi? Or can we persuade governments and medical practitioners or their tools not to participate? Or the public not to believe?

Prudent self-interest, an understanding of shared benefits and costs, a recognition of tradeoffs and internalization of costs can be used with work in international affairs or the pharmaceutical industry. For instance requiring manufacturers to either produce or give up

---

make within a two party model in game theory is to return a good deed with another good deed. Models using an assumption of instigating a bad deed end up with another bad deed in return from the affected party.

[39] *In the late 1990s, thousands of smokers from Florida brought a class action for the damage to their health against America's five biggest cigarette makers under the name of Howard Engle, an 86-year-old paediatrician with respiratory diseases and lymphoma. In 2000, a jury decided the tobacco companies should pay a punitive award of $145bn (£76bn). But the state's appeal court decided that Florida's smokers should not have been allowed to bring a class action. In 1998, New Orleans and Chicago sued gun-makers to force them to cover police and hospital costs incurred by their weapons, arguing that the firearms industry was liable because it made "unreasonably dangerous" products which lacked the safety mechanisms necessary to ensure only their owners could use them. In January 2003, the families of two men killed by the Washington snipers sued the shop where the suspects bought their high-powered rifle. California, sued the six largest carmakers in the US - Ford, General Motors, Toyota, Honda, Chrysler and Nissan - for allegedly creating a "public nuisance" costing it millions of dollars due to vehicle emissions and contributing to global warming.* Glaister Dan California sues car firms for global warming Green campaigners hail landmark action · Six largest manufacturers creating 'public nuisance' The Guardian Thursday September 21, 2006

patents on essential drugs to deal with diseases in the developing world, or to be taxed in some sort of global fund in order to be allowed to develop their products to governments manufacturing drugs themselves. Such products do not make much profit for manufacturers compared to those for chronic diseases in the West and as such no significant developments have taken place in the last thirty years.

With sitting stakeholders around the table, a broad spectrum of solutions might be explored. These might include taxes or voluntary payments (people in the North willing to pay a few cents extra on a bottle of tablets to deal with river blindness), highlighting the positive publicity from the marketplace with corporate generosity, much as the Gates foundation has done, to the promotion of generics.. With operant conditioning we might hope that positive results will reinforce the positive negative behaviours eventually become extinct.

Till recently on environmental issues, it has been the skeptics who are marginalized whose voices aren't heard as loudly in the mainstream media. But that is beginning to change.

Even PR firm Hill & Knowlton recognized a reason to change. Its Chairman and General Manager, Thomas Buckmaster. advises firms after a disaster to "Defusing Sensitive Issues Through 'Risk Communication,' "(1) Acknowledge the concerns of the other side; (2) Encourage joint fact-finding commissions; (3) Offer alternatives to minimize impacts; (4) Accept responsibilities, admit mistakes, and share power; (5) Focus on building long-term relationships; and (6) Act in what will be perceived as a trustworthy fashion." [209] Buckmaster was not advocating changing tactics and truly partnering, but with corporations seeing exposure of activity, they are beginning to change.

In an apparent policy shift, earlier this year Exxon Mobil called climate change "a serious issue," saying that "action is warranted." The oil company also said it would stop funding groups that downplay the risks from global warming or lobby against measures to limit greenhouse gas emissions. While Exxon still funds 40 "skeptic groups," including the American Enterprise Institute, Cato Institute and Heritage Foundation it did cut its donations to such groups by more than 40 percent in 2006 from 2005." [210]

We need to have the individual will to overcome our fears to push for such changes. Let us hope we are getting there in the health, environmental and political sectors.

But we are able to change on at lease an individual level. And once we become aware of a problem must do so to avoid splitting. In a review of Jerome Groopman's book on how physicians think, [211] editor of the *Lancet*, Richard Horton talks of the hubris of "evidence-based medicine" and the need to change. [212] Physicians can guard against these traps by heightening their sense of self-awareness and becoming conscious of their own feelings and emotions, responses, and choices.

We use heuristics when overloaded with information, when don't want to think about a problem, when stakes not important or when we have little or no information. The stakes are high for the planet we should realize that getting rid of scientism and avoiding complicity in corporate distortion and maintaining a healthy skepticism will increase credibility amongst our patients. A little thinking will actually allow us to discard a lot of irrelevant information and ultimately saves time. It will increase credibility among our patients. The same might be true for the pharmaceutical industry, for the military, for the energy sector for politicians. Looking for spin may be convincing in the short term, but in the information age of the Internet, those engaging in such behaviour have a greater risk of exposure.

Change at a Societal Level

When our leaders reverse their public pronouncements as to whether Uncle Joe (Stalin), Noriega or Saddam Hussein are forces of stability, or "better than the alternative," or the "epitome of Evil" as we seek to overthrow them, populations are expected to follow these U-turns like sheep, much as we are expected to do with pharmaceutical industry failures or reversals. Now that we have seen general failures and major new threats are on the horizon,, the search for an alternative becomes more apparent.

We can even apply some of the methodologies of epidemiology and true evidence based medicine to international affairs and a preventive health based model to world affairs. Primordial Prevention in public health involves looking at root causes, the underlying disease processes, not just the proximate causes of death. In international affairs this would refer to what would normally be termed 'risk factors' for conflicts developing in the first place, addressing social causes including lack of political process, over-population, lack of education, human rights abuses, poverty and social inequalities.

Primary prevention concerns prevention in the asymptomatic phase. It would relate to preventing war or violence from breaking out when a situation of conflict already exists, or from escalating to dangerous levels. Limitation of arms, combating propaganda and diplomacy are examples of such efforts. Secondary prevention refers to the situation where war has already broken out (the disease has manifested itself) and methods to make peace are sought (peacemaking and peacekeeping). Tertiary prevention, analogous to rehabilitation in medicine and ecological restoration for environmentalists, would be post 'hot' war peace-building. [213]. Using this public health model with focus on primary prevention may ultimately serve us well. [214]

With non-empirical questions, an systems or ecological approach may help, recognizing feedback loops and uncertainties of risks and benefits. [215] A precautionary approach is not an unreasonable general principle[40] [216] or the Hippocratic injunction to '"First do no harm" should apply across the board to all public and private policy makers and not just to the medical profession. [217, 218] The obligation should be not on citizens and their representatives to demonstrate harm; rather there should be a 'Reverse Onus' [219] on those introducing new products to society to prove that the products themselves are safe, and that clean production processes are used with insignificant discharge of foreign, noxious substances. An analogous reverse onus might be appropriate for medical therapeutics and international affairs. We may allow certain latitude to deal with urgent situations, whether with using a drug with uncertain safety in a pandemic, trying to stop an imminent terrorist attack, dealing with an acute water shortage or famine or in international affairs, in the case of impending or actual genocide, but we must remain wary of those seeking to define every situation as a crisis.

The impact of a drug or therapy is especially difficult to assess more with those concerns including behavioural/social components, such as addiction, weight loss, behavioural interventions - like exercise and cognitive therapy. With these the RCT process can create a

---

[40] "When an activity raises threats of harm to human health or the environment, precautionary measures should be taken even if some cause and effect relationships are not fully established scientifically. In this context the proponent of an activity, rather than the public, should bear the burden of proof. The process of applying the precautionary principle must be open, informed and democratic and must include potentially affected parties. It must also involve an examination of the full range of alternatives, including no action."

highly artificial and distorting milieu. Some have suggested that in the absence of a gold standard, we argue that a convergence of evidence from different types of studies using multiple methods of independent imperfection may provide the best bases for attributing improvements in health outcomes to interventions.[41] These may also be true for environmental or international affairs.

But even making a relatively simple decision like "Will I buy myself an ice-cream now?", all sorts of competing motivations come into play. Desire, hunger, guilt, money, obesity, fun etc - all these thoughts jostle and compete in the mind and eventually you buy the ice-cream, or not, depending on which voices are the most persuasive at that moment in time. When the number of people involved in contributing to a decision increases, the whole process gets much more complex. Arguments get used which do not reflect the real views of the protagonist. Each voice claiming to have the public good in mind when they really are pushing their own barrow. Deconstructing/reconstructing the complex pathways leading to public interest decisions is therefore an enormously difficult task. Even powerful government committees have trouble getting to the bottom of how certain disastrous decisions got make. The PICO model of enquiry (Problem, Intervention, Comparator, Outcome) used in EBM could be employed in international affairs. I am only half-joking when I say that a Cochrane library of international or environmental interventions could truly be established. [220]

Perhaps most important is a philosophical change to one of humility and -simplicity. An analysis of the increase in life expectancy over the last century in the US from 47 to 77 years shows no more than five of these years attributable to improved medical care. Much of the rest is related to public health, hygiene, education and lifestyle measures. And how much of international security vs. insecurity is really provided by national militaries?

In all fields we may have to learn to adapt and adjust to uncertainty rather than predict or control. Forest fires are often worsened by trying to eliminate smaller fires. Monoculture makes fields less sustainable and often requires more intensive care in terms of time and resources. Extremes even of hygiene, may have negative consequences such as asthma and allergies. [221, 222]

In Medicine we have moved from talking about patient compliance to adherence but in terms of decision-making we have not figured out how to mesh the agenda of the patient with our science to develop a common treatment plan to which we can adhere.

A participatory, multidisciplinary approach to decision-making also can lead to more resilient decisions. Bringing all stakeholders to the table, listening to concerns and looking at joint problem solving or conflict resolution may lead to resilient decisions and a more desirable outcome, An open and transparent process establishes some level of credibility up

---

[41] good evidence a safe and effective medicine is being appropriately prescribed; covariation between medicine use and improved health outcomes; being able to discount alternative explanations of the covariation so that medicine use is the most plausible explanation of the improved health outcomes.
The strongest possible evidence would be provided by the coherence of the following types of evidence:
(1)individual linked data showing that patients are prescribed the medicine, there are reasonable levels of patient compliance, and there is a relationship between medicine use and health improvements that is not explained by other factors;
and (2) ecological evidence of improvements in these health outcomes in the population in which the medicine is used. Confidence in these inferences would be increased by: the replication of these results in comparable countries and consistent trends in population vital statistics in countries that have introduced the medicine; and epidemiological modeling indicating that changes observed in population health outcomes are plausible given the epidemiology of the condition being treated

front, though trust still needs to be earned. Such an approach might be applied to environmental and international political decision-making.

Developing a questioning attitude among the general public and advocacy through the media, to highlight these very simple errors of logic, would go a long way towards avoiding many of the past mistakes. It would not undermine the credibility of medical professionals or industry or politicians or the military but lead to joint ownership of decisions. Nothing gives more authenticity than the Truth and decision-makers from politicians to militaries to pharmaceuticals to industry can learn to be sincere.

Such efforts will lead to self-respect which occurs in traditional village inter-dependent societies.

Nobel Prize winning economist, Amartya Sen, using the criteria of number of ailments, surprisingly found that Americans self reported health was worse-much worse than Indians. Furthermore, within India it is in Kerala, the state with the highest level of life expectancy, education, empowerment of women and lowest infant mortality, where people feel the sickest, compared to the poorest state, Bihar. [223]

Those in industrial societies seem to have higher rates of depression and suicide than in developing nations, which may reflect a dis-ease, a lack of empowerment or love. [224] Wealth GDP, stock indexes or oil reserves are inadequate surrogates for health and well being. The short-term drive for wealth is at the expense of the environment; the demand for oil leads to global competition and instability and may compromise health and well being.

In 2005 Australians Clive Hamilton and Richard Denniss wrote *Affluenza* asking

"if the economy has been doing so well, why are we not becoming happier?" (pvii).
"Since the early 1990s, Australia has been infected by affluenza, a growing and unhealthy preoccupation with money and material things. This illness is constantly reinforcing itself at both the individual and the social levels, constraining us to derive our identities and sense of place in the world through our consumption activity." (p178) [225]

Perhaps we could re-focus the energies of our societies on another type of prevention. Americans also spend far more on health care per person than Britons, but Britons are objectively actually healthier. [226] Our perceptions of health often bears little resemblance to the objective measures used by health officials or medical experts. Such an approach might get us to re-focus attention on real public health needs, determinants of health security well being rather than major technological glitter.[42] We could focus resources and time saved on

---

[42]   Stephen Jay Gould from 1980 in an essay from ' The Panda's Thumb' called 'Caring Groups and Selfish genes' (p77-78)
" *I think, in short, that the fascination generated by Dawkin's theory arises from some bad habits of Western scientific thought- from attitudes (pardon the jargon) that we call atomism, reductionism and determinism. The idea that the whole could be understood by decomposition into 'basic' units; that properties of microscopic units can generate and explain the behaviour of macroscopic results; that all objects and events have definitive, predictable determined causes. these ideas have been successful in our study of simple objects, made of few components, and uninfluenced by prior history.... But organisms are much more than amalgamations of genes. they have a history that matters; their parts interact in complex ways. Organisms are built by genes acting in concert, influenced by environments, translated into parts that selection sees and parts invisible to selection. Molecules that determine the properties of water are poor analogues for genes and bodies.*
I may not be the master of my fate, but my intuition of wholeness probably reflects a biological truth."

drug management towards counseling about lifestyle changes. As a society we could meet environmental and developmental challenges with resources wasted on drugs and armaments.

Cookbook medicine has little love in it. Ron McCoy, President of the Nobel Prize winning IPPNW noted,

"A three-thousand-year tradition, which forged a bond of trust between doctor and patient, is being exchanged for a new kind of relationship. Healing is being replaced with treating; caring is being displaced by the technical management of disease; the art of listening to the patient is being supplanted by technological procedures. The human body is seen as the repository of unrelated, malfunctioning organs, often separated from the doctor's healing touch by cold, impersonal machines" [227].

Reallocating resources, time and money may allow us to put caring back into our professions and society.

CONCLUSION

Science should be seen as a tool- one of many such tools we use to make decisions.

'Scientism' is a tool of those with vested interests and undeclared biases, supported by the irrational "worship" of the trappings of science by ordinary citizens. We must be skeptical and have trained, impartial scientists with input from experts from other sectors of society and ordinary citizens to assess any information deemed "scientific." Willa Cather once said [228] *"There are only two or three human stories, and they go on repeating themselves as fiercely as if they had never happened before."* Without such input and considerations we will tragically continue to repeat mistakes in decision-making in medicine, our global environment and international affairs.

ACKNOWLEDGMENTS

Thanks to Peter Mansfield Ralph Faggotter Joel Lexchin Claudia Raichle Jagjit Khosla, Anne Marie Mingiardi John Yee Warren Bell David de Vidi Jim Kutsogiannis Jeff Nagge, Mruna Shah Anita Greig Gordon Guyatt Joanna Santa Barbara John Last David Antebi Sonal Singh for review of this paper, thoughtful comments and critical editing.

REFERENCES

[1]   Health Canada Prepulsid to be withdrawn as a result of cardiac complications May 31, 2000 http://www.hc-sc.gc.ca/ahc-asc/media/advisories-avis/2000/2000_56_e.html

[2]   Griffin JP Prepulsid withdrawn from UK & US Markets. *Adverse Drug React Toxicol Rev.* 2000 Aug;19 (3):177.

[3]   March of Dimes Bendectin makes a Comeback http://www.marchofdimes.com/professionals/681_1820.asp

[4]   National Institutes of Health http://cerhr.niehs.nih.gov/genpub/topics/thalidomide2-ccae.html

[5]   Rosenberg, T.. "What the World Needs Now is DDT," *New York Times Magazine* April 11, 2004

[6]   http://daphne.palomar.edu/calenvironment/ethics.htm

[7]   Holmes OW: The contagiousness of puerperal fever. N Engl Quart J Med Surg, 1842-3, 1:503-540 http://en.wikipedia.org/wiki/Oliver_Wendell_Holmes,_Sr.

[8]   Semmelweiss IP: Die Aetiologie, der Begriff und die Prophylaxis des Kindbettfiebers. Pest, Wien und Leipzig: CA Hartleben, 1861

[9]   Lasser Karen E; Allen Paul D.; Woolhandler Steffie J.; Himmelstein David U.; Wolfe Sidney M.; Bor David H. Timing of New Black Box Warnings and Withdrawals for Prescription Medications *JAMA*. 2002;287:2215-2220. http://jama.ama-assn.org/cgi/content/abstract/287/17/2215

[10] Our Stolen Future http://www.ourstolenfuture.org/Policy/pops/2001-0522popsconvention.htm

[11] US Environmental Protection Agency http://www.epa.gov/international/toxics/pop.htm

[12] US Environmental Protection Agency Montreal Protocol on Substances that Deplete the Ozone Layer in 1987 http://www.epa.gov/ozone/title6/phaseout/index.html

[13] Arya N Pesticides and human health: Why Public Health officials should support a ban on non-essential residential use (Commentary) *Can J Public Health* March/April 2005) 89-92

[14] Demosthenes Wisdom Quotes www.wisdomquotes.com/cat_truth.html

[15] Arya N The end of biomilitary realism? Rethinking biomedicine and international security *Medicine Conflict and Survival* 22(3)220-229 July Sept 2006

[16] Thomas Lewis, What Doctors Don't Know 34 (14) *New York Review of Books* September 24, 1987 http://www.nybooks.com/articles/4677

[17] Guyatt GH. Evidence-Based Medicine[editorial]. *ACP Journal Club* 1991:A-16. (Annals of Internal Medicine; vol. 114, suppl. 2).

[18] Dickersin Kay Straus, Sharon E Bero Lisa A Evidence based medicine: increasing, not dictating, choice *BMJ 2007;334(suppl_1):s10 (6 January)* http://www.bmj.com/cgi/content/full/334/suppl_1/s10

[19] Sackett David L, Rosenberg William M C, Gray J A Muir, Haynes R Brian, Richardson W Scott Evidence based medicine: what it is and what it isn't It's about integrating individual clinical expertise and the best external evidence *BMJ* 1996;312:71-72 (13 January) http://www.bmj.com/cgi/content/full/312/7023/71

[20] The Cochrane Collaboration www.cochrane.org

[21] Helwig Amy, Bower Douglas, Wolff Marie, Guse Clare Residents find Clinical Practice Guidelines Valuable as Educational and Clinical Tools *Education Research and Methods* Vol 30 No 6 p 431-435

[22] Guidelines Advisory Committee http://www.gacguidelines.ca/

[23] Agency for Healthcare Research and Quality http://www.ahrq.gov/clinic/

[24] National Institute for Health and Clinical Excellence http://www.nice.org.uk/

[25] La Haute Autorité de Santé http://www.has-sante.fr

[26] German Agency for Quality in Medicine AEZQ Leitlininien

[27] Guidelines International http://www.g-i-n.net/

[28] Canadian Task Force on the Periodic Health Examination: The periodic health examination. 1986 update. *Can Med Assoc J* 1986; 134: 721-729 http://www.ctfphc.org/

[29] U.S. Preventive Services Task Force: Guide to clinical preventive services: An assessment of the effectiveness of 169 interventions. Baltimore, MD: Williams & Wilkins; 1989 http://www.ahrq.gov/clinic

[30] Grade Working Group http://www.gradeworkinggroup.org/intro.htm

[31] Hippocrates *On The Surgery*

[32] Bradford Hill A "The Environment and Disease: Association or Causation?," Proceedings of the Royal Society of Medicine, 58 (1965), 295-300" http://www.edwardtufte.com/tufte/hill

[33] Sackett David L, Rosenberg William M C, Gray J A Muir, Haynes R Brian, Richardson W Scott. Evidence based medicine: what it is and what it isn't It's about integrating individual clinical expertise and the best external evidence *BMJ* 1996;312:71-72 (13 January) http://www.bmj.com/cgi/content/full/312/7023/71

[34] Di*sease Prevention: Encyclopedia of Public Health* http://health.enotes.com/public-health-encyclopedia/disease-prevention.

[35] Arya N Editorial Ask the Right Questions! *Ottawa Citizen* Mar. 7, 2003

[36] Arya N. Properly Diagnose Terrorism and Work for a Just Response *Medicine and Global Survival* Feb. 2002 56-58 http://www.ippnw.org/MGS/V7N2Aftermath.pdf

[37] Radiation Effects Research Foundation http://www.rerf.or.jp/

[38] Sidel VW, Geiger HJ, Lown B. (1962) 'The medical consequences of thermonuclear war. II. The physician's role in the post-attack period.' *NEJM* 266:1137-45

[39] International Physicians for the Prevention of Nuclear War www.ippnw.org

[40] Arya N. Confronting the small arms pandemic: *Unrestricted access should be viewed as a public health disaster BMJ* 2002; 324: 990-991: (27 April) April 27, 2002 http://bmj.com/cgi/content/full/324/7344/990?eaf

[41] Sloan J Kellermann AL et al Handgun Regulations, crime, assaults and homicide: a tale of two cities *NEJM* 1988 Nov 10:319 (19):1256-62

[42] Kellermann, A.L., Rivara F.P.,. Rushforth N.B. "Gun ownership as a risk factor for homicide in the home", *N Eng J Med* 329, 1993: 1084-1091.

[43] Kellermann, A.L., et al. "Suicide in the home in relation to gun ownership", New Eng J Med 327, 1992: 467-472

[44] Chapdelaine, A., et al. (1991) "Firearm-Related Injuries in Canada: Issues for Prevention", *CMAJ*, vol. 145, no. 10: 1217-1223.

[45] Salvage J. (2002) 'Collateral damage: the health and environmental costs of war on Iraq.' http://www.ippnw.org/CollateralDamage.html

[46] Arya N, Zurbrigg S. Operation Infinite Injustice: The Effect of Sanctions and Prospective War on the People of Iraq *Can J Pub Health* 94 (1) p 9-12Jan/Feb 2003 http://www.humanities.mcmaster.ca/peace-health/Iraqcomm.pdf

[47] Iraq Body Count www.iraqbodycount.org

[48] Roberts L Lafta R Garfield R Khudhairi J Burnham G., (2004) 'Mortality before and after the 2003 invasion of Iraq: cluster sample survey', The Lancet, 364 (9448), pp 1857-1864.

[49] Burnham G, Lasta R, Doocy S, Roberts L, 2006 Mortality after the 2003 invasion of Iraq: a cross-sectional cluster sample survey *Lancet* 368:1421-28

[50] Rossouw JE, Anderson GL, Prentice RL, LaCroix AZ, Kooperberg C, Stefanick ML, et al. Risks and benefits of estrogen plus progestin in healthy postmenopausal women: principal results from the women's health initiative randomized controlled trial. *JAMA* 2002;288: 321-33

[51] Yang YX Lewis JD Epstein S Metz DC Long-term proton pump inhibitor therapy and risk of hip fracture. *JAMA*. 2006 Dec 27;296(24):2947-53.

[52] Bjelakovic G, Nikolova D, Simonetti R Mortality in Randomized Trials of Antioxidant Supplements for Primary and Secondary Prevention: Systematic Review and Metaanalysis. *JAMA*.2007; 297: 842-857 http://jama.ama-assn.org/cgi/content/full/297/8/842

[53] Hirvonen Tero,; Virtamo Jarmo, ; Korhonen Pasi, ; Albanes Demetrius,; Pietinen Pirjo, Alpha-Tocopherol, Beta Carotene Cancer Prevention Study Group. The effect of vitamin E and beta carotene on the incidence of lung cancer and other cancers in male smokers. *New England Journal of Medicine* 1994 Apr 14;330(15):1029-1035

[54] Yusuf S, Dagenais G, Pogue J, Bosch J, Sleight P. Vitamin E supplementation and cardiovascular events in high-risk patients. The Heart Outcomes Prevention Evaluation Study Investigators. *N Engl J Med* 2000;342(3):154-160

[55] Omenn GS, Goodman GE, Thornquist MD, Balmes J, Cullen MR, Glass A, Keogh JP,Meyskens FL, Valanis B, Williams JH, Barnhart S, Hammar S. Effects of a combination of beta carotene and vitamin A on lung cancer and cardiovascular disease.*N Engl J Med*. 1996 May 2;334(18):1150-5.

[56] Beta Carotene Cancer Prevention Study Group. *N Engl J Med* 1994;330(15) 1029-1035.

[57] Fleming, Thomas R and Demets David L. Surrogate End Points in Clinical Trials: Are We Being Misled? *Annals* 125- (7) 605-613 1 October 1996 http://www.annals.org/cgi/content/full/125/7/605

[58] Echt DS, Liebson PR, Mitchell LB, Peters RW, Obias-Manno D, Barker AH, et al. Mortality and morbidity in patients receiving encainide, flecainide, or placebo. The cardiac arrhythmia suppression trial. *N Engl J Med* 1991;324: 781-8

[59] CAST Investigators. Preliminary report: effect of encainide and flecainide on mortality in a randomized trial of arrhythmia suppression after myocardial infarction. N Engl J Med 1989, 321: 406-412.

[60] The Cardiac Arrhythmia Suppression Trial II Investigators. Effect of the antiarrhythmic agent moricizine on survival after myocardial infarction. *N Engl J Med*. 1992; 327:227-33.

[61] Nissen SE and Wolski K. Effect of rosiglitazone on the risk of myocardial infarction and death from Cardiovascular Causes. *N Engl J Med* 2007 Jun 14;[e-pub ahead of print]. (http://content.nejm.org/cgi/content/full/NEJMoa072761)

[62] Singh Sonal Loke Yoon K Furberg Curt D Emerging safety concerns with the – time for urgent regulatory action *Lancet*

[63] Gerstein HC, Yusuf S, Bosch J, Pogue J, Sheridan P, et al. Effect of rosiglitazone on the frequency of diabetes in patients with impaired glucose tolerance or impaired fasting glucose: A randomised controlled trial. *Lancet* /2006; 368:1096-1105.

[64] Nissen SE. The DREAM trial. Diabetes Reduction Assessment with ramipril and rosiglitazone Medication, *Lancet*/ 2006; 368:2049

[65] Committee of Principal Investigators W.H.O. cooperative trial on primary prevention of ischaemic heart disease using clofibrate to lower serum cholesterol: mortality follow-up. *Lancet.* 1980 Aug 23; 2(8191):379-85.

[66] Coronary Drug Project Research Group. Clofibrate and niacin in coronary heart disease. *JAMA.* 1975; 231:360-81

[67] Scandinavian Simvastatin Survival Study (4S). Group.Randomised trial of cholesterol lowering in 4444 patients with coronary heart disease: *Lancet.* 1994; 344:1383-9.

[68] Hayward Rodney A Hofer Timothy P Vijan Sandeep Narrative Review: Lack of Evidence for Recommended Low-Density Lipoprotein Treatment Targets: A Solvable Problem *Annals of Internal Medicine* 3 October 2006 Volume 145 Issue 7 | Pages 520-530 http://www.annals.org/cgi/content/abstract/145/7/520

[69] Huang X, Chen H, Miller WC, Mailman RB, Woodard JL, Chen PC, Xiang D, Murrow RW, Wang YZ, Poole C. Lower low-density lipoprotein cholesterol levels are associated with Parkinson's disease. *Movement Disorders* 2007 Feb 15;22(3):377-81.

[70] "Bayer Voluntarily Withdraws Baycol," U.S. Food and Drug Administration Talk Paper: www.fda.gov/bbs/topics/ANSWERS/2001/ANS01095.html JP Griffin The withdrawal of Baycol (cerivastatin). *Adverse Drug React Toxicol Rev.* 2001 Dec;20(4):177-80.

[71] Collins R, Peto R, MacMahon S, Hebert P, Fiebach NH, Eberlein KA, et al. Blood pressure, stroke, and coronary heart disease. Part 2, Short-term reductions in blood pressure: overview of randomized drug trials in their epidemiological context. *Lancet.* 1990; 335:827-38.

[72] Hypertension Detection and Follow-up Program Cooperative Group. Five-year findings of the hypertension detection and follow-up program. I. Reduction in mortality of persons with high blood pressure, including mild hypertension. *JAMA.* 1979; 242:2562-71.

[73] ALLHAT Collaborative Research Group. Major cardiovascular events in hypertensive patients randomized to doxazosin vs chlorthalidone:the antihypertensive and lipid lowering treatment to prevent heart attack trial (ALLHAT). *JAMA* 2000 April 19; 283:15: 1967-1975.http://www.nhlbi.nih.gov/health/allhat/qckref.htm

[74] Psaty BM, Heckbert SR, Koepsell TD, Siscovick DS, et al. The risk of myocardial infarction associated with antihypertensive drug therapies. *JAMA* 1995;274:620-5.

[75] Held PH, Yusuf S, Furberg CD. Calcium channel blockers in acute myocardial infarction and unstable angina: an overview. *BMJ* 1989;299:1187-9

[76] Yusuf S, Held PH, Furberg CD. Update of effects of calcium antagonists in myocardial infarction or angina in light of the Second Danish Verapamil Infarction Trial (DAVIT-II) and other recent studies. *Am J Cardiol* 1991;67:1295-7.

[77] Wald NJ Law MR A strategy to reduce cardiovascular disease by more than 80% *BMJ* 2003;326:1419 (28 June) http://bmj.bmjjournals.com/cgi/content/full/326/7404/1419

[78] *Reddy K. Srinath* The Preventive Polypill — Much Promise, Insufficient Evidence *NEJM* 356 (3) :212 Jan 18, 2007   http://content.nejm.org/cgi/content/full/356/3/212

[79] Faggotter Ralph Feb 7, 2006 Personal Correspondence.

[80] Taylor Rosie and Giles Jim Cash interests taint drug advice *Nature* Vol 437|20 October 2005, page 1070 http://www.nature.com/nature/journal/v437/n7062/index. html doi: 10.1038/4371070a

[81] Zappa Frank, Album: Joe's Garage, Track: Packard Goose

[82]   Hampton JR. Evidence-based medicine, opinion-based medicine, and real-world medicine. *Perspect Biol Med.* 2002 Fall;45(4):549-68.

[83]   Holmes D,1 Murray SJ, Perron A, Rail G. Deconstructing the evidence-based discourse in health sciences: truth, power and fascism. *Int J Evid Based Healthcare*2006; 4: 180–186

[84]   Mansfield P. Industry-Sponsored Research: A More Comprehensive Alternative. *PLoS Med* 2006;3(10): e463 http://medicine.plosjournals.org/perlserv/?request=get-ocument&doi=10.1371/journal.pmed.0030463

[85]   Genuis Stephen J. The Proliferation of Clinical Practice Guidelines: Professional Development or Medicine-by-Numbers? *The Journal of the American Board of Family Practice* 18:419-425 (2005) http://www.jabfm.org/cgi/content/full/18/5/419

[86]   Sackett David L, Rosenberg William M C, Gray J A Muir, Haynes R Brian, Richardson W Scott Evidence based medicine: what it is and what it isn't It's about integrating individual clinical expertise and the best external evidence *BMJ* 1996;312:71-72 (13 January) http://www.bmj.com/cgi/content/full/312/7023/71

[87]   Faggotter Ralph MD personal correspondence Biojest Nov 11, 2006

[88]   Lexchin J et al. Pharmaceutical industry sponsorship and research outcome and quality: Systematic review. *BMJ* 2003 May 31; 326:1167-70. http://www.bmj.com/cgi/reprint/326/7400/1167.pdf

[89]   Hughes Michael D Williams Paige L Challenges in Using Observational Studies to Evaluate Adverse Effects of Treatment *NEJM* 356(17) 1705-1707 April 26,2007

[90]   Ware James H The Limitations of Statistical Methods as Prognostic Tools *NEJM* 355:25 2015-2017 Dec 21, 2006

[91]   Rothwell PM. External validity of randomised controlled trials: "to whom do the results of this trial apply?". *Lancet.* 2005 Jan 1;365(9453):82-93.

[92]   Hall Wayne D Lauke Jayne Assessing the impact of prescribed medicines on health outcomes *Australia and New Zealand Health Policy* 2007, 4:1 http://www.anzhealthpolicy.com/content/pdf/1743-8462-4-1.pdf

[93]   Groll, D.L. and Thomson, D.J. (2006) Incidence of influenza in Ontario following the Universal Influenza Immunization Campaign. *Vaccine*, 24(24), 5245-5250

[94]   Haynes RB, Sackett DL. Taylor DW Gibson ES Johnson AL. lncreased absenteeism from work after detection and labelling of hypertensive patients. *N Engl J Med* 1978;299:741-4.

[95]   Prentice and Lind, "Fetal heart rate monitoring during labor-- too frequent intervention, too little benefit"[1987:2:1375-1377]

[96]   Baxter, Nancy, with the Canadian Task Force on Preventive Health Care, "Preventive Health Care, 2001 Update: Should Women Be Routinely Taught Breast Self-Examination to Screen for Breast Cancer?" *Can Med Assoc Jrnl* 2001;164(13):1837-1846. June 26, 2001. *http://www.cmaj.ca/cgi/reprint/164/13/1837*

[97]   Canadian Task Force on the Periodic Health Examination, the CTFPHC http://www.ctfphc.org

[98]   Miller AB, To T, Baines CJ, et al. Canadian National Breast Screening Study-2: 13-year results of a randomized trial in women aged 50-59 years. *J Natl Cancer Inst.* 2000;92(18):1490-1499

[99] Miller AB, Baines CJ, To T, Wall C. Canadian National Breast Screening Study: 1. Breast cancer detection and death rates among women aged 40 to 49 years. *CMAJ.* 1992;147(10):1459-1476.

[100] International Health News http://vvv.com/healthnews/mammography.html

[101] Canadian Women's Health Network http://www.cwhn.ca/resources/afi/mammograms. html

[102] Olsen O, Gøtzsche PC. Systematic review of screening for breast cancer with mammography (Gøtzsche PC. Screening for breast cancer with mammography. *Lancet* 2001; 358: 2167-2168

[103] Horton R. Screening mammography—setting the record straight. *Lancet* 2002; 359: 441-442

[104] Ibid. from Jorgensen, KJ and Gotzsche, PC. Presentation on websites of possible benefits and harms from screening for breast cancer: cross sectional study. *British Medical Journal*, Vol. 328, January 17, 2004, pp. 148-53

[105] Wolf AM, Nasser JF, Wolf AM, Schorling JB. The impact of informed consent on patient interest in prostate-specific antigen screening. *Arch Intern Med* 1996; 156: 1333-1336 http://bmj.bmjjournals.com/cgi/content/full/325/7357/216

[106] Feightner John W. Canadian Task Force on Preventive Health Care http://www. ctfphc.org/Full_Text/Ch67full.htm.

[107] Stanford JL, Feng Z, Hamilton AS, Gilliland FD, Stephenson RA, Eley JW, et al. Urinary and sexual function after radical prostatectomy for clinically localized prostate cancer: the Prostate Cancer Outcomes Study. *JAMA* 2000; 283: 354-360

[108] Del Mar Chris Asymptomatic haematuria ...in the doctor, *BMJ* 2000;320:165-166 (15 January)

[109] US National Cancer Institute http://www.cancer.gov/clinicaltrials/results/mayo-lung-project0800

[110] Marcus, P.M., Bergstralh, E.J., Fagerstrom, R.M., Williams, D.E., Fontana, R., Taylor, W.F., Prorok, P.C. (2000, August 16). Lung cancer mortality in the Mayo Lung Project: Impact of extended follow-up. *Journal of the National Cancer Institute, 92*(16), 1308-1316. Aug 16, 2000

[111] Henschke Claudia I. Yankelevitz David F. Libby Daniel M.,Pasmantier Mark W., and Smith James P., Miettinen Olli S. Survival of Patients with Stage I Lung Cancer Detected on CT Screening *NEJM* http://content.nejm.org/cgi/content/ abstract/355/17/1763

[112] Kolata Gina Researchers Dispute Benefits of CT Scans for Lung Cancer *New York Times* March 7, 2007 http://www.nytimes.com/2007/03/07/health/07lung.html

[113] Bach Peter B Jett James R Pastorino Ugo Tockman Melvyn S Swensen Stephen J Begg Colin B Computed Tomography Screening and Lung Cancer Outcomes *Journal of the American Association JAMA* 2007;297:953-961. http://jama.ama-assn.org/cgi/content/abstract/297/9/953

[114] Miser William F. To Treat or Not to Treat Otitis Media - That's Just One of the Questions *Journal of the American Board of Family Practice*

[115] Rosenfeld RM, Vertrees JE, Carr J, Cipolle RJ, Uden DL, Giebink GS, et al. Clinical efficacy of antimicrobial drugs for acute otitis media: meta-analysis of 5400 children from thirty-three randomized trials. *J Pediatr* 1994; 124: 355-

[116] Van Buchem FL, Dunk JHM, van't Hof MA. Appelman CLM, Claessen JQPJ, Touw-Otten FWMM, Hordijk GJ, de Melker RA. Co-amoxiclav in recurrent acute otitis media: placebo controlled study. *BMJ* 1991; 303: 1450-

[117] Burke P, Bain J, Robinson D, Dunleavy J. Acute red ear in children: controlled trial of non-antibiotic treatment in general practice. *BMJ* 1991; 303: 558-562

[118] Boden W. E., O'Rourke R. A., Teo K. K., Hartigan P. M., Maron D. J., Kostuk W. J., Knudtson M., Dada M., Casperson P., Harris C. L., Chaitman B. R., Shaw L., Gosselin G., Nawaz S., Title L. M., Gau G., Blaustein A. S., Booth D. C., Bates E. R., Spertus J. A., Berman D. S., Mancini G.B. J., Weintraub W. S., the COURAGE Trial Research Group Optimal Medical Therapy with or without PCI for Stable Coronary Disease *N Engl J Med* 2007; www.nejm.org on Mar 26, 2007 (10.1056/NEJMoa070829 April 12, 2007 print

[119] Satel Sally and Hoff Sommers Christina The Mental Health Crisis That Wasn't: How the trauma industry exploited 9/11 *Reason* On-line August/September 2005 http://www.reason.com/0508/fe.ss.the.shtml

[120] Hobbs M, Mayou R, Harrison B, Worlock P. A randomised controlled trial of psychological debriefing for victims of road traffic accidents. *BMJ* 1996;313: 1438-9

[121] Enkin Murray Keirse Marc JNC Neilson James Crowther Caroline Duley Lelia,, Hodnett Ellen, Hofmneyr G. Justus Effective Care In Pregnancy and Childbirth: A Synopsis Chapter 50 in *A Guide to Effective Care in Pregnancy and Childbirth* 2000 Oxford University Press 2000 http://www.collegeofmidwives.org/prof_articles01/

[122] Andrew MH, Roty AR Jr. Incidental appendectomy with cholecystectomy: is the increased risk justified. *Am Surg* 1987 Oct;53(10):553-7 found at http://www.qualitymeasures.ahrq.gov/summary/summary.aspx?ss=2&doc_id=6661

[123] Lambert M.L.Cholecystectomy and appendectomy utilisation rates in Belgium: trends 1986-1996 and impact of laparoscopic surgery. Cholecystectomy rates increased by 64% over 7 years (1989-1996) following the introduction of laparoscopic surgery. Appendectomy rates per 100.000 showed a remarkably steady decrease from 282,3 in 1986 to 166,4 in 1996 Belgian trends parallel those observed elsewhere. http://www.iph.fgov.be/aph/abstr200058233240.htm

[124] Jentleson, Bruce. 2000. American Foreign Policy: The Dynamics of Choice in the 21st Century. New York : W.W. Norton & Co.

[125] Mead Walter Russell, "The Case Against Europe The very things that Europeans think make their political judgment better than Americans' actually make it worse", The Atlantic Monthly, 289(4), 2002, p. 26, available at http://globetrotter.berkeley.edu/people3/Mead/mead-con3.html.

[126] Kagan Robert *Of Paradise and Power, America and Europe in the New World Order* Alfred A Knopf, New York, 2003

[127] Gray, John Men Are from Mars, Women Are from Venus: A Practical Guide for Improving Communication and Getting What You Want in Your Relationships Harper Collins 1992

[128] Bergen Peter Cruickshank Paul Iraq 101: The Iraq Effect - War has increased Terrorism Seven-fold Worldwide http://www.motherjones.com/news/featurex/ 2007/03/iraq_effect_1.html Sengupta Kim Cockburn Patrick The War on Terror Is the Leading Cause of Terrorism *The Independent* UK. March 1, 2007. http://www.alternet.org/waroniraq/48620/

[129] Arya N Is military action ever justified? : A Physician Defends the Responsibility to Protect *Medicine Conflict and Survival* 23 (3)

[130] US National Weather Service http://www.lightningsafety.noaa.gov/medical.htm

[131] US National Safety Council http://www.nsc.org/lrs/statinfo/odds.htm

[132] Kahneman Daniel, Renshon Jonathan Why Hawks Win January/February 2007 January 15, 2007 http://www.foreignpolicy.com/story/cms.php?story_id=3660

[133] Holt Jim The Human Factor *New York Times* March 28, 2004 http://www. nytimes.com/2004/03/28/magazine/28WWLN.html

[134] Greenhalgh Trisha, Kostopoulou Olga, Harries Clare *BMJ* 2004;329:47-50(3 July), Making decisions about benefits and harms of medicines http://bmj.bmjjournals. com/cgi/content/full/329/7456/47

[135] Engelhardt Tom 9/11 Life Worth $1.8 million; Iraqi Life, $2,000. What Does It Mean? *Alternet* May 15, 2007 http://www.alternet.org/story/51886/

[136] Herxheimer A (2005) Communicating with Patients about Harms and Risks. *PLoS Med* 2(2): e42 February 22, 2005 http://medicine.plosjournals.org/perlserv/ ?request=get-document&doi=10.1371/journal.pmed.0020042

[137] McNeil BJ Pauker SG Sox HC Jr. Tversky A On the elicitation of preferences for alternative therapies. *NEJM* 1982 May 27;306 (21):1259-62

[138] Gladwell Malcolm Blink: The Power of Thinking Without Thinking Brown Little 2005

[139] Vioxx Recalled Sept 30, 2005 http://www.adrugrecall.com/ US Food and Drug Administration http://www.fda.gov/cder/drug/infopage/vioxx/vioxxQA.htm

[140] US Food and Drug Administration http://www.fda.gov/medwatch/SAFETY/ 2005/safety05.htm#Bextra

[141] Borger Julian Wake-up call *The Guardian* Friday September 6, 2002 http://www.guardian.co.uk/g2/story/0,3604,786992,00.html

[142] Groopman Jerome *How Doctors Think* Houghton Mifflin

[143] Dyer Owen Breast CA: who should be scanned? New MRI and mammography guidelines send mixed messages *National Review of Medicine* 4(8) April 30, 2007 http://www.nationalreviewofmedicine.com/issue/2007/04_30/4_patients_practice_8.ht ml

[144] Doust Jenny, Del Mar Chris Why do doctors use treatments that do not work? *BMJ* 2004;328:474-475 (28 February), http://bmj.bmjjournals.com/cgi/content/full/328/74 38/474

[145] Kahneman Daniel, Renshon Jonathan Why Hawks Win *Foreign Policy* January/February 2007 January 15, 2007 http://www.foreignpolicy.com/story/cms.php? story_id=3660

[146] Simon, Herbert A. 1997. Models of Bounded Rationality. Volume 3. Empirically Grounded Economic Reason. Cambridge, Massachusetts: The MIT Press quoted in Odell John S. Bounded rationality and the World Political Economy: The Nature of Decision Making Chapter 11 in Governing the World's Money, ed. David M. Andrews, C. Randall Henning, and Louis W. Pauly (Cornell University Press, 2002 http://www-rcf.usc.edu/~odell/text%20092101%20web.doc

[147] Barber Benjamin R Jihad vs McWorld *The Atlantic Monthly* March 1992 http://www.theatlantic.com/doc/199203/barber

[148] Scott Tim Stanford Neil Thompson David R, Images of health Killing me softly: myth in pharmaceutical advertising *BMJ* 2004;329:1484-1487 (18 December), doi:10.1136/bmj.329.7480.1484 http://www.bmj.com/cgi/content/full/329/7480/1484

[149] Quoted in PR Watch http://www.prwatch.org/prwissues/2003Q1/monger.html

[150] Payer L. Disease-mongers: How doctors, drug companies and insurers are making you feel sick. New York: John Wiley, & Sons 1992.

[151] Malleson Andrew Whiplash and Other Useful Illnesses McGill-Queen's University Press (April, 2002) reviewed Brian Grottkau, M.D.New England Journal of Medicine, April 3, 2003 http://content.nejm.org/cgi/content/full/348/14/1413

[152] Diseasemongering *PLOS* April 2006 http://collections.plos.org/diseasemongering-2006.php

[153] Moynihan R, Heath I, Henry D. Selling sickness: the pharmaceutical industry and disease mongering. *BMJ* 2002; 324: 886-891

[154] Cassels Alan Moynihan Ray Pharmaceuticals for healthy people US: selling to the worried well *Le Monde Diplomatique* http://mondediplo.com/2006/05/16bigpharma May 2006 adapted from their book *'Selling Sickness. How Drug Companies Are Turning Us All into Patients' (Allen & Unwin, 2005)*

[155] Moynihan R. The making of a disease: female sexual dysfunction *BMJ* 2003;326:45-47(4January) http://bmj.bmjjournals.com/cgi/content/full/326/7379/45

[156] Tiefer Leonore Female Sexual Dysfunction: A Case Study of Disease Mongering and Activist Resistance *PLOS Medicine* www[losmedicine.org April 2006 3 (4) e 178-182

[157] Kolata Gina If You've Got a Pulse, You're Sick *New York Times* May 21, 2006 http://www.nytimes.com/2006/05/21/weekinreview/21kolata.html

[158] Michaels, David Living in a Chemical World: Framing the Future in Light of the Past Volume 1076 published September 2006 *Ann. N.Y. Acad. Sci.* 1076: 149–162 (2006). doi: 10.1196/annals.1371.058 http://www.annalsnyas.org/cgi/content/abstract/1076/1/149

[159] Michaels, David, **DOUBT Is Their Product** *Scientific American*, Jun2005, Vol. 292, Issue 6

[160] Doll R, Hill AB: Smoking and carcinoma of the lung; preliminary report. *Br Med J*, 1950, 2:739-748;

[161] Doll R, Hill AB. The mortality of doctors in relation to their smoking habits. *Br Med J* 1954;228:1451-5. Reproduced in: BMJ 2004;328:1529-3

[162] International Journal of Occupational and Environmental Health http://www.ijoeh.com/ SPECIAL ISSUE Volume II, Number 4 October - December 2005 Feature: Corporate Corruption of Science

[163] Gustave Gilbert "Nürnberger Tagebuch." Nuremberg Diary 18 April 1946 http://www.snopes.com/quotes/goering.htm

[164] Center for Media and Democracy Submitted by Diane Farsetta on Fri, 05/11/2007 http://www.prwatch.org/node/6034

[165] *The European Journal of the History of Economic Thought*, Routledge Volume 8, Issue 1 March 2001, pages 105 - 117

[166] DoD News Briefing - Secretary Rumsfeld and Gen. Pace http://www.dod.gov/transcripts/2001/t12212001_t1221sd.html

[167] Needless Surgery *Consumer Reports on Health* (March 1998) http://www.quackwatch.org/04ConsumerEducation/crhsurgery.html

[168] Bekelman Justin E., Yan Li AB Gross Cary P.Scope and Impact of Financial Conflicts of Interest in Biomedical Research A Systematic Review *JAMA* 2003;289:454-465. Jan 22

[169] Kei Koizumi Chapter 6 R&D in the FY 2005 Department of Defense Budget American Association for the Advancement of Science REPORT XXIX RESEARCH AND DEVELOPMENT FY 2005 (2004) http://www.aaas.org/spp/rd/05pch6.htm

[170] SIPRI *Stockholm International Peace Research Institute* Yearbook 2005 http://yearbook2005.sipri.org/highl/highlights

[171] Hartung William *World Policy Institute* ARMS TRADE RESOURCE CENTER REPORTS - Peddling Arms, Peddling Influence: Exposing the Arms Export Lobby October 1996 World Policy http://www.worldpolicy.org/projects/arms/reports/papi2rep. html

[172] Oil Company Spent Nearly $16 Million to Fund Skeptic Groups, Create Confusion ExxonMobil Report Jan 3, 2007 Smoke, Mirrors & Hot Air: How ExxonMobil Uses Big Tobacco's Tactics to "Manufacture Uncertainty" on Climate Change

[173] JunkScience.com

[174] Brandt Allan"The Cigarette Century http://www.cigarettecentury.com/index.html

[175] *AlterNet, April 16, 2007* http://www.alternet.org/mediaculture/50359/

[176] Beder Sharon Gosden WPP: World Propaganda Power PR Watch 8(2) 2001 Richard http://www.prwatch.org/prwissues/2001Q2/wpp.html

[177] Corporate Watch July 2002 http://www.corporatewatch.org.uk/?lid=395

[178] Cox Teri R Forging Alliances *Pharmaceutical Executive* Magazine, September 1, 2002. http://www.pharmexec.com/pharmexec/article/articleDetail.jsp?id=29974

[179] Burton Bob Rowell Andy Quoted in From Patient Activism to Astroturf Marketing *PR Watch* 4(1) 1997 http://www.prwatch.org/prwissues/2003Q1/astroturf.html Quoted in Burton Bob Rowell Andy Disease Mongering PR Watch 10(1) 2003 http://www.prwatch.org/prwissues/2003Q1/monger.html

[180] Mammography information questioned http://vvv.com/healthnews/mammography. html

[181] Moynihan et al. Op cit.

[182] Source Watch http://www.sourcewatch.org/index.php?title=Front_groups

[183] Fialka John Another Filthy Front Group *Wall Street Journal* April 27, 2007 http://online.wsj.com/article/SB117763193289184191.html

[184] International Atomic Energy Agency http://www.iaea.org/About/statute_text.html

[185] Goldenberg Suzanne Bush administration accused of doctoring scientists' reports on climate change *The Guardian* Wednesday January 31, 2007 http://www.guardian. co.uk/usa/story/0,,2002484,00.html

[186] Rumsfeld Donald http://sadlyno.com/archives/000497.html

[187] Rosenstock IM 1974 http://www.comminit.com/changetheories/ctheories/ changetheories-31.html

[188] Bandura, A. (1977). *Social Learning Theory*. New York: General Learning Press.

[189] Last JM: The Future of Public Health. *Japanese Journal of Public Health*, 1991, 38:10:58-93

[190] Rumsfeld Donald Department of Defense news briefing Feb. 12, 2002, http://www. brainyquote.com/quotes/quotes/d/donaldrums148142.html

[191] Angell Marcia The Truth About the Drug Companies *New York Review of Books* http://www.nybooks.com/articles/17244

[192] 29 September 2006 http://open.imshealth.com/

[193] Angell M. The pharmaceutical industry: to whom is it accountable? *New Engl J Med* 342: 1902-4. http://content.nejm.org/cgi/content/full/342/25/1902

[194] Arya N Letter Reasons to be Fearful *Time* September 23, 2002 http://www.time.com/time/magazine/article/0,9171,1003298-4,00.html http://www.time.com/time/magazine/article/0,9171,1101020923-351218-2,00.html

[195] Rumsfeld Donald Press conference at NATO headquarters, Brussels, Belgium, June 6, 2002," US Department of Defense The Acronym Institute. transcript. www.acronym.org.uk/docs/0206/doc04.htm

[196] Avalon Project Yale University http://www.yale.edu/lawweb/avalon/presiden/speeches/eisenhower001.htm

[197] Bacevich Andrew J. The New American Militarism: How Americans Are Seduced By War Oxford University Press, 2005 http://www.thirdworldtraveler.com/American_Empire/Wilsonians_TNAM.html

[198] Anonymous friend Personal correspondence May 15, 2007

[199] Gladwell Malcolm The Tipping Point: How Little Things Can Make a Big Difference Little Brown 2000

[200] Prochasta James O Norcross John C and Diclemente Carlo C Changing for Good: The Revolutionary Program That Explains the Six Stages of Change and Teaches You How to Free Yourself from Bad Habits

[201] Beck, Aaron T., "Cognitive Models of Depression," in *Journal of Cognitive Psychotherapy,* Vol. 1, No. 1, 1987, pp. 5-37.

[202] *New York Times, May 8, 2007* http://www.nytimes.com/2007/05/08/world/asia/09afghancnd.html

[203] Haditha Investigations Suggest Military Cover-Up *New York Times, May 6, 2007* http://www.nytimes.com/2007/05/06/world/middleeast/06haditha.htm

[204] http://www.prwatch.org/prwissues/1997Q1/risky.html

[205] Rosenblum Jonathan Tracking the Front Group "Boomerang," posted Wed, 03/14/2007 *http://www.prwatch.org/node/5847*

[206] Stauber John and Rampton Sheldon *Toxic Sludge is Good for You* (Common Courage Press, 1995),

[207] Pfau Michael, Haigh Michel, Sims Jeanetta and Wrigley Shelley "The Influence of Corporate Front-Group Stealth Campaigns *Communications Research* February 2007

[208] http://www.nrc.gov/reading-rm/basic-ref/glossary/risk-based-decisionmaking.html

[209] Risky Business: The World According to Hill & Knowlton *PR Watch* 4(1) 1997

[210] Reuters, May 18, 2007 http://www.reuters.com/article/environmentNews/idUSN1843960820070518

[211] Groopman Jerome *How Doctors Think* Houghton Mifflin

[212] Horton Richard What's Wrong with Doctors *New York Review of Books* 54(9)· May 31, 2007 http://www.nybooks.com/articles/20214

[213] Yusuf S, Anand S, MacQueen G. (1998) 'Can medicine prevent war?' *BMJ*; 317: 1669-70. Dec Website. Online. Available: http://bmj.com/cgi/content/full/317/7174/1669.

[214] Arya N. Do no harm: towards a Hippocratic standard for international civilization for 'The end of Westphalia? Re-envisioning sovereignty' for United Nations. Presentation

for University Nations University/ Griffith University Key Centre for Governance April 8-10, 2005 at Canberra Australian National University

[215] Arya N Howard J et al Time for an ecosystem approach to public health? Lessons from two infectious disease outbreaks in Canada *Global Public Health* July 2007

[216] Science and Environmental Health Network - Wingspread Statement on the Precautionary Principle, Jan. 1998. http://www.sehn.org/precaution.html

[217] Arya Neil Do No Harm: Towards a Hippocratic Standard for International Civilization in Re-envisioning Sovereignty Ramesh Thakur and Charles Sampford ed 2007

[218] Arya N. Healing our Planet: Physicians and Global Security *Croatian Medical Journal CMJ* 44 (2) 139-147 March April 2003 http://www.cmj.hr/index.php?D=/44/2/139

[219] Die Off http://dieoff.org/page31.htm Interpreting the Principle

[220] Faggotter Ralph Personal Correspondence May 9. 2007

[221] Sherriff, A Golding J and The Alspac Study Team Hygiene levels in a contemporary population cohort are associated with wheezing and atopic eczema in preschool infants *Archives of Disease in Childhood* 2002;87:26-29 http://adc.bmj.com/cgi/content/abstract/87/1/26

[222] von Mutius Erika The Increase in Asthma Can Be Ascribed to Cleanliness *Am. J. Respir. Crit. Care Med.*, Volume 164, Number 7, October 2001, 1106-1107 http://ajrccm.atsjournals.org/cgi/content/full/164/7/1106

[223] Sen Amartya Health: perception versus observation *BMJ* 2002;324:860-861 (13 April) http://bmj.bmjjournals.com/cgi/content/full/324/7342/860

[224] The WHO World Mental Health Survey Consortium Prevalence, Severity, and Unmet Need for Treatment of Mental Disorders in the World Health Organization World Mental Health Surveys, *Journal of the American Medical Association* 291 (21) 2 June 2004 http://jama.ama-assn.org/cgi/content/full/291/21/2581

[225] 'Affluenza' . see-http://en.wikipedia.org/wiki/Affluenza

[226] Marmot Michael Oldfield Zoe Smith James P Disease and Disadvantage in the United States and England James Banks JAMA 2006:295 2037-2045

[227] McCoy Ronald S. Restoring the Soul of Medicine Oration given at the annual general meeting of the Malaysian Medical Association on 13 June 2002

[228] Cather Willa Carl in '*Oh Pioneers*' Houghton Mifflin 1913.

In: Psychology of Decision Making…
Editor: G. R. Burthold, pp. 69-99

ISBN: 978-1-60021-932-0
© 2007 Nova Science Publishers, Inc.

Chapter 2

DECISION MAKING IN THE IOWA GAMBLING TASK

Gordon Fernie and Richard J. Tunney[*]

University of Nottingham, Nottingham, United Kingdom

ABSTRACT

In recent years the Iowa Gambling Task has become an important tool in the development of theoretical models of decision-making and has greatly added to our understanding of the underlying neural mechanisms. The Iowa Gambling Task is a repeated choice situation in which participants must choose a card from any one of four decks. Two of the decks are advantageous in the sense that although they have a relatively low immediate reward with repeated selection they result in a high overall reward. The remaining two decks are disadvantageous in the sense that they have a higher immediate reward but result in an overall loss with repeated selection. As such, consistent choice of the advantageous decks is rational while consistent choice of the disadvantageous decks is impulsive. These behavior patterns clearly discriminate between clinical and healthy participants. Despite this, behavior in the Iowa Gambling Task, and in particular the motivations for individual choices, are poorly understood. We report two of experiments in which we compared choices between pairs of decks that varied in frequency and magnitude of both reward and punishment to better understand the bases of decision making in the Iowa Gambling Task.

INTRODUCTION

Repeated choice paradigms have a long and important history in decision-making research (see Shanks, Tunney, & McCarthy, 2002; Tunney & Shanks, 2002). One of the most useful aspects of repeated choice paradigms is that they allow an examination of how

---

[*] Address for correspondence: School of Psychology, University of Nottingham, University Park, Nottingham, NG7 2RD, United Kingdom. Email: rjt@psychology.nottingham.ac.uk; Tel: +44 (0) 115 951 5361; Fax: 44 (0) 115 951 5324.

decision-making develops through learning; and as most real life decisions are repeated, provide a closer approximation of how we make decisions outside of the laboratory.

For the most part human decision-making approximates normative expectations. However, when faced with a choice between two alternatives, one of which has a payoff with higher value or utility than the other, both animals and humans will predominantly choose the alternative with the higher value. This seems perfectly rational, in the sense that the agent gains as much from the situation as possible, but it would seem irrational if they continued to do so in a repeated-choice situation when this led to a decrease in overall utility. The problem is one of self-control—preference for a small immediate reward over a larger delayed reward is impulsive (Ainslie, 1975) and is well described by one of the fundamental laws of behaviour – the Law of Effect (Thorndike, 1898). A good deal of research suggests that in animals such behaviour is simply hard wired. Although this explanation can also account for impulsive behaviour in humans it cannot account for the self-evident fact that much of human behaviour is considered and rational. That is, in many situations humans find it easy to make decisions that maximize some future payoff. But in others the lure of an immediate reward can be difficult to overcome even when it can have negative consequences in the future.

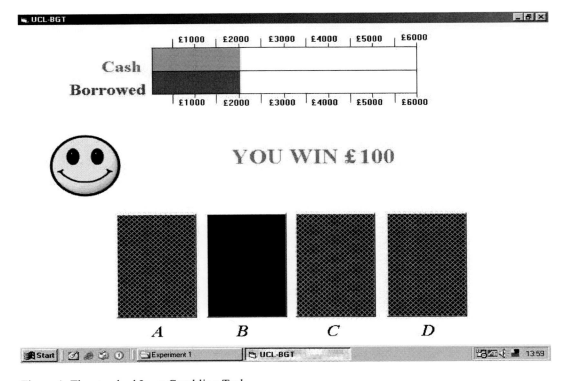

Figure 1. The standard Iowa Gambling Task.

THE IOWA GAMBLING TASK

Recent years have seen an increase in decision-making research using repeated choice paradigms. This has been fuelled by the intriguing finding that patients with damage to specific areas of the frontal-lobes exhibit pathological impulsivity in paradigms where healthy control subjects find it easy to defer gratification (Damasio, Tranel, & Damasio, 1991). Damasio and co-workers developed a standardized task to discriminate between impulsivity and self-control in brain-damaged patients that has become known as the Iowa Gambling task (IGT, Bechara, Damasio, Damasio and Anderson, 1994). Formally it involves two concurrent variable-ratio schedules of reinforcement, and is structurally identical to tasks that have been used to study impulsive decision-making (Tunney & Shanks, 2002).

In the computer version of the IGT (see Figure 1), the participant sees four decks of cards on a screen (early reports used actual decks of cards). The decks are labelled A, B, C, and D. Using a mouse, the participant can click on a card from any of the four decks. After clicking to turn each card, the participant receives some money (the amount is displayed on the screen). On some cards the participant both wins some money and pays a penalty (also displayed on screen). Clicking any card from deck A or B yields £100; turning any card from deck C or D yields £50. However, the ultimate future yield of each deck varies because the penalty amounts are higher in the higher payoff decks (A and B), leading to a net loss, and lower in the low payoff decks leading to a net gain. The 'rational' behaviour is, after an initial period of experimentation, to abstain from the short-term high payoff alternatives (A and B) and to always choose cards from the short-term low payoff decks C and D because in the long-term this leads to a higher overall payoff. Learning is reported to be rapid and the experiment typically ends after 100 choices have been made. Healthy control participants learn to select from the advantageous decks. However, patients with frontal-lobe damage, and many other conditions that are characterized by impulsive behaviour such as drug abuse, consistently select the disadvantageous decks (Damasio, Tranel, & Damasio, 1991; Bechara et al, 1994; Grant, Contoreggi, & London, 2000). That is, healthy participants defer immediate gratification in lieu of a higher long-term reward, while the patient groups prefer immediate gratification irrespective of the long-term consequences.

Although there have been numerous studies documenting pathological decision-making in a wide range of clinical populations the task has not been subject to the same scrutiny as is usual in decision-making research. That is, as research in this domain has focussed on the neuropsychological basis of the task it has done so at the expense of a basic understanding of how, at a basic psychological level, participants actually come to make the decisions that they do. In this chapter we intend to remedy this gap in our understanding of the decision-making in the Iowa Gambling Task.

Fernie and Tunney (2006) suggested that participants' preferences within the advantageous and disadvantageous decks on the Iowa Gambling Task (IGT) were not uniform. Similar results have been found in the relativley few studies where authors have reported deck selection from individual decks (Crone & van der Molen, 2004; O'Carroll and Papps, 2003; MacPherson, Phillips, & Della Sala, 2002; Wilder, Weinberger, & Goldberg, 1998). In these studies participants tended to show a preference for the two decks with infrequent losses (decks B and D) regardless of the long-term value of selecting from these decks; results that are in line with the Law of Effect (Thorndike, 1898). Fernie and Tunney (2006) replicated and extended these findings. They found that if only the mean number of cards selected in an initial 100-trial session were considered, as in MacPherson et al (2002) and Wilder et al (1998), more cards were selected from decks B and D. But in a second 100-trial session the IGT more cards were selected from the advantageous decks. This is the normal behaviour reported by Bechara et al (1994; Bechara, Damasio, Tranel and Damasio,

1997; Bechara, Damasio, Damasio and Lee, 1999). However, the number of cards selected from any individual decks in a session does not tell the whole story. By plotting the number of selections from each deck over 20-trial blocks across the two sessions it appears that participants generally avoided the deck with high immediate reward but frequent higher losses (deck A) and a slightly above chance preference for the deck with low immediate reward but infrequent relatively large losses (deck D) did not change. This added nothing more than the examination of mean number of cards selected. However, looking across block, participants initially preferred the deck with high immediate rewards and infrequent very large losses (deck B) but moved away from it with time (and with increasing losses), and developed a preference for the deck with low immediate rewards but frequent low losses (deck C). Fernie and Tunney (2006) concluded that this change in selection from B to C appeared to underlie participants' learning on the IGT.

Very little work has examined selection from individual decks on the IGT or the relative importance of frequency or magnitude of punishment in choice behaviour. The vast majority of studies have considered the difference in selection from decks based on their expected values. However, some observations of differential selection within the advantageous and disadvantageous decks have been reported (Phillips et al., 2002, Wilder et al., 2002) and others have been reported in more detail.

Mintzer and Stitzer (2002) used the computerised IGT as one of a battery of neuropsychological tests to assess the cognitive performance of patients receiving methodone maintenance treatment for drug addiction. While patients had lower net scores (calculated by subtracting the number of selections from decks C and D from the number selected from decks A and B) than matched controls, their selection pattern differed within the decks with the lowest frequency (B & D), but not the highest frequency (A & C), of loss. Selection bias was measured by subtracting the number of selections of B from the number selected from D. The average score for the patient group (-9.06, sd = 16.25) was significantly different from the control group (2.14, sd = 14.13). This measure indicates that patients preferred deck B to deck D more than controls did. But the interesting measure is that although controls showed a slight preference for deck D (their D-B score was higher than zero), this was not different to zero. The comparable measure for decks A and C, revealed no significant difference between groups, but the C-A measure was greater than zero for the control group (patients = 5.28, sd = 14.69; controls = 9.76, sd = 13.94). This shows that control participants preferred deck C to deck A, and coupled with the D-B selection measure, suggests that increased selection from C as well as decreased selection from B as compared to the patients was in part responsible for the higher net scores in that group. It is also of note that net scores for the control participants are not as high as reported by Bechara and colleagues but are comparable to the lower values reported by others (e.g. Fernie and Tunney, 2006; Bowman, Evans and Turnbull, 2005). Mintzer and Stitzer comment that previous studies of drug addicted populations have not reported differences as a function of loss frequency, but suggest that increasing frequency of loss may eliminate their reported effect. They go on to suggest further examination of this area is needed to understand the performance of their, and presumably other, clinical populations.

Overman (2004) also reported results supporting a role for loss frequency in IGT behaviour, albeit with a gender specific component. All their participants readily avoided deck A, but a difference in selection from deck B between genders was found when the IGT followed administration of the California Weather Task (Reavis and Overman, 2001), a probabilistic learning task where participants must learn the combination of patterned cards that predict either rain or sunshine. Following administration of this task male participants rapidly learned to avoid deck B while female participants did not. When the IGT was administered first this gender-specific pattern was also observed but was not nearly as stark. Overman suggested that female participants were reacting emotionally to losses, regardless of their value, while males were focusing more on the long-term consequences of their choices. This difference was exacerbated by previous experience of the California Weather Task which may have enhanced or focused attention on probability estimation in males but not in females. Differential selection of the advantageous decks was less pronounced, although deck D was selected more often, and much more often in females when the IGT was their first task. These results do seem to suggest that a learned avoidance for deck B is fundamental to success on the IGT.

Fischer, Blommaert and Midden (2005) examined the effect of mood on performance on a manipulated version of the computerised IGT. They found differential selection within the disadvantageous decks with deck A selected below chance and deck B selected above chance. Neither selection from decks C nor D were greater than chance. This contributed to an average monetary loss for participants and a negative mood change over the task (although a positive correlation was found between mood change and final bank balance), and occurred despite the manipulations to the original IGT design. The major changes in their task from the original IGT, aside from the computerisation and payment of real money, were fourfold. Firstly, gains and losses were reported separately in each deck (to facilitate computerisation of the experiment; but see also Peters and Slovic, 2000, discussed below). This meant that in the decks with low loss frequency there were nine gains of (10¢ in deck B; 5¢ in deck D) and one loss (115¢ in deck B; 20¢ in deck D), and in deck A there were five gains of 10¢ and five losses of 15¢. The second major change was in deck C. To avoid net yields of 0¢, the number of gains without loss was increased from five to seven. However, to maintain the expected value of +25¢, five of these gains were of 5¢, one was of 2¢ and one was of 1¢. The 3 losses were all of 1¢. These changes maintained the choice conflict in that decks A and B still had larger immediate gains but decks C and D had positive expected values. However, these manipulations make the probability of gain less certain for the participants (although the number of net gains remains the same) and magnitudes of loss are changed. This is especially relevant for selection from deck C. The third change was the randomisation of reinforcement schedules within each deck. The final major change was the addition of a money transfer aspect. In the original manual version of the IGT participants were required to give the experimenter money when they lost. This feature was restored by making participants move money from the computer dealer's account area to the participant's account area of the screen, or vice versa. This change had an interesting consequence. In a pilot study Fischer et al reported that participants developed a dislike for decks A and C compared to B and D. However, from their observations and debriefings of participants they discerned that participants found the transfer of money with more frequent losses tedious. The authors suggested that the large number of mouse movements involved in these transfers may make avoidance of them indicative of some optimising process. However, this may be only one of the elements involved in the development of dislike since similar patterns have been found in the computerised IGT without the money exchange (Mintzer and Stitzer, 2002).

Crone, Somsen, Van Beek and Van Der Molen (2004) also report evidence of a division in selection behaviour from the four IGT decks on their computerised 'donkey' version of the task developed for children but used with adults in this study They found an interaction between loss frequency and the net gain of the decks, such that participants selected more cards from the deck with the lower rather than the higher frequency of loss within the disadvantageous decks (deck B versus deck A), but no such division was found for the advantageous decks. However, an interaction was also found between loss frequency, net gain and performance group. Further post-hoc ANOVAs found that participants in the best performing group selected less from decks A and B, and more from deck C, with no difference in deck D selection between performance groups. Examination of Figure 2 in this study, shows that participants in the best performing group select a similar number of cards from decks B and C, at chance from deck D and below chance from deck A. The pattern is different in the moderate and worst performing groups where above chance selection from deck B predominates. Selection from the advantageous decks is roughly equal, but below chance in the worst group, and selection from A at chance, whereas the opposite pattern is found in the moderate group. These data suggest that differential selection from the IGT decks may drive overall performance on the IGT. However, no data were presented looking at the change in selection from individual decks across blocks. Trial block was involved in a three-way interaction with performance group and gain amount, as well as the two-way interactions involving these factors. In discussing these results the authors concluded that only the good performers improved (selected more good decks) across trial blocks. This effect could have been driven by decreasing selection from B and increasing selection from C. However, no four-way interaction between factors was revealed.

Recently, Lin, Chiu, Lee and Hsieh (2007) have focused on the preferential selection of deck B noted in the discussion of the studies above. They argue that the persistence of this deck B preference throughout the IGT argues against decision-making based on the long-term outcomes of card choices as maintained by Bechara et al (1994). In an experiment similar in design to our Experiment 1 to be reported below they compared card selection in two versions of the IGT using only two of the four deck schedules. Deck choice in one version was between two deck A's and two deck B's (the AACC condition) and between two deck B's and two deck D's (the BBDD condition) in the other. They report that participants in the AACC condition rapidly learn to select preferentially from deck C, while preferential selection for the advantageous decks does not occur in the BBDD condition. This result supports the hypothesis being developed in this chapter that the frequency of loss is an important influence on IGT deck selection and is suggestive of the importance of decks B and C on the IGT. Our Experiment 1 expands on this theme and tests the relative contribuitions of each deck for the development of learning on this task.

Physiological measures of heart rate and skin conductance were also recorded by Crone et al. (2004) and augmented the information available from the behavioural effects. Generally, heart rate slowed more and skin conductance was increased following infrequent losses. Heart rate has been found to slow in anticipation of an aversive event (Somsen, van der Molen, & Orlebeke, 2004) and skin conductance response is a widely used measure of physiological arousal (Dawson, Shell, & Filion, 1990). Somatic activity of this sort is hypothesised to underlie decision-making on the IGT (Bechara, Tranel, Damasio, & Damasio, 1996; Damasio, 1996; but see Maia and McClelland, 2004; Tomb, Hauser, Deldin and Caramazza, 2002; and Dunn, Dalgleish and Lawrence for a comprehensive review). Crone et al. (2004) performed further analyses to investigate whether heart rate and skin conductance were sensitive to the magnitude or the frequency of the losses compared these physiological measures following losses from decks A and D. In these decks the mean magnitude of losses is the same but the frequencies are different (losses are more frequent in deck A). No differential effects were found suggesting that the physiological measures are sensitive to the magnitude and not the frequency of losses. This absence of an effect is despite the large number of tests carried out to explore all factorial interactions risking an inflation of Type I error.

To some extent these behavioural and physiological findings accord with our previous behavioural results (Fernie and Tunney, 2006) in that little change in selection from decks A and D was found, while changes in selection were apparent following experience of the high magnitude losses in deck B. However, we also reported that selection from D was above chance whereas selection from A was below chance, suggesting that the frequency of loss does influence selection. The results of Crone et al's study suggest that behaviourally, good performance is somewhat mediated by choices from decks B and C.

In a further study, Crone, Bunge, Latenstein and van der Molen (2005) investigated the performance of children and adolescents on the standard and variant versions of the 'donkey' IGT. In the variant IGT (Bechara et al, 1999) the schedule of losses and gains are switched so losses are immediate while gains are the infrequent event. In their experiment participants were randomly assigned within each age group (7-9 years; 10-12 years; 13-15 years) to one of three conditions: a high-complexity condition with 4 options each with punishment frequency at 50% (equivalent to two deck A's and two deck C's); a low-complexity high-punishment frequency condition (equivalent to deck A and C); and a low-complexity low-punishment frequency condition (equivalent to deck B and D). They found that the improvement in performance with increasing age reported in previous studies (e.g. Crone and van der Molen, 2004) were only apparent in the low-complexity low punishment frequency condition where the youngest age group showed chance selection from each deck, whereas the older age groups preferred the deck with the positive expected value. Children in the middle age group were slower to develop this preference. Examining deck switching behaviour Crone et al. found that the younger children switched selection more frequently in this condition. The authors argued that the younger children discounted the infrequent (large) punishment in this condition more quickly than the older age groups. These results demonstrate that punishment frequency does influence selection behaviour, but that it should disappear into adolescence. However, even if a fourth condition with high-complexity and low-punishment frequency (BBDD) had been used it would not be as complex as the standard IGT and where the frequency of punishment influences the behaviour of participants.

Peters and Slovic (2000) have criticised the design of the IGT by commenting that losses, gains and expected values are confounded as the highest magnitudes occur in the disadvantageous decks. According to Peters and Slovic this makes it difficult to determine if participants are selecting on the basis of size of gains, size of losses or expected value. They make no mention of the frequency of losses. Instead they created an alternative task based on the IGT. In this task, two decks have higher gains (B & D) and two have higher losses (B & C), but decks C and D have a positive expected value whereas decks A and B have a negative expected value. Unlike on the IGT gains and losses are not presented together on the same selection. In altering the IGT Peters and Slovic equalised the probability of loss in each of the decks to .5, with the exception of deck C where the probability of loss is .2 (as a result this deck also has a slightly higher expected value). While this task may allow discrimination between the magnitudes of gains, losses and expected values, arguably making it a better task than the IGT, such a manipulation does not tell us anything about the influence of loss frequency on behaviour on the IGT. However, it is of note that the average participant in the Peters and Slovic task chose deck C – the deck with the lowest frequency of loss. But this was also the deck with the highest expected value.

A basic associative learning rule like the Law of Effect (Thorndike, 1898) predicts that decks with the lowest frequency of loss be preferred. This is supported by the results on Peters and Slovic's (2000) modified task. What is not clear is why behaviour on the standard gambling task, with its arrangement of always presented rewards and infrequent losses does not conform all the time. Barron and Erev (2003, Experiment 4), have shown that in small feedback-based decisions decision makers have a tendency to underweight rare outcomes. Small feedback-based problems have three features: they are repeated, each single choice is not very important overall, and there is no objective information – decision makers must rely on the immediate feedback obtained in the situation in the past. Yechiam, Stout, Busemeyer, Rock and Finn (2005) have claimed that the choice on the IGT is an example of a small feedback-based decision situation. They investigated the influence of foregone payoffs on the selection behaviour in two manipulations of the IGT. Foregone payoffs occur when the result of all choices is revealed following selection of one. In their IGT mainpulation foregone payoffs were either included or not and reinforcer magnitude was increased by a factor of 1.5 or not (the non-manipulated condition was equivalent to the standard task). The study was conducted to investigate the influence of foregone payoffs on performance of a high-level drug abusing population (predominantly university students) versus controls. However, the study is of interest in this context because it investigated selection over 150 trials in each IGT deck. The manipulation of reinforcer magnitude produced no significant effects so results were pooled across this condition. For controls in the unmanipulated condition, selection from deck A is always below chance, and actually decreases with time. Selection from B remains above chance, and appears to increase in the first 100 trials. Selection from C is below chance but does show some increase over all blocks, whereas in D selection increases from above chance in the first block. One possible reason for the difference in selection patterns compared to those reported by Fernie and Tunney (2006) is that reward magnitude was ten times higher – participants earned $1 and not 10¢ per selection from decks A and B. Yechiam et al. found that the influence of the foregone payoffs was larger for the drug abusing group in B and D, but a different pattern of results was found – with foregone payoffs selection from B switched from learned avoidance without them to constant above chance selection with them. In A, foregone payoffs resulted in a initial attraction to this deck that reduced over time. This different results pattern lead Yechiam et al. (2005) to caution against aggregating across the disadvantageous decks and to advocate a more detailed examination of selection patterns without collapsing across the frequency difference. Examining Figure 2 in this study reveals that the control participants have similar selection from decks A and B with and without foregone payoffs. But providing foregone payoffs actually increased selection from D and decreased selection from C. This is informative: when participants know what they missed out on they prefer the advantageous deck with the lower frequency of loss.

The reinforcement schedules on the IGT were constructed to contrast decks with positive and negative expected values, but larger or smaller immediate gains. Nowhere in the IGT literature is there any explanation for why within decks with the same expected values, the reinforcement schedules were constructed in the way they were. It can be assumed that the task was constructed with four decks as using two decks would mean that the task was too simple, whereas any more than four would increase the complexity. But it is not clear why within each deck type one deck has an infrequent, but relatively high magnitude loss, whereas the other deck has a more frequent with consequently smaller relative magnitude losses. The task creators believed that since the decks are equivalent in expected value selection would be similar between them. Others have suggested this may not be the case (e.g. Lin et al, 2007; Fernie and Tunney, 2006; MacPherson et al, 2002; Wilder et al, 1998). From these studies it is clear that there is differential selection within decks with negative expected values and possibly within the advantageous decks. The following Experiments were designed to investigate the influence of loss frequency on this choice behaviour on the IGT.

The hypothesis developed in this chapter is that deck selection on the IGT is not merely governed by the long-term consequences of the decks. The contention is that participants readily learn to avoid the disadvantageous deck with the higher frequency of loss and initially prefer the disadvantageous deck with the lower frequency of loss, while within the advantageous decks differential selection is less clear, but participants in general prefer the deck with the more frequent losses (and lower net losses). A possible explanation for this behaviour is the amount of information available to participants about the 'goodness' or otherwise of the decks. This information can only come from the schedule of losses, and the frequency of loss with which loss occurs. In the decks with the less frequent loss there is less information about their 'goodness' as there are less penalties, giving less opportunity to gather information about the long-term 'goodness' of the deck. Whereas in the decks with more frequent losses, there is are more losses and therefore more information about the overall nature of the decks. A further aim of Experiment 2 was to test the hypothesis that the frequency of loss provides information to participants about deck 'goodness' and so affects learning behaviour.

EXPERIMENT 1: ADVANTAGEOUS CARD SELECTION DIFFERS BETWEEN DECK COMPARISONS WHEN CHOICE IS BETWEEN TWO IOWA GAMBLING TASK DECKS

The aim of the Experiment 1 was to investigate participants' deck preferences and their effects on learning in the Iowa Gambling Task by investigating behaviour when a simpler choice was required. In four conditions, choice was examined between one advantageous and one disadvantageous deck from the Iowa Gambling Task. This design permits the examination of learning as measured by the change in preference for the advantageous deck. As the expected values of the decks in each condition are the same, any difference in behaviour implies that the contingencies of the individual decks, and not expected values, are governing selection on this task. Any differential learning between conditions can be attributed to differences in the magnitude and frequency of losses on the individual decks. Table 1 displays the deck contingencies in each condition.

The hypothesis based on previous studies is that changes in selection from decks B and C underlie learning, thus we anticipated that learning would be slowest when the choice is between these two decks. Due to the general avoidance of deck A in earlier studies it was predicted that the fastest learning would be seen when deck A was one of the choice options. Similarly, due to the preference for deck B it was predicted that learning would be slowest in the conditions where it was one of the response options. Differences in learning between conditions where the disadvantageous decks are different and the advantageous decks are the same would suggest that selection from the disadvantageous decks is not uniform and would provide behavioural support for Crone *et al*'s (2004) results. Differences in learning between conditions where the advantageous decks are different but the disadvantageous decks are the same would suggest that selection from the advantageous decks is not uniform. This would conflict with the results from Crone *et al* (2004) but provide support for the hypothesis that change in preference for deck C underlies learning on the IGT.

Table 1. The deck contingencies in each condition in Experiment 1.

	Deck Comparison			
	A:C	A:D	B:C	B:D
Reward Magnitude	10:5	10:5	10:5	10:5
Mean Loss Magnitude	25:2.5	25:25	125:2.5	125:25
Loss Frequency	0.5:0.5	0.5:0.1	0.1:0.5	0.1:0.1

Method

Participants

Forty-eight participants (thirty-nine female) were recruited from the undergraduate and postgraduate populations at the University of Nottingham. Participants were recruited through a poster advertisement that offered the opportunity to earn up to £6 by taking part in a cognitive psychology experiment. Participants were randomly assigned to one of four conditions shown in Table 1.

Apparatus

Participants were tested individually. A PC controlled the experiment. A 2-alternative forced choice task was created and run on the PC. The task was based on published descriptions of the Iowa Gambling Task, except that participants made choices from two rather than four decks of cards. The reinforcement schedules for each deck were the same as those published by Bechara, et al. (1994) for the first 40 cards. For the remaining 160 cards in each deck the reinforcement schedules were based on the format of the first 40 cards: Deck A, five losses totalling £1.25 per ten card selections; Deck B, one loss of £1.25 per ten card selections; Deck C, five losses totalling £0.25 per ten card selections; Deck D, one card selection totalling £0.25 per ten card selections. At the end of the experiment participants were paid the money that they had won in the task.

Design and Procedure

A between-subjects design was used to compare participants' learning between four advantageous deck to disadvantageous deck comparisons. Learning when choosing between decks A and C, decks A and D, decks B and C and decks B and D was compared. The number of selections made from the advantageous decks was recorded for each of twenty ten-trial blocks. From this measure the slope, b, was calculated as an estimate of learning rate. The task lasted for 200 card selections. After 100 card selections participants were invited to take a short break. The length of this break was determined by each participant and was not recorded.

Results

The number of card selections from the advantageous deck (C or D) in each condition was recorded for each participant in each of ten twenty-trial blocks. Table 2 displays the mean number of advantageous selections in each experimental group over the first half, the second half and the whole experiment.

To investigate whether the number of advantageous selections differed between groups, a 4x10 (Condition by Block) mixed design ANOVA was performed. There was no interaction, $F(11.42, 167.43) < 1$, MSE $= 24.88$, $p > .05$. However, ANOVA revealed a main effect of Block, $F(3.81, 305.53) = 12.82$, $p < .001$, indicating that the number of advantageous selections differed between blocks (it increased with block). A main effect of Condition was also found, $F(3, 44) = 3.87$, MSE $= 139.33$, $p < .05$. Pairwise comparisons found that the number of advantageous selections was significantly greater in condition A:C versus condition B:C, $F(3,440) = 6.06$, MSE $= 23.4$, $p < .05$; and in condition A:D versus condition B:C, $F(3,440) = 4.70$, MSE $= 23.4$, $p < .05$. There were no significant differences between any other groups, $F(3,440) < 1$.

Table 2. Mean number of advantageous selections in each group in Experiment 1

Trials	Deck comparison			
	A:C	A:D	B:C	B:D
1 - 100	12.75 (0.80)	12.52 (0.76)	7.43 (0.93)	11.32 (1.09)
101 - 200	15.3 (1.24)	14.73 (1.01)	11.25 (1.71)	13.38 (1.69)
1 - 200	14.03 (0.86)	13.63 (0.83)	9.34 (1.16)	12.35 (1.37)

Note: The maximum number of advantageous selections possible is 20. Figures in parentheses are the standard error of the mean.

Figure 2 shows the mean number of advantageous card selections in each condition across ten twenty-trial blocks. While advantageous selection appears to increase at roughly the same rate in each condition, it is always lower when the choice is between decks B and C. Learning would be indicated by an increase in the number of advantageous selections with increased exposure to the task. As a measure of learning rate the slope, b, was calculated for each participant. Table 3 gives the mean learning rates for the first and second 100 trials and for all trials in each experimental condition and shows that overall learning rate is greatest when the choice is between deck C and a disadvantageous deck.

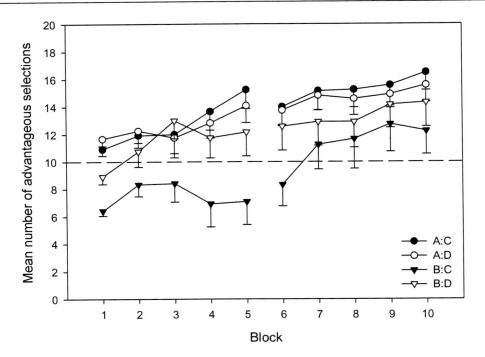

Figure 2. Mean number of advantageous selections across twenty ten-trial blocks in each experimental group in Experiment 1. Error bars are the standard error of the mean.A one-way ANOVA was run to investigate whether learning rate differed significantly between deck comparison conditions. No significant differences in learning rate between conditions were found, $F(3, 44) < 1$, MSE=0.44, $p<.05$.

Table 3: Mean learning rate (*b*) in each experimental condition across first 100 trials, second 100 trials and all trials.

	Deck comparison			
Trials	A:C	A:D	B:C	B:D
1 - 100	1.04* (0.37)	0.54 (0.31)	-0.01 (0.51)	0.75 (0.40)
101 - 200	0.54* (0.24)	0.38 (0.24)	0.93* (0.39)	0.46* (0.20)
1 - 200	0.58* (0.21)	0.45* (0.13)	0.69* (0.25)	0.47* (0.17)

Note: Figures in parentheses are the standard error of the mean.   *indicates significantly greater than 0 at the .05 level using Lorch and Myers regression analyses.

In previous experiments using the IGT selections have most commonly been examined in 100-trial sessions. Examining the data in a similar way reveals that there appears to be no learning in condition B:C (see Table 3). This result is in line with the experimental hypotheses. However, in the second 100 trials participants learn at almost twice the rate of participants in the other conditions. This mirrors the results from our previous experiments where a preference for deck C is found to develop with increased experience of the decks. Table 3 displays a summary of the results of Lorch and Myers (1990) regression analyses on learning rates. These regressions revealed that while learning rate was greater than zero across all 200 trials in all conditions, in the first 100 trials it was almost flat in condition B:C and was no different from zero in conditions A:D and B:D. These results were augmented by comparing mean advantageous selections made in block 5 to zero. For conditions A:D and A:C, the number of advantageous selections were greater than zero in block 5 (A:D: $t(11) = 3.31$, sd $= 4.27$, $p < .05$; A:C: $t(11) = 3.83$, sd $= 4.75$, $p < .05$) but not in condition B:D, ($t(11) = 1.23$, sd $= 6.09$, $p < .05$) or condition B:C ($t(11) = -1.74$, sd $= 5.82$, $p < .05$). In the final block of trials advantageous selections were greater than zero in all conditions (A:D: $t(11) = 4.57$, sd $= 4.23$, $p < .05$; B:D: $t(11) = 2.46$, sd $= 6.11$, $p < .05$; A:C: $t(11) = 5.07$, sd $= 4.44$, $p < .05$) except condition B:C ($t(11) = 1.33$, sd $= 5.88$, $p < .05$).

Discussion

A difference was found between the number of advantageous cards selected in condition A:C and condition B:C. Fewer advantageous selections were made in condition B:C suggesting that participants found it harder to select advantageously due to an increased preference for deck B. This result provides support for the hypothesis that participants' preferences on the IGT distinguished between the disadvantageous decks. However, no significant differences were found in the number of advantageous selections in conditions A:D and B:D, suggesting that the presence of deck C is important.

No differences were found when learning rates between conditions were examined, and learning rate was significantly greater than 0 over all 10 blocks in each condition. However, examination of Figure 2 suggests that condition B:C does differ from the others. Learning rate during the first hundred trial in condition B:C was flat so that by block 5 participants were not selecting advantageously. Despite a large increase in learning rate as measured over 200 trials, in the final block participants were still not showing a preference for the advantageous deck although they were heading in that direction. These results support the experimental hypothesis that due to changes in participants' preferences observed in the IGT this condition would be the hardest for participants to learn on. However, an alternative explanation for these findings is that identifying which option had the better long-term consequences was harder because the deck contingencies varied on both the magnitude and the frequency of loss whereas all other deck contingencies varied on only one (see Table 3; A:C and B:D vary on loss magnitude; A:D varies on loss frequency).

The mean number of advantageous selections was greatest when the deck comparison involved deck A. In all blocks the highest advantageous selections were seen in these two conditions. These results provide support for the hypothesis that participants generally avoid deck A, meaning identification of the deck with better long-term consequences is easier regardless of the advantageous deck it was paired with. Unfortunately because there were no differences in the number of advantageous selections (and consequently disadvantageous deck selections) little can be inferred about the relative contribution of loss frequency or magnitude in the advantageous decks, except that they do not appear to differentially affect learning when the disadvantageous deck is A.

In condition B:D, where only the magnitude of loss differed between decks, advantageous selection did not increase in the first 100 trials and no preference for deck D had been established by block 5. Only after more exposure did a preference for deck D develop. This reflects an effect of loss magnitude. Participants learn to avoid the larger loss despite the larger gain associated with it. Table 3 shows that the lowest overall learning rates are found when deck D is one of the choices. However, this may reflect different processes in conditions B:D and A:D. In condition A:D little change in learning rate reflects the general and unchanging preference for deck D. The later development of a preference for D in condition B:D may reflect the similarity in loss frequency between the decks making it harder to identify the deck selections which will result in greater long-term gains. Something similar was also observed by Lin et al (2007) in the final 20-trial block (of 200 trials) and the differences between their results and ours may be due to several factors. First, Lin et al used two of each deck with the result that their participants' decision-making environment was more complex. This would also have resulted in many more unpunished selections from deck B when considered together. Conceivably this may have clouded their participants' learning that these decks were worse in the long run, or at least postponed their avoidance of them because the option always remained to switch to the other deck B with the chance that it would not be punished. Secondly, in our simpler environment participants were being paid with real money. The incentive to identify the best deck and stick to it may have been increased despite previous findings that reinforcer type does not affect IGT performance (Bowman and Turnbull, 2003; Fernie and Tunney, 2006).

As previously mentioned, Overman (2004) has also identified the differences in deck contingencies as an important factor in behaviour on the IGT. As well as noting the differences in loss frequencies between the decks, Overman has pointed out that due to the size and frequency of losses on deck C very often no overall loss is made when selecting from this deck. This may be the reason that selection from this deck changes across deck: participants learn that while there are frequent losses on this deck, they rarely result in a net loss for that selection, and even when a net loss occurs it is small in comparison to all other decks. As such, deck C varies in a unique respect from the other decks on the IGT: *net loss* frequency. This net loss is lower (it varies between 1 and 4 per 10 card selections) than the frequency of losses (5 per 10 card selections). It may take the participants time to learn this, but it would mirror the apparent initial preference for the decks with infrequent losses (decks B and D) and fit into an explanation utilising the Law of Effect. Of course, the infrequent net losses also means that the magnitude of losses on Deck C are substantially lower than on the other IGT decks and it may be this that influences preference for this deck.

Overman (2004) also reported gender differences in deck selection on the IGT. The majority of our participants were female but no differences in advantageous selections were found across conditions suggesting that this effect did not occur in the 2-choice task. However, due to the small number of male participants the existence of the effect cannot be ruled out.

The results from this experiment provide some support for previous findings that participants' preferences for the disadvantageous decks are not uniform. In a two-choice environment it appears to be harder to select advantageously when deck B is one option. The results also support the hypothesis that learning on the IGT is driven by changes in selection from decks B and C. However, the experiment did not inform on whether the frequency of loss or its magnitude affect card selection on the IGT decks, except to suggest that this relationship may be different in the advantageous and disadvantageous decks. Experiment 2 explores this relationship further.

EXPERIMENT 2: MANIPULATION OF FREQUENCY (AND MAGNITUDE) OF LOSS AFFECTS LEARNING ON THE IGT

The results from Experiment 1 provided some support for the hypothesis that the difference in deck contingencies within the disadvantageous and advantageous decks contributes to learning on the Iowa Gambling Task. Experiment 2 was devised in order to further test this hypothesis by manipulating the reinforcement contingencies in the decks. The hypothesis in these experiments is that participants avoid the disadvantageous deck with the higher frequency of loss and initially prefer the disadvantageous deck with the lower frequency of loss, while within the advantageous decks differential selection is less clear, but participants in general prefer the deck with the more frequent losses (and lower net losses). A possible explanation for this behaviour is the amount of information available to participants about the 'goodness' or otherwise of the decks. This information can only come from the schedule of losses, and the frequency with which losses occur. In the decks with the less frequent loss there is less information about their 'goodness' as there are less penalties, giving fewer opportunities to gather information about the long-term 'goodness' of the deck. Whereas in the decks with more frequent losses, there is are more losses and therefore more information about the overall nature of the decks. A further aim of Experiment 2 was to test the hypothesis that the frequency of loss provides information to participants about deck 'goodness' and so affects learning behaviour. To this end, we created two conditions by manipulating the frequency of losses on the original IGT decks. In a Decreased Frequency condition the frequency of loss in decks A and C was reduced but unchanged in decks B and D. In an Increased Frequency condition the frequency of loss in decks B and D was increased but unchanged in decks A and C. In the Decreased Frequency condition less losses occur across the whole task, giving participants less information about the nature of the decks, whereas in the Increased Frequency condition more information is available. Any difference in learning and in learning rate can be attributed to this difference in frequency of loss. It was predicted that if the frequency of loss is informative then a slower learning rate would be observed in the Decreased Frequency condition. A further prediction is that since participants prefer the lower frequency decks, selection should be higher from those decks within decks with the same expected values. A sign that loss frequency is in part informative would be that this difference is greater in when loss frequency is increased rather than decreased, as participants will still be avoiding the deck with largest loss frequencies.

Method

Participants

Forty-two (twenty-six female) participants were recruited from the undergraduate and postgraduate populations at the University of Nottingham. Participants were recruited through a poster advertisement that offered the opportunity to earn up to £6 by taking part in a cognitive psychology experiment. Data from two participants were excluded from the analysis due to computer error in one case, and an expression by the participant of total misunderstanding of the instructions in the other.

Apparatus

Two modified versions of the Iowa Gambling Task were created. In the Increased Frequency condition the frequency of loss was increased in the two IGT decks with low frequency (but high relative magnitude) losses (decks B and D). In the Decreased Frequency condition the frequency of loss was decreased in the IGT decks with high frequency (but lower relative magnitude) losses (decks A and C). In the original IGT the schedule of losses was fixed. This was maintained in the modified decks and the occurrence of losses was randomly determined within 10 card blocks for each deck with the caveat that the sum of losses did not change the expected value for that deck within a ten card block. Where the magnitude of losses changed (e.g increased with the reduction in loss frequency in modified deck A and decreased with the increase in loss frequency in modified deck B) the same amounts were used in decks with the same expected value e.g. for the disadvantageous decks 5 losses of 15, 20, 25, 30, and 35 or one loss of 125 became three losses of 35, 35, and 55.

Design

A between-subjects design was used to compare participants' learning on the two modified IGT versions. The number of selections made from the advantageous decks minus the number of selections from the disadvantageous decks was calculated for each of ten twenty-trial blocks. From this measure the slope, b, was calculated as an estimate of learning rate. In addition, the number of cards chosen from each of the decks and the change in their selection over time was examined.

Procedure

Participants were randomly assigned to the increased frequency or decreased frequency conditions. The procedure followed that of Experiment 1. Participants took part in only one session of 200 trials and they saw on-screen, and chose between, four decks of cards. After 100 card selections participants were invited to take a short break. The length of this break was determined by each participant and was not recorded.

Table 4. Mean net score in each condition in the first and second hundred trials, and over the whole of Experiment 2

Trials	Decreased frequency	Increased frequency
1 - 100	9.5 (8.40)	3.5 (6.25)
101 - 200	20.3 (10.27)	23.9 (10.88)
1 - 200	29.8 (16.47)	27.4 (16.29)*

Note: Figures in parentheses are the standard error of the mean.
* indicates significantly greater than 0 at the .05 level.

Results

Net score was calculated for each participant over the whole experiment, and for the first hundred and the second hundred trials. Mean net scores in each condition are displayed in Table 4. As the table shows mean net score does not differ much between groups, although contrary to the experimental hypotheses participants in the increased frequency group have a lower net score in the first 100 trials. However, an independent samples t-test found no significant difference in the overall mean net score between conditions, $t(38) < 1.0$.

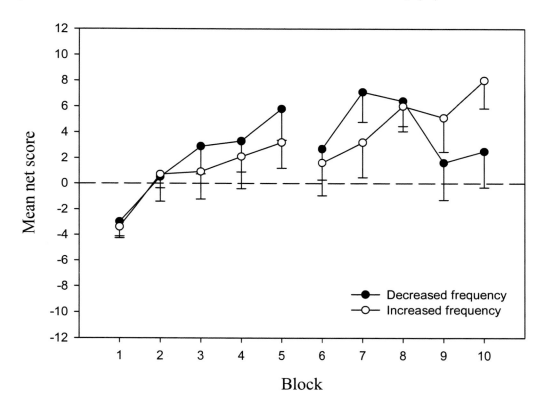

Figure 3. Mean net score across ten twenty-trial blocks in each experimental condition of Experiment 2. Error bars are the standard error of the mean (only negative bars are displayed for ease of viewing).

Table 5. Mean learning rate (*b*) in both experimental conditions across the first 100 trials, second 100 trials and all trials

Trials	Decreased frequency	Increased frequency
1 - 100	2.04 (0.61)*	1.46 (0.55)*
101 - 200	-0.59 (0.56)	1.47 (0.52)*
1 - 200	0.50 (0.29)	0.97 (0.26)*

Note: Figures in parentheses are the standard error of the mean.
* indicates significantly greater than 0 at the .05 level using Lorch and Myers regression analyses.

Figure 3 displays mean net score in each of ten blocks of twenty trials for each experimental condition. Mean net score increases across blocks in both conditions, although only in the Increased Frequency condition does mean net score end above chance. However, contrary to the experimental hypothesis, mean net scores did not differ between conditions. This is confirmed by the results of a 2 x 10 (Loss Frequency by Block) mixed design ANOVA. There was no main effect of Loss Frequency, $F(1, 38) < 1.0$, $MSE = 536.61$, $p > .05$, nor a significant interaction, $F(5.26, 199.72)^1 = 1.57$, $MSE = 86.13$, $p > .05$. A significant main effect of Block was found, $F(5.26, 199.72) = 6.04$, $MSE = 86.13$, $p < .01$, which indicated the tendency for mean net score to increase across blocks.

The main effect of Block does not provide much information beyond showing that mean net score is higher in some blocks than in others. As a result the change in mean net score across block, or the slope b, was calculated as an estimate of learning rate in each condtion. Over the entire experiment learning rate was greater in the Increased Frequency condition, $b = 0.97$ (se $= 0.26$), than in the Decreased Frequency condition, $b = 0.50$ (se $= 0.29$). This supports the experimental hypothesis. However, an independent samples t-test found that this difference was not significant, $t(38) = -1.21$, $p > .05$. This result suggests that, as with the result of the mixed-design ANOVA, there is no strong evidence to support the experimental hypothesis that increasing the frequency of loss in the low frequency decks will lead to faster learning.

In Experiment 1, it was argued that as the structure of the task included a break after 100 trials and as this is the length of the standard administration of the gambling task, learning rate might be examined over the first 100 and second 100 trials. Table 5 displays mean learning rate over the first and second 100 trials, and over the entire experiment, in each condition. Lorch and Myers (1990) regression analyses for repeated measures designs compared these learning rates to zero. These analyses reveal that while there is a significant increase in learning rate in the first 100 trials in both conditions (Decreased Frequency: $b = 2.04$ (se $= .61$), $t(19) = 3.35$, $p < .01$; Increased Frequency: $b = 1.46$ (se $= .55$), $t(19) = 2.67$, $p < .02$), learning rate only continues to increase in the second 100 trials in the Increased Frequency condition, $b = 1.47$ (se $= .52$), $t(19) = 2.82$, $p < .02$. Indeed, learning rate in the second 100 trials in the Decreased Frequency condition is negative, $b = -.59$ (se $= .56$), $t(19) = -1.05$, $p > .05$. An independent-samples t-test found this difference to be significant, $t(38) = -2.69$, $p < .02$ (the same test for the first 100 trials was not significant, $t(38) < 1.0$). This difference and the negative learning rate in the Decreased Frequency condition reflects the decline in mean net score in blocks 9 and 10 in this condition, as illustrated in Figure 3. This decline after 160 trials is what affects the overall learning rate in this condition, and is the reason why it is not significantly greater than zero. Whereas, in the Increased Frequency condition mean net score continues to increase until by the end of the final block, mean net score is significantly greater than chance, $t(19) = 3.70$, $p < .01$. These results give some support to the experimental hypothesis that learning would be greater in the Increased Frequency condition.

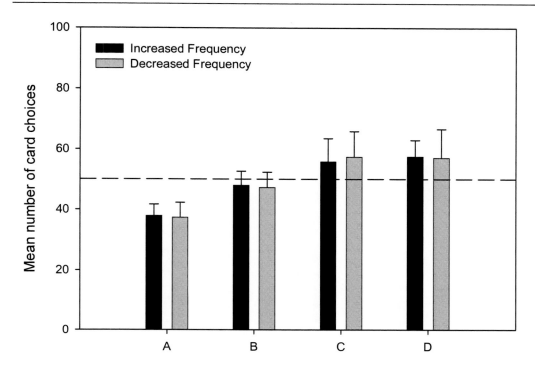

Figure 4. Mean number of cards selected from each deck across all 200 trials in each condition in Experiment 2. Error bars are the standard error of the mean.

Individual Deck Selection

In the standard preparation (e.g. Fernie & Tunney, 2006) participants prefer to select the disadvantageous cards with the least frequent loss, whereas within the advantageous decks, although this general pattern is common early in learning, latter in learning participants prefer to select from the decks with the more frequent loss.

The relevant data are shown in Figure 4. It is clear that participants show a similar deck selection preference in both conditions. This is not surprising given the similarity in net score measures reported earlier. Unlike in previous Experiments there does not appear to be any difference in selection within the advantageous decks. However, within the disadvantageous decks participants still appear to prefer the deck with the infrequent loss. Figure 4 displays deck selection in the first 100 and second 100 trials in both conditions. Deck selection from deck B decreases from the first to the second 100 trials, but unlike those earlier conditions the change in selection from deck D (increases from the first to the second 100 trials), is as large as that found in deck C. This suggests an equivalence in preference within the advantageous decks; a trend not apparent in the disadvantageous decks where deck A is always selected at a level below chance. This implies that within the disadvantageous decks participants prefer the deck with the less frequent losses. Separate 2x2 (Deck by Time) repeated measures ANOVAs for each condition were run to investigate this claim. For the Decreased Frequency condition there was no main effect of Deck, $F(1, 19) = 3.0$, $MSE = 163.26$, $p = .1$; no main effect of Time, $F(1, 19) = 1.15$, $MSE = 104.47$, $p > .05$; nor was there an interaction, $F(1, 19) = 2.43$, $MSE = 29.78$, $p = .14$. For the Increased Frequency condition there was a main effect of Deck, $F(1, 19) = 26.64$, $MSE = 19.89$, $p < .01$; a main effect of Time, $F(1, 19) = 8.49$, $MSE =$

55.40, $p < .01$; but no interaction, $F(1, 19) = 1.68$, $MSE = 26.74$, $p > .05$. In the Increased Frequency condition the selections from B were greater than from A, and the number of selections from these disadvantageous decks was greater in the first hundred than the second hundred trials. That this was not the case in the Decreased Frequency condition implies that participants in this condition did not discriminate between the two bad decks, whereas in the Increased Frequency condition they did.

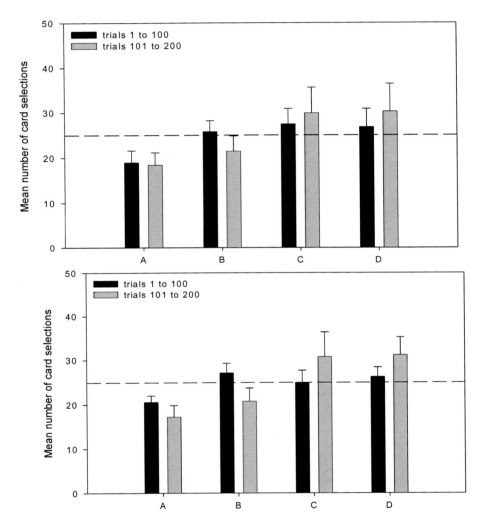

Figure 5. Mean number of cards selected from each deck across the first 100 and second 100 trials in panel A) the Decreased Frequency condition and panel B) the Increased Frequency condition of Experiment 2. Error bars are the standard error of the mean.

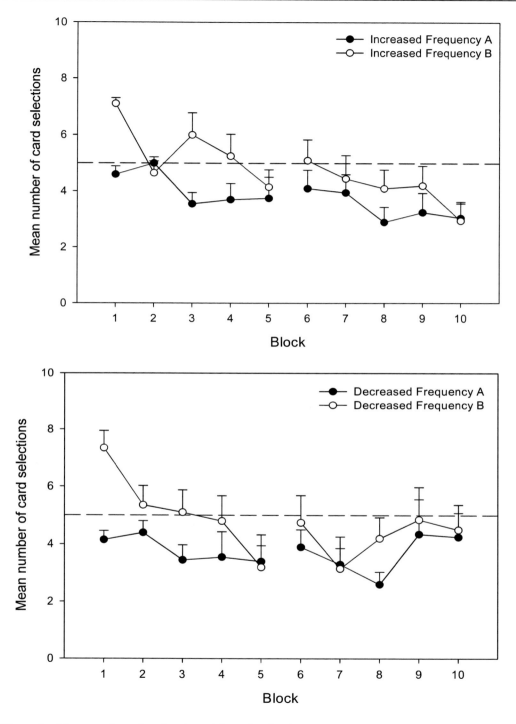

Figure 6a. Mean number of cards selected from the disadvantageous decks in each condition in Experiment 2 (Top: Increased frequency, bottom: decreased frequency). Error bars are the standard error of the mean.

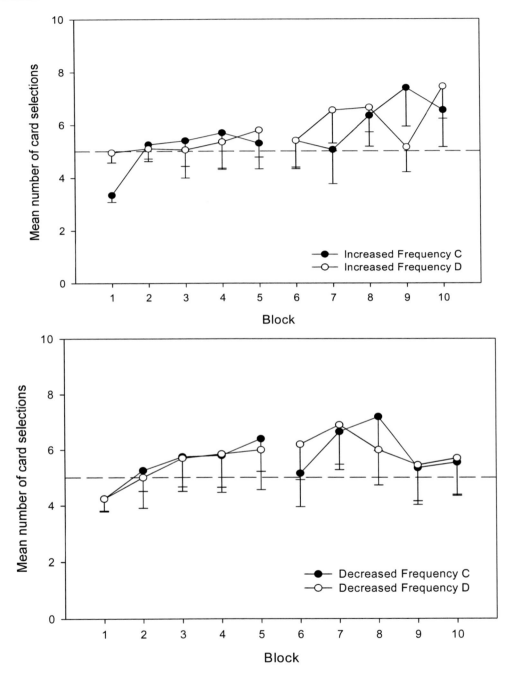

Figure 6b. Mean number of cards selected from the advantageous decks in each condition in Experiment 2 (Top: Increased frequency, bottom: decreased frequency). Error bars are the standard error of the mean.

Table 6. Mean selection rate from each deck in the first and second 100 trials in each condition

	Trial	Decreased Frequency	Increased Frequency
A			
	1 – 100	-.18 (.20)	-.28 (.17)
	101 – 200	.18 (.28)	-.28 (.16)
B			
	1 – 100	-.84 (.27)	-.53 (.18)
	101 – 200	.12 (.22)	-.46 (.17)
C			
	1 – 100	.53 (.34)	.61 (.33)
	101 – 200	-.05 (.23)	.47 (.34)
D			
	1 – 100	.49 (.28)	.20 (.27)
	101 – 200	-.25 (.17)	.27 (.40)

Note: Figures in parentheses are the standard error of the mean.

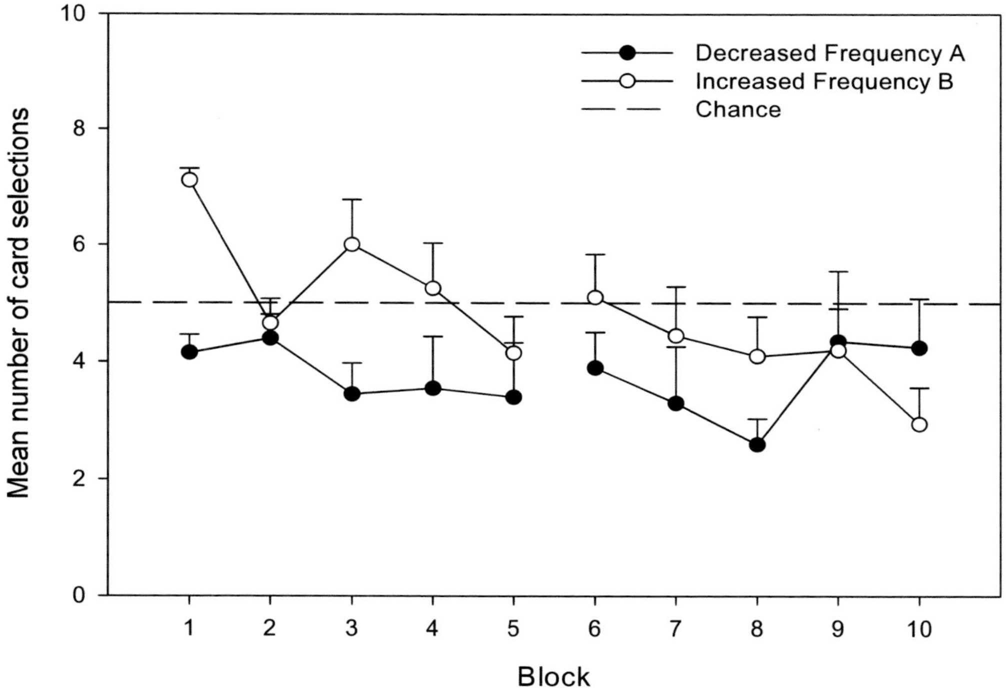

Figure 7. Mean number of card selections across block from the disadvantageous decks with probability of loss of .3. Error bars are the standard error of the mean.

Figure 6 shows the change in selections from each deck across trial blocks. In Figure 6A the change in selections from the disadvantageous decks follow the same trend in both conditions. Selection from deck B begins well above chance in the first block, but by block 5 selection from B is below chance. Selection from A remains below chance in both conditions. However, in the second 100 trials differences emerge between the conditions. Selection from both A and B increases in the Decreased Frequency condition, whereas they continue to decline in the Increased Frequency condition (although this is partly due to the increase in selection between blocks 5 and 6). This difference in selection between conditions would appear to be what underlies the difference in learning between these conditions. Figure 6B mirrors Figure 6A; selection in C and D increases in both conditons in the first hundred trials, but in the Decreased frequency condition selection from both declines in block 8 for deck D and block 9 for deck C. In the Increased Frequency condition selection from both decks continues to increase (although there is a dip in block 9 from D), with selection from both ending above chance.

Table 6 presents the change in selection (the slope, b,) from each deck in the first and second halves of the task. The observations from Figure 5 are borne out. In the Decreased Frequency condition selection from the disadvantageous decks increases and selections from the advantageous decks decreases in the second hundred trials – the opposite to what happens in the Increased Frequency condition. These differences in selection support the experimental hypothesis. With a reduction in the overall frequency of losses (and a consequent increase in magnitude of loss), participants end the task with less differentiation between decks.

It was noted that within the disadvantageous decks participants prefer the decks with the less frequent losses. This is apparent in Figure 6A. Figure 7 displays selections from deck A in the Decreased Frequency condition and selections from deck B in the Increased Frequency condition. These decks have the same probability of a loss, .3, but what differs between them is the context in which they are presented. In the Increased Frequency condition this deck is preferred initially as it has the lowest probability of loss, although selection continues to decline across block, whereas in the Decreased Frequency condition this deck has the greatest frequency of loss and is selected below chance right up until the last two blocks. Figure 7 illustrates that participants initially prefer the disadvantageous deck with the lowest frequency of loss. In the Decreased Frequency condition this is not the case at the end of the task – perhaps because it is more difficult to avoid a deck that provides higher magnitude gains on seven out of ten trials.

Discussion

In Experiment 2 we manipulated the frequency of losses in order to test the hypothesis that learning would be affected by the amount of information participants received about how good or bad their choices were. This hypothesis received some support. Although there was no difference in learning rate across all two hundred trials, in the second half of the task, learning rate was only greater than zero in the Increased Frequency condition. In the Decreased Frequency condition it was negative.

A more detailed examination of selection from the individual decks, revealed that although selection was similar between conditions in the first one hundred trials, in the second one hundred trials participants in the Decreased Frequency condition increased their selection from the disadvantageous decks, whereas in the Increased Frequency condition selection from these decks continued to decline. At the end of the task participants in the

Decreased Frequency condition, were not selecting from any deck above or below chance at the end of the experiment, unlike in the Increased Frequency condition where there was preferential selection from the advantageous decks. This result supports the experimental hypothesis.

It was hypothesised from the results of Experiment 1 that changes in selection from decks B and C drives learning on the IGT. There was no sign of differential selection within the advantageous decks in either experimental condition. However, participants do appear to prefer, at least initially, the disadvantageous deck with the lower frequency of loss. That this preference is associated with frequency of loss and not magnitude of loss was demonstrated in Figure 7 where selection from deck A in the Decreased Frequency condition was compared to deck B in the Increased Frequency condition. Selection patterns from these decks with the same frequency and magnitude of loss differed between groups. Participants in the Increased Frequency condition initially selected more from their deck B, while in the Decreased Frequency condition selection from their deck A remained below chance until the last two blocks. The only difference between these decks was the context in which they were presented. In the Increased Frequency condition, deck B still had the lower frequency of loss relative to the other disadvantageous deck. A possible explanation for this difference, and the higher learning of this group, is that participants in the Increased Frequency condition encountered more losses earlier than participants in the Decreased Frequency group. In the Decreased Frequency group, selections from deck B could go on unpunished for longer than selections from any other disadvantageous deck. This is because in the original task's fixed schedule of losses, the large infrequent loss in deck B occurs after nine selections of a large magnitude gain (in comparison to decks C and D). In the random order of this experiment the schedules of loss were not the same for decreased loss frequency deck A and increased loss frequency deck B. But the first loss was earlier in the modified deck A than in the modified deck B. This suggests that the number of unpunished selections before a loss in the disadvantageous decks may impact on participants' learning.

In conclusion, there was strong evidence that frequency of loss affects learning. Participants in the Increased Frequency condition were preferentially selecting from the advantageous decks by the end of the Experiment while those in the Decreased Frequency condition were not. There was evidence that participants avoid the disadvantageous deck with the more frequent losses. However, this result may have been confounded by the fixed order of losses within decks.

GENERAL DISCUSSION

We have found support in the results of the present Experiments to support the hypothesis that differential selection within the disadvantageous and advantageous decks drives learning on the Iowa Gambling Task. In Experiment 1 participants learned to select from the advantageous deck more slowly when their choice was between deck C and deck B. One possible reason for this was that participants found it easier to identify deck A as one of the worst decks because the frequency of loss was high, whereas in the advantageous decks deck C appeared better because when a frequent loss occurred it was often not a net loss.

In Experiment 2 we also tested the hypothesis that the frequency of loss was influences learning on the Iowa Gambling Task in two conditions. In the Decreased Frequency condition, the identification of deck A as a bad deck and deck C as a good deck was made more difficult by reducing the frequency of loss from .5 to .3, while leaving the other decks unchanged. In Increased Frequency condition, decks A and C were unaltered and the frequency of loss in decks B and D was increased from .1 to .3. Although there were no significant differences between overall learning rates, only learning rate in the Increased Frequency condition was significantly greater than zero, supporting the experimental hypothesis. In the Decreased Frequency condition there were no significant differences in selections from the bad decks suggesting that participants did not select preferentially from between these decks, whereas they did in the Increased Frequency condition. This non-differential selection also appeared to affect participants selection in the Decreased Frequency condition in the few blocks where selection from the disadvantageous decks increased, implying that these participants, on average, had not learned that decks A and B were disadvantageous. However, another possibility is that they had learned that losses were infrequent and thought they could exploit it.

That the frequency of punishment influences deck selection, at least in the disadvantageous decks was further illustrated when selection from decks with the same frequency of loss in the different conditions were compared. There was a clear decrease in selection from deck B, but little change across blocks for deck A (until the last two blocks). The key difference between the decks was that deck B in the Increased Frequency condition had the lower frequency of loss relative to the other disadvantageous deck, whereas deck A in the Increased Frequency condition had a higher frequency of loss. A similar comparison within the altered advantageous decks did not find any differences suggesting that the manipulations to these decks made it more likely that participants would not distinguish between these decks, but gradually increase selections from them.

The issue of what exactly participants are responding to on the Iowa Gambling Task is an important one. As Yechiam et al. (2005) found, differential selection may offer insights into what is affecting selection behaviour on the IGT. Recently, Bechara Tranel and Damasio (2000) have described a modification of the task (the A'B'C'D' version) where the frequency of loss and the magnitude of losses and gains is altered in successive blocks of ten choices from each deck. The manipulations make the differences in expected value between the disadvantageous and advantageous decks greater. In deck A' the frequency of loss is increased 10%, but the magnitude of loss remains the same. In deck B' it is the magnitude of loss that increases every ten cards while the frequency of loss is unchanged. The same pattern is followed in decks C' and D' except that the frequency of loss is reduced in deck C' and the magnitude of loss is reduced in deck D' (Bechara et al, 2000). These changes would appear to make the task easier in that differentiation between what the worst decks are should be clearer. This is certainly so for deck A' where frequency of loss increases. However, patients with VMpfc damage still perform below the level of healthy controls who, if anything, asymptote at a lower level of advantageous deck selections compared to the original task. Performance was analysed using the standard net score measure and no mention was made of any differential selection within the advantageous and disadvantageous decks. However, given the results of Experiments 1 and 2, closer examination of individual deck selection will reveal more information about what is influencing selection.

Yechiam et al. (2005) found that high-level drug abusers showed differential deck selection behaviour. Bechara and Damasio (2002) have reported that both their substance abusing participants and healthy controls could be split depending on their performance on the A'B'C'D' task. However, they do not report any individual deck selection patterns and the possibility has not been ruled out that differences exist between the groups on these measures. Bechara et al. (2000) also created a similar, but more complex, manipulation to their variant EFGH task, in that as well as gains being altered (equivalent to the A'B'C'D' task changes), gains were also increased or decreased in the advantageous and disadvantageous decks respectively. Performance on this task allowed Bechara, Dolan and Hindes (2002) to further divide their substance abusing population into those who were not impaired on either task, a subgroup who were impaired on this task and on A'B'C'D', and those who were normal on E'F'G'H' but had large physiological responses to reward. They concluded that some substance abusers were hypersensitive to reward while others were myopic for future consequences. However, if there was differential selection behaviour between decks then these conclusions may be extended and even supported. For example increased selection from deck B' over deck A', coupled with preference for G' over E' would support a conclusion of hypersensitivity to reward, whereas no differences in A' and B' selection and E' and G' selection would support their conclusion that these participants are myopic for the future.

As mentioned in the introduction, one of the problems with manipulations of the contingencies on the IGT is that gains, loss frequencies and magnitudes and expected values are all confounded with each other. This interdependency of reinforcement magnitude, reinforcement frequency and expected value makes identifying the differential effects of each difficult. Peters and Slovic (2000) successfully removed the confound that the largest magnitudes of reinforcement were in the disadvantageous decks, but their manipulation affected loss frequencies across the decks. In support of an explanation of the importance of the frequency of loss selection was highest from the deck with the lowest losses. They also found individual differences in performance in that selection of decks with high gains correlated with extraversion whereas selection of decks with low losses correlated with high scores on the BIS scale (Gray, 1970). And as neither of their measures correlated with selection from the decks with the highest expected values the suggestion is that this is not the most important factor in determining deck selection. However, the participants who completed the task in this study were the forty with the most extreme scores on the each measure (less than half the total who completed the initial questionnaires, meaning that these participants were a somewhat unrepresentative sample of the normal population even if their performance suggests individual differences are important.

One of the reasons that deck B might be "preferred" so much more than deck A is that with the schedules of reinforcement in the original study, selection from deck B goes unpunished for eight consecutive card selections, whereas the first loss in deck A occurs on the third selection. The same pattern is true in the advantageous decks although the first net loss on deck C occurs later than in deck A. Thus, participants may develop a justifiable preference for the disadvantageous deck with the infrequent loss that is more difficult to overcome because of the unlikelihood of a loss from this deck, although when it comes it is massive. The order of losses in this deck has gone at least some way to explaining the performance of VMpfc patients. Fellows and Farah (2005) found patient performance as measured by net score was no different from controls when the order of losses was altered so that the first loss in deck B occurred earlier. The frequency of loss may contribute to preference for this deck but the schedule of losses is also important. The use of fixed reinforcement schedules has been criticised by Dunn et al. (2006) in their recent review of the clinical use of the IGT. An implication of the order in which participants encounter losses is that the disadvantageous decks are actually the best decks up until the point the accumulated losses are greater than the accumulated gains (Maia and McClelland, 2004). Seen in this way selection from the deck with the infrequent loss is reasonable if the first loss occurs relatively late in that deck. If this were the case then it would also account for the differential selection between decks A and C.

CONCLUSION

This chapter has reviewed some of the studies using the IGT in which differential selection within decks with the same expected value has been reported. These studies suggested that choice on the IGT is not governed solely by an inevital progress towards uniform selection of the decks with a long-term gain. Indeed, the experiments reported in this chapter add empirical evidence to the increasing number of studies observing that the immediate consequences of selection may be more important than has generally been assumed. This is much more apparent for the disadvantageous decks where the difference in the relative frequency of loss appears to determine which is preferred and which is avoided. The number of unpunished selections from the deck would also appear to be a critical factor in determining the number of repeated selections from these decks.

Differences in the immediate outcomes of advantageous deck selections do not appear to create as stark a disparity as in the disadvantageous decks. We have suggested that deck C is perhaps the more important deck in influencing learning. This may be because it takes participants longer to learn that the more frequent losses in this deck do not actually punish them in the longer term. Whereas losses in deck D are so infrequent (and relatively smaller than deck B) that above chance selection does not need to change to gain in the long-term. There may also be a role for individual differences in the relative contibution that loss frequency, loss magnitude, gain magnitude or expected value to individual deck preference and therefore learning on this task. The focus in this chapter has been on the frequency of loss but given the structure of this task it is impossible to alter one component of a deck without a commensurate change in another to maintain a balance. Where the confounds have been removed (Peters and Slovic, 2000) participants have exercised preferrence for the deck with the lowest frequency of loss and the dependent highest expected value, and individual differences in affective processing were found to impact on choices. Despite it's flaws the IGT has become a widely-used test of decision-making. It has drawn attention from many linked but previously disparate fields where the focus has been on the underlying neuropsychology of IGT performance. However, a basic understanding of how participants actually decide on the task has been left behind. This chapter has been an attempt to contribute to this fundamental area.

REFERENCES

Ainslie, G. (1975) Specious reward: a behavioural theory of impulsiveness and impulse control, *Psychological Bulletin*, 82, 463-496.

Barron, G. and Erev, I. (2003). Small feedback-based decisions and their limited correspondence to description-based decisions. *Journal of Behavioural Decision Making*, 16 (3), 215-233.

Bechara, A., Damasio, A., Damasio, H., Anderson, S., (1994). Insensitivity to future consequences following damage to human prefrontal cortex. *Cognition*, 50, 7–15.

Bechara, A., Tranel, D., Damasio, H., Damasio, A.R., 1996. Failure respond autonomically to anticipated future outcomes following damage to prefrontal cortex. Cerebral Cortex 6 (2), 215–225.

Bechara, A., Damasio, H., Tranel, D., & Damasio, A. R. (1997). Deciding advantageously before knowing the advantageous strategy. *Science, 275*(5304), 1293–1295.

Bechara, A., Damasio, H., Damasio, A.R., Lee, G.P., (1999). Different contributions of the human amygdala and the ventromedial prefrontal cortex to decision-making. *Journal of Neuroscience*, 19 (13), 5473– 5481.

Bechara, A., Tranel, D., & Damasio, H. (2000). Characterization of the decision-making deficit of patients with ventromedial prefrontal cortex lesions. *Brain, 123*, 2189-2202.

Bechara, A., Dolan, S., Denburg, N., Hindes, A., Anderson, S.W., Nathan, P.E. (2001). Decision-malting deficits, linked to a dysfunctional ventromedial prefrontal cortex, revealed in alcohol and stimulant abusers. *Neuropsychologia, 39,* 376-389.

Bechara, A., Damasio, H., 2002. Decision-making and addiction (part I): impaired activation of somatic states in substance dependent individuals when pondering decisions with negative future consequences. *Neuropsychologia* 40 (10), 1675–1689.

Bechara A, Dolan S, Hindes A (2002) Decision-making and addiction (part II): myopia for the future or hypersensitivity to reward? *Neuropsychologia* 40:1690–1705.

Bechara, A., Tranel, D., & Damasio, A.R. (2004a). Psychophysiological approaches to the study of decision-making. *International Journal of Psychophysiology*, 45, 53-53.

Bowman, C. H., Evans, C. E. Y., & Turnbull, O. H. (2005). Artifcial time constraints on the iowa gambling task: The eVects on behavioural performance and subjective experience. *Brain and Cognition, 57*, 21–25.

Crone, E.A., van der Molen, M.W., 2004. Developmental changes in real life decision making: performance on a gambling task previously shown to depend on the ventromedial prefrontal cortex. *Developmental Neuropsychology* 25 (3), 251–279.

Crone, E. A., Somsen, R. J. M., Van Beek, B., & Van der Molen, M. W. (2004). Heart rate and skin conductance analysis of antecedents and consequences of decision-making. *Psychophysiology, 41*, 531-540.

Crone, E. A., Bunge, S. A., Latenstein, H., & Van der Molen, M. W. (2005). Characterization of children's decision-making: sensitivity to punishment frequency, not task complexity. *Child Neuropsychology, 11,* 245-263.

Damasio, A.R., 1996. The somatic marker hypothesis and the possible functions of the prefrontal cortex. *Philosophical Transactions Royal Society of London (series B),* 351 (1346), 1413–1420.

Damasio AR, Tranel D, Damasio H (1991) Somatic markers and the guidance of behavior: theory and preliminary testing. In: Frontal lobe function and dysfunction (Levin HS, Eisenberg HM, Benton AL, eds), pp 217-229. New York: Oxford UP.

Dawson, M.E., Shell, A.M., & Filion, D.L. (1990). The electrodermal system. In J.T.Cacioppo & L.G. Tassinary (eds.), Principles of psychophysiology, pp. 295-324. Cambrige: Cambridge University Press.

Dunn, B.D., Dalgleish, T., & Lawrence, A.D. (2006). The somatic marker hypothesis: A critical evaluation. *Neuroscience & Biobehavioral Reviews*, 30, 239-271.

Fellows, L.K., & Farah, M.J. (2005). Different Underlying Impairments in Decision-making Following Ventromedial and Dorsolateral Frontal Lobe Damage in Humans. *Cerebral Cortex*, 15(1):58-63.

Fernie, G., & Tunney, R. J. (2006). Some decks are better than others: The effect of reinforcer type and task instructions on learning in the Iowa Gambling Task. *Brain and Cognition, 60,* 94-102.

Fischer, A.R.H., Blommaert, F.J.J., Midden, C.J.H. (2005). Combining experimental observations and modelling in investigating feedback and emotions in repeated selections. *User Modeling and User-Adapted Interaction*, 15-5, 389-424.

Grant,S., Contoreggi,C.,& London,E. D. (2000). Drug abusers show impaired performance in a laboratory test of decision-making. *Neuropsychologica*, 38(8),1180–1187.

Gray, J. A. (1970). The psychophysiological basis of introversion-extraversion. *Behaviour Research & Therapy*, Vol. 8(3), 249-266.

Lin, C.H., Chiu, Y.C., Lee, P.L. & Hsieh, J.C. (2007). Is deck B a disadvantageous deck in the Iowa Gambling Task? *Behavioral and Brain Functions*, 3, 1-10.

Lorch, R.F., Jr., & Myers, J.L. (1990). Regression analyses of repeated measures data in cognitive research: A comparison of three different methods. *Journal of Experimental Psychology: Learning, Memory, and Cognition, 16*, 149-157.

MacPherson, S. E., Phillips, L. H., & Della Sala, S. (2002). Age, executive function, and social decision making: A dorsolateral prefrontal theory of cognitive aging. *Psychology and Aging, 17*(4), 598–609.

Maia, T.V., & McLelland, J.L. (2004). A reexamination of the evidence for the somatic marker hypothesis: What participants really know in the iowa gambling task, *Proceedings of the National Academy of Sciences of the United States of America* 101 (2004) (45), pp. 16075–16080.

Mintzer, M.L. & Stitzer, M.L., (2002). Cognitive impairment in methadone maintenance patients. *Drug and Alcohol Dependency*, 67(1), 41-51.

O'Carroll, R.E., Papps, B.P., 2003. Decision making in humans: the effect of manipulating the central noradrenergic system. *Journal of Neurology*, Neurosurgery and Psychiatry 74, 376–378.

Overman, W. (2004). Sex differences in early childhood, adolescence, and adulthood on cognitive tasks that rely on orbital prefrontal cortex. *Brain & Cognition, 55,* 134-147.

Peters, E., & Slovic, P. (2000). The springs of action: Affective and analytical information processing in choice. *Personality and Social Psychology Bulletin*, 26, 1465-1475.

Reavis, R., Overman, W.H. (2001). Adult sex differences on a decision-making task previously shown to depend on the orbital prefrontal cortex. Behavioural Neuroscience 115 (1), 196–206.

Shanks, D. R., Tunney, R. J., & McCarthy, J. (2002). A Re-examination of Probability Matching and Rational Choice. *Journal of Behavioral Decision Making, 15*, 233-250.

Somsen, van der Molen, & Orlebeke, 2004.

Thorndike, E. L. (1898). *Animal Intelligence: An Experimental Study of the Associative Processes in Animals* (Psychological Review, Monograph Supplements, No. 8). New York: Macmillan.

Tomb, I., Hauser, M., Deldin, P., Caramazza, A., 2002. Do somatic markers mediate decisions on the gambling task? Nature *Neuroscience*, 5 (11), 1103–1104 (author reply 1104).

Tunney, R. J., & Shanks, D. R. (2002). A Re-examination of Melioration and Rational Choice. *Journal of Behavioral Decision Making, 15,* 291-311.

Wilder, K. E., Weinberger, D. R., & Goldberg, T. E. (1998). Operant conditioning and the orbitofrontal cortex in schizophrenic patients: Unexpected evidence for intact functioning. *Schizophrenia Research, 30*(2), 169–174.

Yechiam, E., Busemeyer, J.R., Stout, J.C., & Bechara, A. (2005). Using Cognitive Models to Map Relations Between Neuropsychological Disorders and Human Decision-Making Deficits. *Psychological Science*, 16 (12), 973–978.

In: Psychology of Decision Making...
Editor: G. R. Burthold, pp. 101-122

ISBN: 978-1-60021-932-0
© 2007 Nova Science Publishers, Inc.

Chapter 3

DEATH QUALIFICATION AND JURY DECISION MAKING IN CAPITAL TRIALS FROM A SOCIAL DOMINANCE ORIENTATION PERSPECTIVE

Christine Marie Shea Adams

University of Wyoming, Department of Psychology

ABSTRACT

Previous research has shown that jurors who are legally considered death qualified (DQ) significantly differ from those considered non-death qualified (NDQ). For example, it has been found that DQ and NDQ jurors differ in punitiveness (including use of evidence and deliberation, conviction-proneness, and sentencing), as well as gender and race. The purpose of this paper is to address the strengths and weaknesses of using social dominance theory to account for these differences. In addition, I suggest other theories, as well as combinations of theories, which may be more appropriate to help researchers understand the differences between DQ and NDQ jurors and in turn how these differences affect jury decision making. Possible areas for future research are also discussed.

DEATH QUALIFICATION FROM A SOCIAL DOMINANCE ORIENTATION PERSPECTIVE

The number of people put on death row in the U.S. and the number of completed executions has increased steadily over the last 30 years (Ogloff & Chopra, 2004). The voting public is seemingly adamant about their support for the death penalty (Sandys & McGarrell, 1995; Steiner, Bowers, & Sarat, 1999). In fact, as of 2000, 63% of adults in the United States supported the death penalty for criminals convicted of first degree murder (Bureau of Justice Statistics, 2002). However, some potential jurors are more willing than others to consider this "ultimate punishment." These jurors, who are legally considered death qualified (DQ;

Lockhart v. McCree, 1986), may not approach a trial with the same amount of legal neutrality as non-death qualified (NDQ) jurors. Therefore, while DQ jurors may not be statistically biased (they do represent the majority of the population), they may be more legally biased than is realized. Differences that have been found between DQ and NDQ jurors include differences in punitiveness (including use of evidence and deliberation, conviction-proneness, and sentencing), and differences between the gender and race of jurors. I will discuss these differences in detail, and I will attempt to explain these differences using social dominance theory.

The purpose of a criminal trial is for jurors to determine what happened in a specific situation while giving the defendant due process. Ideally this process results in the discerning of truth. Jurors in every type of criminal trial are expected to be neutral in their pretrial opinions and to equally consider all evidence presented to them. However, as explained in *Furman v. Georgia* (1972) and again in *Coker v. Georgia* (1977) "death is different" (Haney & Wiener, 2004, p. 374). Unlike other criminal trials, the life of the defendant is legally in the hands of the jury (*Ring v. Arizona,* 2002). Once found guilty, jurors in capital trials must decide between the life and death of a human being, and thus, extra steps must be taken to protect the defendant (Gross, 1996). Specifically, according to *Ring v. Arizona* juries must decide if there is at least one piece of aggravating evidence. Once it is agreed that this evidence exists the defendant can potentially be sentenced to death.

Although due process is always necessary, the maximum measure of due process is essential in capital trials (Nakell & Hardy, 1987). For instance, in *Gregg v. Georgia* (1976) it was established that the discretion that juries express must necessarily be limited in capital trials. This decision was an attempt to cease the prior arbitrary enforcement of the death penalty. Subsequent to this decision, extra steps were added to the jury selection process in an effort to select jurors who were likely to follow the law as it is stated and to willingly follow the oath that they take when chosen. One of the procedures developed to increase the level of due process was death qualification. This step accompanies the standard voir dire process with the goal of finding jurors who will be fair and law-abiding in their decision making. However, research over the last 40 years has produced some cause for concern as to whether DQ jurors are truly following the law as they claim they are willing and able to do. There is evidence that the Constitutional guarantee of due process is not being met as a result of the differences between DQ and NDQ jurors (e.g., differences in how evidence is considered).

To this end, many of the individual differences between DQ and NDQ jurors may be explained with social dominance theory (SDT). The main purpose of this paper is to look at the utility of using SDT to organize the research on death qualification. Specifically, I will discuss the strengths and weaknesses of using SDT to explain the research findings on individual differences and biases associated with willingness to grant the death penalty (i.e., being DQ) in comparison to those considered NDQ. I will first discuss what it means to be DQ and then give a thorough description of SDT. Next, I will describe the differences between DQ and NDQ jurors and demonstrate how some of these findings are consistent with the predictions of SDT. Throughout the paper I will address the strengths and weaknesses of using SDT to account for these differences and will suggest other theories, as well as combinations of theories, which may be more appropriate.

DEFINING THE ISSUES

Death Qualification

The Sixth Amendment of the United States Constitution guarantees a speedy and public trial whereby the defendant is judged by a jury of his or her peers that are representative of the community (Cowan, Thompson, & Ellsworth, 1984). Jurors chosen for capital trials should be willing to abide by the law exactly as it is written, and while this is not unique, capital trials do present a distinct dilemma: the decision of whether or not to take a life. In fact, while the idea of juries making sentencing decisions is not completely extinct (e.g., Virginia and Texas), juries making such decisions in non-capital trials are almost unheard of today (Butler & Moran, 2002). Thus, jurors must be willing to apply the law as stated regarding the decision of guilt, as well as regarding the decision between life and death. This means that each juror must be willing to impartially follow the law (*Wainwright v. Witt,* 1985), which in turn means that they must be willing to sentence the defendant to death. In the 1976 case of *Gregg v. Georgia,* the Supreme Court decided that a defendant can be sentenced to death if at least one aggravating circumstance (facts that increase a defendant's liability for a crime) exists. While there need not be any mitigating circumstances (facts that decrease a defendant's liability for a crime) the defendant can be sentenced to life in prison if the jury feels that there are enough mitigating circumstances to justify such a decision (*Gregg v. Georgia,* 1976). Though the Court intended this decision to assist jurors in applying the law in a consistent and fair manner, I will discuss research which shows this is not always the case.

Although jurors may be willing to decide the guilt phase of a trial without opposition to the law, some potential jurors are excludable because they are unwilling to give the death penalty even when the law suggests that it is an acceptable punishment (Byrne, 1986; Rozelle, 2002). In even rarer situations, jurors may be so in favor of the death penalty for first-degree murder that they are unwilling to consider any other penalty as an alternative (Kadane, 1984) and are thus considered automatic death penalty (ADP) jurors (*Morgan v. Illinois,* 1992). These jurors must also be excluded from capital trials. However, it should be noted that in the current article, NDQ is meant to be in reference to jurors who are unwilling to impose the death penalty.

Because of the uniqueness of capital trials, jurors are asked additional questions during voir dire. These questions are meant to ensure that jurors are fair and yet willing to follow the law specific to the death penalty. However, research suggests that DQ and NDQ jurors may be different in many important ways. For instance, DQ jurors are more conviction-prone than NDQ jurors (e.g., Allen, Mabry, & McKelton, 1998; Butler & Moran, 2002), and are likely to use evidence (e.g., Thompson, Cowan, Ellsworth, & Harrington, 1984) and deliberation differently (Cowan et al., 1984). In addition, available data suggest that race and gender differences exist between the two types of jurors (e.g., Filkins, Smith, & Tindale, 1998).

Social dominance theory may provide a theoretical framework by which to examine the research that has been conducted on the differences between DQ and NDQ jurors. SDT predicts that individuals who strongly support hierarchical group differences will support group inequality (Pratto, Stallworth, & Conway-Lanz, 1998). These differences in support of social hierarchies (differences in social dominance orientation) may account for differences between DQ and NDQ jurors. Before moving to a review of the empirical differences between DQ and NDQ jurors and how SDT may explain these differences, I will discuss the basic premises of the theory.

Social Dominance Theory

Theory Overview

SDT was developed in an attempt to integrate research on personality, observable behaviors, and social structure (Sidanius & Pratto, 1999). This theory attempts to explain why people categorize one another into hierarchical groups (Sidanius & Pratto, 1999). Three primary assumptions are the basis of SDT. The first assumption is that individuals are separated by hierarchical categorizations. There are three main categories of hierarchies, two of which are universal. In general, elders have more power than their younger counterparts and men have more power than women (Sidanius & Pratto, 1999). However, because men and women have intimate relationships with one another that are necessary for reproduction, hostility is not beneficial (Levin, 2004). The third category on which hierarchies may be based is that of arbitrary-set group membership. It is often more difficult to determine membership in these groups with initial observations. Membership within these groups is arbitrarily decided by salient cultural characteristics such as ethnicity, religious sect, or regional grouping, to name a few (Sidanius & Pratto, 1999). Because these groups do not need one another for survival they require more oppression and violence to maintain an established hierarchy. Sidanius and Pratto point out that regardless of societal efforts to rid a culture of an arbitrary hierarchy by establishing programs to force equality (e.g., affirmative action), these arbitrary-set group hierarchies appear to recreate and maintain themselves. Sidanius and Pratto suggest that these hierarchies continue to exist because they are adaptive.

A second assumption of SDT is that most conflicts between groups (especially those which lead to the oppression of one group by another) occur as a means of creating and maintaining a group-based social hierarchy (Sidanius & Pratto, 1999). Prejudice and discrimination cannot be understood without understanding the use of hierarchies. In fact, prejudice against out-group members is often motivated by a drive for dominance (Altemeyer, 2004; Wilson, 2003).

The third and final assumption of this theory is that these social hierarchies are subject to the effects of hierarchy-enhancing and hierarchy-attenuating forces. Hierarchy-enhancing forces serve to maintain the existent hierarchy, and hierarchy-attenuating forces serve to balance the equality of different social groups (Sidanius & Pratto, 1999). Both forces work simultaneously against one another, and are a way of maintaining the conflict between different groups of individuals. One hierarchy-enhancing force is the degree to which an individual is likely to believe in and support a nonegalitarian and hierarchical system. This support is expressed in what theorists have termed "social dominance orientation" (SDO).

Social Dominance Orientation

SDO is a psychological characteristic related to the degree to which an individual supports a group-based hierarchy that leads to the domination of an "inferior" group by a "superior" group (Pratto, Sidanius, Stallworth, & Malle, 1994; Pratto et al., 1998; Sidanius &

Pratto, 1999). Generally speaking, individuals who are high in SDO tend to support group inequality and thus support a structured hierarchy (Pratto et al., 1998). In addition, groups as a whole may display higher levels of SDO than other groups due to group membership (Guimond, Dambrun, Michinov, & Durate, 2003). This hierarchical support may be reflected in prejudicial beliefs and discriminatory behavior. For example, Pratto et al. (1994) found a strong positive correlation between SDO and attitudes related to military support, racism, patriotism, nationalism, chauvinism, cultural elitism, sexism, and political conservatism. In addition, Pratto and her colleagues found a negative correlation between level of SDO and altruism, communality, and tolerance. Thus, the higher one's level of SDO, the more likely he or she is to support ideologies that maintain or increase inequalities between groups (Pratto et al., 1994; Pratto et al., 1998).

Research has generally shown that members of dominant groups exhibit higher levels of SDO than do lower-status group members (Levin, 2004). However, it is important to note that an individual does not necessarily have to be a member of the dominant group to support the hierarchical system (Altemeyer, 2004; Pratto et al., 1994). Instead, when a distinction between groups is believed to be legitimate, both in- and out-group members are likely to favor the high-status group. Conversely, when the distinction is not seen as legitimate it is likely that only the in-group members will favor the high-status group (Levin, Fedrico, Sidanius, & Rabinowitz, 2002). This occurs because low-status group members are unlikely to see the justification of the group distinction and will thus support their own group. Accordingly, ideologies about group equality will influence one's attitudes toward societal policies such as welfare and the death penalty, and in general, those high in SDO will tend to prefer a system of policies that benefits them regardless of the effect these policies have on others (Altemeyer, 2004).

In summary, according to Sidanius and Pratto (1999) SDT is comprised of three assumptions, 1) individuals are separated by hierarchical categories (age, gender, and arbitrary-set groups), 2) group conflicts occur as a way to maintain pre-existing hierarchies, and 3) hierarchies are affected by hierarchy-enhancing and hierarchy-attenuating forces. These three assumptions manifest themselves as variation in individual SDO, which is a hierarchy-enhancing force. Differences in SDO may help to explain differences that have been empirically found between DQ and NDQ jurors. I will now discuss these individual differences including conviction-proneness, use of evidence and deliberation, and race and gender differences between jurors, devoting particular attention to the explanatory value that SDT may contribute to these findings.

DIFFERENCES BETWEEN DEATH QUALIFIED AND NON-DEATH QUALIFIED JURORS

Conviction Proneness

In most criminal trials juries that are purposely mixed in their opinions toward a variety of legal issues decide the fate of defendants. In fact, the Supreme Court consistently maintains the importance of jury representativeness (see *Duren v. Missouri,* 1979). However, in capital trials jurors are deliberately selected to have the same opinion towards one important issue:

they all must be willing to impose the death penalty (Cowan et al., 1984). It has been found that aside from the process of death qualification making jurors more likely to convict the defendant (as opposed to jurors not exposed to DQ questions; Haney, 1984a, 1984b), DQ jurors are more conviction-prone than are excludable jurors (e.g., Allen et al., 1998; Harris, 1971[1]; Jurow, 1971) regardless of the type of case (capital vs. non-capital) being decided. For example, research shows that DQ jurors are more likely to convict a defendant prior to deliberation, and perceive evidence in a more prosecution-favorable manner than their NDQ counterparts (Cowan et al., 1984; Thompson et al., 1984).

Researchers have also proposed that excludable jurors hold different legal values than DQ jurors (Abramson, 2001; Butler & Moran, 2002; Dillehay & Sandys, 1996; Ellsworth, 1993; Fitzgerald & Ellsworth, 1984; Horowitz & Seguin, 1986; Robinson, 1993; Thompson, 1989; Thompson et al., 1984). Ellsworth (1993) argued that a juror's verdict can be predicted from his or her attitude toward the death penalty because this attitude is part of a group of attitudes related to the criminal justice system. These attitude groups closely parallel the legitimizing myth concept of SDT (Sidnius & Pratto, 1999). The legal values are themselves legitimizing myths. Specifically, crime control values will lead to myths meant to enhance the hierarchy whereas due process values will lead to attenuating myths. These attitudes, or legal values, have been examined in terms of which values are more greatly linked to death qualification in jurors.

Fitzgerald and Ellsworth (1984), as well as Thompson et al. (1984), compared individuals with due process values (i.e., those concerned with individual rights and procedural guarantees) to those with crime control values (i.e., those who believe that the most important aspect of the criminal justice system is to repress crime). They found that whereas excludable jurors were significantly more likely to believe that it would be worse to convict an innocent person than to let a guilty person go free, DQ jurors were prone to view leniency errors as more problematic. These beliefs, Thompson and his colleagues suggested, come from a group of attitudes and beliefs toward crime and the criminal justice system that renders interpretation of a wide array of criminal trials simpler for individual jurors. Because high SDO jurors are likely to have hierarchy-enhancing values, they are prone to behave in such a way as to maintain the established hierarchy between the relevant arbitrary-set groups (e.g., defendant and jurors; Quist & Resendez, 2002; Sidanius & Pratto, 1999).

Belief in either hierarchy-enhancing or hierarchy-attenuating myths may also explain why jurors with opposing values may react differently to verdict mistakes. Although it is possible that DQ jurors felt some remorse for their harsh errors (convicting an innocent person by mistake), it is likely that they believed this was the price society must pay to maintain order (Thompson et al., 1984). Because SDO strongly predicts prejudicial beliefs (Altemeyer, 1998; Levin, 2004; Sidanius & Pratto, 1999; Whitley, 1999), which lead to discriminatory behaviors (Capps, 2002; Pratto et al., 1998) such as assuming the guilt of a defendant, jurors with opposing values (hierarchy-attenuating/due process vs. hierarchy-enhancing/crime control) are likely to react differently to mistakes. For instance, Pratto et al. (1994) found that SDO was negatively related to empathy, suggesting that those high in SDO (e.g., DQ jurors) would be less remorseful of mistakes in comparison to those low in SDO (e.g., NDQ jurors).

---

[1] Harris (1971) was never published but is discussed extensively in Fitzgerald and Ellsworth (1984) as well as Cowan et al. (1984).

Overall, excludable jurors are less likely to automatically see criminal intent in a defendant's actions (Goodman-Delahunty, Greene, & Hsiao, 1998) and are less punitive (Fitzgerald & Ellsworth, 1984; Haney, Hurtado, & Vega, 1994) than are DQ jurors. In fact, Fitzgerald and Ellsworth (1984) found that 40% of the excludable jurors in their study believed that even the most heinous criminal should be shown some mercy, whereas 60% of the includable jurors felt that no pity should be displayed toward defendants. It is possible then that the death qualification process inadvertently eliminates advocates of due process, or those who are likely to consider all of the evidence. In essence, the defense may be placed at a disadvantage before the trial's outset.

Right-wing Authoritarianism: A Supplemental Explanation

Right-wing authoritarianism (RWA) may be a useful supplement to SDO in explaining the punitiveness of DQ jurors. As opposed to those high in SDO, individuals high in RWA typically endorse submission to authority without necessarily desiring to be the authority themselves (Altemeyer, 1981, 1988, 1998, 2004), whereas those high in SDO exhibit a drive to dominate (Altemeyer, 2004).

Altemeyer (2004) explains that the similarities between SDO and RWA (e.g., racism, sexism, ethnocentrism) lead individuals high in either or both of these characteristics to be supportive of right-wing political ideals. One may infer that those high in either or both of these attitudes will have the most extreme legal values and will be the most conviction-prone and supportive of the death penalty. It can then be deduced that those who are high in both of these personality characteristics are likely to be overrepresented on death penalty juries due to DQ selection procedures.

Altemeyer (2004) found that these double-high individuals tend to be the most prejudicial group in comparison to any other group (i.e., those high in only one of these traits or low in both traits). Altemeyer went on to explain that double-highs are similar to those who are only high in SDO because not only do they support the idea of a hierarchy, but they also want to be a part of the dominant group. Therefore, although SDO is a strong predictor of punitiveness at the individual level (Altemeyer, 1998) other predictors cannot be ignored (Capps, 2002). Altemeyer (2004) demonstrated that prejudice expressed by those high in SDO is not often due to pragmatic objections as others might assume, but is instead based on preferences for social systems that are beneficial, and that persons high in both SDO and RWA are the most likely to act in a manner that maintains this personally beneficial hierarchy.

Evidence and Deliberation

Differences in Evidence Usage

Thompson et al. (1984) found that DQ jurors interpreted evidence in a more conviction-prone manner than did NDQ jurors. DQ jurors had a lower evidence threshold when determining defendant guilt. Excludable jurors, on the other hand, interpreted evidence in a manner that was more supportive of innocence, or supportive of a lesser, non death-eligible charge. Thompson and his colleagues found that overall DQ jurors gave significantly more weight to pro-prosecution evidence than they did to pro-defense evidence.

Luginbuhl and Middendorf (1988) similarly found that DQ jurors favored aggravating evidence whereas excludable jurors favored mitigating evidence. Jurors in this study were asked a series of questions regarding how much aggravating and mitigating evidence was presented in a trial and whether or not there was enough aggravating evidence to justify the death penalty. Although jurors did not differ in how they perceived the aggravating evidence, they did differ in their perception of the mitigating evidence: the more opposed a juror was to the death penalty, the more likely he or she was to consider mitigating circumstances when making his or her final verdict decision.

More recently Butler and Moran (2002) examined how jurors perceived aggravating factors along with statutory mitigating (e.g., pain from mental/emotional disturbance, person was an accomplice to the crime, no prior criminal history) and non-statutory mitigating (e.g., alcohol or drug use, being a victim of child abuse, prior military service) factors. Although non-statutory mitigating circumstances do not necessarily make an offence excusable, they may reduce the culpability and hence the punishment for a crime. The use of this type of evidence is at the discretion of the jury. However, statutory mitigating factors are circumstances that the jurors are legally required to consider when making their decisions. In general, Butler and Moran found that DQ jurors showed greater acceptance of aggravating evidence, whereas NDQ jurors showed greater acceptance of mitigating circumstances. More precisely, the authors found that all jurors in the study (regardless of DQ status) gave the defendant a break because of statutory mitigators, but only NDQ jurors were willing to consider circumstances that were not statutorily required of them. Instead, DQ jurors saw non-statutory mitigating factors as issues that the defendant should have been able to control.

As previously mentioned by Thompson et al. (1984), findings such as these indicate that one's attitude toward the death penalty may affect how he or she interprets and perceives evidence, and this can lead DQ jurors to be more conviction-prone than NDQ jurors. Thus, when a juror is strongly in favor of conviction and the death penalty, it may be more difficult for them to be merciful for mitigating reasons because the aggravating evidence cannot be overridden. In addition, trial evidence may be used by jurors as verification of prejudicial beliefs that they had prior to the trial. For example, jurors who have crime control values are more likely to be DQ than jurors with due process values (Fitzgerald & Ellsworth, 1984). In addition, jurors who are high in SDO and thus are likely to believe hierarchy-enhancing myths (as opposed to those who are lower in SDO who have more hierarchy-attenuating beliefs; Sidanius & Pratto, 1999) are also more likely to have crime control values than those jurors who are lower in SDO. Therefore, these potential jurors (who are automatically the dominant group because they have power over the defendant) will likely need further persuasive evidence to convince them that the subordinate group member (i.e., the defendant, who is automatically the subordinate simply because he or she is the defendant) does not match the prejudicial beliefs they have about that group (e.g., "If he was arrested, he must be guilty").

SDT suggests that prejudicial beliefs legitimize and maintain a pre-existing social hierarchy (Sidanius, 1993). Quist and Resendez (2002) found that in order to maintain the existing social hierarchy individuals high in SDO are more likely to have stereotypic beliefs and legitimizing attitudes than individuals low in SDO. To maintain this hierarchy, use of stereotypes and belief in legitimizing myths may lead individuals of the dominant group (e.g., those that are likely to be selected as DQ jurors) to oppress members of the subordinate group (e.g., those that are likely to be capital trial defendants) by acting in discriminatory ways (e.g.

finding them guilty and sentencing them to death without considering all of the evidence). It follows then that individuals high in SDO (which DQ jurors are likely to be) will need stronger evidence to change their opinions of subordinate group members.

Differences in Deliberation

Cowan et al. (1984) believed that while deliberation is an important aspect of the trial process, certain issues may never be discussed if NDQ individuals are not given the opportunity to serve on a jury. Hoffman, Burke, and Maier (1965) found that groups composed of individuals with differing abilities, personalities, and experiences participated more in a group activity and produced a better quality product. The presence of varying perspectives may affect how issues are perceived and how evidence is interpreted, leading mixed juries (those with both DQ and NDQ jurors) to consider more information (Clark, Anand, & Roberson, 2000), which will lead them to make a better quality decision (Hoffman et al., 1965) than homogeneous juries.

Cowan et al. (1984) predicted that mixed juries would display more critical views of the evidence in their deliberation and perhaps demonstrate a better memory of the facts and instructions given to them than homogeneous juries. They found that not only were excludable jurors more likely than DQ jurors to find the defendant not guilty prior to deliberation, but they were also more likely to keep their opinions of innocence long enough to express them to the entire jury during deliberation, which helped them contribute more to the final jury decision. In addition, NDQ jurors had greater criticism of witness testimony. Thus, mixed juries were more critical of the evidence than juries composed of only DQ jurors. Therefore, the unquestioning acceptance of guilt or the credibility of witness testimony was not as likely to survive in mixed juries. By including normally excludable jurors who may have different pre-trial beliefs and values (crime control v. due process) about the defendant because they are lower in SDO, juries may be more balanced and better able to consider all of the evidence presented as well as produce more critical arguments that do not necessarily legitimize already existing prejudicial beliefs (Cowan et al., 1984).

Race and Gender Differences

Who will be Chosen for Jury Duty

While the Supreme Court recognizes racial minorities (*Hernandez v. Texas,* 1954; *Batson v. Kentucky,* 1986) and women (*Ballard v. United States,* 1946; *J.E.B. v. Alabama,* 1994) as distinct groups that should not be explicitly excluded from jury duty, the 1986 Supreme Court decision of *Lockhart v. McCree*, made it clear that the court did not feel similarly about NDQ jurors. The Supreme Court felt that there were "serious flaws in the evidence upon which the courts below had concluded that 'death-qualification' produces 'conviction-prone' juries" (p. 1764). Therefore, it was decided that the removal of these individuals from the venire does not violate a defendant's Sixth Amendment right to be judged by a fair cross-section of the community. The Court felt that those being removed are not a distinct group and are thus not protected by the law. Research has demonstrated that racial minorities and women are more likely to have negative views toward the death penalty than White males (Abramson, 2001; Cowan et al., 1984; Fitzgerald & Ellsworth, 1984; Haney et al., 1994; Moran & Comfort,

1986; Mauro, 1992) and are thus more likely to be found NDQ. This brings into question whether or not the exclusion of these jurors is an indirect violation of the previously-stated laws forbidding the exclusion of minorities and women for no other reason than race and/or gender.

Filkins et al. (1998) conducted a meta-analysis to examine individual differences (e.g. gender and race) between DQ and excludable jurors. They found that minorities, especially Blacks, and women were excluded from jury duty because of their attitudes toward the death penalty significantly more often than their dominant peers (i.e., Whites and males; see also Fukurai, Butler, & Krooth, 1991). Filkins and his colleagues demonstrated that although it is statistically unlikely for an all-male jury to be chosen, a defendant may face an all-White jury in some regions. Essentially, those jurors who are likely to be the most similar to the defendant (i.e., members of a subordinate group) have the best chance of being excluded from the venire (Fitzgerald & Ellsworth, 1984).

According to SDT, the law of increasing disproportionality states that the more authority a specific group maintains (e.g., White men), the more likely it is that important and powerful positions (e.g., jurors) will be filled by these dominant group members rather than subordinate group members (i.e., Females or minorities; Sidanius & Pratto, 1999). Thus, because White men are seen as the dominant group in North American culture and are higher in SDO than women and minorities (Levin, 2004; Sidanius & Pratto, 1999; Wilson & Liu, 2003) it is conceivable that they will be more likely to support the death penalty than these other groups (e.g., Filkins et al., 1998) and in turn be chosen for jury duty more often than their counterparts.

Sidanius and Pratto (1999) also found that SDO is strongly correlated with various measures of racism including McConahay's (1986) Modern Racism Scale, as well as Katz and Hass's (1988) Pro-Black and Anti-Black scales (low SDO scores were positively related to Pro-Black scale scores and negatively related to Anti-Black scale scores whereas high SDO scores were negatively related to Pro-Black scores and positively related to Anti-Black scores). Therefore, differences in SDO between Black and White jurors, and thus why White jurors are more likely to be found DQ, may be explained by differences in their levels of racism.

Modern Racism Theories

Modern racism theories are based on the idea that contemporary racists do not see themselves as racist because they define racism in ways that are consistent with old-fashioned (i.e., pre-Civil Rights movement) thoughts and behaviors toward minorities (i.e., being explicit about racist feelings; McConahay, 1986). For instance, McConahay explains that those who are high in modern racism are likely to overtly pronounce discrimination and prejudice as wrong, and claim that minorities deserve the same rights as Whites. However, these same individuals are also likely to believe that many minorities are forcing their way into domains where they are not yet welcome and that this is unfair (McConahay, 1986).

Though not explicit, modern racism may play a role in the courtroom. For instance, some jurors believe that Blacks are more likely to commit certain crimes than are Whites (Sunnafrank & Fontes, 1983). More recently, Sommers and Ellsworth (2000) conducted a study in which the race of the victim and the defendant, as well as the salience of the defendant's race was manipulated. Defendant race was (or was not) made salient in the victim's testimony. The researchers found that White jurors were not affected by the race of the defendant (when race was salient), whereas Black jurors demonstrated in-group favoritism regardless of whether or not the defendant's race was purposely made salient.

Gaertner and Dovidio's (1986) theory of aversive racism can help to explain the behaviors of the White jurors in decision making situations similar to that in the Sommers and Ellsworth (2000) study. They posit that modern White individuals have shifted from overt racism to a more passive racism. White jurors in a situation such as those in the Sommers and Ellsworth study were culturally taught to not express any negative affect they may have towards Black individuals. Thus, when race is salient they are more likely to respond in a socially appropriate manner as opposed to when racial issues are more ambiguous (Gaertner & Dovidio, 1986). However, the behaviors of Black jurors are not as easy to explain with these theories. Gaertner and Dovidio do not address what may influence the behavior of Black individuals in similar situations. Sommers and Ellsworth (2000) speculate that because Blacks have been discriminated against throughout American history their in-group favoritism has become expected and justified.

Note that although modern racism theories may be useful is explaining why jurors respond differently to minority defendants depending on their own race, these theories do not necessarily explain why Black jurors are less likely to be DQ than White jurors. Instead, to explain both aspects of racism within the legal system (racial differences in DQ and NDQ jurors, as well as differences in attitudes towards Black and White defendants) it may be useful to draw on ideas from both modern racism theories and SDT.

Social Dominance Theory and Ideological Asymmetry

Researchers found that SDO is strongly related to biases in favor of the high-status group when the individual being examined is a member of that group, whereas the attitudes of low-status group members are not as closely linked to SDO (Mitchell & Sidanius, 1993; Sidnaius, 1993; Sidanius, Levin, Frederico, & Pratto, 2001; Sidanius & Pratto, 1993; 1999). Sidanius and Pratto (1999) refer to this as the ideological asymmetry hypothesis. The hypothesis states that the extent to which hierarchy-enhancing and hierarchy-attenuating policies drive personal values will differ depending on individual status such that dominant group members will be driven by social dominance values more so than subordinate group members (Sidanius & Pratto, 1999). An example of this can be seen in the results of the Mitchell and Sidanius (1993) study where they found that support for the death penalty was positively related to SDO among Whites (i.e., high-status groups) and negatively related to SDO among Blacks or Hispanics (i.e., low-status groups). The idea, according to social dominance theorists, is that high-status group members have more to gain from a group-based social hierarchy than do low-status group members (Levin, et al., 2002). Thus, preservation of anti-egalitarian attitudes with legitimizing beliefs occurs when it is in one's best interest to maintain the existing hierarchy.

Research has also shown that belief in the legitimacy of a hierarchy affects favoritism toward in- and out-group members, which may affect how potential jurors view defendants of different social groups. For instance, Levin et al. (2002) demonstrated that a legitimate distinction between high- and low-status groups leads individuals to favor the high-status group, whereas an illegitimate distinction will lead individuals to favor their own group. They found that high-status group membership (i.e., Whites) led to a positive relationship between SDO and in-group favoritism regardless of perceived legitimacy of the status hierarchy because the hierarchy favors their position. However, low-status group members (i.e., Blacks) only exhibited a positive relationship between SDO and favoritism for high-status group members when the hierarchy was perceived to be legitimate, because doing so otherwise would not be in the best interest of their own group. The social-reality of status distinctions allows high-status groups to seek distinctiveness via in-group bias. However, the low-status group is not given the same benefit. They are instead forced to favor the out-group when they are unable to argue against the status hierarchy. If there was a way for them to argue that the current hierarchy is illegitimate, however, their level of SDO would be unimportant to the situation.

Thus, in death penalty trials, it seems reasonable that minorities are less likely to be DQ because they are less likely to perceive the hierarchy differences between the defendant and jury as legitimate relative to White jurors. This may be especially true if the defendant is Black and the potential Black jurors feel that this defendant is an example of how society oppresses minorities with a racial hierarchy. In addition, since the majority of capital defendants are male, and female jurors are not likely to see the defendant as an in-group member, differences in SDO between men and women may still explain why women are less likely to be DQ.

Gender Differences in Social Dominance Orientation

In a series of cross-cultural (United States, Sweden, and Israel) studies, Sidanius and Pratto (1999) found that differences between males and females in regard to both hierarchy-enhancing and hierarchy-attenuating social attitudes can be attributed at least in part to gender differences in SDO. Males tend to have higher levels of SDO than females, and this difference is more stable than differences between arbitrary-set groups (e.g., between races; Sidanius & Pratto, 1999). In addition, these differences did not vary between cultures. Thus, differences in SDO between genders may help to explain why discrepancies exist between men's and women's attitudes about political policies such as war, welfare, and the death penalty (Ekehammar, 1985; Marjoribanks, 1981; Pratto, Stallworth, & Sidanius, 1997; Sidanius & Ekehammar, 1980).

Social attitude differences between the sexes include but are not limited to conservatism, punitiveness (including support for the death penalty), and racism, such that men support each of these attitudes more strongly than women. Moreover, Wilson (2003) found that men not only have lower levels of idealism (i.e., the belief that actions should never hurt someone else) than women, but that high levels of SDO are negatively correlated with idealism. This implies that men are more likely than women to view violence against others as necessary in some situations (Wilson, 2003). Thus, if the dominant group's goal (i.e., the jury's goal) is to maintain the existing hierarchy (i.e., between jurors and defendants, especially capital defendants), then it is logical for men to endorse activities, such as executions, that would preserve the hierarchy more than women. These variations in acceptance of harm to another person according to differing SDO levels, can assist in explaining why women are more likely to be excluded from a venire than men.

In addition, researchers found that discrimination against Black men may be motivated by a desire to harm them, and that this same motivation does not exist when the discrimination is against either White or Black women (Ayres, 1991). Thus, as is common in the defendant/jury relationship, arbitrary-set discrimination will be especially harsh when the target is an arbitrary-set subordinate male, rather than a subordinate female (Sidanius & Pratto, 1999). Consequently, Black women will not feel double the aggression from White individuals simply because they are female members of an arbitrary-set group (Sidanius & Pratto, 1999). Instead, arbitrary-set males are in the worst position. Because women are not as aggressive as males, and as previously stated are lower in SDO, they are less likely to feel the same degree of discrimination as male members of an arbitrary-set group (Sidanius & Pratto, 1999).

Within the jury system, aggressive discrimination is likely to exist between the jurors serving on death penalty trials and the defendants because those defendants who are proportionally most likely to face the possibility of death are Black males (especially when their victim was White; Baldus, Woodworth, & Pulaski, 1994; U.S. General Accounting Office, 1990), and jurors who are most likely to be in favor of the death penalty are White males (Abramson, 2001; Cowan et al., 1984; Fitzgerald & Ellsworth, 1984; Haney et al., 1994; Moran & Comfort, 1986; Mauro, 1992). The effect of defendant race on jury decision may also be affected by how strongly jurors identify with their own race as well as their position on the jury.

Social Identity Theory and Gender Differences

Jurors, as individuals, are members of various groups which include but are not limited to race, gender, affluence, and other indicators of social status. Individuals are likely to favor others who they believe are a part of their in-group (Hogg & Abrams, 1988). They will usually support these individuals more than they support members of various out-groups (Brewer, 1979; Wilder, 1981). This is an attempt to appear better than the out-group, and is driven by a need to be a part of the more powerful group (Abrams & Hogg, 1988; Hogg & Abrams, 1988, 1990). Social identity theory (SIT; Tajfel, 1970; Turner, 1978) has been used to sufficiently demonstrate that social-structural conditions (e.g., awareness of group boundaries and group membership) interact with psychological processes to produce behaviors such as out-group discrimination (Sidanius & Pratto, 1999).

Tajfel (1970) would claim that individuals from different groups need not feel a competitive hostility toward one another for there to be an inherent bias against each other. Simply feeling an important link between oneself and a member of the out-group (e.g., recognizing the power the jury has over the defendant) is enough to cause in-group favoritism and out-group hostility (Hinkle & Brown, 1990). This is especially true when in- and out-groups are formed in the presence of one another (e.g., jurors being selected in front of the defendant; Miller & Brewer, 1986). A positive social identity is gained by an individual (e.g., a juror) when the in-group has legitimate status and power over the out-group (e.g., deciding the fate of the defendant), while a negative identity is gained when the out-group has legitimate status and power over the in-group (e.g., because the jury has power over the defendant, the defendant will likely have a negative identity; Levin et al.,, 2002; Turner & Brown, 1978).

Although social dominance theorists do not deny that individuals may prefer the in-group over the out-group in an attempt to appear better than out-group members, SDT would say that these individuals do this to not only maintain a positive self-evaluation but also because these individuals have a drive to dominate the out-group (Levin et al., 2002). Research has shown that high levels of SDO are associated with high levels of in-group favoritism and out-group discrimination while individuals low in SDO are not likely to have these same biases (Pratto et al., 1994; Sidanius, 1993; Sidanius & Pratto, 1993, 1999; Sidanius, Pratto, & Bobo, 1996). These favoritism differences imply that the bias is not simply to identify with the high-status in-group, but rather to maintain power over the low-status out-group. This is especially true when the distinction makes member status explicitly clear (Hinkle & Brown 1990; Mullen, Brown & Smith, 1992; Sachdev & Bourhis, 1987, 1991; Sidanius & Pratto, 1999), as in a courtroom situation.

SDT suggests that when the hierarchy-enhancing myth is pervasive and shared, members of both high-status and low-status groups are likely to reflect positively on the high-status group. This is likely to occur regardless of one's group membership because these attitudes allow everyone in these situations to maintain a positive identity in these areas and help them to maintain the hierarchy itself (Sidanius, 1993; Sidanius & Pratto, 1993, 1999). Similar to this, Hinkle and Brown (1990) point out that contrary to what most would assume SIT to predict, it is not unheard of for out-group favoritism to be displayed. Tajfel and Turner (1979) argue that positive social identities are developed not from in-group favoritism in general, but from favorably comparing oneself to a relevant out-group. In other words, any harm incurred in a negative self-evaluation can be offset by a favorable self-evaluation to a more relevant group. Therefore, perceiving an out-group in a positive manner may not be damaging to the self as long as other, more important out-groups are seen in a negative light (Hinkle & Brown, 1990). Accordingly, if a juror low in SDO does not see the defendant as a member of a group that it is important to compare oneself to, he or she may judge the defendant more fairly than jurors who do see the defendant as a member of a relevant group. A weakness of SDT then is that it does not account for individual identification with a group or the importance of out-groups. It may be beneficial to combine the ideas of SDT (differences in SDO) and SIT (differences in group identification) to better understand why DQ and NDQ jurors view defendants differently.

Social Identity Theory and Gender Differences in Social Dominance Orientation
Wilson and Liu (2003) proposed that the difference between genders in level of SDO is moderated by gender group identification, which the authors of SDT (Sidanius, 1993; Sidanius et al., 2000; Sidanius et al., 1996) fail to address. Based on SIT (Tajfel & Turner, 1979) gender group identification is the extent to which individuals identify and reflect their gender (Wilson & Liu, 2003). Supporters of SIT argue that the fact that men display higher levels of SDO than women as a means of maintaining their dominant position is moderated by the degree to which they identify with their gender. Although men are generally higher in SDO than women regardless of gender identity strength, the more an individual identifies with the male gender the higher their level of SDO, whereas the more feminine an individual is the lower their SDO. As previously discussed, these findings have been demonstrated multiple times in research which found that inter-group aggression is more likely between in-group and out-group males than between female members of the same groups (Altemeyer, 2004; Pratto et al., 1994; Sidanius & Pratto, 1999). Thus, it is reasonable to predict that the more masculine an individual is, the more aggression he or she will feel, the higher his or her SDO level will be, and the more likely he or she will be found DQ. Wilson and Liu (2003) suggest that it would also be plausible for the SDO scores of other low status groups (i.e., ethnic minorities) to be affected by their identity with that group. For example, minorities who strongly identify with their race are expected to be lower in SDO than their White counterparts.

FUTURE RESEARCH

The following research suggestions have not been pursued as of the publication of this book. However, I feel that these are logical next steps in the area of death qualification reserach. I hope that readers will take this chapter, as well as these suggestions, as inspiration for thier own reserach.

Death Qualification and an Ability to Distinguish Differences between Similar Individuals

Brewer and Miller (1984) believe that the amount of inter-group differentiation between in-groups and out-groups can be examined as a continuum of inter-group contact. At one extreme, information about out-group members is processed at a very shallow level using very little information (category-based inter-group contact). At the other extreme, group categories are not distinguished, but instead every individual is differentiated based on unique characteristics that may or may not be similar to the self (personalized inter-group contact). This method of processing is very thorough but is also very time-consuming and it is impractical to think that this approach would be taken with every person that an individual must evaluate. It is the middle level of Brewer and Miller's (1984) model that is the most interesting for future death penalty/death qualification research. At this intermediate level individuals are believed to distinguish between out-group members although the characteristics (e.g., specifics about a crime, specifics about that individual) that make an individual a member of the out-group are recognized (differentiated inter-group contact). For instance, at this level one is aware that others are members of an out-group (e.g., both defendants allegedly committed murder together), however, he or she also notices individual differences between out-group members (e.g., differences in the way the defendants participated in the murder). Because NDQ jurors tend to think more open-mindedly and rely more on due process values than do DQ jurors (Fitzgerald & Ellsworth, 1984), it would be interesting to examine the differences between DQ and NDQ jurors when distinguishing between out-group members (e.g., jurors distinguishing between defendants).

Gender Identification, Social Dominance Orientation, and Death Penalty Support

I would also like to see the research conducted by Wilson and Liu (2003) furthered in a situation specific to jury decision making. In particular, it would be interesting to examine whether or not gender identity (Wilson & Liu, 2003) mediates the relationship between SDO and support for the death penalty. Previous research has resulted in mixed findings as to the relationship between SDO and a new, more sensitive, measurement of DQ (the Death Penalty Attitudes Scale (DPAS); Adams, Perkins, & Bourgeois, 2003; Adams, Tang, Bourgeois, Waack, & Hatz, 2005). It would be interesting to determine if this relationship can be clarified with the inclusion of a mediating factor such as gender identification because this information will help to strengthen researcher's ability to distinguish between truly DQ and NDQ jurors.

The Effect of the Situation on Social Dominance Orientation

A third idea for future research involves examining the effect of the situation referred to when questioning SDO (e.g., being questioned as a juror as opposed to being questioned as the defendant). It is possible that the situation may play a part in how predictive SDO is of other attitudes (i.e., death penalty support). For instance, SDT suggests that people differ in their support for inequality because of differences in a general orientation toward hierarchical social structures (Sidanius & Pratto, 1999). Supporters of SIT will not deny that individuals with higher status are likely to be higher in SDO, however, these same theorists feel that one's status is dependant on the specific context (Schmitt, Branscombe, & Kappen, 2003). In other words, individual group membership will change with the context and his or her level of SDO will depend on who benefits from the current situation. In the previous example, an individual may be higher in SDO when questioned as a juror as opposed to being questioned as a defendant because maintaining the hierarchy would not be in the defendant's best interest.

Although research has examined how the salience of characteristics such as race and sex impact SDO scores (Schmitt et al., 2003), the effect of the capital jury situation has not yet been examined. Guimond et al. (2003) found that social position affects levels of SDO even when social position is arbitrarily assigned. Specifically, individuals given more responsibility (i.e., higher status positions) had higher levels of SDO than those assigned to lower social positions (Studies 3 and 4). Based on these findings, I feel that it would be interesting to examine whether one's level of SDO is affected by being chosen as a capital trial juror or if SDO impacts whether or not a person will be chosen as a juror.

CONCLUSION

As discussed above, research has illuminated numerous differences between jurors who are legally considered DQ and those who are excludable. The differences are explained, at least in part, by SDT, and in particular differing levels of SDO. One strength in using this theory to explain juror differences is that differing levels of SDO can reasonably explain variation in evidence usage and deliberation between those who are and are not DQ. For instance, the fact that those individuals who are high in SDO need more persuasive arguments, or evidence, to change their minds (Sidanius & Pratto, 1999) may explain why jurors who are considered DQ tend to be conviction-prone in comparison with excludable jurors (Fitzgerald & Ellsworth, 1984; Goodman-Delahunty et al., 1998; Haney et al., 1994; Thompson et al., 1984). Specifically, researchers have found that DQ jurors tend to have a lower threshold for guilt, whereas NDQ jurors are more likely to listen to all of the evidence equally before making a decision (Harris, 1971[1]; Jurrow, 1971; Cowan et al., 1984), which is what the law intends.

In addition, Quist and Resendez (2002) showed that in order to maintain an existing hierarchy (e.g., between jurors and defendants) individuals high in SDO are likely to believe in stereotypes and legitimizing myths that confirm these hierarchical differences. Thus, when deliberating about the guilt or innocence of a defendant, jurors who are similar in their high levels of SDO and support for the death penalty are likely to disregard potentially important evidence that may contradict their initial beliefs. This is likely to be especially true if the evidence presented confirms pre-existing stereotypes about the subordinate group member (Clark et al., 2000; Cowan et al., 1984). However, explanatory power in general will be increased when SDT is combined with the ideas behind other theories. For instance, RWA can also contribute to one's support of punitive sentences (or his or her conviction-proneness; Altemeyer, 1998, 2004; Capps, 2002) and thus one's likelihood of being deemed DQ and his or her ability to fairly evaluate evidence.

Combining predictions of multiple theories may also be beneficial to the understanding of race and gender differences between those who are and are not DQ. Combining SDT and modern racism theories, as well as SIT, may allow for a more thorough explanation of these differences. For example, differing views of the legitimacy of a social hierarchy may be affected by one's level of racism. These differences will in turn affect how in- and out-group members are perceived by opposing group members (Levin et al., 2002). Also, gender identification (the degree to which individuals identify with masculine or feminine qualities) moderates the relationship between gender and levels of SDO (Wilson & Liu, 2003). These differences help to explain why women are less likely than men to be found DQ.

The bottom line is that while SDT is useful in explaining some procedural differences between DQ and NDQ jurors (use of evidence and deliberation), this theory does not adequately explain group differences (e.g., race and gender) in and of itself. The best and most useful means of reaching a conclusion on why racial, gender, and other group differences exist between DQ and NDQ jurors can only be drawn when ideas from SDT, RWA, SIT, as well as modern racism theories are combined. The joining of these theoretical perspectives with existing research on death qualification provides a promising pathway for the future of this field of interest.

REFERENCES

Abrams, D., & Hogg, M.A. (1988). Comments on the motivational status of self-esteem in social identity and intergroup discrimination. *European Journal of social Psychology, 18,* 317-334.

Adams, C.M.S., Perkins, J., & Bourgeois, M.J. (2003, June). Validation of the death penalty attitudes scale. *Poster presented at the annual meeting of the American Psychological Society, Atlanta, GA.*

Adams, C.M.S., Tang, C., Bourgeois, M.J., Waack, B.M., and Hatz, J.L. (2005, March). *Further validation of the death penalty attitudes scale.* Talk given at the annual meeting of the American Psychology-Law Society, San Diego, CA.

Abramson, J. (2001). *We, the jury: The jury system and the ideal of democracy.* Cambridge, MA: Harvard University Press.

Allen, M., Mabry, E., & McKelton, D-M. (1998). Impact of juror attitudes about the death penalty on juror evaluations of guilt and punishment: A meta-analysis. *Law and Human Behavior, 22,* 715-731.

Altemeyer, B. (1981). *Right-wing authoritarianism.* Winnipeg: University of Manitoba Press.

Altemeyer, B. (1988). *Enemies of freedom: Understanding right-wing authoritarianism.* San Francisco: Jossey-Bass.

Altemeyer, B. (1998). The other "authoritarian personality." *Advances in Experimental Social Psychology, 30,* 48-92.

Altemeyer, B. (2004). Highly dominating, highly authoritarian personalities. *The Journal of Social Psychology, 144,* 421-447.

Ayres, I. (1991). Fair driving: Gender and race discrimination in retail car negotiations. *Harvard Law Review, 104,* 817-872.

Baldus, D.C., Woodworth, G., & Pulanski, C.A., Jr. (1994). Reflections on the "inevitability" of racial discrimination in capital sentencing and the "impossibility" of its prevention, detection, and correction. *Washington & Lee Law Review, 51,* 359-430.

Ballard v. United States 329 U.S. 187 (1946).

Batson v Kentucky 476 US 79, 90 L Ed 2d 69, 106 S Ct 1712 (1986).

Brewer, M.B. (1979). In-group bias in the minimal intergroup situation: A cognitive-motivational analysis. *Psychological Bulletin, 86,* 307-324.

Butler, B.M., & Moran, G. (2002). The role of death qualification in venireperson's evaluations of aggravating and mitigating circumstances in capital trials. *Law and Human Behavior, 26,* 175-184.

Bureau of Justice Statistics (2002). Attitudes toward the death penalty for persons convicted of murder (By sex, race, age, education, income, occupation, region, religion, and political affiliation, 1978-2000). *Sourcebook of Criminal Justice Statistics, 2001. Section 2. Public Attitudes Toward Crime and Criminal Justice,* 142-143.

Capps, J.S. (2002). Explaining punitiveness: Right-wing authoritarianism and social dominance. *North American Journal of Psychology, 4,* 263-278.

Clark, M.A., Anand, V., & Roberson, R. (2000). Resolving meaning: Interpretation in diverse decision making groups. *Group Dynamics: Theory, Research, and Practice, 4,* 211-221.

Coker v. Georgia, 433 U.S. 584; 97 S. Ct. 2861; 53 L. Ed. 2d 982 (1977).

Cowan, C.L., Thomopson, W.C., & Ellsworth, P.C. (1984). The effects of death qualification on jurors' predisposition to convict and on the quality of deliberation. *Law and Human Behavior, 8,* 53- 79.

Dillehay, R.C., & Sandys, M.R. (1996). Life under Wainwright v. Witt: Juror dispositions and death qualification. *Law and Human Behavior, 20,* 147-165.

Duren v. Missouri, 439 U.S. 357; 99 S. Ct. 664; 58 L. Ed. 2d 579 (1979).

Ekehammar, B. (1985). Sex differences in socio-political attitudes revisited. *Educational Studies, 11,* 3-9.

Ellsworth, P. (1993). Some steps between attitudes and verdicts. In R. Hastie (Ed.), *Inside the juror: The psychology of juror decision making* (pp. 42-64). Cambridge: Cambridge University Press.

Filkins, J.W., Smith, C.M., & Tindale, R.S. (1998). An evaluation of the biasing effects of death qualification: A meta-analytic/computer simulation approach. In R.S. Tindale & L. Heath (Eds.), *Theory and Research on Small Groups: Social Psychological Applications to Social Issues* (pp. 153-175). New York: Plenum Press.

Fitzgerald, R. & Ellsworth, P.C. (1984). Due process vs. crime control: Death qualification and jury attitudes. *Law and Human Behavior, 8,* 31-51.

Fukurai, H., Butler, E.W., & Krooth, R. (1991). Where did Black jurors go? A theoretical synthesis of racial disenfranchisement in the jury system and jury selection. *Journal of Black Studies, 22,* 196-215.

Furman v. Georgia, 408 U.S. 238; 92 S. Ct. 2726; 33 L. Ed. 2d 346 (1972).

Gaertner, S.L., & Dovidio, J.F. (1986). The aversive form of racism. In J.F. Dovidio & S.L. Gaertner (Eds.), *Prejudice, discrimination, and racism* (pp. 61-90). Orlando, FL: Academic Press.

Goodman-Delahunty, J., Greene, E., & Hsiao, W. (1998). Construing motive in videotaped killings: The role of jurors' attitudes toward the death penalty. *Law and Human Behavior, 22,* 257-271.

Gregg v. Georgia. 428 U.S. 153; 96 S. Ct. 2909; 49 L. Ed. 2d 859 (1976).

Gross, S.R. (1996). The risks of death: Why erroneous convictions are common in capital cases. *Buffalo Law Review, 44,* 469-500.

Guimond, S., Dambrun, M., Michinov, N., & Durate, S. (2003). Does social dominance generate prejudice? Integrating individual and contextual determinants of intergroup cognitions. *Journal of Personality and Social Psychology, 84,* 697-721.

Haney, C. (1984a). On the selection of capital trials: The biasing effects of the death-qualification process. *Law and Human Behavior, 8, 121-132*

Haney, C. (1984b). Examining death qualification: Further analysis of the process effect. *Law and Human Behavior, 8,* 133-151.

Haney, C., Hurtado, A., & Vega, L. (1994). "Modern" death qualification: New data on its biasing effects. *Law and Human Behavior, 18,* 619-633.

Haney, C., & Wiener, R.L. (2004). Death is different: An editorial introduction to the theme issue. *Psychology, Public Policy, and Law,* 373-378.

Hernandez v. Texas, 347 U.S. 475, 480 (1954).

Hinkle, S., & Brown, R. (1990). Intergroup comparisons and social identity: Some links and lacunae. In D. Abrams & M. Hogg (Eds.), S*ocial Identity Theory: Constructive and critical advances* (pp. 48-70). New York: Springer-Verlag.

Hoffman, LR., Burke, R,J., Maier, Norman R.F. (1965). Participation, influence, and satisfaction among members of problems solving groups. *Psychological Reports, 16,* 661-667.

Hogg, M.A., & Abrams, D. (1988). *Social identifications: A social psychology of intergroup relations and group processes.* London: Rotledge.

Hogg, M.A., & Abrams, D. (1990). Social motivation, self-esteem, and social identity. In D. Abrams & M. Hogg (Eds.), S*ocial Identity Theory: Constructive and critical advances* (pp. 28-47). New York: Springer-Verlag.

Horowitz, I.A., & Seguin, D.G. (1986). The effects of bifurcation and death qualification on assignment of penalty in capital crimes. *Journal of Applied Social Psychology, 16,* 165-185.

J.E.B. v. Alabama, 511 U.S. 127 (1994).

Jurow, G. (1971). New data on the effect of a death-qualified jury on the guilt determination process. *Harvard Law Review, 84,* 567-611.

Kadane, J.B. (1984). After Hovey: A note on taking account of the automatic death penalty jurors. *Law and Human Behavior, 8,* 115-120.

Katz, I., & Hass, R.G. (1988). Racial ambivalence and American value conflict: Correlational and priming studies of dual cognitive structures. *Journal of Personality and Social Psychology, 55,* 893-905.

Levin, S. (2004). Perceived group status differences and the effects of gender, ethnicity, nd religion on social dominance orientation. *Political Psychology, 25,* 31-48.

Levin, S., Federico, C. M., Sidanius, J., & Rabinowitz, J. L. (2002). Social dominance orientation and intergroup bias: The legitimization of favoritism for high-status groups. *Personality and Social Psychology Bulletin, 28,* 144-157.

Lockhart v. McCree. 106 S. Ct. 1758 (1986).

Luginbuhl, J., & Middendorf, K. (1988). Death penalty beliefs and jurors' responses to aggravating and mitigating circumstances in capital trials. *Law and Human Behavior, 12,* 263-281.

Marjoribanks, K. (1981). Sex-related differences in socio-political attitudes: A replication. *Educational Studies, 7,* 1-6.

Mauro, R. (1992). Tipping the scales toward death: The biasing effects of death qualification. In P. Suedfeld & P.E. Tetlock (Eds.), *Psychology and Social* Policy (pp. 243-254). New York: Hemisphere Publishing Corporation.

McConahay, J.B. (1986). Modern racism, ambivalence, and the modern racism scale. In J.F. Dovidio & S.L. Gaertner (Eds.), *Prejudice, discrimination, and racism* (pp. 91-126). Orlando, FL: Academic Press.

Miller, N., & Brewer, M.B. (1986). Categorization effects on in-group and out-group perception. In J.F. Dovidio and S.L. Gaertner (Eds.), *Prejudice, discrimination, and racism* (pp. 209-230). New York: Academic Press.

Mitchell, M., & Sidanius, J. (1993). Group status and asymmetry in the relationship between ideology and death penalty support: A social dominance perspective. *National Journal of Sociology, 7,* 67-93.

Moran, G., & Comfort, J.C. (1986). Neither "tentative" nor "fragmentary": Verdict preference of impaneled felony jurors as a function of attitude toward capital punishment. *Journal of Applied Psychology, 71,* 146-155.

Morgan v. Illinois. 504 U.S. 719; 112 S. Ct. 2222; 119 L. Ed. 2d 492 (1992).

Mullen, B., Brown, R., & Smith, C. (1992). In-group bias as a function of salience, relevance, and status: An integration. *European Journal of social Psychology, 22,* 103-122.

Nakell, B., & Hardy, K.A. (1987). *The arbitrariness of the death penalty.* Philadelphia: Temple University Press.

Ogloff, J.R.P., & Chopra, S.R. (2004). Stuck in the dark ages: Supreme Court decision making and legal developments. *Psychology, Public Policy, and Law, 10,* 379-416.

Pratto, F., Sidanius, J., Stallworth, L.M., & Malle, B.F. (1994). social dominance orientation: A personality variable predicting social and political attitudes. *Journal of Personality and social Psycology, 67,* 741-763.

Pratto, F., Stallworth, L.M., & Conway-Lanz, S. (1998). Social dominance orientation and the ideological legitimization of social policy. *Journal of Applied Social Psychology, 28,* 1853-1875.

Pratto, F., Stallworth, L.M., & Sidanius, J. (1997). The gender gap: Differences in political attitudes and social dominance orientation. *British Journal of social Psychology, 36,* 49-68.

Quist, R.M., & Resendez, M.G. (2002). Social dominance threat: Examining Social Dominance Theory's explanation of prejudice as legitimizing myths. *Basic and Applied Social Psychology, 24,* 287-293.

Ring v. Arizona 536 U.S. 584, 153 2 Ed. 2d. 556, 122 S. Ct. 2428 (2002).

Robinson, R J. (1993). What does "unwilling" to impose the death penalty mean anyway? Another look at excludable jurors. *Law and Human Behavior, 17,* 471-477.

Rozelle, S. (2002). The utility of Witt: Understanding the language of death qualification. *Baylor Law Review, 54,* 677-702.

Sachdev, I., & Bourhis, R.Y. (1987). Status differentials and intergroup behavior. *European Journal of Social Psychology, 17,* 277-293.

Sachdev, I., & Bourhis, R.Y. (1991). Power and status differentials in minority and majority group relations. *European Journal of Social Psychology, 21,* 1-24.

Sandys, M., & McGarrell, E.F. (1995). Attitudes toward capital punishment: Preference for the penalty or mere acceptance? *Journal of Research in Crime and Delinquency, 32,* 191-213.

Sidanius, J. (1993). The psychology of group conflict and the dynamics of oppression: A social dominance perspective. In S. Iyengar & W.J. McGuire (Eds.), *Explorations in political psychology* (pp. 183-219). Durham, NC: Duke University Press.

Sidanius, J., & Ekehammar, B. (1980). Sex-related differences in socio-political ideology. *Scandinavian Journal of Psychology, 21,* 17-26.

Sidanius, J., Levin, S., Frederico, C.M., & Pratto, F. (2001) Legitimizing ideologies: The social dominance approach. In J.T. Jost & B. Major (Eds.), *The psychology of legitimacy: Emerging perspectives on ideology, justice, and intergroup relations* (pp. 307-331). Cambridge, UK: Cambridge University Press.

Sidanius, J., & Pratto, F. (1993). The inevitability of oppression and the dynamics of social dominance. In P.M. Sniderman, P.E. Tetlock, & E.G. Carmines (Eds.), *Prejudice, politics, and the American dilemma* (pp. 173-211). Stanford, CA: Stanford University Press.

Sidanius, J., & Pratto, F. (1999). *Social dominance.* Cambridge University Press: New York.

Sidanius, J., Pratto, F., & Bobo, L. (1996). Social dominance orientation and the political psychology of gender: A case of invariance? *Journal of Personality and Social Psychology, 67,* 998-1011.

Sommers, S.R., & Ellsworth, P.C. (2000). Race in the courtroom: Perceptions of guilt and dispositional attributions. *Personality and social Psychology Bulletin, 26,* 1367-1379.

Steiner, B.D., Bowers, W.J., & Sarat, A. (1999). Folk knowledge as legal action: Death penalty judgments and the tenet of early release in a culture of mistrust and punitiveness. *Law and Society Review, 33,* 461-505.

Sunnafrank, M., & Fontes, N.E. (1983). General and crime related racial stereotypes and influence on juridic decisions. *Cornell Journal of Social Relations, 17,* 1-15.

Tajfel, H. (1970). Experiments in intergroup discrimination. *Scientific American, 223,* 96-102.

Tajfel, H., & Turner, J.C. (1979). An interactive theory of intergroup conflict. In W.G. Austin & S. Worchel (Eds.), *The Social Psychology of Intergroup Relations* (pp. 33-47). Monterey, CA: Brooks-Cole.

Thompson, W.C. (1989). Death qualification after Wainwright v. Witt and Lockhart v. McCree. *Law and Human Behavior, 13,* 185-215.

Thompson, W.C., Cowan, C.L., Ellsworth, P.C., & Harrington, J. C. (1984). Death penalty attitudes and conviction proneness: The translation of attitudes into verdicts. *Law and Human Behavior, 8,* 95-113.

Turner, J. (1978). Social comparison, similarity and in-group favourtism. In H. Tajfel (Ed.), *Differentiation Between Social Groups* (pp. 235 – 250). London: Academic Press.

Turner, J., & Brown, R.J. (1978). Social status, cognitive alternatives and intergroup relations. In H. Tajfel (Ed.), *Differentiation Between Social Groups* (pp. 201-234). London: Academic Press.

U.S. General Accounting Office. (1990). *Death penalty sentencing: Research indicates a pattern of racial disparities.* Washington D.C.: U.S. Government Printing Office.

Wainwright v. Witt. 469 U.S. 412; 105 S.Ct. 844; 83 L.Ed. 2d 841 (1985).

Whitley, B.E., Jr. (1999). Right-wing authoritarianism, social dominance orientation, and prejudice. *Journal of Personality and Social Psychology, 77,* 126-134.

Wilder, D.A. (1981). Perceiving persons as a group: Categorization and intergroup relations. In D.L. Hamilton (Ed.), *Cognitive processes in stereotyping and intergroup behavior* (pp. 213-258). Hillsdale, NJ: Erlbaum.

Wilson, M.S. (2003). Social dominance and ethical ideology: The end justifies the means? *The Journal of Social Psychology, 143,* 549-558.

Wilson, M.S., & Liu, J. H. (2003). Social dominance orientation and gender: The moderating role of gender identity. *British Journal of Social Psychology, 42,* 187-198.

In: Psychology of Decision Making...
Editor: G. R. Burthold, pp. 123-140

ISBN: 978-1-60021-932-0
© 2007 Nova Science Publishers, Inc.

Chapter 4

IF LOOKS COULD KILL: IDENTIFYING TRIAL OUTCOMES OF MURDER CASES BASED ON THE APPEARANCES OF CAPITAL OFFENDERS SHOWN IN BLACK-AND-WHITE PHOTOGRAPHS

Michael E. Antonio[*]

ABSTRACT

In the present analysis, research subjects were asked to rate four adult males, shown individually in black-and-white photographs, on twelve factors related to physical appearance and personality characteristics (i.e., attractiveness, honesty, etc.). After rating each photograph, research subjects were told that all four of the men photographed were convicted of capital murder and sentenced to either life or death by a capital jury. The research subjects were then asked to decide what punishment a jury imposed on each murderer.

Data gathered by the Capital Jury Project (CJP) provided evidence about the sentencing verdicts reached by juries in 48 death penalty cases. From this information, Department of Corrections' websites in four states were searched to locate photographs of these offenders. Cases were sought to fulfill the following research design: 24 Black murderers (12 from cases resulting in a death sentence and 12 from cases resulting in a life sentence) and 24 White murderers (12 from cases resulting in a death sentence and 12 from cases resulting in a life sentence).

During no part of the experiment did the participants have knowledge about the crime or details about the murder that was committed. Findings indicated that 1) certain factors related to physical appearance and personality characteristics were associated with trial outcomes; 2) offender race significantly impacted ratings on the twelve factors and

[*] Dr. Antonio was the Senior Research Scientist and Lead Project Manager of the Capital Jury Project (Phase II) in the Criminal Justice Research Center at Northeastern University in Boston, MA from September 2000 to May 2005

also students' decision-making about trial outcomes; and 3) accuracy for choosing the correct trial outcome was at a rate greater than expected by chance alone.

INTRODUCTION

"What's in a name?" This was the question posed by William Shakespeare in the tragedy *Romeo and Juliet.* A new question for social scientists to ask is, "What's in a face?" Do people use facial features to make judgments about another's personality, intelligence, behavior, occupation, etc.? Much evidence has been collected that indicates people do. For example, one study showed that capital offenders, who were Black and judged to have stereotypical Black appearances, were more likely to be sentenced to death for their crimes compared to other groups (Eberhardt, Davies, Purdie-Vaughns, and Johnson, 2006). Other research showed that capital defendants, who appeared emotionally involved during their trial (i.e., sorry, sincere, and not bored), were less likely to be sentenced to death compared to defendants who appeared to lack remorse and seemed insincere or bored inside the courtroom (Antonio, 2006). These results suggest that "the outward appearance of the face is used as an index of the inward character" (Strachey, 1933). The present analysis examined how research respondents rated capital offenders featured in black-and-white photographs on a number of factors and how they used these snap judgments to determine trial outcome.

A growing body of literature reveals the importance for further studying facial features that goes far beyond physical appearance alone. In one experiment, facial photographs of individuals were shown to a group of research subjects. The research participants were asked to judge the person photographed on various factors (Goldstein, Chance, and Gilbert, 1984). Responses given in reaction to the facial features reflected stereotypical beliefs of the individual portrayed. For example, some photographs were typically selected to represent "good guys" while others were consistently selected to represent "bad guys." It was found that certain facial features elicited similar responses from research subjects in other empirical studies as well (for example, see Zebrowitz and McDonald, 1991; Lown, 1977). This line of research suggests that, in general, people look at an individual's facial features and extract or interpret something about his or her personality, behavior, or intelligence based solely on those physical attributes. Moreover, given the research findings, it appears that consistency exists within a culture about the meaning of particular facial configurations.

Under normal circumstances, inferences we make about an individual's personality characteristics, behavioral intentions, and temperament based solely on outward appearance seems harmless. In fact, there may even be some advantages for doing this, including saving time and energy to allow for other higher-level cognitive processing (Bandura, Ross, and Ross, 1963). However, are there instances when an over-reliance on an individual's facial features or appearance to assess his or her individuality, character, or attitude would be inappropriate or misplaced? If such circumstances exist, arguably, it would involve the Criminal Justice System (CJS), in particular, our Courts of Law.

STEREOTYPING AND THE CJS

Stereotyping on the basis of facial features could lead to serious problems for the CJS, including blatant violations of an individual's right to due process and even wrongful imprisonment. For example, witnesses to a crime who are asked to select the criminal perpetrator from a lineup could choose the wrong person simply because he or she displays "criminal features" (Shoemaker, South, and Lowe, 1973). This effect extends into the courtroom where jury decision-making could be impaired based on the looks of the defendant and/or plaintiff. Such biased perceptions could impact case outcomes, including guilt and sentencing verdicts (Shoemaker, et al.1973).

The impact that stereotyping plays in the jury box has been recognized for some time (see McArthur, 1982; Bull and Green, 1980; and Bull and Clifford, 1979). For example, Lown (1977) has shown that a defendant's constitutional right to a fair trial may be compromised if jurors rely on stereotypical responses based on physical characteristics rather than on the facts presented to the court during trial. Some may argue that comparing automatic and stereotyped responses drawn from an individual's facial expressions with blatant violations of justice and due process is stretching matters; however, Goldstein, et al. (1984) illustrated this is a potential threat that must be taken seriously.

Results of the study showed that research subjects possessed a "conceptual memory schema that represents their personal prototypic criminal or non-criminal faces." That is, research subjects were shown a series of photos and it was found that one of the photos was selected more frequently to be the "mass murderer" than would be expected by chance, suggesting there exists a "consensual agreement" regarding the appearance of an individual who is capable of killing on a grand scale. Overall, the findings from this study suggested that while facial stereotypes may differ from person to person, there did exist some common themes that contributed to high consensual agreement among subjects. These findings illustrated that "not only do criminal and non-criminal facial prototypes exist, but various subtypes of criminals and non-criminals must also be represented in these memory schemata."

The Goldstein, et al. (1984) findings were consistent with prior research of that time. Specifically, Shoemaker, et al. (1973) found from a stack of portraits of White, middle-aged men, research subjects consistently chose some as being more likely to commit a criminal act and others less likely to do so. In a comprehensive study of facial expressions Goldin (1979) concluded that people did possess cognitive imagery regarding the ideal criminal (murderer, thief, etc.) and these stereotypical beliefs did impact their interpretation of evidence and "processing of criminal stimuli." What these research findings suggest is that nonverbal cues and extralegal factors, including facial features and expressions displayed by individuals, can and do have a significant impact on the CJS.

PHYSICAL APPEARANCE

Physical attractiveness is a highly valued and positive attribute that can influence jury decision-making. A classic study conducted by Stephan and Tully (1977) illustrated the effect of defendant attractiveness on trial outcomes. The researchers had 124 undergraduates read a summary of a trial in which a plaintiff brought a lawsuit against the defendant for damages and injuries caused as a result of a car accident. The student subjects were asked, based on the evidence and facts presented, to find in favor of the plaintiff or defendant and, where appropriate, assign monetary damage awards. To test the influence of attractiveness, the researchers attached a photograph of the plaintiff's face to the case summary. In all, two photos were used, one that was judged to display an attractive plaintiff, the other an unattractive one.

The researchers discovered that the physical attractiveness of the plaintiff significantly impacted the decision-making of the simulated jurors. Specifically, the student subjects more frequently found in favor of the attractive plaintiff than they did for the unattractive plaintiff. In addition, the attractive plaintiff was awarded more monetary compensations for damages than was the unattractive plaintiff. A gender effect was uncovered as well. That is, male subjects awarded the male plaintiffs the largest amount of money, while compensating the female plaintiffs with the smallest monetary awards. This finding did not materialize for females subjects, however, who "did not discriminate on the basis of sex of the defendant and monetary awards" (Stephan and Tully, 1977).

The finding that physical attractiveness impacts trial outcomes has been revealed through other empirical studies (Badzinski and Pettus, 1994; Downs and Lyons, 1991; Pryor and Buchanan, 1984; Stewart, 1980). For example, Zebrowitz and McDonald (1991) have shown that physically-attractive defendants are less likely than physically-unattractive defendants to get convicted; however, even when they were found guilty of committing certain crimes and sentenced for those crimes, the physically-attractive defendants tended to receive more lenient punishments than their unattractive counterparts. This was true not only in civil cases, including a car accident scenario in which monetary damages were awarded, but also for criminal cases where lengthy prison terms would result. Indeed, some studies showed that male jurors were more likely to impose harsh punishments, including longer prison sentences, on criminal defendants charged with committing aggravated assault and rape when the female victim was attractive than when she was not (Villemur and Hyde, 1983; Thornton, 1977).

Are people consciously aware that their decisions and opinions of others are being influenced so strongly by physical appearance? If so, could they correct their behavior and thinking once they realize what they were doing? In one study, researchers found that among a sample of undergraduates, "fewer than 10% of those polled believed that physical attractiveness should have any bearing on judicial decisions" (Efran, 1974). However, when these same research subjects were asked to decide about a student's guilt or culpability for violating a University's honor code, results revealed that student violators who were attractive (regardless of gender) were rated guilty less frequently, received scores indicating less certainty of guilt and, when they were found guilty, received more lenient punishments than their unattractive counterparts. Based on these findings, Efran (1974) concluded that when put in situations where individuals are forced to make rational decisions, "it is a reasonable assumption that decisions will be based on a cognitive assessment of all information available." As findings from this study and elsewhere have revealed, "affectively arousing but irrelevant factors such as physical attractiveness can influence the favorability of an evaluation" and significantly impact the outcome of a trial.

There are certain limits as to how far attractiveness can benefit a litigant inside the courtroom, however. As some research has shown, under certain circumstances and situational factors, one's own physical beauty and personal attributes may lead to harsher sanctions and criminal punishments (Downs and Lyons, 1991). In one experiment designed to test the association between physical attractiveness and culpability, mock jurors deliberated about the guilt and punishment a woman should receive for stealing (Sigall and Ostrove, 1975). Results revealed that the unattractive female defendant was sentenced to more years in prison than was the attractive defendant; however, when the situational factors were changed, including the crime that was committed, different verdicts resulted. Specifically, when the crime was changed from stealing to swindling a man into making a phony investment, the physical attractiveness of the defendant significantly impacted jury verdicts. Using this scenario, the beautiful defendant was sentenced more harshly, which suggests that "the impression created by physical appearance seemed to extend to judgments of criminality" (Sigall and Ostrove, 1975).

Additional research supported the finding that appearance impacts the blameworthiness of certain defendants and that in some criminal cases, attractive defendants will not receive favor from the court and/or jury. Zebrowitz and McDonald (1991) showed in some criminal trials attractive women were sentenced more harshly by juries when their behaviors contributed to serious threats to public safety, including fatal car accidents, and also when they used their physical attractiveness to exploit unsuspecting men (i.e., conning a middle-aged bachelor). Researchers believed that women portrayed as "bad drivers" or "wild" are associated with negative stereotypes of attractive individuals. It is because of this stereotyped or biased mindset that these defendants were subjected to harsher treatment, including strict criminal sanctions, than were the less-attractive defendants in the study.

FACIAL BABYISHNESS

In addition to physical attractiveness, it was found that jurors' decisions also could be swayed by other physical features. Research showed that specific facial features of trial litigants, including those associated with innocence or facial babyishness, could significantly impact decision-making and trial outcomes (for example, see Zebrowitz and Montepare, 1990; Berry and McArthur, 1986). As the name suggests, individuals who are baby-faced are characterized by facial features that resemble the prototypical baby, including "larger eyes, thinner, higher eyebrows, a large forehead, small chin, and a curved rather than angular face" (Berry and McArthur, 1985). These characteristics were found to appreciably impact judicial decisions about one's level of culpability and guilt.

Berry and Zebrowitz-McArthur (1988) found that respondents were more likely to find baby-faced men guilty and responsible for damages caused by an accident involving their own negligence, whereas they were more likely to find mature-faced men more culpable and responsible for damages resulting from accidents caused by their intentional actions. Researchers argued that these findings were consistent with assumptions about baby-faced adults. That is, they are perceived as more honest than the mature-faced adults (thus, less able to cause harm intentionally) and also are viewed as being more naïve (thus, less able to plan intentional harm) and more apt to cause harm through negligence.

Zebrowitz and McDonald (1991) conducted a study in small claims court that extended the findings of defendants' facial babyishness. Overall, their findings were consistent with earlier research which showed that baby-faced adults were perceived as more naïve and more honest than the mature-faced adults; however their findings also revealed that defendants with fewer baby-faced features had to pay larger awards to plaintiffs, but only when the plaintiffs themselves were relatively baby-faced. These findings further suggest that juries want to protect baby-faced plaintiffs from being guilty, while average or mature-faced plaintiffs do not receive this protective treatment.

How could these general findings about facial babyishness and maturity, as well as physical appearance and attractiveness, be extended? What other means exist for testing how facial features are used in decision-making about another person's character, attitude and behavior? This article analyzes data gathered from a sample of undergraduate college students about their ratings on physical appearance and other personality characteristics for a selected group of capital murderers. This analysis will examine the accuracy by which the students were able to identify whether the offenders were sentenced to life or death by an actual capital jury based on nothing other than their judgments about physical appearance and personality. The findings in this analysis raise important questions about how an offender's appearance inside the courtroom during a capital trial impacts jurors' decision-making about guilt and punishment.

METHOD

Two-hundred sixty-six undergraduate college students participated in a research study in which they were asked to rate four adult males shown in black-and-white photographs on twelve factors related to physical appearance and personality characteristics.[1] Each factor was rated using a 10-point scale (i.e., 1-unattractive, 10-attractive). After the ratings were completed, research subjects were told, "suppose each of the individuals you just rated committed a murder, and suppose that two were sentenced to death and two were sentenced to life imprisonment for that crime. On the basis of their facial features as shown in the four photographs, give your best guess for which two got a death sentence and which two got a life sentence."

There was a random assignment of four photographs in the survey each student was asked to complete. The only criteria for inclusion of a certain photograph was to ensure that all 4 race/sentence categorizes (White/death, White/life, Black/death, and Black/life) were represented. The presentation order of photographs also was randomized to ensure that the same race/sentence categories did not consistently follow each other. During no part of the experiment did the research participants have knowledge about the crime or details about the murder that was committed.

---

[1] The twelve factors included: unattractive/attractive; not child-like/child-like; not dangerous/dangerous; not deceptive/deceptive; not friendly/friendly; not frightening/frightening; dishonest/honest; immature/mature; not self-confident/self-confident; insincere/sincere; not warm-hearted/warm-hearted; and not young-at-heart/young-at-heart.

Sample

Preliminary analysis of these data revealed various patterns in responses while controlling for student race and gender. Some of the findings reached statistical significance beyond the .05 probability level, while other findings did not. Presenting all the variations here is beyond the scope of this analysis. The major findings related to ratings on the twelve factors and trial outcome will be restricted to White females only. White females comprised 42.8% (n=107) of the entire student sample. In the last section of the analysis, related to accuracy for predicting trial outcomes, respondents from all students will be explored.

Capital Jury Project

Data gathered by the Capital Jury Project (CJP)[2] provided supplemental evidence about the sentencing verdicts reached by juries in 48 death penalty cases. From this information, internet searches were conducted on Department of Corrections' websites in 4 states to locate current photographs of these inmates.[3] Cases were sought to fulfill the following research design based on defendant race and sentence outcome: 24 Black murderers (12 from cases resulting in a death sentence and 12 from cases resulting in a life sentence) and 24 White murderers (12 from cases resulting in a death sentence and 12 from cases resulting in a life sentence).

Findings for how White females rated the twelve physical appearance and personality factors will be shown first. Next, their ratings on the twelve factors will be examined by the actual trial outcome and the presumed trial outcome. Finally, the accuracy for all the students in the study (N=266) to correctly identify those murderers sentenced to death or life by a capital jury will be revealed.

---

[2] The CJP is a national program of research on the decision-making of capital jurors conducted by a consortium of university-based researchers with the support of the National Science Foundation. The findings of the CJP are based on in-depth interviews with persons who have actually served as jurors in capital trials. The interviews chronicle the jurors' experiences and decision-making over the course of the trial, identify points at which various influences come into play, and reveal the ways in which jurors reach their final sentencing decisions. The CJP has interviewed capital jurors in fourteen states. States were chosen to reflect the principal variations in guided discretion capital statutes. Within each state, twenty to thirty capital trials were picked to represent both life and death sentencing outcomes. From each trial, a target sample of four jurors was systematically selected for in-depth individual interviews. Interviewing began in the summer of 1991. Each juror interview lasted approximately 3 to 4 hours. The present CJP working sample includes 1,198 jurors from 353 capital trials in 14 states. Since 1993, approximately forty articles presenting and discussing the findings of the CJP have been published in scholarly journals, and some of this research has been cited in U.S. Supreme Court decisions. For further details of the sampling design and data collection procedures, see William J. Bowers, The Capital Jury Project: Rationale, Design, and Preview of Early Findings, 70 Ind.L.J. 1043, 1080 nn.200-03 (1995) or www.cjp.neu.edu.

[3] These states included: Florida, Georgia, Kentucky, and North Carolina.

RESULTS

Physical Appearance and Personality Characteristics

Table 1 shows findings for how White female college students rated the murderers by the twelve physical appearance and personality characteristics. Column 1 shows average scores for all White offenders. Overall, the students rated White offenders lowest (under 5.0 out of a scale of 10) on attractiveness (3.54) and appearing child-like (3.90). Offenders also were rated low for other factors, including appearing friendly (4.47), honest (4.93), sincere (4.98), warm-hearted (4.31), and young-at-heart (4.02). The students rated the White offenders higher for appearing dangerous (5.75), deceptive (5.51), frightening (5.58), and self-confident (5.62). The highest rating that White females gave White offenders was for appearing mature (6.52).

Table 1 also reveals ratings on the twelve factors for Black murderers. Column 2 shows that, overall, White female college students rated Black murderers low for appearing attractive (4.23) and child-like (4.77). The murderers were rated in the mid-range for many of the other twelve factors, including appearing dangerous (5.19), deceptive (5.36), friendly (5.43), frightening (5.04), honest (5.43), sincere (5.45), warm-hearted (5.22), and young-at-heart (5.06). White females rated these Black offenders highest for appearing mature (6.11) and self-confident (6.14).

Table 1. Ratings on the Twelve Appearance and Personality Factors for White and Black Murderers

	White Murderers	Black Murderers
	Col. 1[1]	*Col. 2*[2]
	mean	mean
Attractive	3.54	4.23
Childlike	3.90	4.77
Dangerous	5.75	5.19
Deceptive	5.51	5.36
Friendly	4.47	5.43
Frightening	5.58	5.04
Honest	4.93	5.43
Mature	6.52	6.11
Self-Confident	5.62	6.14
Sincere	4.98	5.45
Warm-Hearted	4.31	5.22
Young-at-Heart	4.02	5.06

[1] Scores are based on 209-214 ratings.
[2] Scores are based on 207-214 ratings.

Overall, findings from Table 1 reveal that White female college students rated White offenders lower (on a 10-point scale) on many of the twelve factors compared to Black offenders. When White offenders were rated higher, it was for less flattering attributes, including appearing dangerous, deceptive, and frightening. White offenders also were judged to be more mature than their Black counterparts. Black offenders, on the other hand, were rated higher on two-thirds of the appearance and personality characteristics measured. Many of these factors could be thought of as positive attributes, including appearing attractive, friendly, honest, sincere, warm-hearted, and young-at-heart. Black murderers compared to White murderers also were rated higher for being child-like and self-confident.

Actual Trial Outcome

Table 2 reports *t*-test comparisons for the twelve factors when the actual sentence rendered by a capital jury was considered (i.e., life vs. death). Findings from this comparison show that White female college students rated White murderers sentenced to death by a capital jury as appearing more mature than White murderers sentenced to life (6.84 vs. 6.21) (see columns 1 and 2). This difference was statistically significant beyond the .05 probability level.

Table 2. Ratings on the Twelve Appearance and Personality Factors by *Actual* Trial Outcome for White and Black Murderers

	White Murderers			Black Murderers		
	Death[1]	Life[2]		Death[3]	Life[4]	
	Col. 1	Col. 2		Col. 3	Col .4	
	mean	Mean	diff.	mean	mean	diff.
Attractive	3.52	3.56		4.26	4.20	
Childlike	3.80	3.99		4.21	5.32	***
Dangerous	5.76	5.74		5.46	4.93	*
Deceptive	5.56	5.46		5.51	5.20	
Friendly	4.59	4.35		5.01	5.84	**
Frightening	5.64	5.51		5.39	4.69	*
Honest	4.86	5.01		5.07	5.79	**
Mature	6.84	6.21	*	6.14	6.08	
Self-Confident	5.57	5.67		6.49	5.79	**
Sincere	5.00	4.96		5.27	5.62	
Warm-Hearted	4.18	4.44		4.82	5.63	**
Young-at-Heart	3.94	4.10		4.75	5.37	*

* p < .05, ** p < .01, *** p < .001.
[1] Scores are based on 104-107 ratings.
[2] Scores are based on 105-107 ratings.
[3] Scores are based on 104-107 ratings.
[4] Scores are based on 103-107 ratings.

Columns 3 and 4 reveal findings on the twelve factors by the actual trial outcome for Black murderers. It can be seen that White females judged Black offenders sentenced to death by a capital jury, compared to those sentenced to life, as more dangerous (5.46 vs. 4.93, $p <$ .05), more frightening (5.39 vs. 4.69, $p < .05$), and more self-confident (6.49 vs. 5.79, $p <$ .01). Conversely, Black offenders sentenced to life imprisonment compared to death were rated as more child-like (5.32 vs. 4.21, $p < .001$), more friendly (5.84 vs. 5.01, $p < .01$), more honest (5.79 vs. 5.07, $p < .01$), more warm-hearted (5.63 vs. 4.82, $p < .01$), and more young-at-heart (5.37 vs. 4.75, $p < .05$).

Overall, findings in Table 2 reveal that more positive attributes were associated with Black offenders who were sentenced to life imprisonment, while negative attributes were common to Black offenders who were sentenced to death. Such findings were not uncovered among student responses for the White offenders, however. What could account for these findings, which seem to go against prior research about the perceptions of race in the CJS? Were the photographs of the capital murderers used in this study different in a manner that could explain the students' ratings? Or did the student raters detect that this study focused on offender race, and therefore were more likely to give socially-desirable responses when scoring the twelve factors? Could this also have impacted their decisions about trial outcome as well? Finally, what do these findings indicate about how actual capital jurors reached the punishment decision?

Presumed Trial Outcomes

Table 3 shows ratings on the twelve factors by students' beliefs about trial outcome for the White and Black murderers. Columns 1 and 2 indicate that when White females believed White murderers were sentenced to death by a capital jury, the offenders appeared more dangerous and more frightening than those White murderers sentenced to life (6.29 vs. 5.08 and 6.42 vs. 4.68, respectively). These findings were statistically significant beyond the .001 probability level. Students' ratings for White offenders, believed to be sentenced to life instead of death, showed that offenders were judged to be more attractive (4.04 vs. 3.04, $p <$ .001), more friendly (5.26 vs. 3.69, $p < .001$), more honest (5.52 vs. 4.47, $p < .001$), more mature (6.97 vs. 6.16, $p < .01$), more sincere (5.49 vs. 4.49, $p < .001$), more warm-hearted (4.90 vs. 3.70, $p < .001$), and more young-at-heart (4.46 vs. 3.63, $p < .01$).

Table 3 also reveals findings for Black murderers. Columns 3 and 4 show that White females rated Black murderers who they believed were sentenced to death compared to life as more dangerous and more frightening (5.68 vs. 4.75 and 5.42 vs. 4.72, respectively). These findings were statistically significant beyond the .001 and .05 probability levels. When the students believed the murderers were sentenced to life instead of death, however, the murderers were judged more child-like (5.22 vs. 4.30, $p < .01$), more friendly (6.06 vs. 4.77, p < .001), more honest (5.84 vs. 4.97, $p < .001$), more warm-hearted (5.70 vs. 4.68, $p < .001$), and more young-at-heart (5.40 vs. 4.69, $p < .05$).

Table 3. Ratings on the Twelve Appearance and Personality Factors by *Presumed* Trial Outcome for White and Black Murderers

	White Murderers			Black Murderers		
	Death[1]	*Life[2]*		*Death[3]*	*Life[4]*	
	Col. 1	Col. 2		Col. 3	Col. 4	
	mean	mean	*diff.*	mean	mean	*diff.*
Attractive	3.04	4.04	***	4.23	4.25	
Childlike	3.66	4.16		4.30	5.22	**
Dangerous	6.29	5.08	***	5.68	4.75	***
Deceptive	5.69	5.34		5.54	5.27	
Friendly	3.69	5.26	***	4.77	6.06	***
Frightening	6.42	4.68	***	5.42	4.72	*
Honest	4.47	5.52	***	4.97	5.84	***
Mature	6.16	6.97	**	6.08	6.11	
Self-Confident	5.50	5.77		6.16	6.06	
Sincere	4.49	5.49	***	5.25	5.56	
Warm-Hearted	3.70	4.90	***	4.68	5.70	***
Young-at-Heart	3.63	4.46	**	4.69	5.40	*

* $p < .05$, ** $p < .01$, *** $p < .001$
[1] Scores are based on 100-102 ratings.
[2] Scores are based on 98-101 ratings.
[3] Scores are based on 98-102 ratings.
[4] Scores are based on 98-101 ratings.

Overall, findings from Table 3 suggest that many of the appearance and personality factors impacted White female college students' decision about punishment similarly regardless of race. That is, offenders who appeared dangerous and frightening were believed to be sentenced to death, while offenders who appeared friendly, honest, warm-hearted, and young-at-heart were believed to be sentenced to life. Some differences were found, however, for race of the offender on several factors. For example, White murderers who appeared attractive, mature, and sincere were believed to be sentenced to life, while Black offenders who appeared child-like were thought to have received a life sentence.

Comparing findings shown in Tables 2 and 3 provides valuable insight into how physical appearance and personality characteristics are used inside the courtroom. These findings clearly indicate the importance that physical appearance has on decision-making in capital cases. Indeed, the more favorable the offender appears during a trial, the more likely he will be sentenced to life imprisonment, while the more unfavorable his appearance, the more likely he will be sentenced to death. These findings were true when considering White females' beliefs about trial outcomes.

The same relationships also existed when the actual trial outcomes were considered. This was true at least in cases involving Black murderers. These findings suggest that in some murderer cases (specifically when the defendant is Black), jurors may rely on stereotypical responses based on physical appearance and personality characteristics when reaching a decision about punishment. In murderer cases involving a White defendant, however, there were fewer findings that appearance would significantly impact trial outcome. This may suggest that in cases involving White defendants, jurors are more likely to consider evidence presented during the trial and to use that factual information during their deliberations when rendering a verdict about punishment.

Correctly Identifying Trial Outcomes

The remainder of the analysis will show findings for the full sample of student respondents. Table 4 shows how accurate the entire student sample was for identifying the actual trial outcome reached by a capital jury. As can be seen from the table for White murderers, who actually were sentenced to death by a capital jury, there was significant variation in how accurate the students were at identifying the true outcome of the case. Indeed, the range of accuracy for identifying a death sentence was 0% - 81%. A closer examination showed that for three of the photographs depicting White murderers (#10, #11, and #12), 75% or more of the student raters accurately chose a death sentence (75.0%, 77.3%, and 81.0%, respectively). Also, for two photographs (#1 and #2) the percent accuracy was less than 25%. Indeed, for one of these photographs (#1), all 23 student raters incorrectly guessed that the White murderer photographed was sentenced to life imprisonment. Overall, the percentage of students who accurately chose the White murderer who received a death sentence was 53.9%, which is slightly higher than one would expect by chance alone.

The accuracy for identifying White murderers, who were sentenced to life by a capital jury, fared worse, however. As shown in Table 4, in only one photograph (#24) did more than 75% of the student raters accurately choose a life sentence (85.7%), and in three photographs (#13, #14, and #15) student raters achieved less than 25% accuracy (15.8%, 22.7%, and 23.1%, respectively). Overall, the percentage of students who accurately chose the White murderer, who was sentenced to life by a capital jury, was 45.3%. This was slightly lower than one would expect by chance alone.

Table 4 also reveals findings about how accurate students were for identifying the actual life and death sentences for Black murderers. Students were not able to accurately identify, with a degree of precision greater than 75%, any photographs depicting Black offenders who were sentenced to death. The photograph with the highest percent accuracy for identifying trial outcome was #36 with 72.7%. However, none of the photographs completely deceived the student raters either, as accuracy for choosing a Black murderer, who was sentenced to death, did not fall below 25%. The photograph with the least accurate sentencing identification was #25 with 34.8%. Overall, student accuracy for selecting a Black murderer, who was actually sentenced to death by a capital jury, was 51.9%.

Student accuracy for identifying trial outcome was the highest for Black murderers sentenced to life imprisonment. Student raters were able to achieve 75% accuracy or better for two photographs (#47 and #48) depicting Black murderers sentenced to life (75.0% and 84.0%, respectively), while the photograph with the worst accuracy was #37 with 33.3%, which was still above the lower 25% quartile. Overall, students were able to identify the Black murderer, actually sentenced to life imprisonment, 58.4% of the time, which is higher than one would expect to find by chance alone.

Table 4. Percent of Student Sample Correctly Identifying Trial Outcome

	White, death offenders				White, life offenders		
Photo No.	No. student raters	No. chose death	% correct	**Photo No.**	No. student raters	No. chose life	% correct
1	23	0	.00	**13**	19	3	15.8
2	22	5	22.7	**14**	22	5	22.7
3	25	13	52.0	**15**	26	6	23.1
4	23	12	52.2	**16**	19	5	26.3
5	24	13	54.2	**17**	22	8	36.4
6	22	12	54.6	**18**	21	10	47.6
7	25	14	56.0	**19**	22	11	50.0
8	23	13	56.5	**20**	22	12	54.6
9	23	15	65.2	**21**	26	15	57.7
10	16	12	75.0	**22**	26	16	61.5
11	22	17	77.3	**23**	24	15	62.5
12	21	17	*81.0*	**24**	21	18	*85.7*
			X=53.9				*X=45.3*

	Black, death offenders				Black, life offenders		
Photo No.	No. student raters	No. chose death	% correct	**Photo No.**	No. student raters	No. chose life	% correct
25	23	8	34.8	**37**	21	7	33.3
26	23	9	39.1	**38**	25	11	44.0
27	22	9	40.9	**39**	22	11	50.0
28	23	10	43.5	**40**	22	11	50.0
29	25	11	44.0	**41**	23	13	56.5
30	22	10	45.5	**42**	19	11	57.9
31	19	10	52.6	**43**	24	14	58.3
32	22	12	54.6	**44**	23	14	60.9
33	22	14	63.6	**45**	23	14	60.9
34	23	15	65.2	**46**	20	14	70.0
35	24	16	66.7	**47**	20	15	75.0
36	22	16	72.7	**48**	25	21	84.0
			X=51.9				X=58.4

After examining the individual photographs mentioned above, certain patterns or characteristics among the murderers were observed. For example, photograph #1 depicted an older man with a receding hairline and wrinkled face. Some raters commented informally to test administers after the experiment that the offender looked like a grandfather. Could the offender's appearance account for why 100% of the student raters thought he was sentenced to life? Also observed was photograph #48, which showed a man who noticeably was overweight. His facial features reflected that of a typical baby (i.e., large cheeks and eyes, small chin, bald), which has been found in previous research to impact juror decision-making about culpability and punishment. Could this offender's appearance explain why approximately 85% of the student raters believed this murderer was sentenced to life?

Additional patterns were observed in students' decisions about trial outcome for other murderers who had certain physical characteristics, including being bald, having a beard, or having a mustache. These findings are shown in Table 5. It can be seen in this table that 29.6% of the murderers students believed were sentenced to life were bald compared to only 16.6% of the murderers students believed were sentenced to death. This finding is true for those offenders having a mustache as well. That is, 38.3% of offenders that students believed were sentenced to life had mustaches compared to only 24.5% of offenders believed to be sentenced to death. These findings are statistically significant beyond the .001 probability level. Finally, findings indicated that 19.8% of murderers believed to be sentenced to death had beards compared to 12.0% of murderers believed to be sentenced to life imprisonment (p < .01).

Table 5. Trial Outcome by Physical Appearance

	No. of ratings	Life	Death	Sig.
Bald	246	29.6%	16.6%	***
Beard	169	12.0%	19.8%	**
Mustache	334	38.3%	24.5%	***

** p < .01, *** p < .001

Table 6 shows findings when these three physical appearance characteristics (bald, beard, and mustache) were included in a regression analysis. Findings indicate that being bald had the strongest impact on trial outcome ($B = -.654$). This finding suggests that when the murderer was bald, students believed he was sentenced to life imprisonment by a capital jury. This finding was statistically significant beyond the .001 probability level. Also related to sentencing outcome was having a mustache. That is, when the offender had a mustache, students believed he received a life sentence ($B=-.492$, $p < .01$). While having a beard was related to students' beliefs that the offender was sentenced to death, this finding fell short of the .05 probability level for statistical significance.

Table 6. Logistic Regression with Physical Appearance

	B	Sig.
Bald	-.654	***
Beard	.345	n.s.
Mustache	-.492	**
Constant	.243	

** p < .01, *** p < .001

CONCLUSION AND IMPLICATIONS

A litigant's physical appearance and attitude displayed inside a courtroom can significantly impact the outcome of a trial. Indeed, previous research has shown that capital defendants who appeared emotionally involved during a trial were more likely to be sentenced to life imprisonment by a capital jury, while defendants who appeared emotionally uninvolved were more likely to be sentenced to death. The present analysis examined how a sample of undergraduate college students rated capital murderers on twelve factors related to physical appearance and personality characteristics, and whether these ratings impacted their decision about whether a capital jury rendered a life or death sentence.

The 48 offender photographs included in this study were rated mid-range (on a 10-point scale) for many of the twelve physical appearance factors and personality characteristics. Findings did vary somewhat when offender race was considered, however. White female college students rated Black murderers (compared to White murderers) as more attractive, more child-like, more friendly, more honest, more self-confident, more sincere, more warm-hearted, and more young-at-heart, while they judged White murderers (compared to Black murderers) as more dangerous, more deceptive, more frightening, and more mature. Overall, White offenders, who *actually* were sentenced to death by a capital jury, were judged to be more mature, and Black offenders who were sentenced to death were rated as more dangerous, frightening, and self-confident compared to White and Black offenders sentenced to life. Also, it was found that Black offenders, who actually were sentenced to life by a capital jury, were rated more child-like, more friendly, more honest, more warm-hearted, and more young-at-heart than Black offenders sentenced to death.

This analysis also examined White females' presumptions about trial outcome. Findings showed that regardless of race, when the offender was judged dangerous and frightening, students believed he was sentenced to death; however when the offender appeared friendly, honest, warm-hearted, and young-at-heart, students believed he was sentenced to life. Overall, students believed that White murderers they rated as attractive, mature, and sincere, and Black murderers they rated as child-like, were sentenced to life imprisonment.

The findings shown in this analysis have significant implications for the CJS and suggest that judgments about physical appearance and personality characteristics impact students' beliefs about punishment, but were not related to the actual trial outcome itself— at least not for White murderers. These findings may indicate that capital jurors, like the research participants in this study, rely on stereotypes when deciding the punishment for Black murderers. Since the same relationships were not found among White murderers when comparing responses for the actual trial outcome with students' beliefs about trial outcome, this suggests that jurors also may have relied more on the facts of the case that were presented inside the courtroom during the trial rather than on physical appearance or personality characteristics.

Finally, even though students were able to correctly identify trial outcome over 50% of the time in 3 out of the 4 race/sentence categories (White death, Black life, and Black death), findings were poorer than expected. This suggests, as mentioned above, that for many of the offenders photographed, the actual facts of the case, attorney arguments made during the trial, and jury deliberations about evidence and guilt may ultimately have played a more significant role in how the offender was sentenced than did physical appearance and personality characteristics alone.

Another explanation for the low accuracy to identify trial outcome could be that the photographs of the individual offenders did not accurately reflect how the offender appeared inside the courtroom during the actual capital trial. Indeed, his physical appearance (i.e., haircut, clothes, demeanor, etc.) may have been quite different when standing in front of a jury of twelve men and women who were going to decide his fate, than when posing to be photographed by staff at a state correctional facility. Indeed, in those instances where there was a significant difference in appearance, this could have impacted ratings on the twelve factors and student accuracy for correctly identifying the trial verdicts reached by a capital jury.

Findings uncovered here about how physical appearance impacts trial outcome can be expanded upon with future research. Specifically, during the course of this study, test administrators were consistently questioned by student raters, informally after the experiment, about details of the murder that individual offenders committed. While no details of the crime were provided, students often openly speculated about the killing. Comments received were intriguing. For example, many students identified the murderers as sexual offenders, but could not indicate what features and/or characteristics led them to this conclusion. One student believed that one of the offenders he rated was involved in a murder while committing an armed robbery simply because of the "look in his eyes." Based on the frequency of requests for more information about the killing and the degree of speculation about the crime type, test administrators concluded that further research should evaluate participants' beliefs about crime type and what physical appearance characteristics or features contributed to those decisions.

Overall, findings shown here clearly indicate the strong link that physical appearance and personality characteristics have on judgments about trial outcome. Also, differences were observed for ratings on the twelve factors by trial outcome when offender race was considered. These findings should be important for trial attorneys, who must take into consideration his or her client's appearance and personality when arguing a case in front of a jury. Understanding how a jury may interpret certain characteristics of a plaintiff or defendant will provide a significant advantage inside the courtroom.

REFERENCES

Antonio, M. E. 2006. "Arbitrariness and the Death Penalty: How the Defendant's Appearance During Trial Influences Capital Jurors' Punishment Decision." 24(3) *Behavioral Sciences and the Law*, 215-234.

Badzinski, D. M. and A. B. Pettus. 1994. Nonverbal Involvement and Sex: Effects on Jury Decision Making. *Journal of Applied Communication Research 22*: 309- 321.

Bandura, A., D. Ross, and S. Ross. 1963. Vicarious reinforcement and imitative learning. *Journal of Abnormal and Social Psychology 67*: 601-607.

Berry, D.S. and L. Z. McArthur. 1985. Some opponents and consequences of a babyface. *Journal of Personality and Social Psychology 48*: 312-323.

Berry, D. S. and L. Z. McArthur. 1986. Perceiving character in faces: The impact of age-related craniofacial changes on social perception. *Psychological Bulletin 100*: 3-18.

Berry, D. S. and L. Z. McArthur. 1988. What's in a face? Facial maturity and attribution of legal responsibility. *Personality and Social Psychology Bulletin 14*: 23-33.

Bull, R. and B. R. Clifford. 1979. Earwitness voice recognition accuracy. In G. Wells & E. Loftus (Eds.), Eyewitness testimony: Psychological perspectives. New York: Cambridge University Press.

Bull, R. and J. Green. 1980. The relationship between physical appearance and criminality. *Medical Science Law 20*: 79-83.

Downs, A. C. and P. M. Lyons. 1991. National observations of the links between attractiveness and initial legal judgments. *Personality and Social Psychology Bulletin 17*: 541-547.

Eberhardt, J. L., P. G. Davies, V. J. Purdie-Vaughns, S. L. Johnson. (2006). Research Report; Looking Deathworthy. Psychological Science, 17 (5): 383.

Efran, M. G. 1974. The Effect of Physical Appearance on the Judgment of Guilt, Interpersonal Attraction, and Severity of Recommended Punishment in a Simulated Jury Task. *Journal of Research in Personality 8*: 45-54.

Goldin, S. E. 1979. Facial stereotypes as cognitive categories. Unpublished doctoral dissertation, Carnegie-Mellon University, Pittsburgh, PA. Cited in Goldstein, A. J., et al. (1984).

Goldstein, A. G., J. E. Chance, and B. Gilbert. 1984. Facial stereotypes of good guys and bad guys: A replication and extension. *Bulletin of the Psychonomic Society 22*: 549-552.

Lown, C. 1977. Legal approaches to juror stereotyping by physical characteristics. *Law and Human Behavior 1*: 87-100.

McArthur, L. Z .1982. Judging a book by its cover: A cognitive analysis of the relationship between physical appearance and stereotyping. In A. H. Hastorf & A. M. Isen (Eds.), Cognitive Social Psychology (pp 149-211). New York: Elsevier North-Holland. (Cited in Goldstein, et al. 1984).

Pryor, B. and R. W. Buchanan. 1984. The effects of a defendant's demeanor on juror perceptions of credibility and guilt. *Journal of Communication 34*: 92-99.

Shoemaker, D. J., D. R. South, and J. Lowe. 1973. Facial Stereotypes of deviants and judgments of guilt or innocence. *Social Forces 51*: 427-433.

Sigall, H. and N. Ostrove. 1975. Beautiful but dangerous: Effects of offender attractiveness and nature of crime on juridic judgment. *Journal of Personality and Social Psychology 31*: 410-414.

Stephan, C. and J. C. Tully. 1977. The influence of physical attractiveness of a plaintiff on the decisions of simulated jurors. *The Journal of Social Psychology 101*: 149-150.

Stewart, J. E. 1980. Defendant's attractiveness as a factor in the outcome of criminal trials: An observational study. *Journal of Applied Social Psychology 10*: 348-361.

Strachey, L. 1933. *Eminent victorians*. New York: Modern Library.

Thornton, B. 1977. Effect of rape victim's attractiveness in a jury simulation. *Personality and Social Psychology Bulletin 3*: 666-669.

Villemar, N., J. Hyde. 1983. Effects of sex of defense attorney, sex of juror and attractiveness of the victim on mock juror decision making in a rape case. *Sex Roles 9*: 879-889.

Zebrowitz, L. A. and S. M. McDonald. 1991. The Impact of Litigants' Baby- Facedness and Attractiveness on Adjudications in Small Claims Courts. *Law and Human Behaviors* *15*:603-623.

Zebrowitz, L. A. and J. M. Montepare. 1990. Impressions of males and females across the lifespan as a function of their baby-facedness and attractiveness. Unpublished manuscript. Cited in Zebrowitz, L. A. and S. M. McDonald, 1991.

In: Psychology of Decision Making...
Editor: G. R. Burthold, pp. 141-157

ISBN: 978-1-60021-932-0
© 2007 Nova Science Publishers, Inc.

Chapter 5

MULTIPLE CAUSES OF THE SUNK-COST EFFECT

Edmund Fantino, Anton Navarro, Stephanie Stolarz-Fantino

University of California, San Diego
La Jolla, Californa, U.S.A.

ABSTRACT

The sunk-cost effect describes a common type of non-optimal decision in which humans contribute additional resources to a failing endeavor as a function of previous expenditures of resources (time, effort or money, the "sunk costs"). This phenomenon is intriguing because it appears to result from considering prior costs in decision making rather than basing decisions solely (and rationally) on marginal costs and benefits. We review different types of sunk-cost effects including those embodied in our laboratory's explorations of the factors controlling sunk-cost behavior in both humans and pigeons. These experiments suggested that sunk-cost behavior should be minimized if salient cues directed the participants' attention to the marginal costs and benefits. This finding led to one of the three experiments reported in this paper: By presenting the participant with precise economic forecasts we produced a "reverse" sunk-cost effect in which past expenditure of resources made future spending less (not more) likely. Two additional experiments explored the notion that poor decision-making behavior sometimes reflects inappropriate application of learned aversion to waste (as in "Waste not, want not"). This possibility was explored with both sunk-cost and Ultimatum Game scenarios. In each case support was found for the possibility that non-optimal decisions may be based in part on an aversion to waste. Just as there are different types of sunk-cost behavior, there are multiple causes of these behaviors. From an applied standpoint, however, it appears that presenting information in a complete and transparent manner may minimize such non-optimal decisions.

INTRODUCTION

A sizable literature suggests that people become more likely to persist in questionable courses of action once they have made an investment. Researchers have labeled this phenomenon alternatively the sunk-cost effect (Thaler, 1980) and escalation (Staw, 1976). The sunk-cost effect has intrigued researchers because it involves the inclusion of past costs into decision-making, which counters the maxim that choices should be based on marginal costs and benefits.

Anecdotally, the sunk-cost effect seems to occur in a wide variety of settings. With a small amount of observation or reflection, one may see how people appear to attend to past costs in such diverse endeavors as education, research, and romantic relationships. College students sometimes appear to continue in a major they do not like or need because they have already taken so many classes for the major and studied so many hours. Scientists sometimes appear to persist in failing research projects because they have already invested so much money, time, and creative energy. A more infamous anecdotal example of the sunk-cost effect, and one on a grander scale, is the United States involvement in the Vietnam War (Staw, 1981). The United States arguably was locked in the war for so long because the involvement, or sunk cost, was enormous on many levels—lives spent, billions of dollars spent, countless hours of deliberation and planning by many people, spent. The concern that "lives will be lost in vain" appears to have motivated many cases in which ill-advised military actions have been prolonged.

It is important to note that in each example persistence may have resulted from other factors—in particular, a rational analysis of marginal costs and benefits. An *apparent* sunk-cost effect isn't necessarily a sunk-cost effect. For example, in non-human animals, the sunk-cost effect is called the Concorde fallacy. A review by Arkes and Ayton (1999) concluded that there are no clear-cut instances of the Concorde fallacy in non-humans. They examined purported instances of the Concorde fallacy in the behavioral ecology literature and showed that in every case, behaviors that appeared to be a response to sunk costs could actually be explained in terms of future gains. The reason why that the Concorde fallacy has not been well supported, they proposed, was that the sunk-cost effect depends on social norms, such as "waste not want not", that are unique to humans.

However, certain lines of research with humans suggest the possibility that non-human animals could display this effect. For example, reinforcement history has been shown to affect sub optimal persistence in an investment (Goltz, 1992, 1999). Both the partial reinforcement extinction effect (Goltz, 1992) and behavioral momentum (Goltz, 1999) have been implicated as mechanisms through which reinforcement history could result in persistence. For example, Goltz (1992, Experiment 1) tested persistence in a simulated investment task in which she manipulated participants' past experience of the success or failure of their investments. Participants received returns on their investments (*i.e.*, success) in one of two investment alternatives on one of the following schedules: 1) on every trial; 2) on every other trial; or 3) unpredictably, but averaging out to be on one of every two trials. In behavioral terms, these are equivalent to continuous, fixed partial, and variable partial schedules of reinforcement. When conditions were later altered such that the investment alternative continuously failed to pay off (that is, under conditions of extinction) those participants who were exposed to the least predictable schedule (*i.e.*, the variable partial schedule) persisted in investing significantly longer than those in the two other conditions. Interestingly, Goltz (1992) also included a condition in which the investing participants were given *no* history. These participants persisted about as much as those given variable histories. Goltz (1992) suggested that, in the absence of past experience such as that provided in her persistence-of-commitment task, participants come to the experimental situation with their own histories of variable partial reinforcement for investments and generalize from those histories. Thus, in the absence of an explicit context provided by the experimenter, participants' own past histories provide them with a context for the task. Further support for this view comes from research (*e.g.*, Hantula & Bragger, 1999) suggesting that, when participants are provided with a standard against which outcomes can be compared, there may be less effect of reinforcement history on persistence of commitment. Goltz (1999) also found increases in persistence as participants' past histories included higher rates and greater magnitudes of reinforcement. All of these results are consistent with a behavioral view of the importance of reinforcement history for understanding persistence of commitment. Recent work in our laboratory aimed at developing a pigeon analog to the sunk-cost effect and assessing the conditions under which pigeons and human subjects are most susceptible to it (Fantino, Stolarz-Fantino, & Navarro, 2003) will be reviewed shortly.

It often appears that uncertainty is at the root of persistence. For example, human subjects will persist in an unprofitable research and development project in its early stages, but as losses mount, they *de*-escalate commitment (McCain, 1986). Given that these participants eventually behave correctly by de-escalating commitment, the incorrect persistence in the early stages of the project may indicate that the participants do not yet know in those early stages that the project is unprofitable. McCain (1986) concluded that escalation and de-escalation are learning processes in which optimal behavior surfaces only when the economics of the situation become clear. Bragger and her associates (Bragger, Bragger, Hantula, & Kirnan, 1998; Bragger, Hantula, Bragger, Kirnan, & Kutcher, 2003) explored this hypothesis further in their studies on hysteresis. Their participants had to choose whether to continue with or abandon hypothetical investments while receiving negative economic feedback concerning the investments. In one condition, participants received unambiguous feedback--the investment consistently produced losses of a similar magnitude. In another condition, participants received ambiguous feedback --the investment produced losses of varying magnitude, and occasionally produced a gain, though the average return was equal to that of the former condition. Participants with ambiguous feedback persisted in the project significantly longer than those with unambiguous feedback, and participants with the opportunity to purchase additional feedback quit the project significantly sooner than those without that opportunity. To explain these results, Bragger and her associates cited Bowen's (1987) equivocality theory of escalation. Similar to McCain's (1986) hypothesis, equivocality theory posits that decision-makers in escalation situations are trying to make sense out of uncertain information. While trying to decipher variable feedback on an investment, decision-makers may be better off continuing to invest until it is certain that the investment is sub optimal.

We proposed that if uncertainty and reinforcement history could influence persistence in humans, these variables might plausibly bring about persistence in non-human animals. Thus, Navarro and Fantino (2005) set out to explore conditions of uncertainty and reinforcement history under which pigeons might persist in a losing course of action. To this end, they designed a procedure that models the sunk cost decision scenario. They defined a sunk cost decision scenario as one in which an investment has been made towards a goal, negative feedback concerning the investment has been received, and the investor can persist in the investment or abandon it in favor of a new one. In their procedure, pigeons began a trial by pecking on a key for food. The schedule on the food key arranged a course of action with initially good prospects that turned unfavorable. On a given trial, one of four fixed-ratio (FR) schedules was in effect: short, medium, long, or extra long. On half the trials, the short ratio was in effect; on a quarter of the trials, the medium ratio was in effect; and on a quarter of the trials either of the two long ratios was in effect. With these parameters, after the pigeons emitted the response number required by the short ratio, if no reinforcement had occurred (because one of the longer ratios happened to be in effect), then the initially easy endeavor had become more arduous—the expected number of responses to food was now greater than it had been at the onset of the trial.

Navarro and Fantino (2005) gave pigeons the option of escaping the now less-favorable endeavor by allowing them to peck an "escape" key that initiated a new trial. If the short ratio did not happen to be in effect on a given trial, then once the value of the short ratio had been met the optimal choice was to peck the escape key (and then begin anew on the food key). That is, the expected ratio given escape was lower than the expected ratio given persistence. Notice that at this choice point the pigeons encountered a sunk cost decision scenario. Namely, they had made an initial investment, they had received negative feedback—no reinforcement—and they could either persist in the venture or abandon it in favor of a better one.

This general procedure allowed examination of the role of uncertainty in the sunk cost effect in two ways. One way was through the presence or absence of stimulus changes. If a stimulus change occurred at the moment when escape became optimal, then the economics of the situation should have been more salient than if no stimulus change had occurred. Navarro and Fantino hypothesized that pigeons responding on this procedure with no stimulus change would persist more than pigeons responding on this procedure with a stimulus change present. The results matched our hypothesis—when stimulus changes were absent, the majority of pigeons persisted to the end of every trial. When changes were present, however, all pigeons escaped as soon as it became optimal (this trend appeared once behavior had become stable). A second way to manipulate uncertainty is by varying the difference between the expected value of persisting and the expected value of escaping. The closer these expected values were to each other, the less salient the advantage of escaping and the more likely the pigeons should be to persist. The results again matched our hypothesis—as the advantage of escaping decreased (although still being optimal), persistence rose.

Additionally, by modifying this procedure for use with human subjects, previous findings with human subjects could be extended to a novel format. The above experiments with pigeons were replicated with humans (Navarro & Fantino, 2005; Navarro & Fantino, 2008) in a computer simulation. In the human experiments, the computer keys were the operant and hypothetical money was the reinforcer, and the same contingencies were used. As expected, the human data mirrored those of the pigeons. We suggest that some factors that contribute to the sunk-cost effect—namely, economic salience and the presence of discriminative stimuli—may affect both non-human animals and humans in a similar manner.

Are natural instances of persistence sometimes optimal? Indeed, Rachlin (2000) stresses that persistence is the key to self-control (and to overcoming impulsive behavior). Let us consider the case of a scientist persisting in a research project that has not produced results.

The scientist might persist only when it truly appears to be optimal. In this view, the sunk-cost effect may only be labeled as such *post hoc*. As we have discussed, several studies suggest that behavior in sunk-cost situations is indeed sensitive to true contingencies (Bragger, *et al.*, 1998; Navarro & Fantino, 2005).

Nevertheless, the abundance of anecdotal cases is very suggestive of the "irrational" sunk-cost effect; in support of the anecdotal evidence, a body of empirical findings suggests that the sunk-cost effect is indeed real (see Brockner, 1992, for a review). Consider a classic experiment by Arkes and Blumer (1985), in which a university theater ticket window sold season tickets to customers at one of three prices: $15, $13, or $8. The two lower prices were not advertised, but rather were offered as a promotional discount once a customer had already requested season tickets. Arkes and Blumer measured the number of plays that each group attended throughout the season by counting the number of ticket stubs that corresponded to each price. Normative behavior in this case should result in equal attendance across groups (assuming the groups are equally endowed, which is reasonable). The price of the owned ticket should not affect attendance. However, the results were that for the first six months of the theater season, customers who had paid $15 attended significantly more plays than the other two groups. Indeed, there was a sunk-cost effect.

Other experiments from the same study by Arkes and Blumer (1985) showed the same effect. For instance, in one of several questionnaire experiments (Experiment 1), participants read one of the following questions:

Question A.   As the president of an airline company, you have invested $10 million of the company's money into a research project. The purpose was to build a plane that would not be detected by conventional radar, in other words, a radar-blank plane. When the project is 90% completed, another firm begins marketing a plane that cannot be detected by radar. Also, it is apparent that the airplane is much faster and far more economical than the plane your company is building. The question is: should you invest the last 10% of the research funds to finish your radar-blank plane?

Question B.   As president of an airline company, you have received a suggestion from one of your employees. The suggestion is to use the last $1 million of your research funds to develop a plane that would not be detected by conventional radar, in other words, a radar-blank plane. However, another firm has just begun marketing a plane that cannot be detected by radar. Also, it is apparent that the airplane is much faster and far more economical than the plane your company could build. The question is: should you invest the last million dollars of your research funds to build the radar-blank plane proposed by your employee?

Notice that in both questions, the dilemma is whether to spend $1 million towards a project with a dubious chance for success (this marginal cost is stated explicitly in Question B, but implicitly in Question A). However, in Question A, millions of dollars have already been spent (sunk cost is high), whereas in Question B, nothing has been spent. The results were that 80% of the participants who read Question A answered "yes", compared with only 17% of the participants who read Question B—a strong sunk-cost effect.

Across several studies, Hal Arkes and his associates have developed the hypothesis that the sunk-cost effect is caused by the desire to avoid waste (Arkes & Blumer, 1985; Arkes, 1996; Arkes & Ayton, 1999). Arkes and Blumer (1985) interpreted the two experiments that we have described in terms of waste-avoidance. Subjects in the theater-ticket experiment may have thought that throwing away a discounted ticket was not too wasteful, while throwing away a regular ticket was. Subjects in the radar-blank plane experiment may have thought that quitting a project on which millions of dollars have been spent is a waste of those sunk costs. Consider another experiment by Arkes and Blumer (1985), in which subjects read the following question:

> Assume that you have spent $100 on a ticket for a weekend ski trip to Michigan. Several weeks later you buy a $50 ticket for a weekend ski trip to Wisconsin. You think you'll enjoy the Wisconsin ski trip more than the Michigan ski trip. As you are putting your just-purchased Wisconsin ski trip ticket in your wallet, you notice that the Michigan ski trip and the Wisconsin ski trip are for the same weekend! It's too late to sell either ticket, and you cannot return either one. You must use one ticket and not the other. Which ski trip will you go on?

The results were that more than half the subjects preferred the *less-enjoyable* Michigan trip. Again, a waste-avoidance interpretation is appealing: throwing away the $100 ticket is more wasteful than throwing away the $50 ticket.

Arkes and Ayton (1999) hypothesized more specifically that the desire to avoid waste results from the overgeneralization of a social norm akin to "waste not, want not". Consistent with this hypothesis, those authors pointed out that young children and non-human animals have never been found to display the effect. For example, Webley and Plaisier (1997) found that 5 and 6-year-old children do not attend to sunk costs when making a decision, while children aged 8 and above do. Arkes and Ayton argued that young children and non-human animals are less likely to have the cognitive development necessary to follow abstract social norms; therefore it makes sense that adult humans are the only group for which clear evidence of the sunk-cost effect has been found.

It should be noted that other theories also account for the sunk-cost effect. These include self-justification, which asserts that we experience a psychological need to justify or rationalize our past behavior when it falls short of a goal (Staw, 1976), and Kahneman and Tversky's (1979) Prospect Theory, which, when applied to the sunk cost effect, proposes that individuals treat decisions in the presence of sunk cost as a choice between two losses, leading to risk-seeking behavior with the hope of avoiding a loss (Whyte, 1986). Each of these theories has received some empirical support, although no theory appears to account for all of the data.

EXPERIMENT 1

Presently, we designed an experiment to further test the waste-avoidance hypothesis of the sunk-cost effect. The hypothesis implies that if we hold sunk cost size constant and manipulate the wastefulness of the sunk cost, then we should observe that as the wastefulness goes down, persistence also goes down. How could one manipulate the wastefulness of sunk costs? One way could be to manipulate whether the sunk costs go to charity. Imagine two comparable scenarios—one in which sunk costs have been spent toward a now-undesirable endeavor, and another in which the same costs have been spent toward the endeavor but the costs also happened to go to charity. According to the hypothesis, fewer subjects should persist in the charity condition. We tested this prediction using a variation of the ski-trip experiment by Arkes and Blumer (1985).

Method

Subjects

141 male and female undergraduate students participated in the experiment. All participated in the present experiment as part of a 2-hour session for course credit that involved other experiments.

Procedure

There were two independent variables: 1) the level of sunk cost, and 2) whether or not the sunk cost went to charity. Participants read one version of the following questionnaire:

> Assume that you have spent $200 ($400, $600) on a front row ticket to a professional theater performance. A couple of days later a casual acquaintance gives you a $100 ticket (in a good section) to a rock concert by a band you like. Both tickets were purchased to support a fundraiser put on by your favorite charity. You think you will like to see both these events, although you expect to enjoy the rock concert more. As you are putting the tickets away in your bedroom, you notice that both events are scheduled for the same evening. The tickets are non-transferable and cannot be refunded. You can use only one of the tickets and not the other. Which event will you go to? Write it below.
>
> The design was 3(Sunk Cost) x 2(Charity), for a total of 6 conditions administered between-subjects. The levels of sunk cost were the dollars spent on the theater performance, $200, $400, or $600. The scenario above depicts the "charity" condition. In the "no charity" condition, the sentence mentioning the charity was absent.

Table 1. The Number of Subjects selecting the Theater Ticket Divided by the Total Number of Subjects

	Dollars Spent on Theater Ticket			
	200	400	600	Combined
No Charity	9/21 (43%)	17/21 (81%)	14/24 (58%)	40/66 (61%)
Charity	7/21 (33%)	12/22 (55%)	17/32 (53%)	36/75 (48%)
Combined	16/42 (38%)	29/43 (67%)	31/56 (55%)	

Results

The percentage of participants who selected the theater ticket, combined across levels of charity, was 38 in the $200 condition, 67 in the $400 condition, and 55 in the $600 condition. The effect of Sunk Cost was statistically significant, $F = 3.85$, $p < .05$. The percentages for the "charity" and "no charity" groups, averaged across levels of Sunk Cost, were 48 and 61, respectively. The effect of Charity, while in the predicted direction, was not statistically significant ($F = 2.25$, $p = .136$). No significant interactions were found. Table 1 shows, for each cell, the number of participants who selected the theater divided by the n for that cell.

Discussion

Two main points are evident from the data. Firstly, sunk cost size mattered. The trend was that the more money that had been spent on the theater ticket, the more likely the participants were to select it. This finding is consistent with the typical finding on the sunk-cost effect, and lends further support to the sunk-cost effect as a real phenomenon. The second point is that the charity manipulation had an effect consistent with the waste-avoidance hypothesis, although the effect was not statistically significant. What implication does this have? One possibility is that "waste" has a true but only small effect. Another possibility is that our subjects did not perceive the "charity" sunk costs as being less wasteful than the "non-charity" ones. Pilot data, however, suggested that perceptions of waste (reported by the participants on a numeric scale) *were* affected by the charity manipulation, in the predicted direction. In conclusion, the present data lend mild support to the waste-avoidance hypothesis.

EXPERIMENT 2

Next, we tested the waste-avoidance hypothesis in the context of a different economic activity, the Ultimatum Game (Guth, Schmittberger, & Schwarze, 1982). In this game, a participant is given a sum of money to divide with another (usually unknown) participant. He or she makes an offer to the other that can range from no money at all to the entire sum. If Participant 2 accepts, the money is divided according to the offer; if not, then neither participant receives any money. Generally, participants have been found to accept offers of at least 20-30% of the sum; offers of less than 20% are often refused (for a review, see Camerer, 2003). Will participants who are told that, if the offer is refused, the money will go to a charitable cause (will not really be "wasted") be less willing to accept low offers than those who are told that the money will not be usable for any purpose (that is, will be "wasted")? The current study used hypothetical money, but participants were instructed to behave as if the money in question were real. If participants in the charity condition were more selective about what offers they will accept, it would support the importance of avoiding waste as a motive for economic decisions.

Method

Subjects
Participants were male and female students in psychology courses taught by two different instructors. Students in one course were the Proposers; they were randomly paired with students in another course—the Recipients. Ninety-nine subjects served as Proposers; 48 of

them were assigned to the Waste condition 51 to the Charity condition. There were 118 Recipients; 61 were assigned to the Waste condition and 57 to the Charity condition.

Procedure

The Proposers in the Waste condition received the following instructions:

- This experiment is a simulation of an economic activity: dividing a sum of money between two people. In this case, the money is hypothetical (not real). So try to imagine that it is real money and try to behave as you would if you were given real money.
- In this study, the experimenter gives you $50 and asks you to divide it between yourself (Person 1) and another participant (Person 2). You do not know who Person 2 is and will not meet Person 2 during the study. (In fact, Person 2 is a student in another psychology course.)
- Your task is to make an offer to Person 2 of any amount of the $50, from $0 to $50. The task of Person 2 is to either accept the offer or reject it.
- If Person 2 accepts the offer, he/she gets the amount you have offered and you get the rest.
- If Person 2 rejects the offer, neither one of you will get any money. The $50 will go back to the funding source and the experimenter will not be able to use it for other participants.

Please fill in the blanks below:

1. My offer to Person 2 is _____ dollars. (any amount from 0 to 50)

   Now, answer a question that asks you how you imagine Person 2 might perform his/her part of the task:

2. I think that the smallest amount Person 2 would accept is _____ dollars.

Proposers in the Charity condition received the same instructions, except that, instead of being told that the $50 would "go back to the funding source and the experimenter will not be able to use it for other participants," they were instructed that "Instead, the $50 will go to a university fund that provides tutoring for disadvantaged children."

Recipients in the Waste condition received the following instructions:

- This experiment is a simulation of an economic activity: dividing a sum of money between two people. In this case, the money is hypothetical (not real). So try to imagine that it is real money and try to behave as you would if you were given real money.
- In this study, the experimenter gives a participant $50 and asks him or her to divide it between him/herself (Person 1) and another participant (you--Person 2). You do not

know who Person 1 is and will not meet Person 1 during the study. (In fact, Person 1 is a student in another psychology course.)

- Person 1's task is to make an offer to you of any amount of the $50, from $0 to $50. Your task is to either accept the offer or reject it.
- If you accept the offer, you get the amount Person 1 has offered and he/she gets the rest.
- If you reject the offer, neither one of you will get any money. The $50 will go back to the funding source and the experimenter will not be able to use it for other participants.
- Person 1 has offered you _____ dollars.

Please answer the questions below:

1. I   accept   reject Person 1's offer. (circle one)
2. The smallest amount of money I would accept is _____ dollars.

Again, for subjects in the Charity condition, the instructions were modified as they were for the Proposers.

Results

For Proposers, the mean amounts offered in the Waste and Charity conditions were nearly the same: $20.90 in the Waste condition (SD = 7.08) and $20.81 in the Charity condition (SD = 10.73). Subjects' estimates of the smallest amount the Recipient would accept were also similar: $15.16 in the Waste condition (SD = 9.19) and $17.33 in the Charity condition (SD = 11.17), not a significant difference [t (97 df) = 1.06]. In both conditions, the mean amount offered was greater than the minimum amount Proposers thought Recipients would accept. This was also the case for individual subjects; in all but five instances, the amount offered was more than the smallest amount the Proposer predicted the Recipient would accept. One of these instances occurred in the Waste condition, and four occurred in the Charity condition.

Because the number of students available to be Proposers and Recipients was not equal, the experimenters assigned values to the offers received by some of the Recipients. Thus, the average values of the offers actually received were $24.43 in the Waste condition and $21.84 in the Charity condition; these values are not significantly different [t (116 df) = 0.89].

What offers would Recipients accept and would this differ between the Waste and Charity conditions? Of the 61 offers in the Waste condition, 50 were accepted and 11 rejected. The mean value of accepted offers was $28.60 (SD = 13.59); the mean value of rejected offers was $5.45 (SD = 6.88), a significant difference according to a t-test assuming unequal variances (t 30 df = 8.19, $p < .01$). Of the 57 offers in the Charity condition, 30 were accepted and 27 rejected. Thus, offers were significantly less likely to be rejected in the Waste condition (χ^2 1df = 10.31, $p < .01$). The mean value of accepted offers in the Charity condition was $28.03 (SD = 13.80); the mean value of rejected offers was $14.96 (SD = 15.73). Again, this was a significant difference (t 52 df = 3.32, $p < .01$). Interestingly, in the

Waste condition, 6 of the 11 rejected offers were for $0, and the highest rejected offer was $20. In contrast, in the Charity condition, the rejected offers ranged from $0 to $50, and 12 of the 27 rejected offers were for $20 or more. There was no significant difference between the Waste and Charity groups in the least amount they said they would be willing to accept, which was reported as $15 on average for the Waste group and $14 for the Charity group (t 114df = 0.44).

Discussion

Our results are consistent with the idea that avoiding waste is a factor in economic decision-making beyond its role in the sunk-cost effect. When participants were given the opportunity to avoid wasting a resource (that is, having the money from the rejected offer go to a good cause), they were more selective in the offers they accepted than when the instructions emphasized the possibility of waste. Many offers in the Charity condition were rejected that would not have been rejected in the Waste condition. And, while few Proposers offered less than they thought Recipients would accept, even that difference was in the predicted direction.

We cannot determine whether Recipients in the Charity condition were motivated to reject more offers because they wanted to help disadvantaged children or simply because they felt freer to get back at Proposers making unfair offers. Further work may clarify this issue.

EXPERIMENT 3

Experiment 3 does not directly concern the waste hypothesis, but follows from Experiment 1 in addressing an important question about the sunk-cost effect. The question is whether the effect depends on the qualitative nature of the sunk costs. Researchers have commonly assumed that any type of sunk cost will work—whether of money, time, or effort. Surprisingly, though, from the sizable literature on the sunk-cost effect we could find only one study that has investigated non-monetary costs, a study by Soman (2001). He conducted a series of six experiments contrasting the effects of sunk time with sunk money. In four of the experiments (Experiments 1, 2, 3, and 6), sunk cost information was expressed monetarily in one set of conditions but temporally in another set. Would subjects be equally susceptible to the sunk-cost effect in either case? The results showed that temporal costs did *not* impact behavior, while monetary costs did. Experiments 4 and 5 did produce a sunk-time effect, but only when a wage rate was associated with time or when participants received instruction about economic approaches to time. Soman concluded that, unlike sunk money, sunk time does not impact our decisions. Soman proposed that mental accounting is to blame—we have more difficulty accounting for time spent than for money spent, perhaps for cultural reasons. Thus, a person who has spent money on something is likely to remember having done so, whereas a person who has spent only time on something will sooner forget.

Given that only one study has explored the effect of sunk time, we felt the issue merited more attention. Moreover, intuition and our experience tell us that time is every bit as valuable as money. In a recent study comparing the effectiveness of time and money as reinforcers in economic distribution games (the Ultimatum and Dictator games) we found support for the bromide "time is money" (Fantino, Gaitan, Kennelly, & Stolarz-Fantino, 2007). If individuals weigh sunk costs with respect to money we would predict that they should weigh them when time is the currency as well. In order to assess this hypothesis we conducted an experiment to test the relative effects of time and money sunk costs.

Method

Subjects

One hundred fifty male and female undergraduate students participated in the experiment. All participated as part of a 1-hour session for course credit that involved other experiments.

Procedure

There were three independent variables: 1) the level of Sunk Cost, 2) the level of Completion Cost, and 3) whether the costs were expressed as "time alone" or as "time + money". Variables 1 and 2 were administered within-subjects, and variable 3 was administered between-subjects. Participants received a packet of questionnaires that contained instructions for the present experiment, six scenarios pertaining to the present experiment in counterbalanced order, and other questionnaires pertaining to unrelated experiments. The instructions for the present experiment were as follows:

> Welcome to the mine dig! The year is 1886 and you are the leader of a mining group in Western Utah. You will be digging mines in search of gold. The following information will help you with your task.
>
> You're located in a geographic region that has many mines certain to contain gold. It takes days or weeks of digging a given mine before gold is reached. The average time it takes to dig one whole mine is about 20 days, although it varies widely. All mines have gold. You have plenty of time to spend on digging.
>
> One characteristic of mines in Western Utah is that a wall of quartz surrounds the gold. When your workers hit quartz, they are able to tell exactly how much longer it will take to reach the gold.
>
> As group leader, this is your job: you will dig one mine at a time. You must decide, when your team has hit quartz, whether to A) keep digging the mine you are at, or B) abandon that mine and move all of your workers to another one of the mines in your area. When you abandon a mine, you cannot go back to it and the time you spent on it is lost.
>
> Your goal is to find gold, but of course your bigger goal is to make money overall.
>
> After your session is over, the experimenter will give you a questionnaire asking about what decisions you faced during the mine dig and why you made the choices you did.
>
> If you have any questions, please ask the experimenter now.
>
> Once you begin, you may not turn to previous pages in this booklet (but you can look at this instruction page whenever you want). Each page of your booklet describes a different mine.
>
> If you are ready to begin your job, turn the page and start!

Below is the scenario from the "time-alone" condition with the independent variables shown here in parentheses and boldface:

Good morning!

You have been digging a mine for *(0, 20, 40)* days

Your workers found a vein of gold right away this morning!

Of course, a thick wall of quartz is covering most of the gold. Your workers estimate that it will take another *(8, 32)* days to uncover the rest of the gold.

Do you want to (circle your answer)

A.   continue digging this mine until it is complete (taking *(8, 32)* days)

B.   abandon this mine and move all of your workers to a new one (new mines take on average 20 days to dig)

The number of days spent digging so far was the Sunk Cost, and the number of days left to complete the dig was the Completion Cost. In the "time + money" condition, the instructions were the same except that participants were informed that each day of digging cost $25. Below is the scenario from the "time + money" condition with the independent variables shown here in parentheses and boldface:

Good morning!

You have been digging a mine for *(0 days, and have spent $0; 20 days, and have spent $500; 40 days, and have spent $1000)*

Your workers found a vein of gold right away this morning!

Of course, a thick wall of quartz is covering most of the gold. Your workers estimate that it will take another *(8 days\$200; 32 days\$800)* to uncover the rest of the gold.

Do you want to (circle your answer)

A.   continue digging this mine until it is complete (costing *(8 days\$200; 32 days\$800)*)

B.   abandon this mine and move all of your workers to a new one (new mines cost on average 20 days\$500)

Participants performed the experiment alone in a small room.

Results

The percentage of participants who chose "A" (persisting with the same mine) in each condition is shown in Figure 1. A repeated-measures ANOVA revealed a significant main effect of Sunk Cost, $F(2, 248) = 21.44$, $p < .0001$; Completion Cost, $F(1, 124) = 306.24$, $p < .0001$, and a significant Sunk Cost x Completion Cost interaction $F(2, 248) = 11.66$, $p < .0001$. The average persistence in the low completion cost conditions was 96%, while in the high completion cost conditions it was 40%. With respect to sunk cost, the trend depended on the level of completion cost. When completion cost was low, sunk cost had no effect on persistence. However, when completion cost was high, persistence was inversely related to sunk cost. As sunk cost increased from zero to 20 to 40 days, persistence dropped from 61% to 33% to 27%. There was no significant difference between the "time-alone" and the "time + money" conditions.

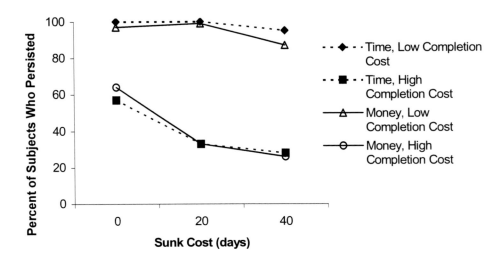

Figure 1. Persistence as a function of sunk cost.

Discussion

There are three points we wish to emphasize. First, participants were sensitive to the economic forecast. In the conditions with high completion cost, the normative choice was to switch to a new mine (completing the already-begun mine was expected to cost more than starting and finishing a new mine). In the conditions with low completion cost, the normative choice was to persist in the already-begun mine (completing the already-begun mine was expected to cost less than starting and finishing a new mine). Behavior was sensitive to these facts. When the completion cost was low, most participants "correctly" persisted. When the completion cost was high, fewer participants persisted. Also in the latter condition, behavior depended more on the sunk cost. As sunk cost increased, participants became more likely to choose normatively and switch to a new mine.

This leads to the second point, which is that we did not find the usual sunk cost effect in which sunk cost size and persistence are positively related. Instead, we found an inverse relationship—a "reverse" sunk-cost effect. Although a rare finding, it is not without precedent. Heath (1995) found a reverse sunk-cost effect when he presented participants with very complete economic information (unlike most sunk-cost experiments reported in the literature, which have kept some information ambiguous). Heath gave his participants the following hypothetical numbers (in millions of dollars) concerning a real estate project:

	Previous costs	Future investment	Sales forecast
Condition A	$6.58	$1.55	$6.66
Condition B	none	$1.55	$6.66

Participants saw information from only one of the two conditions. "Previous costs" were money that had already been spent toward the project. "Future investment" was the amount needed to complete the project. The "sales forecast" was the amount that the project would sell for upon completion. Participants were told that they could either spend the future investment and finish the project, or abandon the endeavor and use the investment toward another project that would yield a 15% return. Therefore, each condition presented the dilemma of whether to spend $1.55 million for a 430% profit, or instead to use the $1.55 million (toward the alternative project) for a 15% profit. Obviously, the normative choice was to complete the already-begun project. The results were startling: while 100% of the subjects in condition B chose to complete the project, only 42% of the subjects in condition A made this choice! The latter number is shocking both because it strongly violates economic norms and because it demonstrates the opposite of the usual, well-established sunk-cost effect. How did Heath explain this result? He hypothesized that individuals create a mental budget for a project provided that they have sufficient economic information. Individuals will continue to spend money toward an endeavor as long as the accumulated expenses are within the budget; once total spending is predicted to exceed the budget, the individuals will quit spending. Heath hypothesized that participants set a mental budget equal to the sales forecast, a notion supported by other experiments from Heath's study.

In the present experiment, it is not clear how participants would arrive at a mental budget. The information that would have been analogous to Heath's sales forecast is the value of the gold, but our scenario did not state this information. In addition, it seems unlikely that the value of the gold would serve as a budget in the time-alone condition. So how do we explain our results? One possibility is that participants formed a budget based on the cost of completing a new mine. This was stated as 20 days on average (20 days and $500, in the money conditions). Perhaps when sunk cost was zero days and the completion cost was 32 days, most participants felt that completing the already-begun mine was a worthwhile gamble since the stated cost of a new mine was after all an average—occasionally, the cost might exceed 32 days. When the sunk cost was 20 days, however, the total spending on the already-begun mine would necessarily be 52 days (20 + 32). In this case, the mental budget would certainly be exceeded. This might explain why the main shift in behavior was observed in the middle condition (as shown in Figure 1). Of course, this analysis is purely speculative. It is clear that further research is necessary to explore the possible factors that contribute to forming a mental budget, and more generally to the reverse sunk-cost effect.

Nevertheless, we wish to emphasize our third point: We found that temporal and monetary sunk costs may impact behavior similarly. Our study provides, to our knowledge, the first such demonstration. Further research is needed on sunk-time costs, as well as the separate effects of sunk time and sunk effort, an issue that has not been addressed in the literature. Also, while the present results suggest time and money investments may have similar effects, it remains to be seen whether this similarity holds true in the "positive" sunk cost effect.

CONCLUSION

The sunk-cost effect is a robust phenomenon that is multiply determined. One goal of the present experiments was to explore the role of perceived waste in promoting the effect. In two experiments involving economic decisions we assessed whether it made a difference if the money lost was wasted or went to a worthy charity. Participants were more likely to incur losses when the money went to charity. A second goal of this paper was to establish whether or not a sunk-cost effect occurred when time was the "commodity" rather than money. In our third experiment we found no difference in participants' decisions between a condition involving time only and one involving both time and money. However, instead of a typical sunk-cost effect we obtained a "reverse sunk-cost effect" in both conditions. These results may be understood in terms of Heath's "mental budget" hypothesis since the precise economic forecasts we provided made the participants' task more transparent. All of the results suggest that the sunk-cost effect is multiply determined. These findings help delineate the conditions under which the sunk-cost effect is likely to occur.

REFERENCES

Arkes, H. R. (1996). The psychology of waste. *Journal of Behavioral Decision Making, 9,* 213-224.

Arkes, H. R., & Ayton, P. (1999). The sunk cost and Concorde effects: Are humans less rational than lower animals? *Psychological Bulletin, 125,* 591-600.

Arkes, H. R., & Blumer, C. (1985). The psychology of sunk cost. *Organizational Behavior and Human Decision Processes, 35,* 124-140.

Bowen, M.G. (1987). The escalation phenomenon reconsidered: Decision dilemmas or decision errors? *Academy of Management Review, 12,* 52-66.

Bragger, J., Bragger D., Hantula, D., & Kirnan, J. (1998). Hysteresis and uncertainty: The effect of information on delays to exit decisions. *Organizational Behavior and Human Decision Processes, 74,* 229-253.

Bragger, J., Hantula, D., Bragger, D., Kirnan, J., & Kutcher, E. (2003). When success breeds failure: History, hysteresis, and delayed exit conditions. *Journal of Applied Psychology, 88,* 6-14.

Brockner, J. (1992). The escalation of commitment to a failing course of action: Toward theoretical progress. *Academy of Management Review, 17,* 39-61.

Camerer, C.F. (2003). *Behavioral game theory: Experiments in strategic interaction.* NY: Russell Sage Foundation.

Fantino, E., Gaitan, S., Kennelly, A., & Stolarz-Fantino, S. (2007). How reinforcer type affects choice in economic games. *Behavioural Processes, 75,*107-114.

Fantino, E., Stolarz-Fantino, S., & Navarro, A. (2003). Logical fallacies: A behavioral approach to reasoning. *The Behavior Analyst Today, 4,* 109-117.

Goltz, S.M. (1992). A sequential learning analysis of continued investments of organizational resources in nonperforming courses of action. *Journal of Applied Behavior Analysis, 25,* 561-574.

Goltz, S.M. (1999). Can't stop on a dime: The roles of matching and momentum in persistence of commitment. *Journal of Organizational Behavior Management, 19,* 37-63.

Guth, W., Schmittberger, R., & Schwarze, B. (1982). An experimental analysis of ultimatum games. *Journal of Economic Behavior & Organization, 3,* 367-388.

Hantula, D. & Bragger, J. (1999). The effects of feedback equivocality on escalation of commitment: An empirical investigation of decision dilemma theory. *Journal of Applied Social Psychology, 29,* 424-444.

Heath, C. (1995). Escalation and de-escalation of commitment in response to sunk-costs: The role of budgeting in mental accounting. *Organizational Behavior and Human Decision Processes, 62,* 38-54.

Kahneman, D. & Tversky, A. (1979). Prospect theory: An analysis of decision under risk. *Econometrica, 47,* 263-291.

McCain, B.E. (1986). Continuing investment under conditions of failure: A laboratory study of the limits to escalation. *Journal of Applied Psychology, 71,* 280-284.

Navarro, A. D. & Fantino, E. (2005). The sunk cost effect in pigeons and humans. *Journal of the Experimental Analysis of Behavior, 83,* 1-13.

Navarro, A.D. & Fantino, E. (2008). The role of discriminative stimuli in the sunk-cost effect. *Mexican Journal of Behavior Analysis,33,*19-29.

Rachlin, H. (2000). *The science of self-control.* Cambridge, MA: Harvard University Press.

Soman, D. (2001). The mental accounting of sunk time costs: Why time is not like money. *Journal of Behavioral Decision Making, 14,* 169-185.

Staw, B. M. (1976). Knee-deep in the big muddy: A study of escalating commitment to a chosen course of action. *Organizational Behavior and Human Performance, 16,* 27-44.

Staw, B. M. (1981). The escalation of commitment to a course of action. *Academy of Management Review, 6,* 577-587.

Thaler, R. (1980). Toward a positive theory of consumer choice. *Journal of Economic Behavior & Organization, 1,* 39-60.

Webley, P., & Plaisier, Z. (1997, August). *Mental accounting childhood.* Paper presented at the 16th Bi-Annual Conference on Subjective Probability, Utility, and Decision Making, Leeds, England.

Whyte, G. (1986). Escalating commitment to course of action: A reinterpretation. *Academy of Management Review, 11,* 311-321.

In: Psychology of Decision Making...
Editor: G. R. Burthold, pp. 159-174

ISBN: 978-1-60021-932-0
© 2007 Nova Science Publishers, Inc.

Chapter 6

EFFECTS OF STRESS, LANGUAGE AND CULTURE ON DECISION-MAKING IN THE CRITICAL CARE ENVIRONMENT

Robert K. Pretzlaff, JoAnne Natale, Jill Joseph

Department of Pediatrics Section of Critical Care Medicine,
University of California, Davis, CA, USA

ABSTRACT

Decision-making capacity is a developmentally regulated process. Among the determinants of that capacity are the age and developmental status of the individual, their relative health, the nature of the choice to be made and the stress under which that person finds themselves. This article will focus on the influences of stress and culture on decision-making by parents whose children are critically ill. The two stressors highlighted in this discussion will be 1) the child's severity of illness and the critical care environment, and 2) potential culture/language discordance between the parents (or surrogates) of the patient and the healthcare team. Treatment decisions for the critically ill child demands the most astute decision-making capacity during a time that that capacity is severely strained. This article will define the environment impacting those decisions and offer some suggestions for improving the ability of parents to make these difficult decisions during a very stressful time.

I. INTRODUCTION

Medical decision-making has been guided by the paradigm of patient autonomy for much of the last forty years. This view of decision-making holds that the final authority for determining the treatment and direction of a patient's medical care lies with the patient or their surrogate. The exercise of that right creates a responsibility for the physician and health care team to provide that the patient, or their surrogate, is sufficiently informed and the resulting healthcare decisions are uncoerced.

This ideal of "pure" patient autonomy is challenged by the realities of the clinical setting, and the competing rights and responsibilities of physicians and patients has evolved into model of 'shared decision-making'. In shared decision-making the health care team and the patient work together as equals to arrive at a mutually agreeable solution to the questions posed. Many of the principles that form the foundation for concepts of patient autonomy and shared decision-making are embodied in the Belmont Report. [1] The Belmont Report, which was released by the National Commission for the Protection of Human Subjects of Biomedical and Behavioral Research in 1979, had the aim of defining the moral basis for the ethical practice of biomedical research, and has had the effect of guiding much of the discourse on autonomy and the ethical treatment of patients.

In the Belmont Report, the Commission clearly differentiated between the general practice of medicine and the performance of research, but the concepts enunciated in the Report have carried over to shape discussions of the patient-physician relationship both in areas of research and bedside care. The three basic ethical principles appealed to in the Belmont Report are: 1) Respect for persons, 2) Beneficence and 3) Justice. Respect for persons was defined as follows: "Respect for persons incorporates at least two ethical convictions: first, that individuals should be treated as autonomous agents, and second, that persons with diminished autonomy are entitled to protection. The principle of respect for persons thus divides into two separate moral requirements: the requirement to acknowledge autonomy and the requirement to protect those with diminished autonomy". [1] Much of the following discussion will focus on the concept of respect for persons.

The concept of autonomy harkens back to the Code of Nuremberg, which stated that research could only be carried out with the consent of the subject of that research, a mandate that was reiterated in the Declaration of Helsinki. [2] [3] These documents were not created in a vacuum, but rather were created in an era of growing interest and respect for individual and patient rights. Much of the examination on medical decision-making has focused on defining those aspects of research participation related to autonomy.

Coincident with these developments in the ethical discourse on research subjects, and more broadly on the role of patients and their surrogates, has been the marked increase in the ability to apply sophisticated technologies to the care of patients. In the last fifty years we have seen the development and refinement of long-term mechanical ventilation, as well as other life-saving and life-preserving modalities that can extend life past a time when it arguably makes sense to do so. The evolution of the concept of brain death is a watershed event in redefining what it means to be alive. [4]

These two currents have met to create a wealth of interest, research and opinion on End-of-Life (EOL) decision-making. EOL discourse includes the concepts of care withdrawal, care limitation and "Do Not Resuscitate" orders, among others. The gravity of these decisions, the relative simplicity of their conception, as well as their importance to the public at large, has made EOL a focus of research in medical decision-making. Less effort has been devoted to the examination of the circumstances and environment surrounding non-EOL decision-making in medical care, which is the focus of this chapter.

This chapter will examine what is known about medical decision-making and the threats to the legitimacy of those decisions. This will be done, not in a broad general sense, but through the lens of what are potentially the most severe threats to the individual adequately participating in shared decision-making. First, we will begin by examining decision-making that is removed one degree by looking at the role of surrogate decision-making. We will concentrate on the decisions that parents or caregivers make for their minor children. Second, we will place the surrogates in a decision-hostile environment, that of a Pediatric Intensive Care Unit (PICU). By setting our discussion in such an environment we can better examine threats to decision-making that threaten the validity and value of those decisions.

II. THE PEDIATRIC CRITICAL CARE ENVIRONMENT

Discussion of the process of decision-making by parents of critically ill children requires the acknowledgment of certain assumptions about the role of the individual and the family in making healthcare decisions. First, it is accepted, in both clinical care and for purposes of research, that a child's parents are the accepted surrogate decision-makers for that child. That children, as they grow older, may have input into their care, but decision-making capacity resides with the parents. Any assault on this assumption is extremely difficult and parents are, in virtually all cases, assumed to have the intellectual, developmental and moral capacity to make appropriate decisions. Second, this chapter assumes a paradigm of patient autonomy common in the United States and not a more paternalistic viewpoint that remains prevalent in a large part of the world. That there is not one unifying concept of medical decision-making in the world adds an additional source of conflict and stress in the healthcare environment. This is readily seen in a multicultural population, like that of the United States. Hence, one of the topics treated in this chapter will be the effect of language and culture on decision-making. To better understand the issues at stake, we will begin with an illustration of the environment of the PICU and then discuss how this milieu jeopardizes different components of the ideal of shared decision-making.

The death of a child is a rare event in the United States. Unintentional injuries, malignancy, and homicide/suicide account for the approximately 2,500 deaths per 100,000 children each year in persons less than 14 years old. (Center for Disease Control – 2002 US Census Data) The majority of these children will die in a hospital intensive care unit. In a study looking at the demographics of death in hospitalized children in the Netherlands, Van de Wal et al. demonstrated that 71% of children who died, did so in the PICU. [5] Further, 39% of these children had some form of limitation in care in place at the time of their death, 14% requested no resuscitation effort prior to their deaths and an additional 17% were declared brain dead. [5] An unpublished study by the author (RP) in his own unit found results that were indistinguishable from those by Van der Wal. Additional published reports in the US echo these findings. [6] Though the majority of children who die do so in an intensive care environment, only 2 to 8 percent of children admitted to an ICU will die. This contrasts with adults admitted to the ICU who have a mortality rate of greater then 13%. [7]

To understand the impact of the PICU environment on the ability of surrogates to make decisions for critically ill and injured children requires some illustration of that environment. It must be understood that the pediatric intensive care environment is utterly foreign to those not working in it. The PICU is a highly technological environment with an absence of privacy where people are working 24 hours a day. The division of night and day at times seems arbitrary when patients are awakened at 2:00 a.m. to draw blood for daily lab tests, and again at 4:00 a.m. to obtain a morning chest X-ray. Each patient is attached to a variety of monitors and machines through wires and tubes. Each monitor and machine has a set of alarms to alert the caregiver when any parameter of the patient or the equipment is outside of its set range. Each of the alarms strives to be unique so that the staff recognizes it. The majority of these alarms are also connected to a central monitoring station in the body of the PICU to alert staff that may have momentarily strayed from the bedside of the patient. The alarms need to be loud enough to catch the attention of the staff and so they are audible from one room to the next. Although the din of alarms may be comforting and familiar to the staff, the alarm cacophony may be extremely distressing to the parent who cannot distinguish the important alarms from the unimportant, or the alarms of their child from the alarms of another. Despite efforts to make the PICU more family friendly, this environment will unlikely ever be able to completely divorce itself from its underlying mission and character.

The often rapid progression of critical illness in children is another stressor for families. A commonly used prediction tool of pediatric risk of mortality, the PRISM-12 score, is able to distinguish with very good reliability the likelihood of survival of admissions to the PICU by accumulating a set of physiologic data obtained in only the first 12 hours after admission. [8] This last sentence points out two important facts. The first is that most patients admitted to an intensive care unit have demonstrable risk of mortality and so the stress of a critical illness in a loved one is very real. Second, because the likelihood of survival can be with some degree of accuracy be predicted in the first twelve hours, it is this early period when care is initiated that may be the most crucial for the patient's survival. Hence, decisions in an PICU environment are often made hurriedly in conditions of grave consequence.

The PICU is a highly specialized location where the patient is not given the opportunity to choose his or her own doctor. To make matters worse intensive care medicine is a 24-hour a day business and so "your" doctor may change frequently. Additionally, the PICU is a complex environment often located in an academic center where information and responsibility is diffused among different services and among different caregivers having very different levels of training. This offers a breadth and depth of knowledge that makes the PICU located in an academic medical center particularly valuable, because admission to such a center offers the availability of many eyes to watch the patient more closely, but this glut of caregivers can significantly impact a parent or surrogates ability to receive information that appears consistent. It is not unusual to see families upset when two physicians expressing agreed upon information, but expressing themselves from their own view-points, having that information interpreted very differently by family members of the patient. This brief illustration was provided because it is not possible to discuss decision-making in the PICU without understanding the environment in which those decisions are made.

III. ELEMENTS OF DECISION-MAKING

The aim of this section will be to describe the minimum required components of a valid or moral decision. In this chapter we are using valid and moral interchangeably and can define such a decision as a healthcare decision that has a potentially significant impact on your life or that of another. Medical decision-making of interest to this discussion has moral significance. Questions of a purely technical nature are not being considered. An example of a technical decision would be the choice of a particular antibiotic for the treatment of a specific infection. This is not open to interpretation and does not require the input of the family or patient. An example of the moral corollary to this question would be whether to initiate antibiotics at all. Treating, or not treating, an infection can be a valid question given the particular circumstances of a patient and is one that is illustrative of shared decision-making. The choice of a particular antibiotic is a wholly technical question.

The first requirement of a valid, or moral, decision is that the individual charged with making that decision needs to be adequately informed. As laid out in the Belmont Report, the components of being adequately informed include: 1) information, 2) comprehension, and 3) voluntariness. Each of these requirements has distinct weaknesses in the milieu of the PICU when making difficult decisions for a critically ill or injured child.

First, the patient, or surrogate, must receive the information necessary to make a decision. Items of information in medical decision-making would include the diagnosis, prognosis and an assessment of the risks, benefits and likelihood of success of different treatment options. Little or no formal medical knowledge is required for an appreciation of the aforementioned data. However, there are two components to receiving such information that should be addressed. The first is that the nature of information in the intensive care environment is necessarily incomplete, and clinical data is in constant evolution. The certainties in life are death and taxes, and earlier in this chapter we declared that our focus was on decisions not at the end of life, but rather on decisions concerned with the evolving care of a critically ill, but not dying, child. The second aspect of information that is necessary to understand is that the complexity of the patient's condition creates often contradictory information. As an example: two hallmarks of an infection are fever and an elevated white blood cell count. Multiple factors, some knowable and others unknowable, influence both fever and the patient's white blood cell count, but if the patient has a fever and normal white blood cell count what information can be provided the parent regarding the presence of infection in their child. The information regarding the presence of infection and the influence that might have on a patient's prognosis and diagnosis is therefore unknowable and only a rough approximation. Hence, the surrogate decision-maker must accept incomplete information as a necessary part of the decisions that are being called on to make.

Delivery of such information is a necessary, but not sufficient condition for the transmission of information. It is necessary to present the information in a clear and coherent manner and also assess whether the informed comprehends the information. Acknowledging that the intellectual capacity, maturity, culture and language of the individual are all components of that person's comprehension. [9] Additional factors such as disease severity also impact comprehension and recall. In a study of adults being enrolled in four different research studies both the amount of information and the type of information was affected by the severity of disease of the participants. In this study the sickest subjects remembered the most about the procedures and were motivated by the purpose of the treatment. [10] In a further study examining more then three hundred patients with four different diagnoses but similar prognoses decisions regarding resuscitation were significantly different. [11] It is not much of an extension to believe that parents of sick children have a similar response to information presented to them. Also, the comprehension of families on information delivered depended on diagnosis prognosis and knowledge of the language of the predominant language in the unit. [12] A review examining a total of 42 trials aimed at improving understanding and communication in research studies demonstrated that techniques including multimedia presentations had a limited benefit. [13]

Third, voluntariness, as written in the Belmont Report, refers to a person's decision-making capacity that necessarily needs to be free of coercion, undue stress, and self-interest if it is to be considered autonomous. Coercive forces also apply to non-research medical decision-making. The intensive care environment as detailed in the last section has significant impacts on each of these factors. The rapid timeframe and incomplete nature of information available to the surrogate decision-maker can place measurable stress on the parent or surrogate and potentially influence their decision-making capacity. [14] [15] Often the need for patient care interventions may arise before the family member has had time to adapt to their child's illness. With an average length of admission of only a few days decisions are often made quickly. Other aspects of the environment, such as sensory overload from alarms and sleep deprivation, make the situation of the parent more analogous to a person exposed to intense interrogation then it is to being given the chance to make an informed decision.

Finally, making a decision requires an element of certainty so as not to be paralyzed into inaction. The results of no decision in the PICU also have significant and immediate consequences. In a study on healthcare workers in the PICU, except for those patients near death or practically healthy, even experienced intensive care physicians demonstrated a high degree of uncertainty when it came to quantifying a patient's prognosis. [16]

This section demonstrates a few of the difficulties in combining the ideal of autonomous decision-making with their reality of the PICU environment. No component of ethical decision-making, from information to comprehension or voluntariness, may be satisfied. The next two sections will look at what is known about the effects of stress and culture/language on decision-making.

IV. FAMILY CENTERED CARE PARADIGM

Placing the health care needs of a child and the delivery of services to meet those needs in the context of a family is the foundation of a family centered care model of health care delivery. In the model of family centered care, the child's family is a dynamic and driving force for health care delivery. In this critical role, parents need to be well informed and involved in the health care needs of their child. The benefits of family centered care include greater parent and provider satisfaction with the care of the child, improved parent coping with their child's illness, more collegial decision-making, and decreased length of hospitalization. Based on these benefits, the concept of family-centered care has become a central organizing paradigm for delivering pediatric health care.

An essential component of the decision-making process in the PICU is the ability of physicians and surrogate decision makers to meaningfully communicate. This is necessary for the exchange of information, to ascertain the degree of comprehension, and of voluntariness of the decisions. In the SUPPORT trial, a trial designed to improve EOL decision-making in adults, the services of a specially trained nurse were used to facilitate EOL discussions and provide information to the patients and the care team. Using this model, no significant improvement in communication was observed. This study demonstrated that barriers to communication are significant and culturally engrained. These cultural barriers exist within the context of the physician-patient relationship. In a study examining information given to families during EOL discussions in intensive care units families that were less educated were provided less information. Further physicians failed to provide prognostic information in a substantial number of cases. [17] One ethicist has defined this as a crisis of prognostication. [18]

Attempts to improve communication and understanding include increasing a family's involvement in the care of the patient, such as involving families in the bedside care of the patient. One study in France demonstrated opposition from both caregivers and family members. Significantly, only a third of families wanted to participate. [19] This study was done in France and may represent a more paternalistic model of decision-making when compared to the US. Family participation in care, not just decision-making, is perhaps more appropriate for children then adults, but data do not exist regarding its application and acceptability. An increase in family involvement may be a way to inform families independent of structured meetings. [19]

V. EFFECTS OF STRESS ON DECISION MAKING CAPACITY

Measurable symptoms of anxiety or depression are seen in parents of patients admitted to the PICU. One study comparing mothers of patients in the PICU with those on a general care unit demonstrated that mothers of the PICU patients experienced greater stress during the hospitalization. Additionally, many of the environmental issues described earlier added considerably to the mother's stress, such as the alarms and too many people providing information. [14] In a study looking at both pediatric and adult ICU's evidence of anxiety and/or depression was present in between 25 and 80% of family members. [20] A recent, and very good review of the literature on family impact of critical illness in a child concluded that critical illness has demonstrable effect on the whole family. [15] The study further stressed that improved research needs to be done in this area and that improved methods and attention should be paid to family support. Evidence of stress, including measures of post-traumatic stress disorder, following the ICU experience can still be detected in follow-up studies as long as six months following PICU admission. [21] [22]

The PICU environment and the stress of having a child admitted limits the ability of surrogate decision makers to absorb, retain and comprehend information given. In the sickest children, which are likely the ones where decision-making is most crucial; the effects of stress on evaluating information are the most marked. Further, family members have symptoms of anxiety and depression that are measurable during the PICU admission. The effects of which can be seen long after discharge from the PICU. These factors figure significantly in the ability of parents to make decisions for their critically ill children.

Figure 1 provides a model of communication and decision-making. Using this construct, communication and decision-making by any family are shaped by their access to information, by their concepts of health, disease and medical treatment, by their values, and by their psychological state. The task of the medical care team generally and for physician providers specifically is to "map" their interactions onto these four domains as they are conceptualized by the family in order to promote communication and decision-making. Inattention to, or incongruity between, the provider and the family in any of these domains can disrupt the coherent circle of communication and decision-making.

A variety of techniques for addressing issues that affect communication and, therefore, decision-making by parents of critically ill children are provided in Table 1. The suggestions presented are by no means comprehensive, nor are they applicable to every family and every situation. However, they do provide a starting place for thoughtful provider responses.

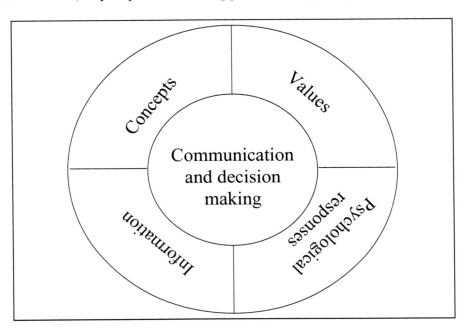

Figure 1.

Table 1. Suggestions for addressing issues that affect communication and decision-making for parents of critically ill children

---

Information

- Negotiate a shared agenda at the beginning of each meeting with the parents by asking them what they want to know, understand, or communicate.
- Be explicit about your own agenda, particularly if you are anticipating some response or decision by the parents based on the information you are communicating.
- Inquire about and identify each family's preferences regarding information exchange. Relevant issues to be considered include:
  - "Route" for information transmission and flow (e.g. initial information transmitted to parents who assume responsibility for communicating to other family members versus larger family meetings.)
  - Timing and pacing of family meetings (e.g. avoid the impression that such meetings always mean "bad news".)
  - Location of meetings (e.g. bedside versus conference room: some families are concerned that their child will be adversely affected by any "bad news", while others are reluctant to leave the bedside.)
- Plan and coordinate multidisciplinary communication.

Concepts

- Ask frequent questions regarding family understanding in a way that makes apparent you are doing so to assess your communication abilities rather than the family's ability to understand.
- Anticipate within-family variability in the concordance to provider definitions of key concepts.
- The family understanding of a concept such as a treatment modality may not correspond perfectly with that of the medical team. In this circumstance, assess whether their understanding is nonetheless sufficient for participation in decision-making (e.g. exactly understanding the reasons for respiratory failure and the mechanisms are ventilatory support may not be required for discussion of the advantages and disadvantages of a tracheotomy.)

Values

- Practice "team intensive care", incorporating the skills of social work and chaplaincy as appropriate for assessing core family values.
- As requested or identified as a preference, welcome extended family members, community leaders, and religious leaders into key meetings.
- There may be variability in the values or religious expressions of different family members. In this circumstance, ask the family to help the team understand the implications of such variability for any communication and decision-making.

Psychological responses

- Practicing "team medicine" is essential. As appropriate, consider incorporating consultation-liaison psychiatry into the intensive care team.
- Psychological responses are likely to evolve and fluctuate over time. Adequately understanding how a family feels at one point in time may provide little information regarding their psychological state later. The intensive care team needs to anticipate and respond to such fluctuations.
- Dealing with some families and situations is highly stressful for team members. There should be methods for validating and responding to such distress on the team. (e.g. assigning a single team member for primary communication with the family may make sense or it may impose an excessive burden on a single individual.)

VI. EFFECTS OF LANGUAGE AND CULTURE ON DECISION MAKING CAPACITY

A Family's Story

Mr. and Mrs. Q are Hmong parents of a 19-month-old girl with Down syndrome who was admitted to the pediatric ward with pneumonia. Mr. Q understands conversational English although he is uncomfortable speaking English, while Mrs. Q speaks only Hmong. Approximately 24 hours after hospital admission, the child's condition worsened and she rapidly developed respiratory failure requiring rescue breathing with a mask held over her nose and mouth. The child was transferred emergently to the PICU, and because of her severe pneumonia, she was placed on a specialized ventilator that required her to remain immobile. Medications were used to ensure comfort, and to prevent movement as a means to keep the child safe while receiving this intensive treatment. Because this sudden change in the child happened in the early morning hours when on-site interpreters were not available, the medical team used telephonic interpreting to explain the child's critical condition and the emergency treatments she was receiving to Mr. and Mrs. Q. Later that morning, with the help of an in-person Hmong interpreter, the PICU physician attempted to explain their daughter's condition and engage them in discussion. This was minimally successful, and the parents seemed both withdrawn and hostile, although no obvious reasons for their reactions could be elicited. Over a period of the next 3 days, the same interpreter and physician spent considerable time with the parents, explaining the use of sedatives to keep the child comfortable and immobile, pointing out the various tubes and machines that were connected to their daughter, and describing the treatment plans. When told on the fourth day that their daughter was doing somewhat better, the parents seemed surprised and the mother commented, "but she is dead." This surprising and alarming statement leads to a long conversation, which revealed the source of the parents' discomfort and withdrawal. They had attributed the child's acute worsening on her first hospital day to the use of rescue breathing with a mask that "suffocated" the child. In the PICU, they understood that a machine was breathing for their daughter, but believed that such inability to breathe combined with the immobility of her body, meant that she was dead. With the assistance of the Hmong interpreter who had worked daily with the family, these concerns and misconceptions were addressed, and the family became actively involved in the care and decision-making for their daughter.

Family centered care is the extension of shared decision-making to pediatrics. Provision of culturally and linguistically appropriate care is fundamental to family centered care. The growth in size of the U. S. population, with the coincident broadening in diversity of culture and language effects the practice of family centered care in pediatric critical care medicine.

Large populations of immigrant Americans are found in virtually all American cities. Specifically, US census data (2004) demonstrate that 18.7% of Americans over age of 5 years live in a home where a language other than English is spoken. It is not unreasonable to assume that many of these families have limited English proficiency (LEP) particularly with respect to conversations with medical providers regarding diagnosis, management prognosis of critical illness/injury of their children. In many major urban centers the situation is even more dramatic. For example, 20% of the population over the age of 5 years living in Philadelphia, 28% living in Denver, and 34% living in Chicago speak a language other than English at home. Eight metropolitan areas, among the 68 U.S. cities with a 2004 population of at least 250,000, report more than half of all adults over age of 5 come from homes where a language other then English is spoken. Not surprisingly, these LEP-dense areas are in the boarder states of Florida, Texas, and California. Even states with a predominately rural population, such as West Virginia have a more than 2% of the population speaking a language other than English at home.

Several additional points help to lay the groundwork for the subsequent discussion of culture and language in decision-making for families with critically ill children. First, Hispanic persons in the U.S. tend to be younger as a group than the overall population (median age Hispanic origin 27.2 years compared to 36.2 years for overall population in 2005). Furthermore, 18% of Hispanic families have three or more children compared to 10% of families in the overall population. Therefore, US Census data cited above under represent the proportion of children whose parents speak a language other than English. Second, although there has been considerable attention to Latino immigration, many urban areas have remarkably diverse ethnic minorities with LEP. For example the racial/ethnic distribution in Sacramento California, the location of our PICU, is 40% white, 22% Hispanic, 16% Asian,

15% black, 4% report two or more races, 1% American Indian, and 1% Pacific Islander. Imposed on this racial distribution is broad linguistic diversity. For instance, within the white racial group in Sacramento, Eastern and Western European languages are spoken in many households rather than English. Third, census data are known to under represent several populations, notably including undocumented immigrants. This too contributes to underestimating the number of families with LEP that may require intensive care for their children. Fourth, although exact incidence figures are not available, it has long been appreciated that illness and injury are differentially experienced by those of lower SES. [23] Taken together, there are, therefore, multiple reasons for those of us delivering medical care to critically ill and injured children to anticipate interactions with families whose command of English is limited. Whether occurring in urban areas where such interactions are the norm or in scattered communities where they are less uncommon, our task remains the same: providing culturally competent, compassionate, family-centered care for all families.

"Culture is a pattern of learned beliefs, shared values, and behavior; it includes language, styles of communication, practices, customs, and vies on roles and relationships". [24] Culture provides the context where decisions are made. Yet although culture cannot be dissociated from decision-making, understanding a series of beliefs common to an ethnic group is insufficient for knowing what any individual, or family believes. Integrating the range of potential responses within a culture into health care communication, particular in the setting of a family with a critically ill child, adds to the challenges faced by the PICU team. Culturally skilled practice, where the beliefs of the family and the clinician are negotiated to reach mutually acceptable goals, lays the groundwork for shared decision-making.

The culture, language, and recognized authority of medicine create inherent barriers to effective communication with all patients and their families. Furthermore, health care providers are disproportionately white and of high socioeconomic status, thereby creating sharp divides with those burdened by the morbidity experienced by communities of color and the socioeconomically disadvantaged. [25]

The burden and challenge created by discordant language and cultural differences between the provider and the patients they care for fall into two broad categories: 1) specific and unique difficulties, and 2) exacerbations of difficulty confronted in the care of all patients. We will use the term limited English proficiency-non-dominant culture (LEP-NDC) to refer to these diverse patients.

The U. S. Census Bureau defines a household as "linguistically isolated" when no person over the age of 14 in the household speaks English "very well." In this chapter, we use the term to refer to the manifold ways in which families with LEP exist apart from routine patterns of communication in the PICU. Even when adequate interpretation is provided, frequently such families are less able to participate in the continuous, on-going exchange of information, questions/answers, and support from bedside nursing staff. For example, "in the moment" questions about why a heart rate monitor is alarming when an EKG lead inadvertently becomes disconnected are poorly addressed by the daily formal, interpretive discussion with the PICU physician. Even when there is some English proficiency, both the context of an acute medical care setting and cultural patterns of deference can combine to make frequent, informative, exchanges of questions and answers less likely. When referring to the model of communication and decision-making (Figure 1), it is apparent that linguistic isolation affects both the acquisition of information and shared medical concepts while also limiting provider ability to respond to the values and psychological state of these families.

A specific challenge that can appear from discordant culture and language arises from the historical mistrust of the dominant group. Such mistrust has been well-documented in the African American community particularly with respect to clinical research, but should also be considered as a factor in other groups [26]. Specific historical, political, or current events can significantly impact trust in providers from the dominant group. For example, anti-Latino immigrant initiatives may reduce the likelihood that recent immigrants (both documented and undocumented) seek care or can compromise the trust required for effective communication and decision-making. As others have noted, it may be difficult for physician to recognize and/or address this issue openly [27].

Finally, working with families whose culture and language are not those of the dominant society can also be complicated by varying levels of acculturation. As pediatricians, our focus is on providing appropriate care for children. When applied to adolescents, this includes granting them a degree of autonomy and self care which may be consistent with their needs but not those of their parents. More generally, the intensive care environment often includes discussions and decision-making that incorporates multiple generations, drawing further attention to the acculturation continuum within even a single family. Furthermore, there are cultures characterized by respect for or reliance on elders, thereby further increasing the need for careful consideration of this issue.

In addition to these challenges which are specific to families who language and culture are not those of the dominant group, there is a broader point to consider. For such families, the ordinary challenges of shared communication and decision-making are exacerbated. Several will be considered here. First, family response to the critical illness or injury in their child evolves over time and requires appropriately fluctuating responses by the care team. The family who was initially quiet and overwhelmed may become angry and suspicious only later to be engaged and involved in care. The intensive care team will need to make special effort to understand the responses and needs of a patient's family when relying on interpreters to working across wide divides of culture and often of social class. It is tempting is to assume that such effort is sufficient and that ongoing re-evaluation is not required. In the story told at the beginning of this section, the initial breakthrough in understanding and responding to the family's needs could easily have been followed by another phase in their adaptation to the PICU that was only appreciated through openness to this possibility and on-going appropriate dialogue. For any family, communication and involvement in decision-making is a process that requires an accurate understanding of their current responses and needs. For LEP-NDC families, such reevaluation is especially challenging.

A second common challenge that is exacerbated in LEP-NDC families is temptation by health care providers to view the family as part of a cultural group without seeing the patient and their family as a unique case. Few providers would assume that one European American, English-speaking family would closely resemble the next. Even as providers attempt to become "culturally competent" there is an appreciable hazard of losing such attention to individually focused interactions. Far too often, presentations of cultural differences focus on contextual practices (e.g. coining), beliefs (e.g. empatcho), and family needs (e.g. restrictions on between gender contact between Orthodox Jewish and Muslim patients). Similarly, while it is true in many societies women defer to their husbands, there is always individual variability in such matters that require careful consideration. Even as providers acquire knowledge about cultural norms, beliefs, and practices, the risk arises that they will stereotype those from a specific cultural background and a specific group in a way they would never do in their own culture.

Table 2. Suggestions for addressing issues that affect communication and decision-making arising among to LEP-NDC parents of critically ill children

Information
- Insist on use of an appropriately trained and certified interpreter for all communication.
- Establish the policy that any critical care team member (nurses, respiratory therapists, chaplains, etc.) should, as needed, request an interpreter for interactions with the parents.
- As possible, consistently use a single interpreter who can build relationships with the family and assume more of a role as a "cultural broker" facilitating communication with the family.
- When there is variability in English language skills (e.g. the father is more comfortable with English than the mother), always provide services so that the least comfortable family member is able to be supported.

Concepts
- Never assume that interpretation of words and sentences is equivalent to assuring a shared understanding of key concepts such as the reasons for treatment decisions and the purpose of specific interventions (e.g. extracorporeal life support).

Values
- Information regarding relevant family values obtained from discussions with the family should be shared throughout the team and, as appropriate, documented.
- Encourage family use of the bedside for displaying cultural and/or religious images that are comforting to them.

Psychological responses
- Understand that the experience and expression of psychological state is heavily influenced by culture. Therefore, the family experience needs to be contextualized by appropriate care provider expectations.
- Family distress and pain should never be ignored because its expression is assumed to be "culturally appropriate". (e.g. a generally silent and withdrawn young Chinese immigrant mother may be seen as expressing behavior consistent with her culture, when she is actually experiencing post-partum depression.)

Finally, the all too often problematic dynamics within health care teams and communication can be especially difficult for LEP-NDC families. Providing all families with a coordinated, consistent, and carefully explained discussion of their child's diagnosis, prognosis and treatment plan is challenging. Subspecialists and the intensive care team may disagree, plans may shift abruptly without explanation, and care providers come and go as their schedule demands. To watch multiple providers and teams move in and out of the child's room, to hear their child's name mentioned, to have obvious changes in treatment arise can be especially distressing and perplexing when the family does not understand what is happening. The ability of LEP-NCD families to participate in decision-making may require frequent use of interpretive services and insisting that subspecialists take the time to participate in family conferences with such interpreters, and a high level of attentiveness to team communication.

In conclusion, communication and decision-making in the context of pediatric critical care requires attentiveness to each individual family. The information available to them, their concepts to health and disease, their values and psychological responses are all conditions by language and culture. Recommendations for such a "culturally skilled practice" are listed in Table 2. These suggestions for promoting communication and decision-making are directed to the particular circumstances and needs of the LEP-NDC family. Even as providers work to acquire cultural competence, they must remain constantly attentive to the specific and evolving needs of each family.

VII. CONCLUSION

The paradigm of shared decision-making in the healthcare environment is a noble ideal. Shared decision-making recognizes the concepts of respect for persons and that medicine is not merely a technical pursuit, but one in which the goals of the individual may be at odds with the goal of prolonging life. However, in the most extreme circumstances, such as that of the PICU, the ability to fully realize the ideal of shared decision-making is under assault. This chapter has detailed the some of the notable threats to attaining this ideal. These threats include an incomplete and evolving base of information, comprehension that might be limited by culture, environment and stress, and the effects of limited time and environment on the voluntariness of a surrogate's decision-making capacity.

In addition to the recommendations to providers included in Tables 1 and 2, we conclude with a broader consideration of methods for better understanding and improving decision-making by families in the unique environment of the PICU. Concentration should be placed on the issues that demand shared input and leave those issues that are of a more technical nature off the table. The goals of treatment, and more globally the goals parents have for their children, should be the subject of more communication. As a part of this physicians should provide prognostic information even in the absence of perfect certainty. Further, caregivers should prepare for the emotional dynamics that families face and work toward comprehension and not the delivery of information.

As seen in this chapter much of the research on decision-making has concentrated on the patient specific factors in decision-making. Physician caregiver factors have not been as well studied and deserve attention as part of the dynamics of decision-making. To do this consistently and systematically the application of quality improvement principles and guidelines in caregiver training and in the structure of Intensive Care unit policy is advocated.

With respect to LEP-NDC families, a few additional general recommendations should be made. First, a widely disseminated and adequately supported institutional commitment to family centered, culturally skilled care is essential. Concretely, this means an adequate number of skilled medical interpreters must be available to meet the evolving local demographics of immigrant populations. Similarly, staff should be trained in culturally skilled practice which is reinforced by institutional norms and supervisory standards. Second, greater racial, ethnic, and linguistic diversity of nursing and medical staff will overcome some of the barriers to communication and decision-making. Finally, in addition to the general call for research on decision-making among parents of critically ill/injured children, specific studies are needed to better appreciate the barriers to and facilitators of communication for LEP-NDC families.

REFERENCES

[1]   National Commission for the Protection of Human Subjects of biomedical and Behavioral Research.., *The Belmont Report.* 1979, Department of Health, Education, and Welfare.

[2]   Tribunals, N.M., *The Nuremberg Code.* 1947, Nuremberg Military Tribunals.

[3]   Association, W.M. *Helsinki Declaration.* in *18th World Medical Assembly.* 1964. Helsinki, Finland.

[4]   Beecher, H.K., *Experimentation in man.* J Am Med Assoc, 1959. *169*(5): p. 461-78.

[5]   van der Wal, M.E., et al., *Circumstances of dying in hospitalized children.* Eur J Pediatr, 1999. *158*(7): p. 560-5.

[6]   Garros, D., R.J. Rosychuk, and P.N. Cox, *Circumstances surrounding end of life in a pediatric intensive care unit.* Pediatrics, 2003. *112*(5): p. e371.

[7]   Zimmerman, J.E., et al., *Acute Physiology and Chronic Health Evaluation (APACHE) IV: hospital mortality assessment for today's critically ill patients.* Crit Care Med, 2006. *34*(5): p. 1297-310.

[8]   Pollack, M.M., K.M. Patel, and U.E. Ruttimann, *PRISM III: an updated Pediatric Risk of Mortality score.* Crit Care Med, 1996. *24*(5): p. 743-52.

[9]   Pretzlaff, R.K., *Should age be a deciding factor in ethical decision-making?* Health Care Anal, 2005. *13*(2): p. 119-28.

[10]   Schaeffer, M.H., et al., *The impact of disease severity on the informed consent process in clinical research.* Am J Med, 1996. *100*(3): p. 261-8.

[11]   Wachter, R.M., et al., *Decisions about resuscitation: inequities among patients with different diseases but similar prognoses.* Ann Intern Med, 1989. *111*(6): p. 525-32.

[12]   Azoulay, E., et al., *Half the families of intensive care unit patients experience inadequate communication with physicians.* Crit Care Med, 2000. *28*(8): p. 3044-9.

[13]   Flory, J. and E. Emanuel, *Interventions to improve research participants' understanding in informed consent for research: a systematic review.* Jama, 2004. *292*(13): p. 1593-601.

[14]   Board, R. and N. Ryan-Wenger, *Stressors and stress symptoms of mothers with children in the PICU.* J Pediatr Nurs, 2003. *18*(3): p. 195-202.

[15]   Shudy, M., et al., *Impact of pediatric critical illness and injury on families: a systematic literature review.* Pediatrics, 2006. *118 Suppl 3*: p. S203-18.

[16]   Marcin, J.P., et al., *Prognostication and certainty in the pediatric intensive care unit.* Pediatrics, 1999. *104*(4 Pt 1): p. 868-73.

[17]   White, D.B., et al., *Prognostication during physician-family discussions about limiting life support in intensive care units.* Crit Care Med, 2007. *35*(2): p. 442-8.

[18]   Rich, B.A., *Defining and delineating a duty to prognosticate.* Theor Med Bioeth, 2001. *22*(3): p. 177-92.

[19]   Azoulay, E., et al., *Family participation in care to the critically ill: opinions of families and staff.* Intensive Care Med, 2003. *29*(9): p. 1498-504.

[20] Pochard, F., et al., *Symptoms of anxiety and depression in family members of intensive care unit patients: ethical hypothesis regarding decision-making capacity.* Crit Care Med, 2001. *29*(10): p. 1893-7.

[21] Board, R. and N. Ryan-Wenger, *Long-term effects of pediatric intensive care unit hospitalization on families with young children.* Heart Lung, 2002. *31*(1): p. 53-66.

[22] Rees, G., et al., *Psychiatric outcome following paediatric intensive care unit (PICU) admission: a cohort study.* Intensive Care Med, 2004. *30*(8): p. 1607-14.

[23] Marmot, M.G., M. Kogevinas, and M.A. Elston, *Social/economic status and disease.* Annu Rev Public Health, 1987. *8*: p. 111-35.

[24] Davidson, J.E., et al., *Clinical practice guidelines for support of the family in the patient-centered intensive care unit: American College of Critical Care Medicine Task Force 2004-2005.* Crit Care Med, 2007. *35*(2): p. 605-22.

[25] Cooper, L.A., et al., *Patient-centered communication, ratings of care, and concordance of patient and physician race.* Ann Intern Med, 2003. *139*(11): p. 907-15.

[26] Gamble, V.N., *Under the shadow of Tuskegee: African Americans and health care.* Am J Public Health, 1997. *87*(11): p. 1773-8.

[27] Kagawa-Singer, M. and L.J. Blackhall, *Negotiating cross-cultural issues at the end of life: "You got to go where he lives".* Jama, 2001. *286*(23): p. 2993-3001.

In: Psychology of Decision Making...
Editor: G. R. Burthold, pp. 175-184

Chapter 7

USE OF THE HIGH PERFORMANCE DEVELOPMENT MODEL IN DECISION MAKING

Marc Wooten[*]

Indiana University School of Medicine, Indiana, USA

ABSTRACT

The high performance development model (http://vaww.va.gov/hpdm/) enables leaders within the Veterans Health Administration (VHA) to function more effectively in the highly competitive environment in which they operate. The model is based on eight core competencies expected of VHA leadership, including personal mastery, interpersonal skills, creative thinking, technical skills, flexibility, systems thinking, organizational stewardship, and customer service. The impact of each of these on decision making is significant both for the individual leader and for healthcare leadership. A 360-degree assessment is used in the VHA to compare actual performance (as perceived by the rater) and preferred performance. This model encourages continuous growth of leaders and is an effective and efficient way of teaching and effecting good decision-making skills.

The high performance development model (HPDM) is widely used in the Department of Veterans Affairs as a way to illustrate the core competencies needed in order to be a successful manager and leader. Figure 1 shows the tool, with each of the eight core competencies—personal mastery, systems thinking, technical skills, creative thinking, organizational stewardship, customer service, flexibility, and interpersonal effectiveness. Each of these directly influences managerial decision making, and, additionally, a manager's decision-making preferences are reflected in these core competencies. The model's intent is

[*] Address correspondence and reprint requests to: Marc Wooten, MD, FACP, FACR, Chief of Staff, VA Northern Indiana Healthcare System, 2121 Lake Avenue, Fort Wayne, Indiana 46805; Phone: 260-460-1311; Fax: 260-421-1827; E-mail: marc.wooten@va.gov.
"The views expressed in this article are not those of the Department of Veterans Affairs or of the United States Government."

that leadership development occurs at all levels of the organization, and that successful organizations develop at all levels along a common set of core competencies.

The model's six spokes represent the activities by which the effective leader not only grows in his or her own development, but also develops those who work for him. These activities include competency development, continuous learning opportunities, coaching/mentoring, continuous assessment, performance management, and performance-based interviewing. Each of these activities is used in the organization to help guide individuals to greater levels of accomplishment.

The eight core competencies can also be viewed as a spectrum from the foundation issues of dealing with self through the capstone issue of holistic leadership (Figure 2). They bridge the spectrum from controlled accountability to global accountability. In this model, the leader must demonstrate all of the core competencies in order to truly demonstrate organizational stewardship.

This commentary will briefly examine each of the eight core competencies and its impact upon decision making. In addition, the role of the 360-degree feedback process for the purpose of enhancing performance will be discussed.

PERSONAL MASTERY

Personal mastery is the quality of a leader which assumes responsibility for personal development and career goals. In this competency, the leader actively seeks information on how s/he is perceived by others, and takes initiative for continuous learning. This competency is demonstrated when the leader learns from setbacks and failures as well as from successful efforts.

Not only does this competency mean that individuals set aside time to reflect on their own personal development, but it also means that they encourage those they supervise to pursue self-development opportunities and growth. In short, this competency reflects on the overall organizational health of the enterprise. A manager with this competency demonstrates a passion for personal excellence in him or herself and in those s/he leads.

In decision making, the leader seeks, both formally and informally, continuous feedback about the impact of his actions on others. Each decision is weighed with a view to both the benefits and risks attendant to it, and the impact on those served and those who provide the service. The true leader is a servant leader. Rather than seeking to only maximize his or her personal gain, the servant leader looks for the good of those around him. Where tradeoffs exist, the effective leader makes decisions that enhance the overall development of the staff impacted by the decision.

The spokes that most clearly relate to this core competency are continuous assessment, coaching/mentoring, and competency development. A mentor or coach will help the effective leader to get objective feedback regarding decisions, as well as help develop options for decision making in the future.

TECHNICAL SKILLS

Tandem with personal mastery in the model of the core competencies is the competency of technical skills, since this also has to do with dealing with oneself (Figure 2). The leader with this core competency displays knowledge and skills necessary to perform assigned duties, and also keeps current on new developments in the field of expertise. The area of health care is burgeoning with new ideas and developments including flow improvement, advanced clinic access, six sigma, and lean thinking. The effective leader will harness these tools, and find opportunities to master them.

Multiple organizations exist which advance the leader's skills in decision making and health care administration. Included in these are the American College of Physician Executives and the American College of Health Care Executives. Each offers a route of advancement by which the decision maker develops practical skills which enable him or her to make more effective decisions. The effective leader nurtures innovations that are recognized as best practices or models, both within one's own organization and from without. This leader also provides his or her employees with time, resources, and opportunities to master new material so that collaboratively the decision-making process is improved.

Often the issues reflected in decision making are complex and require full examination of the options based on data. The effective leader with this core competency fosters and rewards high standards for accuracy, safety, and continuous improvement in all areas of the organization. This is accomplished through a constant reappraisal process. The most commonly employed model is the PDSA ("plan, do, study, act") model, involving multiple rapid-cycle changes in response to observations made during the third phase of the model.

The effective leader with this core competency is ultimately recognized as a consultant or advisor in a regional or national basis regarding topics dealing with his field of expertise. The spokes on the HPDM model which most clearly address this core competency are those of continuous learning opportunities, competency development, and performance management. Becoming a lifetime learner enables the effective leader not to stagnate in his or her decision-making skills, but rather to grow in the knowledge of tools which are present to enhance the decisions that he makes.

INTERPERSONAL RELATIONSHIPS

In the functional model of the core competencies, the next level demonstrated by the effective leader is that of dealing with others. This is intertwined with the competencies directed at dealing with oneself and becoming others-oriented. The core competency of interpersonal relationships deals with the ability to build and sustain positive relationships among individuals within the manager's scope of supervision (while personal mastery addressed the manager's development of these individuals). While the core competency of personal mastery had as an element a focus on the development of individuals within one's scope of supervision, this core competency focuses on the relationship aspect of this supervision. Lack of interpersonal effectiveness correlates with failure in leadership and derails the leader's ability to make good decisions.

One of the key components of this core competency is that of encouraging shared decision making. In this arena, the servant leader is not one who dictates to those below him or her, but views his or her responsibility to them as effectively drawing them into the decision-making process, including building consensus around the final decision. Often this involves finding champions for a given process or idea, who will assist in rolling the idea out through the organization.

This core competency is demonstrated when the leader exhibits negotiation skills required to achieve cooperation among those that they lead. Often the most difficult phase of decision making is the implementation phase, when staff must execute the plan. Being able to negotiate with key leaders throughout this phase and provide timely feedback to senior leadership harnesses the potential of transformation within the organization. Other activities which demonstrate this core competency with regard to decision making include clear, candid, and open communication in staff meetings (such as town halls or all employee meetings) when decisions are of a magnitude as to affect all or a majority of staff, and seeking to break down barriers to communication.

Ultimately this core competency is about collaboration, both within the organization and outside the organization utilizing networks that are both hierarchically and functionally based. Sometimes champions for a change idea come from within the organization, and sometimes they come from outside its structure. These are individuals who will carry forth a decision and a change idea into the infrastructure of the organization to facilitate buy-in by those staff who may be reluctant to implement the change. Use of these people in team projects is one way to integrate them into the overall impact of the decision. Actively soliciting feedback from staff can effectively anticipate or circumvent obstacles to implementation.

The spokes of the HPDM model which most clearly relate to this core competency are coaching and mentoring, continuous assessment, and performance-based interviewing (especially when done collectively). This is one area where personality types tend to have the most influence, with extroverts being the most likely to view themselves as successful. Coaching/mentoring, and performance assessment, provide objective feedback, and reveal areas for potential improvement.

CUSTOMER SERVICE

The next core competency, customer service, deals with the responsiveness of the decision maker to the constituents of the organization. In the functional model, this focuses on becoming others-oriented, as well as developing recovery systems when service delivery is not adequately handled to the satisfaction of the customer. The nucleus of this competency is building a service that incorporates customer feedback into the planning and provision of services and products.

One particular obstacle in effective use of this competency is determining who are the customers of a given service. While external customers are often focused upon, many decisions rely upon an accurate assessment of who are the internal customers of the organization. As the effective leader stresses and models the need to be customer-focused throughout the organization, he or she clarifies the mission of the organization. In turn, this provides the opportunity to hire staff who also embrace this vision. Placing the customer first, regardless of whether the customer is internal or external, is the hallmark of servant leadership.

An effective leader bases strategic planning on customer feedback and projected needs, and decision making is in turn driven by this strategic planning. The identification of key barriers which impede good service delivery is a part of this planning process. Encouraging feedback from customers prior to implementation of a major decision is also an effective way of anticipating these barriers. Clearly the effective leader must remain highly visible and accessible to all customers, including staff. The effective leader also searches for and recognizes staff who excel in customer service delivery within and outside their own organization.

When service delivery systems fail, it is important to have as a key component of the service delivery system an opportunity for service recovery. This demonstrates to the customer that the organization recognizes that the system has failed, and that the organization is interested in, and committed to, the satisfaction of its customers. The influence of including this in the overall decision-making strategy is ultimately not felt on the individual level, but as a result of the impressions conveyed to all of the potential customers of that organization.

The spokes of the HPDM model which most closely correlate with this competency are the same ones which correlated with interpersonal skills—coaching and mentoring, continuous assessment, and performance-based interviewing. Use of feedback through all of these methods will result in the decision maker becoming more skilled and competent in all that he or she does.

FLEXIBILITY/ADAPTABILITY

Flexibility and adaptability are inserted as a core competency because of the need for the decision maker and leader to appropriately respond to a new or changing environment. The effective decision maker is able to make the most of limited resources, as well as demonstrate resilience in the face of setbacks. Above all, this decision maker must be able to understand the principles of change management.

In the foundational model of the core competencies, this competency falls within the realm of becoming comfortable with unpredictability. In the language of flow improvement, this involves dealing with two kinds of variability, natural and artificial. The effective decision maker addresses artificial variability and seeks to redress this form of variability causing disruption in utilization of resources. Management of natural variability becomes the goal of decision making, including proactively addressing this in planning, and compensating for this when it occurs outside the ranges of what was expected.

Part of flexibility and adaptability involves looking for better alternatives, and fostering flexibility through cross-training and developmental work assignments. In addition, the effective leader responds to changing priorities and resources with optimism, and encourages the staff to respond positively and proactively to these changes. This person stays abreast of, and educates staff about, changing conditions in the health care market, and understands change management principles.

Foundational Model of the Core Competencies
(courtesy of Linda Belton, Network Director, VISN 11)

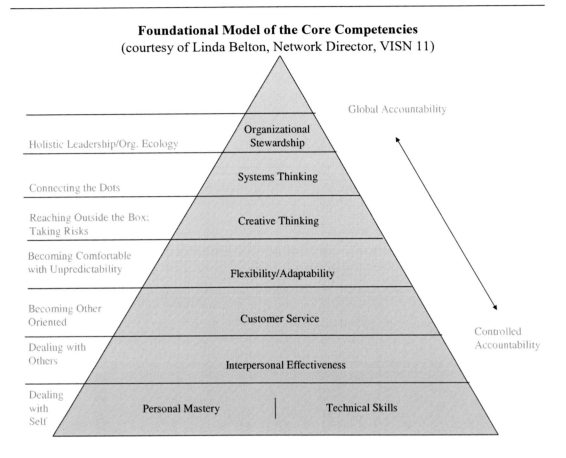

The inability to make timely changes as part of decision making hampers the organization's ability to respond appropriately to a changing climate. In addition, in the foundational model there is the expectation that those with this competency demonstrate controlled accountability for their actions.

The spokes of the HPDM model which relate to this core competency are continuous assessment, performance management, and coaching/mentoring. The manager must adapt to the information and feedback gained through these activities. The servant leader must be willing to allow changes to planning to accommodate the needs of staff as well as the customers. The model allows for the leader to progress in the decision-making process with a view to the ultimate goal.

CREATIVE THINKING

This core competency is sandwiched in between that of flexibility/adaptability (because of the frequent need to demonstrate creative thinking in these situations) and systems thinking (which often embraces creative thinking). In the foundational model of the core competencies, this represents reaching "outside the box" and taking risks.

Good creative thinking can create new approaches to problems or invest new systems or approaches with the tools they need in order to be successful. Creative thinking requires an appreciation for new ideas and approaches, thinking or acting innovatively, and looking beyond the current reality and the status quo. Creative thinking can be risky, both from the standpoint of taking action which does not meet the market forces which affect the organization, and also the standpoint of failing to take action when timing is critical. Yet this risk must be balanced against the risk of the situation or problem remaining the same or the system used being dealt with in the usual fashion. Creative thinkers look beyond the current reality to prepare the organization for alternative futures.

Creative thinkers often have difficulty dealing with those who are not creative, and vice versa. A harmony must be struck between change for change's sake, and "we've always done it that way." In the conceptual field of change management, it is important to reward those who are risk takers in decision making, even if a disillusionment phase associated with implementation of a changed process occurs. Also, the decision maker must recognize that the twenty percent of individuals who usually are on the front end of change usually represent the creative thinkers in the organization, and that the challenge is finding champions who will facilitate rollout of the idea into the remainder of the organization, even to those who do not readily embrace change.

Those decision makers who do not have creative thinking skills will do well to surround themselves with people who do have this talent, and seek ideas from them actively in the decision-making process. These same decision makers will need to encourage and reward risk-taking and entrepreneurial behavior within the organization.

The spokes of the HPDM model which most clearly relate to this core competency are competency development and coaching and mentoring. The ability to adjust one's system and thinking is necessary in order to adapt to the changing environment of decision making. Feedback in a non-threatening way from observers provides the opportunity for the decision maker to see how s/he incorporates creative thinking into day-to-day decision making.

Systems Thinking

The core competency of systems thinking is the ability to integrate the impact of the parts on the whole. It involves knowledge of how one's role relates to others within the organization, as well as an appreciation of the consequences of specific actions on other parts of the system. The decision maker demonstrating this core competency will ask questions that help others to think in a broader context, and will encourage and reward collaboration.

In the foundational model of the core competencies, this competency represents "connecting the dots" within the organization so that the parts are able to work together. It represents a progression toward the global accountability that is expected of an experienced leader. Systems thinking embraces creative thinking (immediately beneath it in the model), and serves as the foundation for organizational stewardship.

Knowledge of the parts of the system with which the decision maker is least familiar requires the ability to ask critical questions prior to making a decision or implementing a plan. Often it is critical to have all potentially impacted services come together and hold a meeting of the minds regarding the impact of potential decision. In health care there tend to be "invisible" customers who may be impacted, either positively or deleteriously. In addition, there is the need to consider the whole of the organization, if the institution is part of a larger entity such as a managed health care organization.

A key piece of the decision maker's role is in sharing the "big picture" with staff, including the consequences of not thinking holistically. This, in turn, is part of servant leadership, where the leader views his or her job as communicating decisions down to the lowest level in the organization and facilitating training and resources for those most impacted by the decision. It also involves breaking down "silos" within the organization of groups viewing themselves as having a vested interest in the outcome of a particular decision, and averting a decision which has narrow interests in view rather than that of the organization as a whole.

The spokes of the HPDM model which most impact systems thinking are coaching/mentoring, continuous assessment, and performance management. This is an ideal place for the personal coach or mentor to assist the coachee or mentee to see things from the perspective of someone higher up in the organization or outside the organization. Continuous assessment of the impact of a decision and rapid cycle changes are ways to help improve decision making for the future. Obviously, the decision maker accepts the global consequences of his or her every decision.

ORGANIZATIONAL STEWARDSHIP

The last core competency encompasses being genuinely committed to the overall health and welfare of the organization. An effective leader with organizational stewardship will provide a clear vision of the future and will lead the organization through necessary changes. In so doing, s/he will demonstrate commitment to people, empower and trust others, and develop team-based improvement processes within the organization.

This competency represents the highest level of accountability within the foundational model of the core competencies. The emphasis will be on holistic leadership, as well as the ecology of the organization as a totality. The decision maker will focus on managing physical, fiscal, and human resources to increase the value of products and services, and will engage in strategic planning. In developing staff, the leader will provide links between individuals and groups in the organization and will integrate the organization into the community. The leader accepts accountability for self, others, and the organization's development; s/he works to accomplish the organizational business plan. S/he needs to be familiar with organizations outside his or her own with similar missions and/or structures.

More than any other, the decision maker must model this core competency in order to be fully successful. While aspects of this competency can be learned, it is most often "caught rather than taught." Healthy organizations and their decision makers have a high level of commitment to seeing the prosperity of their organization as a whole and within the greater community of organizations of like commitment. The decision maker who embodies this core competency will be perceived by others as being truly trustworthy.

Having a personal coach or mentor is an invaluable aid to the decision maker at this stage. The impact of the decision beyond a local level is easy to overlook, and a coach can often offer ways to make the impact of a decision even greater in the community or among the constituencies which support the organization. This core competency also builds upon all of the other seven, and the decision maker with this competency synthesizes information from all of the other core competencies to come to a truly beneficial decision, having weighed all the risks and benefits, as well as the pros and cons of a particular decision.

In a servant leadership model, the effective decision maker views every member of the organization as important, and seeks to effect an outcome which will improve or advance those staff. The impact of this will be that staff will view leadership as being less distant and self-focused, and will be more willing to embrace the decisions which are made.

USE OF THE 360-DEGREE ASSESSMENT TOOL

The Veterans Health Administration has developed the 360-degree assessment tool, which evaluates leaders on each of the core competencies mentioned above. This particular tool asks for feedback from four sources—supervisors, peers, and staff supervised, as well as self. Questions based on each of the eight core competencies are answered first by the individual himself. There is also an element with each question which asks for a rating of his or her desired behavior. The rated individual is then asked to identify others from within these three areas who would also complete this rating of him or her. These ratings are rolled up based on areas of strength identified across the raters and areas of potential development. The ratee is blinded to the actual raters in the feedback, as their responses are pooled in the evaluation. Respondents are also given the opportunity to make verbatim comments to the ratee on any area observed within each of the eight core competencies.

The ratee is given the opportunity to be briefed on the results of the instrument and to address any areas of cognitive dissonance between perceived and actual behaviors. A copy of the results is then provided to the individual being rated. The use of this tool can facilitate a personal development plan for each of the eight core competencies through the development of goals and activities which will further enhance the decision-making skills of the leader.

The use of this tool often identifies three areas of strength, which then become the core competencies that the decision maker can turn around and use to influence others from within the organization on (such as through coaching/mentoring). Significant gaps also indicate areas for development of the decision maker. In this manner, the leader is given feedback to improve performance in a non-threatening way (based on other's and one's own perceptions). This instrument can be repeated cyclically or throughout an organization's top management.

CONCLUSIONS

Each of the eight core competencies is influential in effective decision making. Clearly, a versatile and responsive decision maker who is accountable to the organization and sees his or her organization in the totality of the marketplace will need to develop all eight of these competencies. This model, then, becomes an effective construct upon which decision making may be based. The successful organization will develop its leaders at all levels with these core competencies, in part to enhance their decision-making ability. Leadership is not all about "position," since there are multiple levels of organizational leadership represented within the model between the spokes. Yet the core competencies are the "glue" along the outside and the spokes are the tools which support the model. Use of these tools in the pursuance of developing the leader's core competencies is what enhances decision making.

Individualized personal development plans are key tools to enable leaders to develop in areas identified as relative weaknesses or preferences that may serve as barriers to effective decision making. One such instrument is the 360-degree assessment, where the individual is rated by a spectrum of individuals in that leader's work environment. This provides consistent feedback in perception of areas of excellence as well as need for development across a multiplicity of individuals.

The end result is that the Veterans Health Administration seeks to develop qualified leaders who will continue to provide the best possible health care in an ever-changing arena

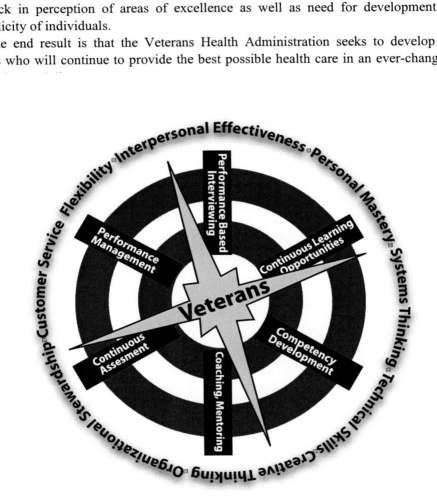

In: Psychology of Decision Making...
Editor: G. R. Burthold, pp. 185-201

ISBN: 978-1-60021-932-0

© 2007 Nova Science Publishers, Inc.

Chapter 8

THE IMPACT OF NOTE-TAKING AND JUSTICE-VENGEANCE MOTIVES ON JUROR DECISION-MAKING IN A CRIMINAL MURDER TRIAL

Lynne ForsterLee, Robert ForsterLee, Hollie Wilson, and Robert Ho
Central Queensland University

ABSTRACT

This study examined the effects of note-taking and justice-vengeance motives on juror decision making in a criminal trial. The study predicted that (1) jurors who took notes would render more appropriate decisions and recall more evidentiary content, (2) jurors high in vengeance would sentence the defendant more harshly and recall less probative information, and (3) note-taking would interact with justice and vengeance motives and impact upon sentencing and the recall of information. The sample of 149 jury eligible participants recruited from the Central Queensland community were assigned to one of two conditions (note-taking or non note-taking). All participants viewed the same murder trial and subsequently, rendered a verdict and sentencing decision, as well as recalled the trial facts. Lastly, they completed the Justice-Vengeance scale (Ho, ForsterLee, ForsterLee, & Crofts, 2002). Results of the study indicated that (1) jurors who took notes recalled more probative information than their non note-taking counterparts, (2) jurors high in vengeance sentenced the defendant more harshly and recalled fewer case-related facts, and (3) note-taking offset the vengeance motive for punishment, suggesting that note-taking would be a useful memory aid for vengeance-oriented jurors. The implications of these findings are discussed, as well as recommendations for future research in the field of juror decision-making.

INTRODUCTION

Throughout the criminal justice system, there has been much controversy regarding the competency of the jury to adjudicate complex criminal proceedings. Jurors have the responsibility of deciding whether a person is guilty or innocent of a particular crime without prior training or expertise within the field of criminal justice. In fact, a fundamental assumption is that the jurors will ignore personal biases and act as impartial fact finders, who are able to render verdict outcomes according to legal guidelines. Nevertheless, there have been a number of criticisms concerning the process of jury decision-making, particularly with regard to the inexperience of community members to render an impartial verdict in a criminal case. Opponents against the jury system also argue that numerous factors such as pre-trial publicity (Douglas & ForsterLee, 2003) and the gender of the defendant (ForsterLee, Fox, ForsterLee, & Ho, 2004) have been shown to influence juror decision-making.

In contrast, advocates for the jury system such as Lempert (1993) contend that the use of basic memory tools to aid jurors' comprehension of complex case facts is an essential element that is necessary for improving juror decisions. The inclusion of such strategies has been shown to augment the underlying cognitive processes involved in juror decision-making. Thus, to enhance juror decision-making, procedural reforms have been proposed. Illustrations of such reforms or strategies to improve juror comprehension include allowing jurors access to trial transcripts or providing them with bottom-line summary statements of expert witness testimony. These basic cognitive tools or memory aids allow jurors to process information more efficiently and accurately and have proven to be effective methods, particularly in aiding recall (ForsterLee, Horowitz, Athaide-Victor, & Brown, 2000; Horowitz & ForsterLee, 2001). Another promising strategy to improve juror information processing is note-taking.

NOTE-TAKING

The influence of note-taking on juror decision-making has been widely researched with various outcomes. An early study by Fisher and Harris (1973) found that note-taking increased the efficiency of college students by significantly increasing the recall of information, apparently serving as an encoding device and memory aid. In a subsequent study Einstein, Morris, and Smith (1985) found that note-takers within an educational setting recalled more messages of higher importance as compared to those not permitted to take notes.

Nevertheless, while Peper and Mayer (1978) also found that note-taking had a significant effect on overall learning outcomes, such as remembering broad concepts, it did not result in better performance on a recall measure. Similarly, Kierwa (1985) found that the immediate effect of note-taking was not significant in a sample of students who viewed a video-tape of a lecture and were subsequently tested on the recall of the information presented. Clearly, the research has produced mixed results for the possible benefits of note-taking in general within educational contexts.

The controversy surrounding the beneficial effects of note-taking has also generated much debate within research in the psycholegal arena. For example, Heuer and Penrod (1994) found no significant differences between the note-taking and non note-taking conditions for mock jurors in the recall of case facts. In addition, Heuer and Penrod's (1988; 1994) examination of 34 civil and 33 criminal trials in the Wisconsin circuit courts failed to support juror note-taking facilitating the comprehension or recall of the trial facts. However, their methodology did not allow a direct test of whether note-taking improved comprehension and recall, as those in the various conditions decided different cases (ForsterLee, Horowitz, & Bourgeois, 1994).

In contrast, other studies have shown that note-taking is advantageous for mock jurors, in particular serving as a memory aid by facilitating recall (Flango, 1980). One illustration is a study by Horowitz and ForsterLee (2001), who investigated the impact of note-taking and trial transcript access in a complex civil trial. They found that note-takers were better able to organize the case facts according to legal principles and consequently, distinguished among the plaintiffs and assigned compensatory damage awards that were consistent with each complainant's medical and economic claims. This was not the case for those juries who had access to the trial transcript. Further, note-taking juries were more likely to recognize case-related facts and reject plausible lures (statements that were not actually in the trial) as opposed to their counterparts who were not allowed to take notes. In addition, they found that note-taking juries were more satisfied with the trial process than those not permitted to take notes (Horowitz & ForsterLee).

Another study which demonstrates the effectiveness of note-taking as a cognitive aid was conducted by Rosenhan, Eisner, and Robinson (1994). In this study, mock jurors were assigned to two conditions (note-taking or non note-taking) where they viewed a trial. They found that mock jurors, who were permitted to take notes while watching a video-taped trial, recalled more trial information, and reported greater involvement in the case than mock jurors not allowed to take notes. Furthermore, the accuracy, quantity, and organization of the notes all had a positive effect on recall (Rosenhan et al.).

Although the results of previous studies indicate that note-taking improves jurors' elaboration and subsequent recall of the evidentiary content (Flango, 1980; Horowitz & ForsterLee, 2001), there is no current legislation in Australia that requires a judge to inform a jury of the possible benefits of note-taking (*Jury Act, 1995*). Nevertheless, jurors are often provided with note-taking materials in order to assist them with the recall of important trial information.

Thus, it is apparent that there is a body of research suggesting that taking notes does improve comprehension and recall. To this end, a primary aim of the present study is to test the effects of note-taking on recall of probative information. It is expected that note-taking should augment juror information processing.

In addition to note-taking, other factors that effect juror decision-making also need to be examined. One such factor that influences juror decision-making is whether jurors may be motivated by either justice or vengeance motives to process the trial facts.

JUSTICE-VENGEANCE

An important aspect of juror decision-making is whether jurors are influenced by justice or vengeance motives (Ho, ForsterLee, & ForsterLee, 2004). Recently, a justice-vengeance scale was developed to identify and clearly delineate the motives of jurors when deciding a criminal case (Ho, ForsterLee, ForsterLee, & Crofts, 2002). This has important implications for the legal system as it may determine whether punishment is rendered on the basis of justice or vengeance.

A study conducted by Ho et al. (2004) concluded that justice motives are based on fairness and legal aspects of a case, whereas vengeance motives are based on sentencing and emotion. Within the context of a criminal trial, they found that vengeance-oriented jurors tended to sentence the defendant more harshly than those who were justice oriented. However, it was not apparent whether jurors' sought 'clear cut' punishment based on justice or vengeance motives, or if these factors overlapped (Ho et al.). Indeed, the ambiguous nature of jurors' motives for punishment make it difficult to determine whether their decisions are based on justice, vengeance, or a combination of the two (Ho et al., 2002).

Thus, the current study further investigates the possibility of an overlap in justice-vengeance motives by determining how high or low a juror may be on both scales. If a particular juror is high in justice, for example, the same juror may also be high in vengeance. In this instance, such a juror might be objective in considering the case facts according to legal guidelines, while also being motivated by retribution. Considering the complex nature of juror decision-making, clearly delineating between justice and vengeance motives has potentially important pragmatic implications for the justice system.

Given the historial expectations of unbiased processing of jurors, the examination of the potential underlying motives of jurors is a recent exception to the studies of influences to juror decision-making previously discussed. As such, there is a paucity of information examining the differences between justice-oriented and vengeance-oriented punishment of offenders by jurors in criminal or civil proceedings. The present study should therefore provide additional information about the justice-vengeance motives of jurors within the context of a murder trial.

One theoretical model that may be useful in accounting for the influence of justice and vengeance motives on the severity of punishment imposed and the recall of evidence is the Elaboration Likelihood Model.

ELABORATION LIKELIHOOD MODEL

The Elaboration Likelihood Model (ELM) is a dual process model that posits two distinct information processing routes (Petty & Cacioppo, 1984). The first information processing route, called central processing, involves active and analytical consideration of the message (in the present study, the evidentiary content of the trial). Central processors therefore need to be motivated to think about the possible meanings of the message and respond to the quality and strengths of the arguments presented (Petty, Cacioppo, & Schumann, 1983). This process, then, involves the elaboration of information and careful consideration of the arguments. In the current study, jurors who closely examine all the evidence and make an informed decision based on all the facts available to them would be categorized as central processors.

In contrast, peripheral processors do not consider all of the possible alternatives, have difficulty understanding the content of the message, and are persuaded by cues such as the perceived credibility of the source (Petty & Cacioppo, 1984). Peripheral processors are also not motivated to think or elaborate upon a particular message and tend to be influenced by factors that are not relevant to the content of the message, such as the gender or race of the person delivering the message or argument (Petty & Cacioppo). This alternative mode of information processing requires less attentional resources and cognitive effort than central processing (Petty et al., 1983). For example, in a complex trial, jurors are often presented with cognitively dense testimony (e.g., DNA evidence). Faced with such complex evidentiary content, receivers (or jurors), who are peripheral processors are likely to rely on peripheral cues or heuristics that are not associated with the message content to render a decision (Petty et al.)

The potential application of the ELM to juror decision-making in a courtroom setting, where lay people are required to deliver verdicts on the accused based on the presentation of the case facts and testimony, is evident. Jurors who are central processors are more likely to elaborate on all of the case information presented throughout the trial proceedings. In contrast, jurors who are peripheral processors are more likely to be swayed by other unimportant variables or heuristic cues.

Thus, it is apparent that the ELM provides a theoretical framework for understanding juror information processing in a criminal trial. Central processors should be able to comprehend and elaborate upon all the information during the course of the trial, and make an informed decision based on the facts of the case. Conversely, peripheral processors, who are unable to elaborate on all the information presented to them during a trial, may make decisions based on factors that are not relevant.

Elaboration Likelihood Model and Note-taking

The underlying assumptions of the Elaboration Likelihood Model may be used to account for the differences in information processing or decision-making in jury trials. Specifically, providing jurors with a memory aid such as note-taking is more likely to enable jurors to process the trial facts centrally. Conversely, jurors not allowed to take notes are more likely to process the trial material relying on peripheral factors.

Research conducted by Horowitz and ForsterLee (2001) supports this contention. They found that note-takers recalled more case-related information as compared to their non note-taking counterparts. Indeed, their body of research (e.g., ForsterLee et al., 1994; ForsterLee & Horowitz, 1997; ForsterLee & Horowitz, 2003) demonstrates that allowing jurors to take notes during a civil trial can aid in decision-making and recall. That is, note-taking is a cognitive tool that enhances the likelihood that jurors elaborate on and process the trial facts centrally, leading to better decisions and improved recall. In contrast, non note-takers are less likely to process relevant trial facts, suggesting that jurors who do not take notes are more likely to process information peripherally (Horowitz & ForsterLee).

Thus, the present study expects that note-taking should provide jurors with a cognitive framework that allows them to elaborate upon and comprehend the information presented at trial. In this case, jurors should process the case facts centrally leading to better recall of the evidence.

Elaboration Likelihood Model and Justice-Vengeance

The Elaboration Likelihood Model may also provide a theoretical foundation for jurors' motives for punishment. Ho, ForsterLee, and ForsterLee (2004) found that justice oriented individuals attended to the trial information more than other heuristic cues, such as the source's characteristics, whereas vengeance-oriented individuals focused more on mitigating factors than the actual case facts. The current study proposes that jurors high in justice are likely to be central processors, as seeking justice in the trial should motivate jurors to accurately process the case facts.

Central processors should therefore render a sentencing decision that is based on fairness and legal principles. Central processors should also recall more probative case facts. Conversely, jurors high in vengeance are more likely to be peripheral processors, whose rendering of a verdict is likely emotionally based and involves heuristic cues. In sum, justice-vengeance motives should influence how the jurors process the case facts and the subsequent decisions and recall of information.

Thus, the current study examines the influence of note-taking and justice-vengeance motives on juror decision-making using the ELM as a theoretical framework. Specifically, the focus of this study is to examine the effects of note-taking and justice-vengeance motives on probative recall.

Empirical Questions

1. Does note-taking impact juror decision-making? For example, are note-takers more likely to render appropriate sentencing decisions, as well as accurately recall more of the trial information?
2. Are jurors' motives justice- or vengeance-oriented? For example, are jurors low in justice and high in vengeance more likely to sentence harshly and recall less of the evidentiary content?
3. Do the variables of note-taking and justice-vengeance interact? For example, are non note-takers who are low in justice and high in vengeance less likely than jurors in other conditions to render an appropriate sentence and recall more of the trial facts?

METHOD

Participants

The sample consisted of 149 jury eligible participants selected from the Central Queensland community. The 93 female and 56 male participants varied in age, from 18 to 64 years, with a mean age of approximately 31 years. Participants included a large proportion of community members, as well as university students.

Trial Materials

The participants viewed a criminal murder trial that has been used in previous research (ForsterLee, Horowitz, ForsterLee, King, & Ronlund, 1999; Ho et al., 2002). The murder trial, based on an actual case (ForsterLee et al., 1999), describes the torture and subsequent death of a victim (Mrs. Janine Hallman) by her husband (Dr. Jason Hallman). The defendant was a physician, who was impotent and suffered from depression and paranoia. On the suspicion that his wife, a former beauty queen, was having affairs with other residents of their apartment complex, Dr. Hallman viciously 'operated' on his wife with the intent of disfiguring her and making her repulsive to other men. He showed her a note after tying her up which advised her not to scream, threatening that he would make her even more repulsive. To drown out the noise made by his wife's screams, the defendant had previously purchased stereo equipment. The victim died 21 days after the incident from the wounds inflicted by her husband.

All participants viewed the trial in its entirety. The videotaped trial, which was approximately 20 minutes long, included the facts of the case, the prosecution summation, the defence summation, and the judicial instructions. Paid actors played the various participants of the trial.

The prosecution argued that Dr. Hallman was responsible for his actions as the attack was premeditated, which was indicated by the following facts. Dr. Hallman purchased a stereo prior to the assault, and had a note written to his wife telling her not to scream. In addition, Dr. Hallman had gloves and acids readily available in his home, which were consequently used in the attack. Furthermore, they argued that as a doctor, the defendant would have been able to reasonably foresee the lethal consequences of his actions.

The defense counsel argued that Dr. Hallman was suffering from temporary insanity and therefore was not responsible for his actions at the time of the crime. Defense counsel argued this on the basis of his previous psychological history, along with the fact that he was a well-respected doctor (one of the mitigating factors), and that he seemed disoriented when they found him at his home. Finally, the judge provided the participants with the substantive (case-related) judicial instructions on how to reach a verdict, as well as explaining the legal precedents involved in coming to this decision. The defendant in this case was clearly guilty. In previous research by ForsterLee et al. (1999), a pre-test on the case transcript with third year law students showed strong agreement that the defendant was guilty (Kappa coefficient 0.91). The trial transcript comprised 1542 words.

Experimental Design

The design used in this study was a 2 (note-taking – yes or no) x 4 (justice-vengeance -- justice high/vengeance high, justice high/vengeance low, justice low/vengeance high, justice low/vengeance low) between subjects design.

Independent Variables

Note-taking

All participants were randomly assigned to either a note-taking or non note-taking condition. Participants in the note-taking condition were allowed to take notes throughout the trial, whereas participants in the non note-taking condition were not permitted to take notes.

Justice-Vengeance Scale

Each participant was asked to answer the questions comprising the Justice-Vengeance Scale (Ho, ForsterLee, ForsterLee, & Crofts, 2002). This multivariate scale assesses the four motives of vengeance-emotion (V/E), vengeance-sentence (V/S), justice-legal (J/L), and justice-fairness (J/F). The four motive sub-factors are delineated by the 20-items in the scale (e.g., V/E in deciding a criminal case, it is alright to allow your anger to play a part in your decision; V/S in deciding a criminal case, all convicted sexual offenders should be castrated; J/L in deciding a criminal case, it is important to make your decisions according to legal principles; J/F in deciding a criminal case, it is important to be objective when considering the evidence). A six-point Likert-type scale ranging from 1 (strongly agree) to 6 (strongly disagree) was utilized, with higher scores indicating stronger support toward the varying justice and vengeance motives.

For the purpose of this study, the scores along the two primary dimensions (Justice and Vengeance) were derived by summing the ratings for the items that comprise each of the scales. These summative scores for each dimension were subjected to a median split technique to assign the participants into a high or low group along that dimension. Participants were then partitioned into one of four possible conditions of interest for this study depending on their assignments (high or low) on the two motives justice and vengeance. This resulted in four groups representing those who rated themselves as: justice high/vengeance high, justice high/vengeance low, justice low/vengeance high, or justice low/vengeance low.

Dependent Variables

Verdict Decision

The case clearly shows that the defendant was guilty; therefore, the verdict decision was not expected to be influenced by the independent variables. Nevertheless, participants indicated their verdict decision by circling '1' (not guilty by reason of insanity), '2' (guilty, manslaughter on the basis of diminished responsibility), or '3' (guilty, murder).

Recommended Sentencing Decision

Participants, who found the defendant guilty of murder or manslaughter, were asked to indicate a recommended sentencing decision on a seven-point scale with the following outcomes: '1' (jail term of one year or less), '2' (jail term of 1 to 5 years), '3' (jail term of 5 to 10 years), '4' (jail term of 10 to 15 years), '5' (jail term of 15 to 20 years), '6' (jail term of 20 to 25 years), and '7' (life sentence without the possibility of parole). This scale has been used in previous research by ForsterLee et al. (1999).

Recall Measure

Subsequent to rendering a verdict and sentencing decision, each participant was asked to write down any trial facts that they considered when arriving at their verdict outcomes. Jurors were specifically requested to note trial facts that may have impacted their decisions. The content of these responses was then analyzed by breaking each sentence down into single units of information. Each unit of information was categorized as probative or directly related to the case facts.

As an illustration, consider the following sentence: 'The police found Mrs. Hallman tied to a bed, naked, horribly mutilated but still alive." This statement contains four units of *probative* information: 1 = 'The police found Mrs. Hallman,' 2 = 'tied to a bed,' 3 = 'mutilated' and 4 = 'alive.' This would be scored as four pieces of evidence. Each of the probative units of information for each participant was tallied to attain an overall score.

Procedure

Prior to the presentation of the trial, participants were advised that they would watch a criminal murder trial, which included the facts of the case, prosecution and defense summations, and the substantive judicial instructions. All of the participants were given an information sheet detailing the purpose of the research, as well as a form for informed consent to participate in the study. The participants were then asked to carry out their task as a juror would in an actual trial context, and also informed that they could withdraw at any time throughout the experiment.

Participants, who were randomly assigned to each of the two experimental conditions, (i.e., note-taking or non note-taking) watched the video of the murder trial on a large screen television. All participants viewed the same video and were treated identically with regard to the presentation of the trial and materials.

Participants in the note-taking condition were provided with note-taking materials and informed that they could take notes during the trial. Those in the non note-taking condition were not provided with note-taking materials.

At the conclusion of the trial, participants indicated a verdict decision. Those who found the defendant guilty then recommended a sentencing decision. After rendering these decisions, participants were asked to write down the trial events, focusing on those aspects of the trial that helped them to make their decisions. Participants then filled out the manipulation check. In this case, the manipulation check asked whether or not the participant took notes during the presentation of the trial. Lastly, participants were required to complete the justice/vengeance scale.

All of the participants were debriefed by the experimenter and thanked for their participation in the study. Any questions or concerns were responded to at this stage.

RESULTS

Reliability Analysis

Reliability analyses on the two JV subscales indicated that the seven items comprising the Justice scales yielded (α = .65) and the nine items comprising the Vengeance subscales showed (α = .82). These results indicate that in the present sample the Justice items were responded to in a marginally consistent manner; while the Vengeance items demonstrate adequate stability with the sample.

Manipulation Check

A chi square analysis conducted on the manipulation check for note-taking revealed that jurors correctly assessed whether or not they took notes, χ^2 (1, N = 149) = 8.22, p = .004.

Verdict Decisions

A 2 (Note-taking) x 4 (Justice-Vengeance) analysis of variance (ANOVA) was carried out on the verdict scores. As expected, and considering the weight of the case facts, there were no significant effects of the independent variables on the verdict given.

Recommended Sentencing Decisions

To analyze the recommended sentencing decisions, a 2 (Note-taking) X 4 (Justice-Vengeance) analysis of variance was performed on the recommended sentencing decisions. Mock jurors who rendered a "not guilty" verdict decision were not included in the analysis, as they did not recommend a sentence.

Results revealed a main effect for Justice-Vengeance, $F(3, 138)$ = 3.90, p < .05. The main effect of Note-taking and the interaction between Note-taking and Justice-Vengeance were not significant.

Multiple comparisons for the significant effect of Justice-Vengeance indicated that mock jurors low in both justice and vengeance-oriented motives rendered significantly lighter sentences to the defendant (M = 4.94, SD = 1.44), than those participants high in both justice and vengeance-oriented motives (M = 6.15, SD = 1.27), $F(3, 138)$ = 9.60, p < .01, and their counterparts low in justice and high in vengeance motives (M = 5.81, SD = 1.41), $F(3, 138)$ = 7.16, p < .01.

These findings suggest that mock jurors high in vengeance delivered harsher sentences (as would be anticipated), than individuals low in vengeance and low in justice. While not significant, there was a similar trend seen between the high vengeance-high justice cohort and the low vengeance-high justice group (M = 5.48, SD = 1.31), $F(3, 138)$ = 3.35, p < .07. Thus, it appears that the present findings support the contention that participants with higher vengeance motives tend to render longer sentences relative to their low vengeance peers.

Recall Measure

The probative or case-related recall responses were analyzed using a 2 (Note-taking) X 4 (Justice-Vengeance) analysis of variance. The analyses yielded two main effects for Note-taking, $F(1, 141) = 11.55$, $p < .01$, and for Justice-Vengeance, $F(3, 141) = 3.48$, $p < .05$. The interaction between Note-taking and Justice-Vengeance was also significant, $F(3, 141) = 4.02$, $p < .01$. The relationship between Note-taking and Justice-Vengeance is displayed in Table 1.

Main Effects
The main effect of Note-taking indicates that note-takers ($M = 10.09$, $SD = 4.35$) recalled more case-related information about the trial than those not permitted to take notes ($M = 7.21$, $SD = 4.39$).

To further analyze the significant effect of Justice-Vengeance, multiple comparisons were conducted. Mock jurors low in justice and high in vengeance ($M = 6.50$, $SD = 4.32$) recalled significantly fewer trial facts than respectively, those participants high in both justice and vengeance-oriented motives ($M = 10.70$, $SD = 4.84$), $F(3, 141) = 9.38$, $p < .01$, and those who were low in both justice and vengeance ($M = 8.74$, $SD = 4.79$), $F(1,141) = 4.23$, $p < .05$.

A similar trend, approaching significance, was observed between the mock jurors low in justice and high in vengeance who remembered less probative information as opposed to their counterparts high in justice and low in vengeance ($M = 8.89$, $SD = 3.98$), $F(3, 141) = 3.31$, $p < .08$. Overall, these findings suggest that mock jurors who are low in justice and highly vengeance-oriented engaged in peripheral processing as they recalled fewer case facts than any other group.

Two-way Interaction
All of the proceeding results were informed by the relationship between Note-taking and Justice-Vengeance, which suggests the beneficial effects of allowing note-taking particularly when jurors are vengeance prone.

Table 1. Mean Sentencing as a Function of Justice/Vengeance

	n	Mean	SD	Std. E
Yes Notes, J Hi V Hi	9	10.78	4.63	1.54
Yes Notes, J Hi V Low	19	8.90	3.81	.88
Yes Notes, J Low V Hi	16	9.69	4.24	1.06
Yes Notes, J Low V Low	14	11.71	4.86	1.30
No Notes, J Hi V Hi	11	10.64	5.22	1.57
No Notes, J Hi V Low	27	8.89	4.16	.80
No Notes, J Low V Hi	32	4.91	3.43	.61
No Notes, J Low V Low	21	6.72	3.65	.80

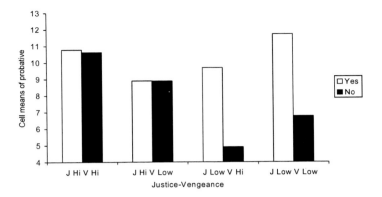

Figure 1. Graphed means of probative recall as a function of the interaction between justice-vengeance and note-taking.

Multiple comparisons indicated that a key finding of this study was that mock jurors who did not take notes and were low in justice but high in vengeance ($M = 4.91$, $SD = 3.43$) recalled significantly less probative trial information than, respectively:

- note-takers high in both justice and vengeance ($M = 10.78$, $SD = 4.63$), $F(1, 141) = 14.45$, $p < .01$;
- note-takers high in justice but low in vengeance ($M = 8.90$, $SD = 3.81$), $F(1,141) = 11.31$, $p < .01$;
- those who took notes and were low in justice but high in vengeance ($M = 9.69$, $SD = 4.24$), $F(1, 141) = 14.55$, $p < . 01$;
- note takers low in both justice and vengeance ($M = 11.71$, $SD = 4.86$), $F(1, 141) = 26.93$, $p < . 01$;
- non note-takers who were high in justice and vengeance ($M = 10.64$, $SD = 5.22$), $F(1, 141) = 16.04$, $p < .01$; and
- non note-takers high in justice but low in vengeance ($M = 8.89$, $SD = 4.16$), $F(1, 141) = 13.86$, $p < .01$.

These findings indicate that mock jurors who were low in justice, but high in vengeance processed the evidence peripherally resulting in poor recall as compared to six of the seven conditions (the exception being non note-takers low in both justice and vengeance). Further, the importance of allowing mock jurors to take notes is clearly evident as individuals within the low justice note-taking conditions recalled significantly more information than their counterparts who did not take notes. Specifically, support for this contention was provided by the multiple comparison showing that mock jurors who took notes and were low in both justice and vengeance ($M = 11.71$, $SD = 4.86$) scored higher on the recall measure than their non note-taking counterparts also low in both justice and vengeance ($M = 6.76$, $SD = 3.65$), $F(1, 141) = 12.29$, $p < .01$.

Taken together, the findings confirm that jurors who take notes or are justice-oriented are central processors, and are therefore more likely to elaborate upon the trial facts in a comprehensive and meaningful fashion. In contrast, those who do not take notes and are vengeance prone appear to be peripheral processors, who are less likely to expansively elaborate on the information presented to them. Additional supporting evidence for this conclusion can be seen with the multiple comparisons between note-takers who were high in justice and vengeance (M =10.78, SD = 4.63) and their non note-taking counterparts low in justice and vengeance (M = 6.76, SD = 3.65), $F(1, 141) = 6.06$, $p < .05$, and non note-takers who were high in justice and vengeance (M =10.64, SD = 5.22) and low on both the justice and vengeance scales (M = 6.76, SD = 3.65), $F(1, 141) = 6.47$, $p < .05$. Certainly, providing jurors with cognitive aids such as note-taking materials appears to significantly improve recall, particularly when mock jurors are vengeance oriented.

DISCUSSION

This study examined the impact of note-taking and justice-vengeance motives on juror decision-making in a murder trial. The empirical questions of this study were generally supported, and the findings have potentially important pragmatic implications for the criminal justice system.

Recommended Sentencing Decision

Contrary to expectations, there was no significant effect of note-taking on the recommended sentencing decisions. This suggests that in this instance taking notes did not result in more appropriate sentencing of the defendant. A significant effect for Justice-Vengeance was revealed, indicating that jurors high in vengeance tended to render harsher punishment relative to those low in vengeance. This finding is consistent with previous research carried out by Ho et al. (2004).

Specifically, the findings of this study indicated that jurors low in both justice and vengeance-oriented motives rendered significantly lighter sentences towards the defendant than those high in both justice and vengeance-oriented motives, and their peers low in justice and high in vengeance motives. Again, these results suggest that mock jurors high in vengeance delivered harsher sentences than individuals low in vengeance and low in justice.

Clearly, where a juror falls along both the justice and vengeance orientations continuum has important implications. That is, individuals who were high in vengeance seemed to process the trial information peripherally as opposed to those who were high in justice. Consequently, they were more likely to judge the defendant based on mitigating factors (e.g., source characteristics) rather than case information. Taken together, these findings confirm the research conducted by Ho et al. (2004). As was demonstrated in this study, in the context of the courtroom verdict decisions whether a juror is justice or vengeance oriented may affect the outcome of the trial.

The interaction between note-taking and Justice-Vengeance was not significant for the recommended sentencing decisions.

Recall Measure

The primary aim of this study was to identify the effects of note-taking and justice-vengeance motives on recall of probative information. As anticipated, note-takers recalled substantially more case-related information than their non note-taking counterparts. This finding confirmed the prediction that note-taking serves as a memory aid and significantly enhanced comprehension and the ability to elaborate upon the trial information. Indeed, note-taking appeared to facilitate central processing whereby jurors actively elaborated on the case facts resulting in better recall.

Conversely, those individuals who did not take notes recalled less information relating to the trial, clearly indicating peripheral processing of the trial information. These findings support previous research indicating that note-taking improves comprehension and recall (e.g., Rosenhan, Eisner, & Robinson, 1994; ForsterLee, Horowitz, & Bourgeois, 1994; ForsterLee & Horowitz, 1997; Horowitz & ForsterLee, 2001).

Another important finding was that justice and vengeance motives impacted on the amount of probative information recalled. Jurors who were low in justice and high in vengeance recalled significantly fewer case-related facts than any other group. It is apparent then that this group did not exert as much cognitive effort and likely processed the trial information peripherally, as reflected in the recall of less trial information. These findings are consistent with the research carried out by Ho et al. (2004).

These results were informed by the significant interaction between note-taking and justice-vengeance motives on the recall of probative information. The principle finding was that jurors who were not permitted to take notes and were low in justice and high in vengeance, recalled fewer trial facts than all individuals high in both justice and vengeance-oriented motives, and all individuals high in justice but low in vengeance, as well as note-taking jurors low in both justice and vengeance. While not significant, there was also a trend between low justice-high vengeance jurors recalling less than those jurors high in justice and low in vengeance.

Collectively, these findings suggest that when jurors high in vengeance are not provided with a cognitive aid they are unable to actively process and elaborate on the trial events, resulting in poor recall of the evidence. In this case, it is likely that the participants engaged in peripheral processing.

Thus, an important finding of this study was the beneficial effect of note-taking in counteracting vengeance motives. That is, when vengeance was high, note-taking proved to be an effective strategy or cognitive aid that eliminated the biasing effects of vengeance and resulted in enhanced recall. These findings suggest that providing jurors with the opportunity to take notes assists them, particularly if they are vengeance-oriented. It also further supports the prediction that note-taking facilitates central processing as a memory aid that can easily be implemented to augment juror decision-making. These findings confirm previous research (e.g., Rosenhan et al., 1994; ForsterLee et al., 1994; ForsterLee & Horowitz, 1997; Horowitz & ForsterLee, 2001).

Limitations and Future Research

In addition to providing a number of significant contributions informing the psychological and legal academic communities, the current study is highlighted by two important strengths. One was the use of a video-tape which simulated reality rather than relying on a trial transcript. In fact, the video-taped trial appeared to provide a more realistic courtroom setting for the mock jurors. Furthermore, participants in this study were instructed to act as though they were in an actual trial, which also made their experience more realistic. The second strength was the sample size, comprising 149 jury eligible participants. This sample was most likely representative of the pool from which future jurors would be drawn.

Nevertheless, there are a number of limitations that should be considered. One limitation of this study was that the jurors did not deliberate as a jury; rather they made their decisions as individual jurors. This is an important aspect of jury decision-making as group dynamics can play an important role in this process. Lloyd-Bostok (1988), for example, contends that as a group, juries have a better chance of accurately recalling the case facts. Future research should therefore investigate the findings of the present study in the context of a jury group rather than as individual jurors.

Another limitation was the presentation of the trial on a television. A television presented trial may not capture the attention of a juror, as would a normal criminal trial played out in court.

Lastly, this study found that note-taking counteracts the vengeance motive for punishment. Future studies could examine the impact of introducing note-taking as a procedural reform into the courtroom in order to facilitate juror comprehension, particularly for vengeance oriented individuals. Prospective research in juror decision-making could also investigate whether other strategies such as providing trial transcripts or summary statements of expert witness testimony are effective as cognitive aids for individuals who are more prone toward vengeance than justice.

CONCLUSION

The jury based justice system is inexorably linked to the notion that the individual juror is capable of approaching the task without bias or prejudice. The present results demonstrate that this may not be completely possible, but there are means to minimize the potential negative impact to verdict decision-making. The key finding of this study is the beneficial effect of note-taking in offsetting vengeance motives. In particular, when vengeance was high, note-taking proved to be an effective memory aid that reduced the biasing effects of vengeance as reflected in better recall of the evidence. Thus, it is apparent that allowing jurors to take notes assists their abilities to process information via the central route, particularly if they are vengeance-oriented. It also further supports the body of research indicating that note-taking provides jurors with a cognitive framework that promotes effective comprehension and the elaboration of the case facts resulting in better verdict decisions.

Lastly, the findings of this study reaffirm the positive outcomes from the provision of note-taking materials in the courtroom. Note-taking is a cost-effective memory aid that could easily be implemented to improve information processing and ameliorate the potentially damaging impact of jurors who are vengeance-oriented.

REFERENCES

Douglas, K. M., & ForsterLee, L. (2003). Pre-trial publicity in Australian print media: Eliciting bias effects on juror decision making. *Australian Studies in Journalism, 12,* 104-128.

Einstein, G. O., Morris, J., & Smith, S. (1985). Note-taking, individual differences, and memory for lecture information. *Journal of Educational Psychology, 77*(5), 522-532.

Fisher, J. L., & Harris, M. B. (1973). Effect of note taking and review on recall. *Journal of Educational Psychology, 65*(3), 321-325.

Flango, V. E. (1980). Would jurors do a better job if they could take notes? *Judicature, 63*(9), 436-443.

ForsterLee, L., Horowitz, I. A., & Bourgeois, M. (1994). Effects of note-taking on verdicts and evidence processing in a civil trial. *Law and Human Behavior, 18,* 567-578.

ForsterLee, L. & Horowitz, I. A. (2003). The impact of procedural strategies on information processing in civil litigation. *Judicature, 86*(4), 184-190.

ForsterLee, L., & Horowitz, I. A. (1997). Enhancing juror competence in a complex trial. *Applied Cognitive Psychology, 11*(4), 305-319.

ForsterLee, L., Fox, G. B., ForsterLee, R., & Ho, R. (2004). The effects of a victim impact statement and gender on juror information processing in a criminal trial: Does the punishment fit the crime? *Australian Psychologist, 39,* 57-67.

ForsterLee, L., Horowitz, I. A., Athaide-Victor, E., & Brown, N. (2000). The bottom line: The effect of written expert witness statements on juror verdicts and information processing. *Law and Human Behavior, 24,* 259-270.

ForsterLee, L., Horowitz, I. A., ForsterLee, R., King, K., & Ronlund, L. (1999). Death penalty attitudes and juror decisions in Australia. *Australian Psychologist, 34*(1), 64-69.

Heuer, L., & Penrod, S. D. (1988). Increasing jurors' participation in trials: A field experiment with jury notetaking and question asking. *Law and Human Behavior, 12,* 231-262.

Heuer, L., & Penrod, S. D. (1994). Juror notetaking and question asking during trials: A national field experiment. *Law and Human Behavior, 18*(2), 121-150.

Ho, R., ForsterLee, L., & ForsterLee, R. (2004). The impact of justice and vengeance motives on sentencing decisions. In S. P. Shohov (Ed.), *Advances in Psychology Research*, (Vol 28.). Hauppauge, NY: Nova Science Publishers, Inc.

Ho, R., Forsterlee, L., Forsterlee, R., & Crofts, N. (2002). Justice versus vengeance: Motives underlying punitive judgements. *Personality and individual differences*, *33*(3), 365-377.

Horowitz, I. A., & ForsterLee, L. (2001). The effects of note-taking and trial transcript access on mock jury decisions in a complex civil trial. *Law and Human Behavior, 25,* 373-391.

Jury Act. (1995). Reprint No. 2E. [Electronic version]. Queensland: Office of the Queensland Parliamentary Counsel.

Kierwa, K. A. (1985). Students' note-taking behaviors and the efficacy of providing the instructor's notes for review. *Contemporary Educational Psychology, 10,* 378-386.

Lempert, R. (1993). Civil juries and complex cases: Taking stock after twelve years. In R. Litan (Ed.), *Verdict: Assessing the civil jury system*. St Paul, MN: West.

Lloyd-Bostok, S. (1988). *Law in practice*. London: The British Psychological Society.

Peper, R. J., & Mayer, R. E. (1978). Note-taking as a generative activity. *Journal of Educational Psychology, 70*(4), 514-522.

Petty, R. E., & Cacioppo, J. T. (1984). The effects of involvement on responses to argument quantity and quality: Central and peripheral routes to persuasion. *Journal of Personality and Social Psychology, 46*(1), 69-81.

Petty, R. E., Cacioppo, J. T., & Schumann, D. (1983). Central and peripheral routes to advertising effectiveness: The moderating role of involvement. *Journal of Consumer Research, 10,* 135-146.

Rosenhan, D. L., Eisner, S. L., & Robinson, R. J. (1994). Note-taking can aid juror recall. *Law and Human Behavior, 18*(1), 53-61.

In: Psychology of Decision Making…
Editor: G. R. Burthold, pp. 203-218

ISBN: 978-1-60021-932-0
© 2007 Nova Science Publishers, Inc.

Chapter 9

DEVELOPMENT AND APPLICATION OF FEEDBACK-SYSTEMS TO SUPPORT CLINICAL DECISION MAKING IN OUTPATIENT PSYCHOTHERAPY

Wolfgang Lutz[1,] and Niklaus Stulz[1,2,†]*
[1]Department of Psychology, University of Trier, Germany
[2]Department of Psychology, University of Berne, Switzerland

ABSTRACT

The implementation of feedback systems into routine clinical practice has been recognized as a promising way to enhance treatment outcomes in outpatient psychotherapy. These feedback systems rely on the monitoring of individual treatment progress during the course of psychotherapy and the feedback of this information to therapists in a timely manner. If necessary, therapists can then use this information for adaptive treatment planning. However, since the problems of the clients seeking psychotherapy are manifold and, hence, not all clients have the same prospect for treatment success (at least not within the same amount of time), such feedback systems should also take into account an estimation of how much change or improvement can be expected for a given client until a given point of time in therapy based on his or her individual characteristics. By contrasting the actual treatment progress of an individual client and his or her expected treatment response, the actual client state is set into perspective. The approaches to predict individual treatment courses on the basis of client intake characteristics and previous treatment progress can be classified into two broad classes: *Rationally-derived decision rules* are based on judgments of experts, who determine the amount of progress that a client has to achieve until a given treatment session to be considered 'on track'. *Empirically-derived decision rules,* on the other hand, are based on statistically-derived expected recovery curves. In this chapter, examples of such decision support systems are presented and their potential to identify clients at risk

---
[*] Phone: +49 (0)651 201 28 84; Fax : +49 (0)651 201 28 86; E-mail: wolfgang.lutz@uni-trier.de
[†] Phone: +41 (0)31 631 53 64; Fax: +41 (0)31 631 82 12; E-mail: niklaus.stulz@psy.unibe.ch

for treatment failure during ongoing treatment courses is demonstrated. Furthermore, the potential of providing feedback to therapists based on these decision rules with respect to the enhancement of treatment outcomes is discussed.

1. INTRODUCTION

While the majority of clients who undergo psychotherapy have a positive treatment outcome, there is also a significant minority of clients who fail to clearly improve or even deteriorate while enrolled in therapy (estimations for deterioration range between 5 and 10%, Hansen, Lambert, & Forman, 2002; Lambert & Ogles, 2004). In combination with the questionable predictive validity of therapists' prognostic ratings (Breslin, Sobell, Sobell, Buchan, & Cunningham, 1997; Meyer & Schulte, 2002), these findings have led to the development of quality management efforts aimed at improving the outcomes of psychological services. The implementation of feedback systems into routine clinical care has been recognized as a promising way to support clinical decision making in outpatient psychotherapy and, hence, to enhance the likelihood of positive treatment outcomes (Lambert et al., 2003; Lutz, Lambert et al., 2006). These feedback systems are typically based on the monitoring of individual treatment progress by means of repeated assessments of clients' state during the course of psychotherapy and the feedback of this information to therapists and other mental health providers in a timely manner (e.g., Howard, Moras, Brill, Martinovich, & Lutz, 1996; Lambert, 2007; Lutz, 2002). The therapists can then use this information for early identification of clients at risk for treatment failure (i.e., clients who are likely to fail) and, if necessary, to initiate adaptive treatment planning during the ongoing treatment course.

However, the problems of the clients seeking psychotherapy are manifold (different psychological problems, symptoms and disorders, different social and vocational situations and circumstances etc.). Therefore, not all clients have the same prospect of treatment success, at least not within the same amount of time. As a result, feedback systems to support clinical decision making should not only consider the actual treatment progress of a client but also take into account an estimation of the amount of change or improvement that can be expected for that given client until a given point of time in therapy based on his or her individual characteristics. By contrasting the actual treatment progress of a client and his or her expected treatment response the actual state of the client is set into perspective. This information can then be used to develop decision support systems for outcome management and to generate feedback to therapists in routine clinical settings.

In this chapter, we will illustrate the development of different types of feedback systems based on comparisons between the actual and the expected treatment progress, and we will demonstrate their potential to identify clients at risk for treatment failure (as well as clients who are likely to have positive treatment outcomes) during the ongoing treatment course. In a subsequent section, we will then also discuss the potential of providing feedback to therapists based on these decision rules with respect to enhancement of positive treatment outcomes and reduction of treatment failures.

2. DEVELOPMENT AND VALIDATION OF FEEDBACK-SYSTEMS TO SUPPORT CLINICAL DECISION MAKING

As aforementioned, sound clinical decision support and feedback systems should account for individual client characteristics and circumstances and, therefore, rely on comparisons between the actual treatment progress and the treatment response that can be expected for a given client based on his or her individual characteristics and circumstances. To enable such comparisons, different approaches to generate predictions of individual treatment progress on the basis of client intake characteristics and previous treatment progress have been developed during the last decade. These approaches to generate client-specific predictions and the decision rules basing on these predictions can be classified into two broad classes:

– *Rationally-derived decision rules* are based on judgments of experts, who determine the amount of progress that a client has to achieve until a given treatment session to be considered 'on track'.
– *Empirically-derived decision rules,* on the other hand, are based on statistically-derived expected recovery curves (so-called expected treatment response profiles).

In the subsequent sections, some examples of such rationally-derived and empirically-derived decision support systems will be presented.

2.1. Rationally-derived Feedback-systems to Support Clinical Decision Making

A group of experts in clinical psychology and psychotherapy developed a rationally-derived decision support system to provide therapists with feedback on their clients' treatment progress and to assist them in evaluating this previous treatment progress (Lambert, Whipple, Bishop et al., 2002; Lambert, Whipple et al., 2001; Lutz, Lambert et al., 2006). Based on information about early response to treatment, the assumption of a negative accelerated dose-response relationship in psychotherapy (Howard, Kopta, Krause, & Orlinsky, 1986) and the concept of reliable and clinical significant change (cf. Jacobson, Roberts, Berns, & McGlinchey, 1999; Jacobson & Truax, 1991), these experts created a set of decision matrices for different treatment phases (e.g., for sessions 2 to 4). These matrices enable the clinicians to classify every client into one of four feedback categories on the basis of the initial score on the 45-item Outcome Questionnaire (OQ-45, Lambert et al., 2004) and on change on this instrument at the session of interest. The OQ-45 is a widely used self-report questionnaire to evaluate psychotherapy (Lambert, 2007). In a subsequent study Lutz, Lambert et al. (2006) furthermore adapted the decision matrices for a 30-item short form of the OQ-45, the Outcome Questionnaire-30 (OQ-30; Lambert, Hatfield, Vermeersch, & Burlingame, 2001), which might be better suited to assess data on a session-by-session basis since its completion takes less than five minutes. The vertical axis of the decision matrices is used to plot the OQ-45 or the OQ-30 score at the beginning of treatment and the horizontal axis represents the OQ-45 or OQ-30 change score at the session of interest. The areas of the matrices are color coded and they represent different feedback categories resulting in different recommendations to therapists. White feedback is given if the client is within the range of normal functioning and it includes the recommendation to consider termination of therapy. The higher the initial impairment of a client is, the more he or she has to improve on the OQ-45 or on the OQ-30 to reach the white area of the matrices, that is, the range of normal functioning. Green feedback signifies that the client is making satisfactory treatment progress, whereas yellow feedback indicates that the client's progress may be insufficient. Red feedback signifies even more serious concern and the therapist is invited to seriously reconsider the ongoing treatment regimen.

These rationally-derived decision rules were shown to be effective in identifying clients at risk for treatment failure as well as clients with positive treatment outcomes. For example, using the OQ-45 and the corresponding decision matrices in an sample of $N = 492$ outpatients of an university counseling center in the United States, overall 79% of the clients were correctly identified as having positive or negative treatment outcome, respectively (Lambert, Whipple, Bishop et al., 2002).

2.2. Empirically-derived Feedback-systems to Support Clinical Decision Making

Empirically-derived decision support systems are based on expected treatment response curves (ETR curves) as shown in Figure 1 to which the actual treatment progress of the client under consideration can be compared in order to evaluate treatment progress during ongoing treatment courses. Before Figure 1 will be explained in detail, firstly, we will demonstrate how ETR curves can be generated for individual clients on the basis of their individual characteristics.

Generating ETR Curves: Growth Modeling Procedures

During the last decade, new statistical methods have become available, which allow to model and predict individual change during treatment using a latent growth curve analysis framework (e.g., Bryk & Raudenbush, 1992; Raudenbush, 2001; Singer & Willett, 2003). These growth modeling procedures (which are referred to by different names in literature: hierarchical linear models, random coefficient regression models, mixed models or multi-level models) assume an underlying trajectory of change over time, and they are able to deal with the nested structure of longitudinal psychotherapy data (repeated assessments of treatment progress are nested within each client and clients are nested within therapists). In a first step of analysis (level 1 model), a repeatedly observed outcome variable (e.g., treatment progress on a outcome indicator) is related to time or a time-related variable (e.g., the number of treatment sessions). Individual variation in growth is captured by the fact that growth factors (e.g., intercepts and slopes in a linear model) are random coefficients and can, therefore, vary across individuals resulting in an individual model of change for every client. In a second step of analysis (level 2 model), the interindividual variation in these growth parameters is set into relation to potential predictors of change by treating the growth parameters as dependent variables on a second level of regression. Following this, the level-two regression model allows to evaluate the impact of client intake characteristic on development over time. For incoming clients this information can then be used to generate expected treatment response profiles on the basis of their intake characteristics. These hierarchical regression models include a series of advantages over traditional analytic techniques for longitudinal data: Whereas the latter (like, for example, repeated measures ANOVA or ANCOVA) require a fixed assessment schedule for each client and cases with missing values have to be excluded or treated with an imputation strategy, which might artificially reduce the error variance, hierarchical linear models allow to deal with missing values and with different between-assessment intervals. These characteristics make them specifically appropriate to analyze practice-based data.

Trough the application of hierarchical linear models to a large-scale dataset (N = 890 psychotherapy outpatients) deriving from a national provider network of a managed care company in the United States, Lutz, Martinovich and Howard (1999) identified a set of client intake characteristics (well-being, symptom distress and life functioning, treatment expectations, amount of prior psychotherapy, chronicity of problems and therapists' global assessment of functioning ratings) which allow to predict individual differences in treatment progress on a global outcome indicator (the Mental Health Index [MHI], Sperry, Brill, Howard, & Grissom, 1996). Following the dose-effect model in psychotherapy (Howard et al., 1986), which proposes a negative accelerated relationship between the amount of treatment (the number of treatment sessions) and treatment progress on global outcome indicators, these predictors were then used to forecast individual change as a log-linear function of the session number for new incoming clients. Figure 1 shows the expected treatment response profile and the actual treatment progress for a virtual client. As can be seen there, in session 10 the actual treatment progress of the client is much worse than expected according to his or her intake characteristics and it falls below a pre-defined failure boundary (that is, outside of a defined confidence interval around the predicted treatment course).

In their study, Lutz et al. (1999) demonstrated that the higher the number of observed values falling below this failure boundary is, the higher is the probability of treatment failure – a finding replicated in subsequent studies (e.g., Finch, Lambert, & Schaalje, 2001; Lambert, Whipple, Bishop et al., 2002; Lueger et al., 2001). Following this, comparisons between the actual treatment progress and the ETR curve can be used to inform clinical decision making during ongoing treatments. For the client shown in Figure 1, for example, the deviation from the expected treatment response profile in session 10 might result in the following feedback to the therapist: "The client is not progressing as expected. Therapy might not be successful. Please reconsider your treatment regimen." Based on this feedback, the therapist can reevaluate his or her treatment strategy for this client and this might help to reestablish treatment progress as expected and, hence, to enhance chances for a positive final treatment outcome. Moreover, given that the empirically-derived decision support systems provide accurate predictions of the treatment courses and that the necessary information is available in the dataset of a clinic, one might also use the ETR curve (the expected client improvement on the outcome measurement over time) to determine for an incoming client which treatment modality (e.g., medication, psychotherapy or a combination of psychotherapy and medication) or which treatment setting (e.g., individual or group) is most likely to result in positive change (Lutz, 2003; Lutz, Grawe, & Tholen, 2003). And finally, ETR curves may also be used to estimate how many sessions are expected to be enough to reach a desired level of improvement on a outcome indicator.

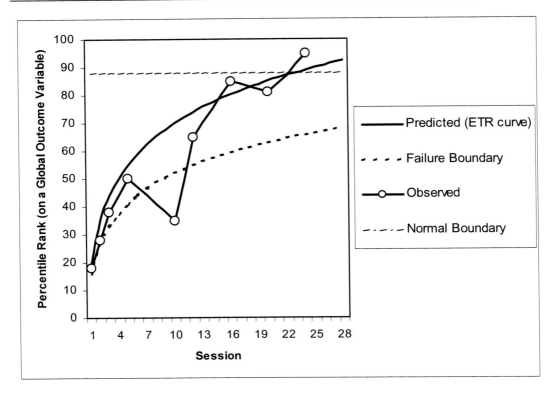

Figure 1. Observed and predicted (i.e., expected) treatment course of a virtual patient. In session 10 the client falls bellow the failure boundary around the predicted treatment course resulting in a warning signal for the therapist that the therapy might not be successful.

As was shown in subsequent studies, the ETR method to generate treatment response profiles for individual clients can be validly applied to different measures of client progress (Lutz, Lowry, Kopta, Einstein, & Howard, 2001), to different diagnostic groups (Lueger, Lutz, & Howard, 2000) and the predictive accuracy of the method can be further enhanced by also taking into account information on previous client change (Lutz, Rafaeli, Howard, & Martinovich, 2002). Compared to the rational method described above, the ETR technique was essentially equivalent in predicting final client treatment outcome, though it was marginally more accurate with respect to the prediction of client treatment failure. On the other hand, the rational method developed trough the consensual opinions of expert judges turned out to be faster in identifying clients at risk for treatment failure, that is, clients likely to have poor outcomes were identified earlier in treatment by the rational method (for details see Lambert, Whipple, Bishop et al., 2002).

Using the ETR curve methodology described so far implies that the predictors identified in a large sample of clients are predictive for the treatment courses of *all* individuals. That is, one implicitly assumes that a client intake characteristic has the same effect on treatment progress in all clients. However, there might also be client intake characteristics that are not that global, that is, predictors which are predictive for the individual treatment progress only in specific subsets of clients (Krause, Howard, & Lutz, 1998). Following this, the validity of the use of growth curve prediction weights for any particular client depends on the extent to which the study sample is representative of the population of which that client is a member.

Nearest Neighbor Techniques

To address this problem, Lutz et al. (2005) used an extended growth curve methodology that employs nearest neighbor (NN) techniques to predict individual treatment courses (see also Lutz, Lambert et al., 2006; Lutz, Saunders et al., 2006). The NN approach is derived from alpine avalanche occurrence research (e.g., Brabec & Meister, 2001), where large databases with many potentially relevant parameters (e.g., temperature, barometric pressure, depth of snow, recent rainfall) recorded on a daily basis are used to make predictions of alpine avalanche risk for a given day. By choosing the most similar days based on these climatic parameters and using the relative frequency of avalanches among those nearest neighbors as a prediction, the probability of alpine avalanche occurrence for a given day is estimated.

This NN methodology was adapted by Lutz et al. (2005) to predict treatment courses in psychotherapy. In a sample of $N = 203$ psychotherapy clients seen in routine practice settings in the United Kingdom, those previously treated clients who most closely match the target client on the following intake variables were chosen: age, gender, severity of depression (measured by the Beck Depression Inventory [BDI], Beck, Ward, Mendelson, Mock, & Erbaugh, 1961), severity of anxiety (measured by the Beck Anxiety Inventory [BAI], Beck, Epstein, Brown, & Steer, 1988), severity of interpersonal problems (measured by the 32 item-version of the Inventory of Interpersonal Problems [IIP-32], Barkham, Hardy, & Startup, 1996), and overall symptom severity (measured by the Clinical Outcome in Routine Evaluation - Outcome Measure [CORE-OM], Barkham, Gilbert, Connell, Marshall, & Twigg, 2005). Closeness among cases was defined in terms of Euclidean distances between the values in these six variables. In a subsequent step of analysis, the slopes of the growth models of the most similar already treated clients were then aggregated and the resulting mean slope served as prediction of treatment progress for the target client.

In the British sample mentioned above, this NN approach was shown to generate more accurate predictions of individual treatment courses than the ETR model using the same six demographic and psychometric pretreatment measures as predictors (Lutz et al., 2005). Depending on the number of nearest neighbors selected (10, 20 or 50) and on the growth model used (linear or log-linear), the correlations between the observed slopes and the slopes predicted with the NN method ranged between $r = .70$ and $r = .72$ and were, therefore, clearly higher than the correlations between the observed slopes and the slopes predicted by the ETR model (all r's = .34). Following this, the strategy of basing predictions on small subsamples of cases with similar pretreatment characteristics seems to be superior to the strategy of basing predictions on optimally weighted combinations of pretreatment characteristics. In a subsequent study using a sample of $N = 4365$ outpatients in the United States, the NN technique also outperformed the rational method with respect to the prediction of final treatment outcomes (Lutz, Lambert et al., 2006). For example, as can be seen in Table 1, using a 75% confidence interval (failure boundary) around the ETR curve, the NN method was superior to the rational method in all measures of prediction accuracy (positive and negative predictive value, sensitivity and specificity, correct identified cases).

Table 1. Indicators of the accuracy of predictions of the final treatment outcome based on the rational method and on the NN method with different confidence intervals representing different failure boundaries

		Empirical (NN method)						
	rational	67 % CI	75% CI	84% CI	90% CI	95% CI	97.5% CI	99.5% CI
Positive predictive value	60.4	63.2***	65.8***	69.9***	73.1***	75.7***	77.5***	78.8***
Negative predictive value	63.1	75.4***	70.3***	65.1***	61.8***	58.3***	56.1***	53.9***
Sensitivity	57.4	79.0***	68.4***	53.1***	41.1***	27.5***	17.8***	7.3***
Specificity	65.9	58.3***	67.8*	79.3***	86.3***	92.0***	95.3***	98.2***
Correct identified	61.9	68.2***	68.1***	66.8***	64.8***	61.4	58.5***	55.0***

* p ≤ .05 (two-tailed significance).
*** p ≤ .001 (two-tailed significance).
CI = confidence interval.
Differences between different empirical decision rules an the rational decision rule were compared using McNemar's Chi^2-Test.

According to these findings, the NN technique can be seen as a viable alternative to predict individual treatment progress and to identify client at risk for treatment failure. By using a homogeneous subgroup of similar already treated clients to generate predictions of treatment progress for a target client, the NN technique mirrors the way clinicians often talk about how they use their clinical experience: confronted with a new client, they are looking for some similar already treated cases and use the experiences they had with these past cases to develop an optimal treatment regimen for the incoming client. However, bearing in mind that decisions based on clinical experience are typically less accurate than statistical predictions and, in the case of predicting eventual treatment failure, woefully underpredict such outcomes (Hannan et al., 2005), the NN technique (as well as the other prediction methods presented in this chapter) may provide valuable support to enhance treatment outcomes. At present, the necessary extensive computational efforts as well as the lack of a easy-to-handle software do not make the NN technique feasible for implementation into routine clinical practice. But this may be overcome by the creation of appropriate software packages.

3. IMPLEMENTATION OF FEEDBACK-SYSTEMS TO SUPPORT CLINICAL DECISION MAKING INTO ROUTINE CARE AND THEIR INFLUENCE ON TREATMENT OUTCOME

The rationally-derived method as well as the empirically-derived methods presented so far both indicated their potential to predict individual treatment courses and to identify clients at risk for treatment failure early during the ongoing treatment courses through the comparison of the actual and the expected treatment response. However, the correct identification of clients at risk for treatment failure (and of clients likely to have positive outcomes) does not necessarily imply that feedback of this information to therapists enhances treatment outcomes. To address this issue, a series of three studies (Lambert, Whipple et al., 2001; Lambert, Whipple, Vermeersch et al., 2002; Whipple et al., 2003) evaluated the effects of providing therapists with feedback on client progress based on the rational method to identify clients at risk for treatment failure (for an overview, see Lambert et al., 2003). The findings of these three studies taking into account a total of $N = 2610$ outpatients of an university counseling center in the United States are summarized in Table 2. As can be seen there, providing therapists with feedback on their clients' progress resulted in an increased number of improved clients (39% vs. 38%) and a reduced proportion of negative treatment outcomes (5% vs. 8%). While these differences in the complete sample are not overwhelming, among those clients at risk for treatment failure, that is, among those clients for whom an alert signal to the therapist was generated, the effects of providing therapists with feedback were clearly more accentuated. Here, the percentage of improved clients increased from 21% to 35% and the percentage of deteriorated clients decreased from 21% to 13% when providing therapists with feedback (see Table 2). Since, moreover, feedback indicative of possible treatment failure resulted in extended treatment durations in all three studies, it appears that therapist behavior is changed due to feedback at a minimum in terms of keeping clients with warning signals in treatment longer. On the other hand, among those clients predicted to have a positive treatment outcome the number of sessions was reduced without diminishing positive treatment outcomes.

Table 2. Classification of treatment outcomes depending on whether therapists were provided feedback or not and depending on whether an alert signal (a negative feedback) was generated (or would have been generated in the no feedback condition) during the course of treatment or not (Lambert et al., 2003)

Experimental condition	Type of feedback	Outcome classification[1]					
		Improved		No change		Deteriorated	
		n	%	n	%	n	%
Feedback	Alert signal	104	35%	154	52%	40	13%
	No alert signal	419	40%	588	57%	29	3%
	Total	523	39%	742	56%	69	5%
No feedback	Alert signal	60	21%	165	58%	61	21%
	No alert signal	426	43%	524	53%	40	4%
	Total	486	38%	689	54%	101	8%

[1] Classification of outcomes according to the concept of reliable change (Jacobson et al., 1999; Jacobson & Truax, 1991).

Whipple et al. (2003) further extended and refined the rationally-derived decision support system. Whenever the rational decision rule identified a client to be 'not on track' (yellow or red feedback), the responsible therapist had the option of using a clinical support tool. This clinical support tool included a decision tree, a series of psychometric instruments to asses therapeutic relationship, motivation to change and social support network, and handouts with lists of possible interventions for problems in these three areas (for details, see Whipple et al.,

2003). The application of this clinical support tool in addition to the feedback system resulted in better treatment outcomes when compared to only providing therapists with feedback on clients' progress.

4. CONCLUSION

This chapter aimed at presenting the development and application of feedback-systems to support clinical decision making in outpatient psychotherapy. In a series of studies, the implementation of a rationally-derived feedback system – that is, of a feedback system basing on experts' judgments of sufficient progress – into routine clinical care was shown to be a promising way to support clinical decision making in outpatient psychotherapy and to enhance the likelihood of positive treatment outcomes. Moreover, by extending the therapies among those clients predicted to fail (resulting in better outcomes) and shortening treatment durations among clients with good predictions (without diminishing treatment outcomes), providing therapists with feedback on their clients' progress can not only enhance treatment outcomes but also foster a better allocation of resources, which may have economic implications for insurance companies, clients and providers (Lambert, Whipple et al., 2001).

As compared to the rationally-derived method, empirically-derived ETR curves turned out to be essentially equivalent with respect to the prediction of final treatment outcomes, though they were shown to be marginally more accurate in predicting client treatment failure. The NN technique as another instance of an empirically-derived model was shown to provide even more accurate predictions of individual treatment progress than ETR curves and it turned out to be most accurate in predicting final treatment outcomes and, hence, in identifying clients whose positive response to treatment is in doubt. However, the effects of feedback to therapists basing on these empirically-derived methods have still to be evaluated in routine clinical care. Therefore, at least until the availability of an easy-to-handle software to generate ETR curves and to calculate the nearest neighbors in large datasets, the decision matrices of the rational system seem to be the best method for clinical practice.

Although the results presented so far indicate that providing therapists with feedback on their clients' progress on a routine basis is a viable way to enhance treatment outcomes, of course, one need not to choose between providing therapists with feedback and the use of empirically supported treatments (i.e., treatments that turned out to be effective in randomized controlled clinical trials and/or naturalistic studies comparing different interventions and control groups). In effect, the 'traditional' efficacy and effectiveness research and the research on decision support and feedback systems presented here are not mutually exclusive but represent complementary approaches to enhance the quality of psychological services.

However, it should also be noted that, despite their strengths, the feedback systems discussed here also have some limitations and difficulties. Firstly, the research presented in this chapter is limited to self-report measures of improvement and treatment progress is treated in terms of one single global measure of client state (usually the total score of a self-report questionnaire) which includes different aspects of therapeutic progress (e.g., symptom remission, enhancement of life-functioning, etc.). While this is a field-tested way to track client progress during treatment and to report this information in an easy to handle way to therapists, further developments might also consider other views of the impact of therapy on clients (e.g., therapist ratings). Furthermore, therapeutic progress might also be modeled as a multidimensional phenomenon including change in different areas in order to better account for the differential nature of change during therapy (Barkham, Stiles, & Shapiro, 1993; Kopta, Howard, Lowry, & Beutler, 1994; Lutz et al., 2001; Stulz & Lutz, 2007).

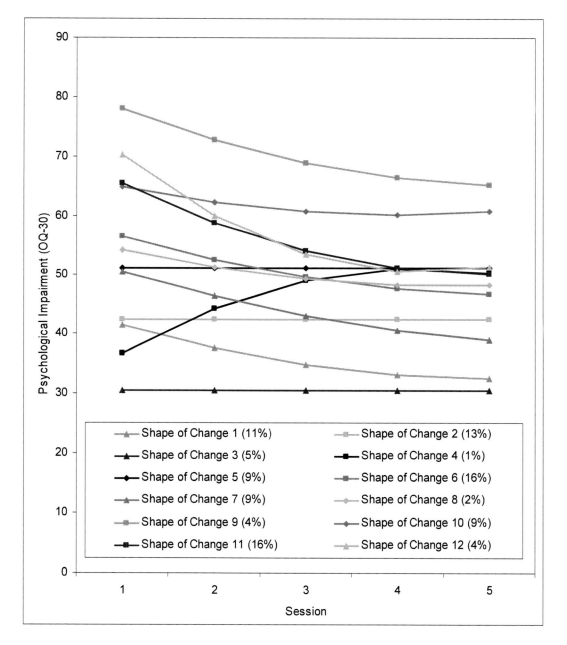

Figure 2. Typical shapes of early change on a global outcome indicator (OQ-30) during the first five treatment sessions in a sample of psychotherapy outpatients (N = 2206) in the United States and the proportion of clients following these shapes of early change.

Moreover, while the empirically-derived decision support systems presented in this chapter take into account that not for every client the same treatment progress can be expected and thus use individually varying ETR curves as a benchmark to inform clinical decision making during ongoing treatment courses, these decision support systems are still built on the assumption of one specific shape of change (e.g., log-linear) for all clients in the sample (and then aim at predicting individual deviation from this overall mean growth curve). To overcome this assumption of one general trend for all clients and to allow for a more intensive disaggregation of longitudinal client data, recent research started attempts to identify subpopulations of clients with distinct but typical shapes of change over the course of treatment (Lutz, Stulz, Smart, & Lambert, 2007; Stulz, Lutz, Leach, Lucock, & Barkham, submitted). Figure 2, for example, shows the typical shapes of early change that were identified in a sample of $N = 2206$ psychotherapy outpatients in the United States (Lutz et al., 2007). The identification of these shapes of change was accomplished using Growth Mixture Models (Muthén, 2001, 2004; Muthén & Muthén, 2000).

However, this research on shapes of change in psychotherapy is still at the beginning and further efforts will be necessary to implement their findings into clinical decision support systems. For example, it still has to be examined whether these shapes of early change or decision rules relying there upon allow for better predictions of final treatment outcomes than the existing decision support systems presented above.

There are some further limitations and difficulties concerning the practical applicability of feedback systems. For instance, the feedback systems depend on frequent assessments of clients' state. Although the instruments are usually short, their completion requires an additional effort of the clients and the therapists. On the other hand, both the therapist and the client can benefit from such assessments: the therapist gains additional and objective information on the progress of his or her client and may be provided with recommendations for therapeutic action. The client, in turn, may benefit of a more adequate psychological intervention and thus a better treatment outcome in consequence of this feedback to the therapist. Despite this potential deriving from frequent assessments over the course of treatment, therapists' confidence in their own clinical judgments may hinder the implementation of monitoring and feedback systems into routine clinical care – although therapists' predictions of final treatment outcomes were shown to be questionable (Breslin et al., 1997; Meyer & Schulte, 2002). If this hindrance would be overcome, with the incorporation of technologically advanced information systems into routine care and a growing interest in empirical outcomes assessment, large databases documenting response to psychotherapy across time would become available. This would allow researchers to improve the prediction models and the feedback systems to assist clinical decision making. Clinicians would gain from such systems in terms of the possibility of integrating research information into everyday clinical practice and, as already mentioned, clients may benefit in terms of better treatments.

REFERENCES

Barkham, M., Gilbert, N., Connell, J., Marshall, C., & Twigg, E. (2005). Suitability and utility of the CORE-OM and CORE-A for assessing severity of presenting problems in psychological therapy services based in primary and secondary care settings. *British Journal of Psychiatry, 186,* 239-246.

Barkham, M., Hardy, G. E., & Startup, M. (1996). The development of the IIP-32: A short version of the Inventory of Interpersonal Problems. *British Journal of Clinical Psychology, 35,* 21-35.

Barkham, M., Stiles, W. B., & Shapiro, D. A. (1993). The shape of change in psychotherapy: Longitudinal assessment of personal problems. *Journal of Consulting and Clinical Psychology, 61,* 667-677.

Beck, A. T., Epstein, N., Brown, G., & Steer, R. A. (1988). An inventory for measuring clinical anxiety: Psychometric properties. *Journal of Consulting and Clinical Psychology, 56,* 893-897.

Beck, A. T., Ward, C. H., Mendelson, M., Mock, J., & Erbaugh, J. (1961). An inventory for measuring depression. *Archives of General Psychology, 4,* 53-63.

Brabec, B., & Meister, R. (2001). A nearest-neighbor model for regional avalanche forecasting. *Annals of Glaciology, 32,* 130-134.

Breslin, F. C., Sobell, M. B., Sobell, L. C., Buchan, G., & Cunningham, J. A. (1997). Towards a stepped care approach to treating problem drinkers: The predictive utility of within-treatment variables and therapist prognostic ratings. *Addiction, 92*(11), 1479-1489.

Bryk, A. S., & Raudenbush, S. W. (1992). *Hierarchical linear models: Applications and data analysis methods.* Newbury Park: Sage Publications.

Finch, A. E., Lambert, M. J., & Schaalje, B. G. (2001). Psychotherapy quality control: The statistical generation of expected recovery curves for integration into an early warning system. *Clinical Psychology and Psychotherapy, 8,* 231-242.

Hannan, C., Lambert, M. J., Harmon, C., Nielsen, S. L., Smart, D. W., Shimokawa, K., & Sutton, S. W. (2005). A lab test and a algorithmus for identifying patients at risk for treatment failure. *Journal of Clinical Psychology, 61*(2), 155-163.

Hansen, N. B., Lambert, M. J., & Forman, E. M. (2002). The psychotherapy dose-response effect and it's implication for treatment delivery systems. *Clinical Psychology: Science and Practice, 9,* 329-343.

Howard, K. I., Kopta, M., Krause, M. S., & Orlinsky, D. E. (1986). The dose-effect relationship in psychotherapy. *American Psychologist, 41,* 159-164.

Howard, K. I., Moras, K., Brill, P., Martinovich, Z., & Lutz, W. (1996). The evaluation of psychotherapy. *American Psychologist, 52,* 1059-1064.

Jacobson, N. S., Roberts, L. J., Berns, S. B., & McGlinchey, J. B. (1999). Methods for defining and determining the clinical significants of treatment effects: Description, applications, and alternitives. *Journal of Consulting and Clinical Psychology, 67*(3), 300-307.

Jacobson, N. S., & Truax, P. (1991). Clinical significance: A statistical approach to defining meaningful change in psychotherapy research. *Journal of Consulting and Clinical Psychology, 59*(1), 12-19.

Kopta, S. M., Howard, K. I., Lowry, J. L., & Beutler, L. E. (1994). Patterns of symptomatic recovery in psychotherapy. *Journal of Consulting and Clinical Psychology, 62*, 1009-1016.

Krause, M. S., Howard, K. I., & Lutz, W. (1998). Exploring individual change. *Journal of Consulting and Clinical Psychology, 66*(5), 838-845.

Lambert, M. J. (2007). Presidential address: What we have learned from a decade of research aimed at improving psychotherapy outcome in routine care. *Psychotherapy Research, 17*(1), 1-14.

Lambert, M. J., Hatfield, D. R., Vermeersch, D. A., & Burlingame, G. M. (2001). *Administration and scoring manual for the Life Status Questionnaire (LSQ) [Draft Version]*. Orem, UT: American Professional Credentialing Services L.L.C.

Lambert, M. J., Morton, J. J., Hatfield, D., Harmon, C., Hamilton, S., Reid, R. C., Shimokawa, K., Christopherson, C., & Burlingame, G. M. (2004). *Administration and scoring manual for the OQ-45.2 (Outcome Questionnaire)*. Orem, UT: American Professional Credentialing Services L.L.C.

Lambert, M. J., & Ogles, B. M. (2004). The efficacy and effectiveness of psychotherapy. In M. J. Lambert (Ed.), *Bergin and Garfield's handbook of psychotherapy and behavior change* (5 ed., pp. 139-193). New York, NY: Wiley.

Lambert, M. J., Whipple, J. L., Bishop, M. J., Vermeersch, D. A., Gray, G. V., & Finch, A. E. (2002). Comparison of empirically-derived and rationally-derived methods for identifying patients at risk for treatment failure. *Clinical Psychology and Psychotherapy, 9*, 149-164.

Lambert, M. J., Whipple, J. L., Hawkins, E. J., Vermeersch, D. A., Nielsen, S. L., & Smart, D. W. (2003). Is it time for clinicians to routinely track patient outcome? A meta-analysis. *Clinical Psychology: Science and Practice, 10*, 288-301.

Lambert, M. J., Whipple, J. L., Smart, D. W., Vermeersch, D. A., Nielsen, S. L., & Hawkins, E. J. (2001). The effects of providing therapists with feedback on patient progress during psychotherapy: Are outcomes enhanced? *Psychotherapy Research, 11*, 49-68.

Lambert, M. J., Whipple, J. M., Vermeersch, D. A., Smart, D. W., Hawkins, E. J., Nielsen, S. L., & Goates, M. (2002). Enhancing psychotherapy outcomes via providing feedback on client progress: A replication. *Clinical Psychology and Psychotherapy, 9*, 91-103.

Lueger, R. J., Howard, K. I., Martinovich, Z., Lutz, W., Anderson, E. E., & Grissom, G. (2001). Assessing treatment progress of individual patients using expected treatment response models. *Journal of Consulting and Clinical Psychology, 69*, 150-158.

Lueger, R. J., Lutz, W., & Howard, K. I. (2000). The predicted and observed course of psychotherapy for anxiety and mood disorders. *The Journal of Nervous and Mental Disease, 188*, 127-134.

Lutz, W. (2002). Patient-focused psychotherapy research and individual treatment progress as scientific groundwork for an empirical based clinical practice. *Psychotherapy Research, 12*, 251-273.

Lutz, W. (2003). *Die Wiederentdeckung des Individuums in der Psychotherapieforschung: Ein Beitrag zur patientenorientierten Psychotherapieforschung und Qualitätssicherung [Rediscovering the individual in psychotherapy: A contribution to patient-focused psychotehrapy research and quality assurance]*. Tübingen: dgtv-Verlag.

Lutz, W., Grawe, K., & Tholen, S. (2003). Empirische Unterstützung der differentiellen Indikation für unterschiedliche Behandlungsmodalitäten in der Verhaltenstherapie

[Empirically supporting the differental indication of different treatment modalities in behavior therapy]. *Zeitschrift für Klinische Psychologie, Psychiatrie und Psychotherapie, 51*, 51-70.

Lutz, W., Lambert, M. J., Harmon, S. C., Tschitsaz, A., Schürch, E., & Stulz, N. (2006). The probability of treatment success, failure and duration - what can be learned from empirical data to support decision making in clinical practice? *Clinical Psychology and Psychotherapy, 13*, 223-232.

Lutz, W., Leach, C., Barkham, M., Lucock, M., Stiles, W. B., Evans, C., Noble, R., & Iverson, S. (2005). Predicting change for individual psychotherapy clients based on their nearest neighbors. *Journal of Consulting and Clinical Psychology, 73*(5), 904-913.

Lutz, W., Lowry, J., Kopta, M., Einstein, A., D., & Howard, K. I. (2001). Prediction of dose-response relations based on patient characteristics. *Journal of Clinical Psychology., 57*, 1-12.

Lutz, W., Martinovich, Z., & Howard, K. I. (1999). Patient profiling: An application of random coefficient regression models to depicting the response of a patient to outpatient psychotherapy. *Journal of Consulting and Clinical Psychology, 67*, 571-577.

Lutz, W., Rafaeli, E., Howard, K. I., & Martinovich, Z. (2002). Adaptive modeling of progress in outpatient psychotherapy. *Psychotherapy Research, 12*, 305-327.

Lutz, W., Saunders, S. M., Leon, S. C., Martinovich, Z., Kosfelder, J., Schulte, D., Grawe, K., & Tholen, S. (2006). Empirically and clinically useful decision making in psychotherapy: Differential predictions with treatment response models. *Psychological Assessment, 18*(2), 133-141.

Lutz, W., Stulz, N., Smart, D. W., & Lambert, M. J. (2007). Die Identifikation früher Veränderungsmuster in der ambulanten Psychotherapie [Patterns of early change in outpatient therapy]. *Zeitschrift für Klinische Psychologie und Psychotherapie, 36*(2), 93-104.

Meyer, F., & Schulte, D. (2002). Zur Validität der Beurteilung des Therapieerfolgs durch die Therapeuten [The validity of therapists' judgements of therapy success]. *Zeitschrift für Klinische Psychologie & Psychotherapie, 31*, 53-61.

Muthén, B. O. (2001). Second-generation structural equation modeling with a combination of categorical and continuous latent variables. In L. M. Collins & A. G. Sayer (Eds.), *New methods for the analysis of change* (pp. 291-332). Washington, DC: American Psychological Association.

Muthén, B. O. (2004). Latent variable analysis: Growth mixture modeling and related techniques for longitudinal data. In D. Kaplan (Ed.), *Handbook of quantitative methodology for social sciences* (pp. 345-368). Newbury Park, CA: Sage Publications.

Muthén, B. O., & Muthén, L. K. (2000). Integrating person-centered and variable-centered analyses: Growth Mixture Modeling with latent trajectory classes. *Alcoholism: Clinical and Experimental Research, 24*(6), 882-891.

Raudenbush, S. W. (2001). Comparing personal trajectories and drawing causal inferences from longitudinal data. *Annual Review of Psychology, 52*, 501-525.

Singer, J. D., & Willett, J. B. (2003). *Applied longitudinal data analysis: Modeling change and event occurence.* New York, NY: Oxford University Press.

Sperry, L., Brill, P. L., Howard, K. I., & Grissom, G. R. (1996). *Treatment outcomes in psychotherapy and psychiatric interventions.* New York: Brunner/Mazel.

Stulz, N., & Lutz, W. (2007). Multidimensional patterns of change in outpatient psychotherapy - the Phase Model revisited. *Journal of Clinical Psychology, 63*(9), 817-833.

Stulz, N., Lutz, W., Leach, C., Lucock, M., & Barkham, M. (submitted). Shapes of early change in psychotehrapy under routine outpatient conditions.

Whipple, J., Lambert, M. J., Vermeersch, D. A., Smart, D. W., Nielsen, S. L., & Hawkins, E. (2003). Improving the effects of psychotherapy: The use of early Identification of treatment failure and problem-solving strategies in routine practice. *Journal of Counseling Psychology, 50*(1), 59-68.

In: Psychology of Decision Making...
Editor: G. R. Burthold, pp. 219-231

ISBN: 978-1-60021-932-0
© 2007 Nova Science Publishers, Inc.

Chapter 10

CAN CONSOLIDATION AND RECONSOLIDATION DETERMINE THE DYNAMICS OF THE RANKING OF MEMORIES IN DECISION-MAKING PROCESSES?

Alex Stolberg [*]

Mahshov Research Center R.Israeli Ltd., 13 Alpha Building, Tel-Aviv, 61571, Israel

ABSTRACT

Reactivation and the subsequent transformation of previously established memories are among the major topics of current psychobiological research [1, 7, 10, 26, 31]. Despite controversy about the nature of reconsolidation, there is growing acceptance that memory is a dynamic in nature and that reactivation returns a consolidated engram to a labile sensitive state, in which it can be modified, strengthened, or possibly even erased [9-11, 26]. Whereas significant efforts were applied to pharmacological dissection of reconsolidation, in an attempt to discover clear distinctions between cellular-molecular mechanisms of consolidation and reconsolidation [1, 6-7, 14-15, 17, 39, 41], the variety of roles that systemic consolidation and reconsolidation can play in actual-choice behavior is still largely unknown [1, 5, 10, 41]. Recently, we reported several new findings on hidden learning and ranking of memories and behavioral strategies in the matching-to-sample task on the radial maze [34]. Initially, the possible function of consolidation and reconsolidation, underlying these phenomena was not elucidated. In the current paper, the new extended research framework has been delineated. According to this, hidden learning and ranking can be explained by systemic consolidation and reconsolidation of matching skill, and by its effect on post-reactivation dynamic interactions of engrams in working memory. It is suggested that in a choice process, ranking of co-existing memories and behavioral strategies can be an important function of consolidation and reconsolidation. Further research for understanding the features and the functional significance of systemic consolidation and reconsolidation was shown to be critical for grasping dynamic aspects of decision-making in multiple-choice situations.

---

[*] Email: Stolberg@prontomail.com

INTRODUCTION

Understanding the dynamics of memory and temporal evolution of decision-making is one of the central, complex and exciting challenges that psychobiology and cognitive neuroscience confronts today. A dynamic approach is the most adequate for studying the temporal aspects of decision-making, effortful information processing and choice behavior. Dynamic system analysis provides a set of mathematical and conceptual tools that help to explain how the system changes over time [40]. A good dynamic theory goes beyond the description of the pattern of events towards a real explanation of why events unfold as they do. In cognitive neuroscience, the perspectives of understanding the dynamics of memory and cognition are largely associated today with reconsolidation research.

Over the last decade the interest of psychologists and neuroscientists in the phenomenon and concept of reconsolidation has increased dramatically [1, 7, 9-11, 19, 24, 26, 28-29, 31]. Reconsolidation implies the process and the result of additional engram consolidation, activated by the retrieval of previously consolidated memory trace. Although the finding that an already stabilized engram can become sensitive following retrieval is not new, the most important aspect of the current wave of interest in reconsolidation is a substantial paradigm shift in memory research.

The vulnerability of previously consolidated memory to electroconvulsive shock (ESC) following memory reactivation was discovered about forty years ago [11, 26, 31]. After about a decade of studies and controversy, which focused on ESC-induced amnesia, it was concluded that reconsolidation is a problematic phenomenon in a sense of its repeatability, generality and theoretical significance [10, 30]. In addition, the conclusion was reached that amnesia was the result of ECS action itself and was not related to memory reactivation and retrieval [30].

Although the initial debates on memory loss versus retrieval failure in amnesia models of reconsolidation are still relevant today [2, 4, 20-21, 33], the current interest in reconsolidation is growing on the basis of a new paradigm, according to which the reactivation of consolidated memory, the retrieval itself, is considered the source of plasticity. The modern approach emphasizes the investigation of cellular-molecular and functional aspects of this active temporal and malleable state of consolidated memory, following retrieval.

The emerging paradigm presents a more dynamic view of memory-processing after retrieval, than ever. According to the standard classical point of view each memory trace undergoes two phases until stabilization [1, 10, 18, 21-22, 26, 28, 32, 42]. The first stage is a short-term memory, which results in an encoding of a new memory trace. The new engram is initially unstable, can be disrupted by pharmacological agents, ESC, is susceptible to interference and can be wiped out by reinforcement withdrawal. The second stage that stabilizes the encoded engram after certain time frame is consolidation. The consolidated memory trace cannot be destroyed or transformed further and should not undergo the same process again in the future. It is stored in long-term memory as a stable, irreversible engram, which can later be retrieved in an appropriate context.

The direction of development of psychology and cognitive science was towards more dynamical models. Already, in 1930s, Bartlett demonstrated that memories are fundamentally dynamic. According to him, during the process of retrieval, memory is integrated into the flow of ongoing emotions and experiences, leading thereby to the emergence of new memories [4, 26, 30]. Incorporation of new memories as a feedback of outcomes of action into the stream of experience processing and adaptation was the main feature of the goal-directed behavior model, proposed by P. Anokhin, in his functional system analysis [3].

For a long time the main topic of memory studies was the "storage versus retrieval" debate. Encoding and storage problems were considered to be the main source of learning difficulties and memory impairment [11, 21, 33]. The formulation of the principle of encoding specificity by Tulving was a major contribution to dynamic understanding of interactions between encoding and retrieval [42]. He showed that retrieval is an active process. The inability to recall certain item does not imply its absence in memory, because an appropriate reminder or retrieval cue is able to activate a "forgotten" item, proving its presence in the memory store [28, 42].

Over the last four decades great efforts have been devoted to discovering the dynamics of memory trace transformation from being labile to being stable [18, 22, 26]. However, the framework of the old model of memory was too narrow to recognize post-retrieval dynamic processes, it did not reflect interactions of long-term and short-term memories during the acquisition of a new skill and it considered long-term memory a rigid, passive store that cannot be modified over time.

Modern reconsolidation research was the last development, marking progress towards a dynamic theory of memory. It opened the gate for investigation of post-retrieval and post - reactivation sensitivity. The reconsolidation hypothesis was initially advanced mainly on the basis of experimental amnesia studies [1, 7, 10, 26]. In various kinds of one-day avoidance, fear or aversion training paradigms, it was shown that protein synthesis blockers cause amnesia, if administered after reactivation of existing memory by conditioned stimulus, while they have no effect without prior memory reactivation. The results were confirmed in experiments with a wide variety of species, including rodents, chicks, fishes, snails and crabs [2, 10, 26]. Simple models of experimental amnesia research were for a long time the primary tools for the study of reconsolidation. These studies made a significant impact in discovering reconsolidation as a phenomenon and in the investigation of its cellular-molecular mechanisms. However, actual choice and decision-making experiments were not sufficiently studied in reconsolidation research and still need to find their way into the investigation of memory dynamics.

Unlike simple models of experimental amnesia, actual choice research presupposes modeling of real decision-making processes in uncertainty situations when memories and expectations in the process of consolidation and reconsolidation determine behavioral dynamics. In multiple-choice situations, new mechanisms of latent expression of memory traces, other than storage deficit, retrieval failure and trace inaccessibility may be discovered,

Recently, we have found two dynamic processes that reflect the acquisition of matching-to-sample on the radial maze and actual choice behavior: hidden learning and ranking of memories [34, 36]. Hidden learning and subsequent ranking were demonstrated when animals were allowed a second attempt, following an error in the first testing choice of matching procedure. We found that, in the early phase of training, when erroneous performance continued and no visible signs of acquisition of the matching skill could be noted in the first testing choice, the "absent" learning could be observed during the second testing attempt. It was observed that finding a reward on the second attempt became progressively sooner over time, until the memory for the location of the informational arm, visited in the study phase of the trial, captured the highest dominant position among concurrent memories from the very beginning, in the first testing choice.

To check the supposed ability of animals to build a hierarchy of acquired memories and strategies, the retroactive interference task, based on a consolidated win-stay strategy, was used. In the matching-to-sample task rats were trained to remember the location of the recent informational arm and return to it in the testing run. After learning the skill at a success rate of 90-95%, the group of experienced animals was exposed to a second informational run in a study phase of the matching task. This procedure was intended to create interference and cause the rats to choose between alternatives, related to two memory traces. The relevant strategy to solve this task in the testing phase was to change their habit of returning to the location of the most recent informational arm and go to the next-to-recent visited informational arm. Typically, a retroactive interference procedure is used to cause the deterioration of the original skill and to demonstrate its dependence on working memory. In our experiments, after an initial significant increase in erroneous choices, the rats were able to recover and solve the task by rearranging the ranks of memories that they remember [34, 36].

The aim of this article is to examine the possibility that consolidation and reconsolidation determine ranking and hidden learning in the matching-to-sample task on the radial maze and whether this is one of their functions in decision-making processes.

SIMPLE MODELS OF EXPERIMENTAL AMNESIA AND ACTUAL CHOICE EXPERIMENTS ON RECONSOLIDATION

Experimental amnesia research has outlined basic elements and revealed a number of important molecular signatures and cellular circuits of reconsolidation [1, 8, 10, 14, 26]. The hypothesis has been advanced that reactivation and retrieval of already consolidated memory in the case of reinforcement withdrawal triggers two opposing processes: extinction and reconsolidation. When extinction is incomplete, reconsolidation is responsible for spontaneous recovery. Some authors point out the conflicting processes of reconsolidation and extinction. For them, reconsolidation can be detected only in the absence of significant extinction. However, there is also evidence that extinction cannot prevent reconsolidation from occurring. It suggests that retrieval during a non-reinforced test trial could initiate reconsolidation even in place of extinction of mnemonic trace [11, 37]. Research on simple models of experimental amnesia has been focused mainly on molecular and cellular mechanisms of reconsolidation. Its findings were regularly discussed and extensively covered by numerous review articles [1, 10, 26, 31]. However, the theoretical significance and variety of possible applications of the reconsolidation hypothesis cannot be fully covered by the investigation of simple models based on one-day training. Such studies are unable to delineate the boundaries of existence and the variety of functions that systemic reconsolidation can play in actual choice behavior. Therefore, studies of effortful information-processing, actual choice behavior, incentive learning and ranking should complement them.

It is reasonable to expect that following reactivation, consolidated memories could be sensitive, not only to pharmacological blockers or ESC, but to external events as well. Reactivation of traces in response to retrieval cues and endogenous states is a common, natural way of memory functioning. It can lead to either activation of multiple related engrams that compete for the control of behavior or a remodeling of all kinds of memory, including human [26]. Recently, incentive learning, in which animals had to update the changes in the values of reward, was shown to be dependent on protein synthesis in amygdala for both consolidation and reconsolidation [38]. In addition, the reconsolidation hypothesis was tested in some relatively complex spatial memory tasks [10-11, 23].

Until now, experiments on more complex behavioral models and spatial memory have led to suggestions for the following determinants and boundaries for reconsolidation: 1) age of memory, 2) mismatch necessity, 3) dominance of memory trace at retrieval as a condition for reconsolidation, and 4) the need for an active encoding mode [10-11].

It was demonstrated that the probability of reconsolidation initiation depends on the age of reactivated memory [10-11, 37]. Younger memories are more likely reconsolidate than older memories. Older traces may not be susceptible to reconsolidation at all. This evidence indicates that several levels of consolidation probably exist and that at each level, the susceptibility of reactivated state of memory to pharmacological agents or to dramatic events is different. Investigation of complex behavior in multiple-choice situations can allow a detailed study of different stages of consolidation and their functions.

The necessity of mismatch indicates the role of the emotional component of reactivation and its power to cause modification and subsequent reconsolidation. Weak reactivation, lacking mismatch can barely initiate reconsolidation. Mismatch, in turn, can activate an encoding mode of memory, causing both re-encoding and reconsolidation of an already consolidated engram.

With regard to the dominance of consolidated memory trace as the determinant of reconsolidation, I would point out that it is not a necessity for the process. Memory does not have to be dominant in order to be encoded or consolidated. The processes of consolidation and reconsolidation of memory trace before it acquires dominant rank could very likely be a mechanism of new learning and relearning. It could be suggested that in multiple-choice situations different memories can co-exist and compete, and the more memory trace is consolidated, the more chances it has for dominance. Dominance of memory trace could be necessary for the final achievement of the reconsolidation process. Research on ranking and hidden learning is one of the ways to study consolidation and reconsolidation functions in decision-making processes.

RANKING, HIDDEN LEARNING AND HYPOTHESIS ON MULTIPLE STAGES OF CONSOLIDATION

As was already mentioned, we found ranking and hidden learning, using matching-to-sample task on the radial maze [34, 36]. Ranking can be defined as a capacity and a process for dynamic hierarchical organization of memory traces or behavioral strategies, in accordance with the context and endogenous state of organism.

Ranking occurs when all reminders and retrieval cues for each alternative memory trace are present in the environment. Therefore, it cannot be explained by retrieval failure and problems of memory trace accessibility. In fact, there is no failure in ranking. Instead, the order of trace or behavioral strategy expression depends on its ranking. In many cases, we are not what we remember – rather, we are how we rank what we remember.

The original explanations of possible mechanisms of ranking referred to the dynamics of retrieval, depending on the strength of competing memory traces [34]. Possible sources of this strength and the role of consolidation and reconsolidation were not elucidated. Taking into account the fact that these experiments were performed under conditions of stable motivation and in a stress-free environment, the only factor that could affect the strength of memory traces is the dynamics of learning and memory formation.

It is well known that the acquisition of new learning is frequently challenged by interference from previous experience. Our experiments, dealing with the influence of previous experience on new learning in the maze, demonstrate that with a continuous reinforcement schedule, there are three stages for relearning and singling out dominant reaction [12, 35]. In the first stage, in spite of non-reinforcement, initial long-term memory traces persist, can become even stronger and dominate behavior. In the second stage, initially dominant memories lose their highest position. As a result, behavioral persistence is replaced by the sensitive stage - selective exploration and search activity. In the third stage selective exploration comes to an end, the initial strategy loses its high rank completely and the new behavioral strategy prevails [12, 34-35]. It is likely that consolidation and reconsolidation of encoded new skills are responsible for the dynamics of behavioral changes during relearning.

Three stages of learning a new skill were also demonstrated for the acquisition of matching-to-sample on the radial maze [34]. At the beginning, win-shift bias dominated the behavior of animals. In the second stage, an encoding of win-stay strategy and selectivity in search behavior following errors was observed. The distinctive feature of this training procedure was the use of a second testing attempt that allowed an unlimited search for reward after an erroneous first choice. In the second attempt we found hidden learning effect, when an encoding of win-stay strategy and increase in its rank became visible earlier in the course of learning, than it had been observed in the first testing choice. The dominance of the win-stay strategy in the first testing choice and acquisition of matching behavior to the level of almost perfect matching score was the last stage of learning. It is very likely that the progressive consolidation of encoded win-stay strategy was responsible for the dynamics of hidden learning and ranking effects.

Reconsolidation of the original matching skill might be the component necessary to overcome interference. We found that in a retroactive interference task, experienced animals with matching skill in each testing choice remember two or three arm locations simultaneously before they decide which one to choose [34, 36]. The correct choice is the return to the location of the next-to-recent informational arm. To learn this task, the previous matching skill of returning to the most recently visited informational arm should be re-encoded and reconsolidated.

It is worth mentioning the connection between ranking hypothesis and multiple trace memory theory [25, 42]. Tulving outlined in detail the dichotomy between the multiple memory systems approach and the concept of a unitary memory system [42].

There are several classifications of memory and models of multiple memory systems [15, 25, 42]. One includes explicit and implicit memory systems that can interact and compete. While explicit memory is an attribute of exclusively human memory, implicit memory can be found in both humans and animals. The effects of ranking and hidden learning described in our experiments should be attributed to features of implicit memory.

Another concept makes a distinction between semantic and episodic memory (in humans). Both are the attributes of human memory. However, in animals an episodic-like memory is described. It implies a memory of specific events and contains components answering three questions: what, where and when [13].

In a retroactive interference matching-to-sample task on the radial maze animals demonstrate all aspects of episodic-like memory. Rats are able to solve the task and their memories respond to all three questions: what, where and when [13]. Long-term memory responds to the question of what to do (to return to the place of reinforcement, received in the informational run), working memories serving long-term strategy, respond to the question of where to run (the exact location of the informational arm). The temporal discrimination on "when the informational arm should be counted as the true one" requires a decision and depends upon interactions between long-term and working memories. The correct choice is to go to the location of the first informational arm of the study phase (the next-to-recent), which can be viewed as a "reconsolidation" arm. The erroneous choice is to go to the location of the second informational arm of the study phase (the most recent) that can be viewed as an "extinction" arm.

Thus, ranking and hidden learning as they are observed in a matching-to-sample task on the radial maze constitute the features of implicit and episodic-like memory.

It is not a matter of debate as to whether each type of memory mentioned in multiple-trace memory theory shares the two basic stages of memory formation: encoding and consolidation. However, systemic consolidation is dependent upon more processes, including several levels of molecular consolidation and sequencing of processes in each brain structure involved. It can be suggested that each type of memory can go through various kinds or stages of consolidation: consolidation dependent on protein synthesis (common for all and correspondent with intermediate and long-term memory), consolidation dependent on hippocampus (early consolidation), consolidation dependent on REM sleep, consolidation dependent on amygdala (it may be part of relearning process), neocortical consolidation (corresponding to long-term memory) [9-10, 15, 17-18, 25]. In a multiple-choice situation, different memories simultaneously undergo conflicting or synergic processes, in numerous directions.

My assumption is that in a matching task, decision-making each time depends on the stage of consolidation and reconsolidation of long-term win-stay behavioral strategy, which simultaneously directs several competing working memories.

Here is a proposed general schema for the dynamics of acquisition of new matching skill. As new memories are encoded, they are not dominant. In spite of their low ranking, they undergo consolidation. Visualization of this hidden consolidation can be allowed by a second testing attempt. In the course of learning, the rank of the old behavioral strategy is lowered, while the new encoded win-stay strategy, because of its subsequent consolidation, gets a higher rank and prevails in decision-making and in competition over the control of behavior. The level and stage of consolidation and reconsolidation of win-stay strategy may determine the rank of multiple competing working memory traces in decision-making. Ranking itself appears to be one of the important functions of consolidation and reconsolidation that affects retrieval features in effortful processing and the dynamics of choice.

Activation Time-Frame Window in Consolidation and Reconsolidation Research

How could consolidation and reconsolidation be made accessible for the purpose of experimental analysis in actual choice situations? Numerous studies show that molecular mechanisms of consolidation and reconsolidation are very similar: both depend on protein synthesis, require translation and transcription, both are close in posttranslational modifications, modulation of gene expression and morphological synaptic remodeling [1, 10, 14, 22]. It is not clear yet whether they differ at the level of DNA and gene regulation. The evidence for dissociation in molecular consolidation and reconsolidation was reported for the DNA recombination, the transcription Zif268 factor effect and the subset of genes involved in both processes [5, 17, 43]. Blockers on all levels of molecular consolidation and reconsolidation can affect the learning course and expose underlying processes.

On a systemic level, the main distinction between consolidation and reconsolidation appears to be in the shorter time-frame window and smaller neural networks, activated by reconsolidation. During systemic reconsolidation, there is no total repetition of the original consolidation process and the brain areas involved in consolidation after initial training are not required for reconsolidation [2, 10]. Reconsolidation is faster and this is probably one of its roles - to allow more rapid information processing and integration at the time of memory retrieval and decision-making.

Because reconsolidation does not always last for a long period of time, it cannot always be detected in experiments [5, 11]. A short time-frame window is one possible factor that can prevent the detection of reconsolidation or other post-reactivation processes (linking, hidden stages of ranking) in the course of learning. Repeatability or detection difficulties still do not mean that reconsolidation is absent. More refined experimental methods and procedures could be required for the detection of systemic reconsolidation, because of the relatively short reactivation time-frame window.

There are some differences in theoretical approaches to the nature of reconsolidation [1, 10, 26]. According to one of them reconsolidation is not an independent process. It is viewed as a term to designate one of the phases of classical consolidation [1, 41]. All experimental data describing reconsolidation are in fact deal with encoding, consolidation new traces and linkage of them to old memories. Consequently, the labile state of the old engram, following retrieval is seen as a part of the linking and stabilization process. Similarities in biochemical signatures confirm the idea that reconsolidation is no different from consolidation. Shorter neural circuits underlying systemic reconsolidation compared to consolidation only confirm the basic priority of the latter.

According to another view, the post-reactivation state of the engram is an independent sensitive memory phase that allows not only stabilization, but also the modification, strengthening or even disruption of a previously consolidated engram [26]. The problem with this approach is that reconsolidation effects are not always replicated or detected, especially if the memory trace was consolidated a long time ago.

In spite of their differences all approaches agree on the existence of a post-reactivation sensitive phase following retrieval. Differences in interpretations show only the present lack of basic knowledge about reconsolidation and its functions, especially in complex forms of choice and behavior.

In an attempt to resolve existing theoretical contradictions, the lingering consolidation hypothesis has been proposed [11]. It is based on the evidence that younger memories are better at undergoing reconsolidation, than older traces. The lingering consolidation hypothesis makes a distinction between fast molecular-cellular consolidation and systems consolidation that lingers and cannot be completed within a short period of time. The hypothesis tends to avoid the unnecessary elements of controversy of the dual-trace classical consolidation concept versus the paradigm of reconsolidation. It is close to the view that consolidation passes through several stages. It implies that the outcome of various consolidation blockers should vary as consolidation advances. Today it is common to classify memory as a three-stage process: short-term memory, intermediate-term memory and long-term memory [15]. Though this classification is acceptable today, it will hardly prove to be sufficient tomorrow. Systemic consolidation can take much longer periods than so far assumed and it is still unknown how many stages of consolidation exist.

The lingering consolidation hypothesis and the concept of multiple stages of systemic memory consolidation provide a framework for further investigation of reconsolidation, linking, ranking and hidden learning. It can be a heuristic tool to discover new stages and new functions of consolidation, related with intermediate and long-term memories. A key factor in dissociating multiple stages and memory systems, responsible for differences between consolidation and reconsolidation is investigation of the active time-frame window for each type of memory formation.

PERSPECTIVES IN MEMORY REACTIVATION, RANKING AND THE DYNAMICS OF CHOICE RESEARCH

The first inclusive presentation of the problem of dynamics of cognition in cognitive and artificial intelligence science appeared about a decade ago [40]. In contemporary cognitive neuroscience, the dynamics of learning and memory is described mainly through consolidation theory and reconsolidation paradigm.

According to an emerging new paradigm, memory formation includes encoding (labile period during acquisition of memory trace), consolidation (stabilization of encoded memory, intermediate-term memory and a stable period, after formation of long-term memory) and reconsolidation (labile period and process of stabilization, following retrieval and reactivation of long-term memory trace). It could be suggested also that re-encoding and linking can precede reconsolidation and can be accomplished by the rearrangement of ranks of competing memories. For a long time the problems of encoding, storage deficit or retrieval failure were considered the only sources of recall difficulties and memory impairment. Today, initial memories can be controlled or observed by researchers and we can analyze post-retrieval activation of already consolidated memories, parallel processing of selective engrams in different stages of memory consolidation and the hidden dynamics of acquisition processes.

As previously mentioned, simple models of experimental amnesia research based on one-day training are limited in providing an analysis of the dynamics of acquisition, relearning, actual choice behavior and complex decision-making. The questions - how memories change, when they persist, how they interact and how their changes affect decision-making in ecologically adequate settings – can be studied and addressed mainly by complex tasks, involving choice and effortful information-processing. It appears that consolidation and reconsolidation play a key functional role in the decision-making processes and memory remodeling.

For the time being our knowledge of the dynamics of choice processes is quite limited. Future studies are necessary for further development of dynamic models of learning and cognition. Studies of ranking, hidden learning and stages of consolidation are some of the important areas of future research.

It has already been shown that protein synthesis inhibition does not block the learning process irreversibly [10, 27, 30]. The effects of blockers are reversible and transient [10, 30]. It can be predicted therefore, that protein synthesis blockers and other inhibitors will broaden the time-frame window of hidden learning, instead of blocking consolidation and the learning process. The time-frame window of hidden learning can be pharmacologically analyzed and its experimental detection can be facilitated for a wide range of tasks. The process of ranking is going through a dynamic phase of selective search and rank elevation to stabilization. Could we anticipate that dynamical ranking would occur during the time-frame window, related with completion of the specific stage of consolidation? Could it be that consolidation and reconsolidation stabilize not only neuronal representation of the engram, but also its position among other engrams? Blockers of consolidation and reconsolidation can test the hypothesis that ranking depends on both of them.

It is possible that ranking in the retroactive interference task on the radial maze contains both linking, re-encoding and reconsolidation. Although it needs to be investigated in neurobiological experiments, it is already clear that either encoding problems or solely retrieval failure explanations are insufficient for understanding of the phenomenon and the dynamics of ranking. Broad investigation and pharmacological analysis by blockers at all levels of molecular processing are necessary in order to find out in more detail the functions and interactions of consolidation and ranking at different stages of their dynamics.

An important way of developing dynamic models of choice is mathematical modeling and computer simulation of experiments [40]. Whereas our data on the three stages of relearning process are valid with the continuous reinforcement schedule, the question arises as to what will happen and when, if the partial reinforcement schedule is applied? Because partial reinforcement can imitate real life situations the best, mathematical models and computer simulation can be very important parts of the solution to these questions. The combination of experiments and computer simulation is a powerful tool for the development of reconsolidation and ranking research [40]

Ranking and reconsolidation research should not be confined to the framework of animal behavioral studies. Animal research investigates the dynamics of implicit and episodic-like memory. Reconsolidation and ranking should also be studied in other memory systems, including humans. Interactions between rankings in different memory systems are a very interesting issue for analysis. It is clear that functional neuroimaging techniques combined with relevant tasks are ideal for reconsolidation and ranking research, because both phenomena are systemic and circuit dependent.

The consequences of change toward dynamic paradigm of memory research combined with the study of ranking in different memory systems can be far-reaching in finding numerous practical applications.

The disruption of a reactivated trace that constitutes a procedure for experimental amnesia was successfully used to attenuate cocaine addiction [16]. In spite of the evidence of a positive effect on drug addiction, this procedure should be used much more carefully in the treatment of traumatic memories and PTSD, because of the possible disruptive effect on relearning capabilities and bioethical problems. The revival of traumatic memories in different contexts in order to move them to the past might be a better technique for re-processing them and overcoming their painful effect. Modifying, strengthening or changing the rank of the engram following reactivation might be a refined method for treatment, reducing the shortcomings of the biomedical model. Without reactivation there can be no modification of a memory trace with its motivational and emotional components. The same principle of modification through reactivation may be important in the teaching practices of modern multicultural societies, which could help to utilize the different cultural backgrounds of students in order to activate their inherent learning abilities.

Thus, consolidation and reconsolidation might determine mechanisms of ranking of memories in decision-making. Rearranging the ranks of memories could be one of their main functions in the process of choice. The experimental study of functions that consolidation and reconsolidation have in ranking and hidden learning may reveal the essential role and the boundaries of both phenomena, having many practical applications.

ACKNOWLEDGEMENTS

I would like to thank Colin and Ann Marks for their assistance in the manuscript preparation.

REFERENCES

[1]   Alberini, C.M. (2005) Mechanisms of memory stabilization: are consolidation and reconsolidation similar or distinct processes? *TRENDS in Neurosciences*, 28, 51-56.

[2]   Anokhin, K.V., Tiunova, A.A., Rose, S.P.R (2002) Reminder effects – reconsolidation or retrieval deficit? Pharmacological dissection and protein synthesis inhibitors, following reminder for a passive avoidance task in young chicks. *European Journal of Neuroscience*, 16, 1750-1766.

[3]   Anokhin, P.K. (1968) Biology and Neurophysiology of the Conditioned Reflex. *Meditsina, Moscow.*

[4]   Bartlett, F.C. (2004) Remembering: A Study in Experimental and Social Psychology. *Cambridge University Press: Second Edition.*

[5]   Cammarota, M., Bevilaqua, L.R.M., Medina, J.H., Izquierdo I. (2004) Retrieval Does Not Induce Reconsolidation of Inhibitory Avoidance Memory. *Learning & Memory,* 11, 572-578.

[6]   Colon-Cesario, M., Wang, J., Ramos, X., Garcia, S.G., Davila, J.J., Laguna, J., Rosado, G., de Ortis, S.P. (2006) An Inhibitor of DNA Recombination Blocks Memory Consolidation, But Not Reconsolidation, in Context Fear Conditioning. *Journal of Neuroscience*, 26 (20), 5524-5533.

[7]   Debiec, J., LeDoux, J.E., Nader K. (2002) Cellular and Systems Reconsolidation in the Hippocampus. *Neuron*, 36, 527-538.

[8]   De Hoz, L., Martin, S.L., Morris, R.G.M. (2005) Forgetting, Reminding and Remembering: The Retrieval of Lost Spatial Memory. *PLoS Biology*, 2(8), 1233-1242.

[9]   Dudai, Y. (2002) Molecular bases of long-term memories: the question of persistence. *Current Opinion in Neurobiology*, 211-216.

[10] Dudai, Y. (2006) Reconsolidation: the advantage to be refocused. *Current Opinion in Neurobiology*, 16, 174-178.

[11] Dudai, Y., Eisenberg, M. (2004) Rites of Passage of the Engram: Reconsolidation and Lingering Consolidation Hypothesis. *Neuron*, 44, 93-100.

[12] Grigoryan, G.E., Stolberg, A.M. (1991) Comparative analysis of spatial orientation in changing media in rats with different preliminary experience. *Zhurnal Vysshey Nervnoy Deyatelnosti im.I.P.Pavlova*, 41, 717-723.

[13] Hupbach, A., Gomez, R. Hardt, O., Nadel, L. (2007) Reconsolidation of episodic memories: A subtle reminder triggers integration of new information. *Learning & Memory*, 14, 47-53.

[14] Kelly, A., Laroche, S., Davis, S. (2003) Activation of Mitogen-Activated Protein Kinase/ExtraCellular Signal-Regulated Kinase in Hippocampal Circuitry Is Required for Consolidation and Reconsolidation of Recognition Memory. *The Journal of Neuroscience*, 23(12), 5354-5360.

[15] Lee, I., Kesner, R.P. (2003) Time-Dependent Relationships between the Dorsal Hippocampus and the Prefrontal Cortex in Spatial Memory. *The Journal of Neuroscience*, 23 (4), 1517- 1523.

[16] Lee, J.L., DiCiano, P., Thomas, K.L., Everitt, D.J. (2005) Disrupting reconsolidation of drug memories reduces cocaine-seeking behavior. *Neuron*, 47, 795-801.

[17] Lee, J.L., Everitt, D.J., Thomas, K.L. (2004) Independent Cellular Processes for Hippocampal Memory Consolidation and Reconsolidation. *Science*, 304, 839-843.

[18] McGaugh, J.L. (1966) Time-Dependent Processes in Memory Storage. *Science*, 153, 1351-1358.

[19] Milekic, M.H., Alberini, C.M. (2002) Temporally Graded Requirement for Protein Synthesis following Memory Reactivation. *Neuron,* 36, 521-525.

[20] Miller, C.A., Sweatt, D.J. (2006) Amnesia or retrieval deficit? Implications of a molecular approach to the question of reconsolidation. *Learning & Memory*, 13, 498-505.

[21] Miller, R.R., Matzel, L.D. (2006) Retrieval failure versus memory loss in experimental amnesia: Definitions and processes. *Learning & Memory*, 13, 491-497.

[22] Milner, B., Squire, L.R., Kandel, E.R. (1998) Cognitive Neuroscience and the Study of Memory. *Neuron*, 20, 445-468.

[23] Morris R.G.M., Inglis J., Ainge J.A., Oliverman H.J., Tulloch J., Dudai Y., Kelly P.A.T. (2006) Memory Reconsolidation: Sensitivity of Spatial Memory to Inhibition of Protein Synthesis in Dorsal Hippocampus during Encoding and Retrieval. *Neuron*, 479-489.

[24] Myers, K.M., Davis, M. (2002) Systems-Level Reconsolidation. Reengagement of the Hippocampus with Memory Reactivation. *Neuron*, 36, 340-343.

[25] Nadel, L., Samsonovich, A., Ryan, L., Moscovitch, M. (2000) Multiple Trace Theory of Human Memory: Computational, Neuroimaging and Neuropsychological Results. *Hippocampus,* 10, 352-368.

[26] Nader, K. (2003) Memory traces unbound. *TRENDS in Neurosciences*, 28, 66-71.

[27] Pedreira, M.E., Maldonado, H. (2003) Protein Synthesis Subserves Reconsolidation or Extinction Depending on Reminder Duration. *Neuron*, 863-869.

[28] Riccio, D.S., Millin, P.M., Bogart, A.R. (2006) Reconsolidation: A brief history, a retrieval view and some recent issues. *Learning & Memory*, 13, 536-544.

[29] Rossato, J.I., Bevilaqua, L.R.M., Medina, J.H., Izuierdo, I., Cammarota, M. (2006) Retrieval induces hippocampal-dependent reconsolidation of spatial memory. *Learning & Memory*, 13, 431-440.

[30] Rudy, J.W., Biedenkapp, J.C., Moineau, J., Bolding, K. (2006) Anisomycin and Reconsolidation Hypothesis. *Learning & Memory*, 13, 1-3.

[31] Sara, S.J. (2000) Retrieval and Reconsolidation: Toward a Neurobiology of Remembering. *Learning & Memory*, 7, 73-84.

[32] Shettleworth, S. (2001) Animal cognition and animal behaviour. *Animal Behaviour*, 61, 277-286.

[33] Squire, L.R. (2006) Lost forever or temporarily misplaced? The long debate about the nature of memory impairment. *Learning & Memory*, 13, 522-529.

[34] Stolberg, A. (2005) Ranking of memories and behavioral strategies in the radial maze. *Acta Neurobiologiae Experimentalis (Wars.)*, 65, 39-49.

[35] Stolberg, A.M., Grigoryan, G.E. (1991) Singling out of the dominant in white rats at elaboration of win-stay strategy in three-arm maze. *Zhurnal Vysshey Nervnoy Deyatelnosti im. I.P.Pavlova*, 41, 364-371.

[36] Stolberg, A., Roberts, W.A. (1995) Matching to Sample on the Radial Maze. *Abstracts of Annual Meeting of Psychonomic Society, Los Angeles*.

[37] Suzuki, A., Josselyn, S.A., Frankland, P.W., Masushige, S., Silva, A.J., Kida, S. (2004) Memory Reconsolidation and Extinction Have Distinct Temporal and Biochemical Signatures. *The Journal of Neuroscience*, 24(20), 4787-4795.

[38] Szu-Han Wang, Ostlund, S.B., Nader, K., Balleine, B. (2005) Consolidation and Reconsolidation of Incentive Learning in the Amygdala. *The Journal of Neuroscience*, 25(4), 830-835.

[39] Torras-Garsia, M., Lelong, J., Tronel, S., Sara, S.J. (2005) Reconsolidation after remembering an odor-reward association requires NMDA receptors. *Learning & Memory*, 12, 18-22.

[40] Townsend, J., Busemeyer, J. (1995) Dynamic Representation of Decision-Making. *In Port, R., Van Gelder (Eds) Mind and Motion. Exploration in the Dynamics of Cognition, MIT Press*, 102-119.

[41] Tronel, S., Milekic, M.H., Alberini, C.M. (2005) Linking New Information to a Reactivated Memory Requires Consolidation and Not Reconsolidation Mechanisms. *PLoS Biology*, 3, 1630-1638.

[42] Tulving, E. (1999) Study of memory processes and systems. *In Foster, J.K., Milicic, M (Eds) Memory: Systems, Process or Function? NY: Oxford Unoversity Press*, 11-30.

[43] Von Hertzen, L.S.J., Giese, P.K. (2005) Memory Reconsolidation Engages Only a Subset of Immediate-Early Genes Induced during Consolidation. *The Journal of Neuroscience*, 25(8), 1935-1942.

In: Psychology of Decision Making...
Editor: G. R. Burthold, pp. 233-248

ISBN: 978-1-60021-932-0
© 2007 Nova Science Publishers, Inc.

Chapter 11

EXPERTS AND LAYPERSONS' DECISION MAKING PROCESSES IN INFORMATION-RICH SETTINGS: THE CASE OF HR SELECTION

Leehu Zysberg [*]

Tel Hai Academic College, Department of Psychology

Anna Zisberg

University of Haifa, Department of Nursing

ABSTRACT

While research focusing on decision making by laypersons is quite ample, research focusing on the decision making processes conducted by experts is a bit less abundant. This is especially true for studies conducted in actual life settings instead of the popular excerpt or hypothetical bets settings used in most existing studies. The two studies depicted herein examined decision making processes conducted by laypersons and personnel psychologists regarding the congruence of candidates' various characteristics with the requirements and demands of a professional job.

One hundred and six candidates applying for prestigious legal positions in a large government agency participated in the first study. They have taken a selection test battery including aptitude tests as well as personality and interpersonal skill tests. The results were judged by I/O psychologists specializing in HR selection. To test the decision-making processes of these experts, the information sources (the test scores) were used as predictors of the final decision criterion in a series of stepwise regression models.

In the second study, 68 candidates for a service oriented position in a technological organization were screened using a standard aptitude battery, and then were screened using an assessment center, observed by both skilled psychologists and HR managers from the organization. The candidates accepted were followed up until the end of their

[*] Correspondence regarding this chapter should be addressed to: Dr. Leehu Zysberg, 53A Haviva Reich street # 4; Haifa ISRAEL 32541; Phone: 011-972-54-8054529; Email: LeehuZysberg@yahoo.com or Leehu@telhai.ac.il

training program in the organization. The training course grades served as a performance criterion.

The same method as described above was used to compare the structure and validity of the psychologists' decision making process vis-à-vis the HR managers decision making (based on a simple averaging formula).

The results show patterns consistent with existing research on human perception and decision making: Experts showed the same biases as laypersons in their decision making process. Moreover – the validity of the experts' decision was found to be lower than the validity of a simple averaging formula utilized by the HR managers.

The results are discussed in light of existing research on human perception and information processing. In addition suggestions for additional research and possible practices in the field of HR decision making are raised.

INTRODUCTION

Decisions making and human judgment processes have been the focus of interest in psychological research for quite a while now (Kahneman & Tversky, 1983; Ramsey, 1999; Keren & DeBruin, 2003). Researchers and theoreticians have provided us with a complex, yet fascinating view of how people judge information presented to them and make decisions.

A decision is about choice: "An act or process of making a choice or reaching a conclusion, among several options" (Chermack, 2003, p. 365). In most life situations, the choice of any option means leaving out alternative routes of action or preferences. Therefore it seems like psychologically speaking, real-life decision making is a sort of a logical "catch 22": Without having all the information needed to make a fully-informed decision, people have to make a choice knowing it will carry with it the risk of overlooking better alternatives, choices and possible losses. Herein lays the basis for our understanding of the human paradox of decision making in real life situations.

This paradox is of great significance in organizational settings where decisions may influence the lives of numerous persons, beyond the individuals who make them. This chapter focuses on decision making in screening for hiring. More and more organizations are realizing that hiring decisions are pivotal in building human capital, recruiting talent and maintaining competitive advantage (LaVigna, 2002; Marques, 2006). This realization creates a high-risk environment for HR related decision-making. As a result numerous organizations turn to HR and organizational experts for support in making those crucial decisions. How well do experts do in such settings? This chapter takes a look into this question with a sequence of studies aimed at examining laypersons and experts' decision making processes in corporate hiring settings.

THEORIES OF DECISION MAKING

The realization noted above creates a divide in how psychologists and behavioral scientists conceptualize decision making. Traditionally we tend to differentiate 'Normative' theories – depicting the ideal process, the one that may lead to more efficient process and outcomes from 'Descriptive' theories focusing on people's actual decision making process, identifying typical biases and fallacies in the process (Keren & DeBruin, 2003; Debenham, 2004). This chapter focuses mainly on the latter type of conceptualization: depicting real-life decision making processes while attempting to outline pitfalls, biases and fallacies that are typical of the process.

WHAT MAKES A "GOOD DECISION" IN REAL LIFE SETTINGS?

A 'good decision' is one that supplies the decision maker with the best results that could be expected from the decision. In corporate settings this means maximal or at least optimal return on the investment involved in decision making (e.g.: time, money paid to employees and experts etc.). In this respect we are discussing the issue of the decisions' predictive validity: to what extent were the decision-makers capable of predicting the employees' future contribution to the organization? (Schmidt & Hunter, 1989). Though the validity of psychological measures and instruments supporting hiring decision making have been tested in the past (Schmidt & Hunter, 1989; Jereb, Rejkovic & Rejkovic, 2005) there's only meager research focusing on the processes underlying the actual decision making process in this domain (McCauly, 1991; Zysberg & Nevo, 2004).

In the absence of direct evidence, studies have also focused on evaluation of the two main aspects of decision making: 1) The process of decision making – assuming that proper process leads to more effective outcomes. A substantial body of research looks into the process as key to the quality of decisions made in real-life contexts. (2) The outcomes of decisions – in terms of benefits and costs to the decision maker or the entity he or she represents (in our case – the organization) (Keren & DeBruin, 2003).

This chapter takes the first approach – examining the process. More specifically, comparing the one that is suggested by "normative" theories according to which information from diverse and multiple sources is to be weighted and considered before drawing conclusions to the one actually conducted.

TYPICAL BIASES IN DECISION MAKING PROCESSES

The literature supplies us with a partial understanding of the types of pitfalls decision makers tend to fall for. Here is a short summary, which is anything but exhaustive, to give us the foundation from which to build on:

- In most cases decision makers do not use pure utility function to make a choice among alternatives. Two reasons are often quoted to account for this phenomenon – one is our limited capacity of processing information and the other – "hidden agendas" or alternative motivations, biasing our decisions (on a more or less conscious level), mainly influenced by context (Tverskty & Kahneman, 1983; Peters, 2001).
- Not being able to process all the information available creates a constant state of uncertainty for the decision maker. Under such condition, studies show personal and emotional biases become even more salient (Kahneman & Tversky, 1984).

- It seems like the main principle accounting for the heuristics underlying people's decision making is the perception of risk and gain. People tend to avoid risk taking in decisions for which they will be held responsible and will prefer smaller assured reward than a risky decision with a much higher expectancy value. Paradoxically, this tendency is inverted once people try to minimize loss (Kahneman & Tversky, 1984; Ramsey, 1999; Keren & DeBruin, 2003).
- This perception, biased already, is given to numerous further perceptional biases, for example – people may drive across town to save 5$ on a 15$ shirt but will not be willing to do the same to save 5$ on a 125$ coat. Further down the perceptual biases road lay additional typical fallacies such as the perception of contingency between independent events ("illusory correlations"), biased perception of chances and more (Bernstein, 1996).

These findings have lead laypersons and corporate organizations to turn to professionals and experts, assuming their decision making process offer a more systematic, less biased and therefore more valid process.

EXPERTS AND LAYPERSONS' DECISION MAKING PROCESSES

Studies comparing the quality of laypersons and experts' show mixed results: While some studies have shown higher decision-making quality among experts (i.e.: a more methodological approach, more thorough review of the available information, more valid results), compared to laypersons (Levin, Prosansky & Heller, 2001) there is a substantial body of evidence pointing to the opposite. Studies focusing on diverse domains of decision making have suggested that experts, just like novices or laypersons, tend to use heuristics very often, show perceptual biases and fallacies, tend to be more conservative that laypersons in their decision-making style and what's worse – they often are unaware of these shortcomings (Aspel, Willis & Faust, 1998; Levin, Prosansky & Heller, 2001; Marshall, Stone & Jawahar, 2001). Studies examining expert and novice clinical decision making in various settings as well as in HR selection paradigms have consistently shown experts and novices vary only slightly in their judgments, with experts being more conservative and less willing to take risks (Ramsey, 1999; Peters, 2001; Marshall, Stone & Jawahar, 2001). Additional evidence points to typical biases in experts' decision making processes, mainly related to the effect of 'bounded rationality' (Morecroft, 1983). 'Bounded rationality' is a term referring to people's limitation in their capacity to process information in decision making processes. This can be broken down into a few components: 1) limited capacity of including and processing information, (2) limited capacity of identifying and weighing all the relevant alternatives and (3) limited capacity of anticipating the consequences of a decision. Now, most reasonable readers may say: "But of course, no one expects experts to know it all – just know more than most others". What seems to make the above points serious, though, is a reoccurring finding suggesting that often experts are unaware of those limitations and their potential consequences (Aspel, Willis & Faust, 1998).

THE PROCESS AND PREDICTIVE VALIDITY OF EXPERT VS. OTHER METHODS OF JUDGMENT IN DECISION MAKING

Contrary to the utility of clinical decision making processes focusing on individuals in various settings, studies that examined the predictive validity and utility of the 'clinical decision making' processes in both clinical and selection settings have shown that experts only marginally surpass the validity of decision made by novices or laypersons (Peters, 2001; Marshall, Stone & Jawahar, 2001; Allen, Shore & Griffeth, 2003). In selection settings, a handful of studies that ventured into this rarely examined area, have suggested that experts provide little added value beyond the predictive strength of the measures and information sources they use. To make things worse – evidence suggests that a simple regressions formula utilizing the same data sources, and at times, simple mean scores will provide higher predictive value than the expert 'clinical judgment' (Daws & Corrigan, 1974; Tversky & Kahneman, 1984; Schmidt & Hunter, 1989; McCauly, 1991; Peters, 2001; Chermack, 2003; Zysberg & Nevo, 2004). Another example of studies casting a worrying shadow over the validity of experts' decision making effectiveness is the one focusing on the validity of vocational and job interviews. Studies comparing expert interviewers and a computer program simulating an interview have shown that candidates revealed more personal information and that the programs provided more valid information compared with the expert interviewers (Cascio, 1991). What are we to conclude then? Are experts' decisions of no added value beyond the information they are based upon? It seems like the answer depends on the context. When it comes to analyzing results and drawing conclusions, especially post-hoc, there is no substitute to 'human touch'. However, the empirical evidence suggests that experts, just like any other person, may fall victims to the very same decision-making biases plaguing us all.

DECISION-MAKING IN INFORMATION-RICH ENVIRONMENT

Authors in the fields of business and management have termed the last two decades or so "the information age" (Mason, 1986). The reason for that is quite self-evident – in today's world we are immersed in information. Decision-makers anywhere are dealing with large amounts of information. Integration of information to achieve what authors have often referred to as 'a well-informed decision' (Debenham, 2004, p. 147) is a treacherous task for more than one reason:

- *Focusing on the essential* – Large amounts of information means more and less relevant information within any given context. Focusing on what's relevant while 'filtering out' irrelevant information is a substantial challenge to decision makers.
- *Relying on unreliable information* - Multiple sources of information may provide varying levels of information quality. This is especially correct in open information systems such as on-line bulletin boards, discussion groups, mass media sources, internet news or websites. How reliable is the information we use? This is a question any decision maker is dealing with on a daily basis.

- *Partial information* – In a world that is becoming more and more complicated, information too gets more complicated, less complete and comprehensive in nature. In other words, even though we may be swamped in information, it, at best, provides a partial, segmented picture of the world; and we are left to make decisions in conditions of extreme uncertainty.
- *The limitations of human cognition* – Psychological research has often explored the gaps between an environment that is constantly changing becoming more and more sophisticated and challenging and the human psyche, which tends to evolve and change at a much slower rate (Myers, 2004). Cognitive psychologists explored people's limits in retaining information in working and short term memory, retrieving information in various decision making settings and eventually being able of achieving a cognitive product truly based on vast quantities of information (Myers, 2004; Nickerson, 2004).

The main relevant challenges arising from the empirical evidence are: a) Limited storage capacity in our short term memory (b) Limited capacity of using various modes of data (e.g.: integrating and processing visual, auditory and tactile information) (c) Limited capacity of weighing and integrating vast amount of information items and lastly – (d) A limited insight into the shortcomings of our decision making process (Aspel, Willis & Faust, 1998; Myers, 2004; Zysberg & Nevo, 2004).

THE STUDIES

The studies reported herein are yet another attempt at exploring this uncharted territory of expert vs. non-expert decision making processes in real life settings and in an information-rich environment. The studies build upon previous studies reviewed above and examine the implications of findings from adjacent areas and other settings in a real-world, business decision making environment which is dynamic, risky, information-rich (though the quality of the information provided varies), imbued with uncertainty and requires the added value associated with expert intervention and services.

Consider this: large scale organizations often invest substantial resources in recruiting and selecting appropriate candidates for positions of high risk or responsibility. In such cases, emphasis is often put on the selection process since its products will determine the quality and fit of the human capital "acquired" by the organizations to the tasks and challenges it has to face. Human resource selection for hiring purposes is, therefore, the general decision making process we look into in these studies.

Decision Making Information Sources in HR Selection

Almost a century of research stands behind the complex system of information sources utilized by decision makers in the domain of HR selection. These sources may include: biographical information, references from previous jobs or acquaintances, candidates' résumé's as well as psychological measures such as personality tests, interviews, aptitude and skill tests (GMA) and various types of job and work environment simulations (Schmidt & Hunter, 1989). This body of research, however, only strengthens the assumptions mentioned above regarding the nature of HR selection decision making. Experts (e.g.: organizational and HR psychologists) as well as non-experts (hiring managers) are faced with multiple options to choose from, immersed in information of at best moderate reliability and validity.

Here are just a few of the major findings that demonstrate the typical paradoxical decision making space HR experts and non-experts face:

- Job interviews, especially of the open ended questions type are of low to null predictive validity (Schmidt & Hunter, 1998; Krell, 2005). However, most decision makers insist on relying on interviews in their decision making and attribute much more validity to them than objective evidence show.
- Most personality measures consistently show very low predictive validity in work related settings (Murphy & Dzieweczynski, 2005). Some promise is evident from the "Big 5 personality factors" theory showing sporadic evidence of predictive value in work related settings (Barrick & Mount, 1991). Despite this evidence, the majority of experts will use personality inventories based on traditional measures as well as projective measures to support their decisions.
- Various methods of psychological testing for vocational purposes exist, with no "golden standard" to point to an acceptable industry-wide procedure. Among them:
  a) *Individual assessment* (Highhouse, 2002) – A procedure in which each individual candidate goes thorough a series of psychological testing batteries typically consisting of aptitude tests, personality tests, interviews and a standardized group simulation or role play at the end of which a vocational psychologist analyses the tests' results and writes an integrative assessment of the candidates characteristics and an evaluation of their fit to the job requirements.
  b) *Assessment centers* (AC's) have gained much popularity in research and practice, especially in the selection of executives and managers (Bowler & Woehr, 2006). In a typical AC, psychological assessment vis-à-vis a specific job description is conducted by 2 or more judges of which at least one would be a psychologist and others will be representatives of the hiring organization. During a typical AC, candidates go through individual and group activities such as: A Case analysis in a group, an In-basket priority setting and decision making simulation (usually individually and in writing), an interview, a leaderless group activity with other candidates, a presentation and role play simulations taken from the job-related domain. The empirical evidence regarding the internal validity of AC's is at best inconsistent, however there is some evidence suggesting AC's are quite valid when it comes to predicting managerial performance with coefficients ranging from .21 to .48 (Goffin, Rothstein & Johnston, 1996).
  c) *Personality and vocational interest batteries* (self report measures administered in person or online). As mentioned above, most self report personality inventories show moderate to null predictive validity (with one exception agreed upon in recent literature). The added value of vocational interest inventories is yet another much debated issue. Generally, vocational interest inventories are

aimed at identifying people's interest areas, assuming that a good fit between one's personal preferences or interests and the job characteristics will promise better performance on the job, less turnover and other positive outcomes (Gottfredson & Holland, 1990). Logical and intuitive as these assumptions may seem, research seems to refute most of these assumptions with the exception of lesser turnover and higher job-related satisfaction. The most frustrating finding? Person and job congruence fails to consistently predict job performance (for example see: Verplanken, 2004).

The Decision-makers in HR Selection

These studies focus on two specific samples of decision makers in HR selection: organizational-personnel psychologists and hiring managers. While psychologists are assumed to be experts (in both training and practice) in such decision making procedures, the hiring managers may be experts in their field of practice but are usually assumed to be laypersons or at least non-experts in hiring decisions.

The Decision-making Process

Decisions regarding the hiring of candidates are considered risky and complex in the HR literature (LaVigna, 2002; Chermack, 2003). Such decisions are considered even ore challenging then most others due to a few points repeatedly mentioned in the literature: a) timelines pay a crucial role in HR decision making (b) decisions and their results are inter-dependent and (c) moist decisions are iterative in nature rather than anecdotal (Chermack, 2003; Jereb, Rajkovic & Rajkovic, 2005). Therefore, expertise in HR decision making is growing in its importance and so are the expectations of HR experts (Marques, 2006).

These study examine the quality and validity of decision making processes in HR selection according to standards defined by Keren & DeBruin (2003): a) How standardized and reliable is the process? b) How well are various information sources utilized and weighed during the process? c) To what extent do systematic biases plague the process (random vs. systematic error)?

STUDY 1

The first study focused on the decision making of industrial/organizational psychologists within the framework of individual assessment of candidates for professional legal expert positions. Candidates took an aptitude test battery as well as a job interview, and personality measures. The psychologists were requested to make an integrative decision based on the information provided and determine the fit of candidates to the position on a scale from 1 (not fit for the position) to 5 (highly recommended). It was hypothesized that:

a. Experts' decisions will not bring into consideration the full range of information sources available to them.
b. Experts will tend to give higher importance and priority to aptitude tests in their decisions.

Sample

The Applicants

One hundred and six applicants for a professional legal position in a government agency were included in this study. Mean age was 28.6 (s.d.=4.86), 64% were men, all with at least a bachelor's degree in law, economics or business administration. All the applicants took all the tests and selection procedures depicted in the 'measures' section. Applicants who did not complete all the needed screening stages were excluded from the sample.

The Decision Makers

Five psychologists, all experts in personnel selection participated in the study. They all had a Masters degree from a major University and at least 4 years experience in personnel selection.

Measures

All the participants included in the study took all the following tests and measures as a part of their selection procedure:

* *Aptitude tests*: three computerized tests of aptitude were used in this study: 1) A standard test of formal-series testing basic analytic and integrative abilities. Test takers are presented with a series of forms changing according to a given principle. They are requested to understand the underlying principle and apply it to find the correct next form in the series out of a few options provided to them. Tests of this type are considered in the literature a relatively valid measure of general intelligence (Schmidt & Hunter, 1998; Zysberg & Nevo, 2004). (2) A test of understanding verbal instructions, and (3) A standard test of mathematical skills, focusing on solving math problems of 12th grade high school level. The tests show high reliability coefficients and moderate to good validity indices (Schmidt & Hunter, 1989; Bartua, Anderson & Salgado, 2005).
* *Job Interview:* A semi-structured job interview was conducted by trained interviewers, all with a masters' degree in the social sciences, after professional training in job interviews and at least 1 year's experience in conducting job interviews. The interviews focused on identifying the candidates' motivation bases, background experience and personality related strengths and weaknesses given the job description. The interviews lasted typically about 45 minutes each. The interviewers graded the participants on "personal attributes" and "level of fit to the organization" on a scale ranging 1-5 as depicted above.

- *Personality test:* A computerized self-report objective personality inventory based on the PRF (Jackson, 2007) consists of questions to which participants answered by choosing either "true for me" or "not true for me" yielding 6 personality scales dubbed: service orientation, agreeableness, sensitivity to others, cooperation, assertiveness, and independence.
- *The psychologist's final report:* The summarizing individual assessment report includes subscales depicting in a numerical manner the results of the tests and interview, accompanied by open text providing the psychologists' insight and interpretation of the information provided. The report also includes a summarizing section in which the psychologists provide a numerical and verbal assessment of the candidates' fit for the position to which they applied. Only the numerical assessment was included in this study with grades ranging 1-5 as depicted above.

Procedure

Following a post-hoc quasi-experimental design, the researcher obtained the data from the applicants' files at the end of the candidate selection process. Both the client and the institute conducting the tests provided their consent to share information for the purpose of this study. The data was retrieved in such a manner that none of the participants' identity, personal or confidential information were exposed or compromised at any stage.

Rationale for Data Analyses

In an attempt to bypass some of the typical biases raised in previous studies that might obscure the actual processes underlying experts' decision making in HR selection, a multiple regression model was used based on the methodology and rationale offered by Zysberg and Nevo (2004): The various sources of information available to the decision makers are used as predictors and the final recommendation score (reflecting the experts' decision outcome) is used as the dependent variable in the regression model. The outcomes of the analyses allow for accurately assessing the weight given to each information source in the formation of the final decision.

To make this possible one has to assume the psychologists involved in the decision-making process show high inter-rater reliability in their information weighing patterns. To establish this assumption, the information provided by the various psychologists involved in the process was compared and no differences were found among raters.

Results

The variables representing the information sources were entered into the regression formula twice: once as separate, raw grades and at the second time an average grade was calculated for each of the types of information sources: Mean aptitude grade, Mean interview grade (representing the overall level of perceived fit between the candidates' characteristics and the position) and mean personality fit grade were used to predict the psychologists' recommendation. Since both the detailed and the summarized regression models showed identical results Table 1 shows the results of the summarized stepwise regression test:

The data demonstrates a significant influence of the aptitude test information source on the final decision made by the psychologists. Moreover – the other information sources seem to have played an insignificant role in the process. To examine other possible co-relations among the variables, a correlation matrix was produced, as depicted in Table 2. The correlation matrix reveals a significant association between the interview and personality scores although none of them associated significantly with the psychologists' decision.

Table 1. Regression coefficients, R-square values and significance level of information sources as predictors of the psychologists' decision (n=106)

Predictor	Regression coefficient (b)	R square	Significance
Mean aptitude	.85	.31	.001
Interview	-.02	-.02	NS
Personality	.02	.03	NS

Constant value = -.26.

Table 2. Inter-correlations among the study variables (n=103)

	Aptitude	Interview	Personality	Final (Psychologists' decision)
Aptitude	--	.14	.02	.56*
Interview		--	.46*	.05
Personality			--	.00
Final (Psychologists' decision)				--

* Significant at the .01 level or better.

STUDY II

In the second study the predictive validity of expert and laypersons' decisions were compared within the framework of candidate selection for the positions of service personnel for a large scale international communications corporate. The study utilized a prospective design in which the selection information and decisions were documented and kept for the period of training of the accepted candidates. Training course grades served as performance criterion, in this study.

Sample

The Candidates
An original pool of applicants for a customer service position in a world-wide communications corporate, including 346 potential participants served as the preliminary frame of reference. The candidates participated in an assessment center. Based on the results of the AC, 68 candidates were accepted and went through the training period in the organization. This group consisted of the study sample. The participants' mean age was 23.00 (s.d.: 4.32). Most of them were women (73.5%). They all had high school diploma.

The Expert Decision Makers
Three psychologists, working as project managers for the hiring company participated in the study. They all had a Masters degree in psychology and at least 2 years experience in personnel selection and assessment center management.

The 'Layperson' Decision Makers
Two HR personnel from the hiring company participated in the study. Both have been working for the company for over 2 years in the field of HR. Both have a BA degree in the social sciences. Both have no formal or informal training or expertise in psychological testing and assessment.

Measures

The predictors included the following measures: 1) The total score of a cognitive aptitude test assessing learning skills based on formal series logic (see Study I for details). (2) Six summarizing scores based on the assessment center activities – service orientation, level of motivation for the job, coping with difficulties, expressiveness, assuming responsibility for assignments, and emotional stability. (3) The psychologists' decision regarding each candidate's fit for the position was documented as a final recommendation score ranging 1-5 as mentioned in study I.

The performance criterion included 3 different course grades reflecting the candidates' performance throughout the 2 month training period. The grades were averaged to produce a general criterion score.

Procedure

At the end of each assessment center, the psychologists documented their decision as a recommendation grade. After receiving the information form the psychologists, HR managers reviewed the raw information provided by the AC selection measures. The HR managers reported a sense of inadequacy analyzing the raw data on their own and therefore utilized a simple mean score calculated across the various grades provided by the AC reports and an interview they conducted with each candidate.

In this study the researcher used both the expert psychologists' decision scores as well as the laypersons' (HR managers) decision grades to predict the mean training course score using regression models.

Results

Inter-correlations among the Study Variables

A simple correlation matrix was computed to examine the inter-relations among the predictors. The matrix revealed inter-correlations ranging from -.08 (NS) to .61 (p<.01) between the predictor scores, eliminating the danger of co-linearity. The final decision scores (the psychologists and the HR managers') did not show any significant correlation between them! (r =-.21; p<.14).

At the next step of the analysis the correlations of each of the decision scores with the criterion grade were compared. Table 3 provides the details of these comparisons. The results suggested that the 'layperson model' basically averaging the various sources of information provided higher predictive power and validity than the 'expert model' based on the psychologists' clinical decision making process (Z=1.78; p<.05).

Additional analyses examined the mental models used by psychologists and HR managers in weighing the information provided. A series of step-wise regressions followed the rationale underlying study I to examine the relative weight given to each of the information sources in each of the two decisions. The analyses summarized in Table 4 show that while psychologists gave service orientation and cognitive aptitude priority in their decision making, the HR managers' averaging model gave much less weight to both while weighing in all the other information sources (which is to be expected by definition of the HR managers' choice of process).

Table 3. Correlations among decision and criterion scores (n=68)

	Pearson's r	r-square
Psychologists' decision score	.33*	.11
HR managers average score	.57**	.32

* p<.040
** p<.001

Table 4. Unique correlation coefficients comparing Psychologists' and HR managers' weighing of selection information

	Psychologists	HR managers
Cognitive aptitude	.41*	.13
Service orientation	.57*	.18
Motivation	.32*	.09
Coping w/ difficulties	.21	.16
Expressiveness	.20	.13
Assuming responsibility	.30*	.07
Emotional stability	-.02	.11
HR Interview	--	.17

* p<.05 or better.

CONCLUSION

The two studies reported herein set out to examine the effectiveness of decision-making processes of experts and laypersons in a complex, information-rich environment. The results suggest that the biases known to psychologists from other fields of decision-making studies may be at work in this case too: Experts often failed to include a wide range of data in their decision making. Moreover, when we compared a simple averaging model used by laypersons and the 'clinical' model of decision making in their ability to predict performance in organizations, the data suggested that the simple averaging model fared better than the one employed by the experts. These result patterns are congruent with patterns emerging from previous studies in adjacent fields (Cascio, 1991; Highouse, 2002; Zysberg & Nevo, 2004).

Should we ignore expert advice and decision making from now on then? Of course not. However, results such as the ones reported here should remind us that expert decision making is not free of human biases. Understanding these biases and the way they undermine the efficiency and validity of our decisions may help reduce such biases and develop advanced evidence-based models of decision making in HR psychology.

Evidence Based Practice

Evidence based practice is a method of designing and planning courses of action, relying solely on empirical evidence, as opposed to theoretical basis (Allen et al., 2005). Prevalent in health care, it is yet to have an established following in HR management and HR practices. Such a change would be nothing short of a paradigm shift. Allow such a paradigm shift in HR practices, many more studies focusing on HR decisions and their outcomes in various fields. Preliminary work already emerges in recent years suggesting HR measures and indices making it possible not only to assess outcomes but also to study factors influencing outcome measures and predicting them effectively (Cascio, 1991; Becker, Huslid & Ulrich, 2001).

Limitations of Current Studies

The current studies are not free of limitations: though conducted in two different organizations, and samples were taken from different job-strata, the samples were of moderate size and may raise the question of generalizability. In addition, the standardized test batteries used in these studies as well as the criteria for performance may not apply to certain job-markets or segments.

However, since the results found here correspond nicely with other study results from various fields of study, we may suggest a consistent pattern deserving some more attention in the future.

To sum it up: As our world becomes more and more complex and challenging, we are exposed to more and more information, supposedly as means of supporting decisions. While information technology takes quantum leaps forward let us remember that our capacities and limitations do not change as frequently. The increasing gap between technological advances and human performance is one that will draw more and more attention in research and practice. So are we doomed to ever lapse behind technology? Not necessarily. Future research may suggest means of training and adapting decision-making processes and techniques to allow decision makers to make better use of the wide range of supportive information sources at their disposal.

REFERENCES

Allen, D. G., Shore, L. M., & Griffeth, R. W. (2003). The role of perceived organizational support and supportive HR practices in the turnover process. *Journal of Management,* 29(1), 99-118.

Aspel, D. A., Willis, W. G., & Faust, D. (1998). School psychologists diagnostic decision making process. *Journal of School Psychology*, 36(2), 137-149.

Barrick, M. R., & Mount, M. K. (1991). The big 5 personality dimensions and job performance. *Personnel Psychology*, 44(1), 1-26.

Bertua, C., Anderson, N., & Salgado J. F. (2005). The Predictive validity of cognitive ability tests: A UK Meta Analysis. *Journal of Occupational and Organizational Psychology*, 78, 387-409.

Bowler, M. C., & Woer, D. J. (2006). A Meta-analytic evaluation of the impact dimension and exercise factors on assessment center ratings. *Journal of Applied Psychology*, 91(5), 1114-1124.

Cascio, W. F. (1991). *Applied Psychology in Personnel Management*. 4th edition. Englwood cliffs, NJ: Prentice Hall.

Chermack, T. J. (2003). Decision making expertise at the core of HR development. *Advances in Developing HR,* 5, 365-379.

Debenham, J. (2004). Multi-issue bargaining in an information rich context. *Knowledge based Systems*, 17, 147-155.

Goffin, R. D., Rothstein, M. G., & Johnston, N. G. (1996). Personality testing and the assessment center: Incremental validity for managerial selection. *Journal of Applied Psychology*, 81(6), 746-756.

Gottfredson, G. D., & Holland, J. L. (1990). A longitudinal test of the influence of congruence. *Journal of Consulting Psychology*, 37(4), 389-398.

Highouse, S. (2002). Assessing the candidate as a whole: A historical and critical analysis of individual psychological assessment for personnel decision making. *Personnel Psychology*, 55(2), 363-397.

Jackson, D. N. (2007) *Personality Research Form*. Research Psychologists Press, Inc.

Jereb, E., Rajkovic, U., & Rajkovic, V. (2005). A hierarchical multi-attribute system approach to personnel selection. *International Journal of Selection and Assessment*, 13(3), 198-206.

Kahneman, D., & Tversky, A. (1984). Choices values and frames. *American Psychologist*, 39(4), 341-350.

Keren, G., & DeBruin, W. (2003). Decision Quality. In: Hardman, D. & Macchi, L. (eds.) *Thinking: Psychological Perspectives on Reasoning, Judgment and Decision making*. NY: Wiley & Sons, LTD.

Krell, E. (2005). Personality Counts. *HR Magazine*, 50(11), 46.

LaVigna, R. (2002). Best practices in public sector human resources. *Human resources Management*, 41(3), 369-384.

Levine, I. R., Prosansky, C. M., & Heller, D. (2001). Prescreening of choice options in positive and negative decision making tasks. *Journal of Behavioral Decision making*, 14, 279-293.

Lopez, S. P., Peon, S. M. M., & Vasquez-Ordes, C. J. (2006). Human resources management as a determining factor in organizational learning. *Management Learning*, 37(2), 215-241.

Marques, J. F. (2006). The new HR department. *Human Resource Development Quarterly*, 17(1), 117-124.

Marshall, G. W., Stone, T. H., & Jawahar, I. M. (2001). Selection decision making by slaes managers and HR managers. *Journal of Personal selling and Sales Management*, 21(1), 19-28.

Mason, R. O. (1986). Four Ethical issues of the information age. *Management Information Systems Quarterly*, 10 (1), 5-12.

McCauly, C. (1991). Selection of NSF graduate fellows. American *Psychologist*, 46(12), 1287-1291.

Murphy, K. R., & Dzieweczynski, J. L. (2005). Why don't measures of broad dimensions of personality perform better as predictors of job performance? *Human Performance*, 18(4), 343-357.

Myers, D. (2004). *Exploring Psychology*. 5th. Edition. NY: Worth Publishers.

Nickerson, R.S. (2004). *Cognition and chance: The psychology of probabilistic reasoning.* Mahwah, NJ, US: Lawrence Erlbaum Associates Publishers.

Peters, D. F. (2001). Examining child sexual abuse evaluations- the types of information affecting expert judgment. *Child Abuse & Neglect*, 25, 149-178.

Ramsey, S. D. (1999). Evaluating evidence from a decision analysis. *Journal of the American Board of Pharmaceutical Practice*, 12(5), 395-402.

Schmidt, F. L., & Hunter, J. E. (1998). The validity and utility of selection methods in personnel psychology. *Psychological Bulletin*, 124 (2), 262-274.

Tversky, A., & Kahneman, D. (1983). Extensional vs. Intuitive reasoning: The conjunction fallacy in probability judgment. *Psychological Review*, 90(4), 293-316.

Verplanken, B. (2004). Value congruence and job satisfaction among nurses. *International Journal of Nursing Studies*, 41, 599-605.

Zysberg, L., & Nevo, B. (2004). The Smarts that counts. *Journal of Business and Psychology*, 19(1), 117-124.

INDEX

D

E

F

H

I

J

K

L

M

N

P

O

Q

R

T

Y